Get the eBook FREE!

(PDF, ePub, Kindle, and liveBook all included)

We believe that once you buy a book from us, you should be able to read it in any format we have available. To get electronic versions of this book at no additional cost to you, purchase and then register this book at the Manning website.

Go to https://www.manning.com/freebook and follow the instructions to complete your pBook registration.

That's it!
Thanks from Manning!

Rust Web Development

Rust Web
Development

WITH WARP, TOKIO, AND REQWEST

BASTIAN GRUBER

MANNING
SHELTER ISLAND

For online information and ordering of this and other Manning books, please visit
www.manning.com. The publisher offers discounts on this book when ordered in quantity.
For more information, please contact

> Special Sales Department
> Manning Publications Co.
> 20 Baldwin Road
> PO Box 761
> Shelter Island, NY 11964
> Email: orders@manning.com

Manning Publications Co.	Development editor:	Elesha Hyde
20 Baldwin Road	Technical development editor:	Tanya Wilke
PO Box 761	Review editor:	Mihaela Batinić
Shelter Island, NY 11964	Production editor:	Kathleen Rossland
	Copy editor:	Sharon Wilkey
	Proofreader:	Jason Everett
	Technical proofreaders:	Troi Eisler and Jerry Kuch
	Typesetter:	Dennis Dalinnik
	Cover designer:	Marija Tudor

ISBN: 9781617299001
Printed in the United States of America

To Emily, Cora, and Marlo

brief contents

contents

preface

I am a pragmatist at heart. My introduction to programming was inspired by a neighbor in my small hometown, who sold websites for businesses for a (back then) large sum of money. I thought, if he can earn money with that, I can do it, too. I started a business at the age of 17 with a friend, and we built websites for companies. Seeing this amount of value unlocked for these companies from the comfort of my home made me fall in love with this industry.

However, programming was never my favorite subject, never something I wanted to dive deep into. It was a means to an end, something I had to do so I could deliver an application or a website. I went from writing PL/I on the mainframe to JavaScript for browser applications, while doing backend APIs in between. I just love developing for the internet. This passion led to Rust. It's the first time a language and its compiler had my back so I could focus on what's important: creating value for others.

Rust Web Development is written from this pragmatic view about our industry: creating value with the best tools currently available. This book shows why Rust, even if not obvious at first sight, is a perfect match for the future generation of web applications and APIs. *Rust Web Development* is not just about syntax, but offers guidance and deep dives, and enables you to confidently start and finish your next project with Rust.

I want to lift the curtain and look behind the scenes of a Rust crate, the language itself, and of the web frameworks we choose. The level of detail will always aim to be pragmatic: how much do you need to know to make a difference, to understand a solution so you can adapt it in your own project, and let you know where to look further.

To quote one of my former colleagues, "Writing Rust is like cheating!" My hope is that this book inspires you to see the beauty of developing for the web, with a language that has your back and empowers you to do things faster and safer than you could have done before. I am honored to take you on this journey!

acknowledgments

First, I have to thank my wife, Emily, for believing in me, pushing me forward, and never giving up on trusting that I could finish this book. Writing this book took a lot of hours away from our already limited time, and I will be forever grateful for your support. Thank you for always having my and our family's backs. I love you.

Next, I have to thank Mike Stephens, for reaching out to me and making this book happen. The first calls with you were truly inspiring and made me believe that I could actually write a book. Your wisdom and experience influenced this book and my writing for years to come.

To my editor at Manning, Elesha Hyde: thank you for your patience, your input, your constant following up with emails and invaluable suggestions and guidance throughout this journey. I always looked forward to our meetings and I will truly miss them.

Thank you to the developers who inspired me on this journey: Mariano, your wisdom and insights carried me not only through this book but also through a good chunk of my developer career. Knut and Blake, our time at smartB and the discussions afterward shaped the way I approached the readers of this book. Simon, you taught me a lot about what it takes to be a developer and take one's craft seriously. And thank you, Paul, for providing an outlet, recharging my energy, and getting me excited about our craft through our conversations. Dada, studying together with you was one big cornerstone of being able to write this book. And last but not but least, Sebastian and Fernando, our time together shaped me more than anything else to be the developer and person I am today.

To all the reviewers: Alain Couniot, Alan Lenton, Andrea Granata, Becker, Bhagvan Kommadi, Bill LeBorgne, Bruno Couriol, Bruno Sonnino, Carlos Cobo, Casey Burnett, Christoph Baker, Christopher Lindblom, Christopher Villanueva, Dane Balia, Daniel Tomás Lares, Darko Bozhinovski, Gábor László Hajba, Grant Lennon, Ian Lovell, JD McCormack, Jeff Smith, Joel Holmes, John D. Lewis, Jon Riddle, JT Marshall, Julien Castelain, Kanak Kshetri, Kent R. Spillner, Krzysztof Hrynczenko, Manzur Mukhitdinov, Marc Roulleau, Oliver Forral, Paul Whittemore, Philip Dexter, Rani Sharim, Raul Murciano, Renato Sinohara, Rodney Weis, Samuel Bosch, Sergiu Răducu Popa, Timothy Robert James Langford, Walt Stoneburner, William E. Wheeler, and Xiangbo Mao; your suggestions helped make this a better book.

about this book

Rust Web Development will help you write web applications (be it an API, a microservice, or a monolith) from start to finish. You'll learn everything you need to open an API to the outside world, connect a database to store your data, and test and deploy your application.

This is not a reference book; it should be considered a workbook. The application we are building will make sacrifices in its design so concepts can be taught at the right time. It takes the whole book to finally be able to ship it to production.

Who should read this book

This book is for people who have read the first six chapters of *The Rust Programming Language* by Steve Klabnik and Carol Nichols (No Starch Press, 2019) and then asked themselves, "What can I do with that?" It is also meant for developers who have built web applications in the past with a different language and are wondering if Rust would be a good choice for their next project. And last, it is a great book to help onboard yourself or a new hire to a new job requiring you to write and maintain web applications in Rust.

How this book is organized: A road map

Rust Web Development has three parts with 11 chapters and one appendix.

Part 1 covers the why and how of writing Rust:

- Chapter 1 covers for which environment and team Rust is a great fit and explains the mindset behind choosing Rust for your team or next project. It compares the language with others and gives a sneak peek into its web ecosystem.

- Chapter 2 talks about the Rust language foundations and knowledge needed to complete the book and understand the code snippets presented. It also covers the web ecosystem foundations and explains the extra tooling needed to write asynchronous applications in Rust.

Part 2 is about creating the business logic of the application:

- Chapter 3 creates the foundation that we will build on later in the book. It introduces Warp, the web framework we are using, and how to respond to HTTP GET requests with JSON.
- Chapter 4 covers HTTP POST, PUT, and DELETE requests and how to read fake data from in-memory. This chapter also covers the differences between url-form-encoded and JSON bodies.
- Chapter 5 is all about modularizing, linting, and formatting your code. We split large chunks of code into their own modules and files, use the Rust commenting system to annotate our codebase, add linting rules, and format it.
- Chapter 6 introspects your running application. We explain the difference between logging and tracing and show various ways of debugging your code.
- Chapter 7 gets rid of the in-memory storage and adds a PostgreSQL database instead. We connect to a database on localhost and go through the process of creating a connection pool and sharing it among our route handlers.
- Chapter 8 connects to an external service, where we send data and process the received answer. We discuss how to bundle asynchronous functions and deserialize JSON responses.

Part 3 makes sure everything is ready to bring your code in production.

- Chapter 9 talks about stateful versus stateless authentication and how it manifests in our codebase. We introduce the user concept and add token validation middleware.
- Chapter 10 parameterizes our input variables such as API keys and database URLs and prepares the codebase to be built on various architectures and for a Docker environment.
- Chapter 11 closes the book with unit and integration testing, and how to start and wind down a mock server after each test.

The appendix adds guidance for auditing and writing secure code.

The book can be read in parts. The code repository can be used to check out chapters and get set up for the part you are currently reading. The application is built chapter by chapter, so you might miss some information if you jump ahead. However, chapters can be used as a soft reference guide.

About the code

The code examples in *Rust Web Development* are written with the 2021 Rust edition and have been tested on Linux and macOS with both Intel and Apple chips.

This book contains many examples of source code, both in numbered listings and inline with normal text. In both cases, source code is formatted in a `fixed-width font like this` to separate it from ordinary text. In addition, **bold** is used to highlight code that has changed from previous steps in the chapter, such as when a new feature adds to an existing line of code. In some cases, ~~strike-through~~ is used to indicate code that is being replaced.

In many cases, the original source code has been reformatted; we've added line breaks and reworked indentation to accommodate the available page space in the book. Additionally, comments in the source code have often been removed from the listings when the code is described in the text. Code annotations accompany many of the listings, highlighting important concepts.

You can get executable snippets of code from the liveBook (online) version of this book at https://livebook.manning.com/book/rust-web-development. The complete code for the examples in the book is available for download from the Manning website at https://www.manning.com/books/rust-web-development, and from GitHub at https://github.com/Rust-Web-Development/code.

liveBook discussion forum

Purchase of *Rust Web Development* includes free access to liveBook, Manning's online reading platform. Using liveBook's exclusive discussion features, you can attach comments to the book globally or to specific sections or paragraphs. It's a snap to make notes for yourself, ask and answer technical questions, and receive help from the author and other users. To access the forum, go to https://livebook.manning.com/book/rust-web-development/discussion. You can also learn more about Manning's forums and the rules of conduct at https://livebook.manning.com/discussion.

Manning's commitment to our readers is to provide a venue where a meaningful dialogue between individual readers and between readers and the author can take place. It is not a commitment to any specific amount of participation on the part of the author, whose contribution to the forum remains voluntary (and unpaid). We suggest you try asking the author some challenging questions lest his interest stray! The forum and the archives of previous discussions will be accessible from the publisher's website as long as the book is in print.

about the author

BASTIAN GRUBER is a runtime engineer at Centrifuge, working full-time with Rust. He was part of the official Rust Async Working Group and founded the Rust and Tell Berlin Meetup group. He worked for one of the largest crypto exchanges in the world on the core backend with Rust. He is also a writer with 12+ years of experience, and writes on a regular basis about Rust for LogRocket and gives interviews and talks that have been collected on this book's website (https://rustwebdevelopment.com). Through his experience, Bastian developed the ability to teach complex concepts in an easy way, and his articles are liked for being both easy to digest and in-depth at the same time.

Bastian can be found on social media through his Twitter handle @recvonline. Feel free to send an email to foreach@me.com if you want to get in touch with him.

about the cover illustration

The figure on the cover of *Rust Web Development* is "Femme de Stirie," or "Woman from Styria," taken from a collection by Jacques Grasset de Saint-Sauveur, published in 1788. Each illustration is finely drawn and colored by hand.

In those days, it was easy to identify where people lived and what their trade or station in life was just by their dress. Manning celebrates the inventiveness and initiative of the computer business with book covers based on the rich diversity of regional culture centuries ago, brought back to life by pictures from collections such as this one.

Part 1

Introduction to Rust

This first part of the book sets you up with the foundation of the language. To be able to use Rust for web development, you need an understanding of the language and of the tooling needed to write asynchronous server applications with it. Part 1 covers both topics.

Chapter 1 takes care of the "why." It shows how Rust can be more performant than other languages, and at the same time, enable you to easily and safely create applications with it. It shows how to set up Rust locally, what the toolchain looks like, and importantly, what the async and web ecosystem looks like in Rust.

Chapter 2 then goes further to cover all the foundational knowledge required to not only follow the code snippets throughout the book, but also feel comfortable enough to start a new project in Rust.

Why Rust?

This chapter covers

- The tooling that comes bundled with a standard Rust installation
- A first glimpse of the Rust compiler and what makes it so unique
- What is needed to write web services in Rust
- Features that support the maintainability of Rust applications

Rust is a systems programming language. Unlike an interpreted language like JavaScript or Ruby, Rust has a compiler like Go, C, or Swift. It combines running with no overhead (like active garbage collection in Go or a virtual machine, like Java), but offers easy-to-read syntax from Python and Ruby. Rust therefore performs as languages like C. This is all possible because of the compiler that safeguards any type errors and makes sure to eliminate many classical runtime errors, such as use-after-free, before you run your application.

Rust offers performance (it has no runtime nor garbage collection), safety (the compiler makes sure everything is memory safe, even in asynchronous environments), and productivity (its built-in tooling around testing, documentation, and the package manager makes it a breeze to build and maintain).

You might have heard about Rust, but after trying to go through the tutorials, the language seemed too complex and you gave up learning it. However, Rust comes up as the most-loved programming language on the yearly Stack Overflow surveys, and has found a large following in corporations like Facebook, Google, Apple, and Microsoft. This book will unblock you and show you how to become comfortable with the basics of Rust and how to build and ship solid web services with it.

> **NOTE**   This book assumes you have written a few small Rust applications and are familiar with the general concepts of a web service. We will go through all the basic Rust language features and how to use them in this book, but more as a refresher than as a deep learning experience. If you have read through chapter 6 of *The Rust Programming Language* by Steve Klabnik and Carol Nichols (No Starch Press, 2019, https://doc.rust-lang.org/book), for example, you are fine and won't face any trouble following along with the exercises presented in this book. The book covers Rust 2021, and is backward compatible with version 2018.

For you as a developer, Rust provides a unique chance to broaden your horizons. You might be a frontend developer who wants to get into backend development, or a Java developer who wants to learn a new language. Rust is so versatile that learning it can expand the kinds of systems on which you are able to work. You can use Rust wherever you can use C++ or C, but also in a situation where you would use Node.js, Java, or Ruby. It is even beginning to find a foothold in the machine learning ecosystem, where Python has dominated for years. In addition, Rust is great for compiling to WebAssembly (https://webassembly.org), and many modern blockchain implementations (Cosmos, Polkadot) are written in Rust.

The longer you spend writing code and the more programming languages you learn, the more you realize that the most important things are the concepts you learn and using the programming language best suited to the problem. This book, therefore, does not stop at just showing you which lines of Rust code enable you to make HTTP requests. It describes how web services work in general, as well as the underlying concepts behind asynchronous Rust, so that you can pick the Transmission Control Protocol (TCP) abstraction that works best for you.

1.1   *Batteries included: Rust's tooling*

Rust comes with the right amount of tooling to make starting, maintaining, and building applications straightforward. Figure 1.1 gives you an overview of the most important tools you need to get started writing Rust applications.

You can download Rustup and install Rust by executing the command on the terminal shown in listing 1.1. This works on macOS (via `brew install rustup-init`) and Linux. For an up-to-date way to install Rust on Windows, follow the instructions on the Rust website (www.rust-lang.org/tools/install).

Toolchain/ version manager	Rust compiler	Code formatter	Linter	Package manager	Package registry
Rustup	Rustc	Rustfmt	Clippy	Cargo	crates.io

Figure 1.1   All the tools you need to write and deliver Rust applications with

Listing 1.1   Installing Rust

```
$ curl --proto '=https' --tlsv1.2 -sSf https://sh.rustup.rs | sh
```

The command-line tool curl is built to transfer data with URLs. You can fetch remote files and download them onto your computer. The option `--proto` enables the use of protocols, like Hypertext Transfer Protocol Secure (HTTPS), which we use. With the parameter `--tlsv1.2`, we use Transport Layer Security (http://mng.bz/o5QM) in version 1.2. Next comes the URL, which, if we open it via the browser, offers a shell script to download. This shell script is getting *piped* (via the `|`) to the sh command-line tool, which executes it.

This shell script will also install the tool Rustup, which lets you update Rust and install helper components. Updating Rust is as easy as running the command `rustup update`:

```
$ rustup update
info: syncing channel updates for 'stable-aarch64-apple-darwin'
info: syncing channel updates for 'beta-aarch64-apple-darwin'
info: latest update on 2022-04-26,
      rust version 1.61.0-beta.4 (69a6d12e9 2022-04-25)

...

  stable-aarch64-apple-darwin unchanged - rustc 1.60.0
(7737e0b5c 2022-04-04)
    beta-aarch64-apple-darwin updated -
    rustc 1.61.0-beta.4 (69a6d12e9 2022-04-25)
    (from rustc 1.61.0-beta.3 (2431a974c 2022-04-17))
  nightly-aarch64-apple-darwin updated -
  rustc 1.62.0-nightly (e85edd9a8 2022-04-28)
  (from rustc 1.62.0-nightly (311e2683e 2022-04-18))

info: cleaning up downloads & tmp directories
```

And if you want to install more components, like the code formatter mentioned in figure 1.1, you use `rustup` as well.

Listing 1.2   Installing Rustfmt

```
$ rustup component add rustfmt
```

Running this tool via `cargo fmt` will check your code against a style guide and formats the code accordingly for you. You have to specify the folder or file you want to run it for. You can, for example, navigate to the root folder of your project, and run `cargo fmt .` (with a dot) to run it for all directories and files.

After executing the `curl` command in listing 1.1, we not only have the Rust library installed, but also the package manager Cargo. This will let us create and run Rust projects. With this in mind, let's create and execute our first Rust program. The following listing shows how to run a Rust application. The command `cargo run` will execute `rustc`, compile the code, and run the produced binary.

Listing 1.3   Running our first Rust program

```
$ cargo new hello
$ cd hello
$ cargo run

   Compiling hello v0.1.0 (/private/tmp/hello)
    Finished dev [unoptimized + debuginfo] target(s) in 1.54s
     Running `target/debug/hello`
Hello, world!
```

Our new program prints `Hello, world!` to the console, and we see shortly why. Looking inside our project folder hello, we see the files and folders listed in listing 1.4. The command `cargo new` creates a new folder with the name we specify, and also initializes a new Git structure for it.

Listing 1.4   Folder contents of a new Rust project

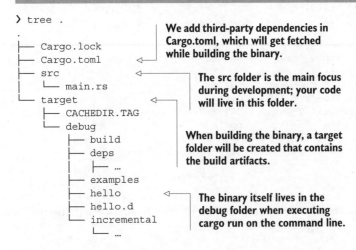

```
> tree .
.
├── Cargo.lock
├── Cargo.toml        ◁
├── src               ◁
│   └── main.rs
└── target            ◁
    ├── CACHEDIR.TAG
    └── debug
        ├── build
        ├── deps
        │   ├── ...
        ├── examples
        ├── hello     ◁
        ├── hello.d
        └── incremental
            └── ...

9 directories, 28 files
```

We add third-party dependencies in Cargo.toml, which will get fetched while building the binary.

The src folder is the main focus during development; your code will live in this folder.

When building the binary, a target folder will be created that contains the build artifacts.

The binary itself lives in the debug folder when executing cargo run on the command line.

The command `cargo run` will build the application and execute the binary, which lives inside the ./target/debug folder. Our source code lives in the src folder. Depending on the type of application we are building, this folder has either a main.rs or lib.rs file in it with the following content.

Listing 1.5 The autogenerated main.rs file

```
fn main() {
    println!("Hello, world!");
}
```

In chapter 5, you will see the difference between the lib.rs and main.rs files, and when Cargo creates which one. The folder target contains another folder called debug, which contains our compiled code, generated by the `cargo run` command. A simple `cargo build` would have had the same effect but would just build and not execute our program.

When building a Rust program, the Rust compiler (Rustc) is creating Rust byte-code, and passes it on to another compiler, called LLVM (https://llvm.org), to create machine code (LLVM is also used by languages like Swift and Scala and turns byte-code produced by the language compiler into machine code for the operating system to run). This means Rust can be compiled on whatever operating system LLVM supports. The whole stack is shown in figure 1.2.

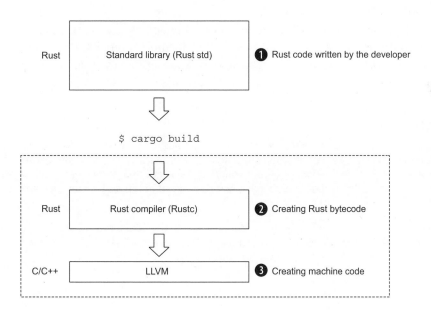

Figure 1.2 After installing Rustup, you have the Rust standard library on your machine, which includes the Rust compiler.

Another important file is Cargo.toml. As we see in listing 1.6, it contains the overall information about our project, and specifies the third-party dependencies if necessary.

> **NOTE**   When developing libraries, the Cargo.lock file should not get checked into your version control system (like Git). But when creating an application (binary), you should add the file to your version control system. Applications (binaries) are often dependent on specific versions of an external library, and therefore other developers you are working with need to know which versions are safe to install or have to be updated to. Libraries, on the other hand, should function on the latest version of used libraries.

Listing 1.6   Contents of a Cargo.toml file

```
[package]
name = "check"
version = "0.1.0"
edition = "2021"

# See more keys and their definitions at
# https://doc.rust-lang.org/cargo/reference/manifest.html
[dependencies]
```

Installing third party libraries happens by adding the names of the dependencies under the [dependencies] section, and running cargo run or cargo build. This will fetch the libraries (called *crates* in the Rust community) from crates.io, the Rust package registry. The actual fetched version of the installed packages appears in a new file, called Cargo.lock. If the file is in the root folder of your project, Cargo will fetch exactly the version of the packages specified in the Cargo.lock file. This will help developers working on the same codebase to replicate the exact same state across different machines.

TOML file

The *TOML* file format is, like JavaScript Object Notation (JSON) or YAML Ain't Markup Language (YAML), a configuration file format. It means *Tom's Obvious Minimal Language*, and as the name suggests, should make configurations easy to read and parse. The package manager Cargo uses this file to install dependencies and populate information about the project.

To quote one of the Rust core members: "It is the least terrible option" (http://mng.bz/aP9J). This doesn't mean that TOML is bad, but just that there are always tradeoffs when handling configuration files.

The last tool in our belt is the official code linter Clippy. This tool is included now by default when installing Rust. It can also be installed manually if you operate on older Rust versions.

Listing 1.7 Installing Clippy

```
$ rustup component add clippy
```

Chapter 5 introduces the use of Clippy and details how to configure it.

1.2 *The Rust compiler*

The advantages of using Rust versus other languages is its compiler. Rust compiles down to binary code with no garbage collection invoked at runtime. This gives you C-like speed. In contrast to C, however, the Rust compiler enforces memory safety at compile time. Figure 1.3 shows the differences between popular programming languages used for server-side programming, and C.

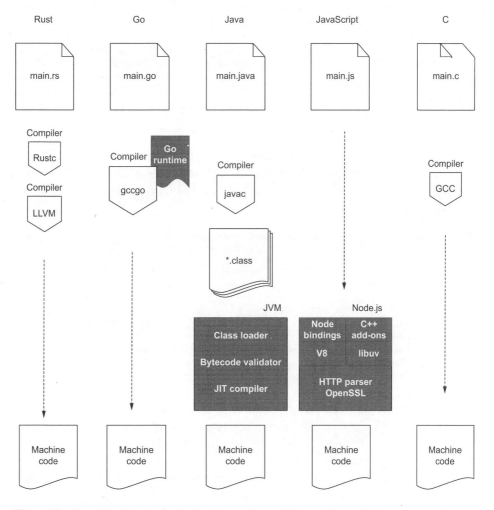

Figure 1.3 Comparing Rust and other languages in compiling machine code from source code

Each language has tradeoffs. Go is the newest of the demonstrated languages and comes closest to the speed of C. It uses a runtime for garbage collection and therefore operates with a bit more overhead than Rust does. Go's compiler is faster than Rustc. Go aims for simplicity and takes a small runtime performance hit to do so.

You see that Rust offers no runtime overhead, and because of the compiler, offers more comfort and safety while writing code than Go or JavaScript, for example. Java and JavaScript require a (sort of) virtual machine for running the code. This results in a heavy performance penalty.

One of the adjustments you will have to make when writing programs in Rust is to work with the Rust compiler to build applications. When you come from a scripting language, this is a huge shift in mindset. Instead of starting an application in a few seconds and debugging it until it fails, the Rust compiler will make sure everything works fine before it starts. For example, consider this code snippet (from later in the book, just printed here for demo purposes).

Listing 1.8   Checking for an empty ID

```
match id.is_empty() {
    false => Ok(QuestionId(id.to_string())),
    true => Err(Error::new(ErrorKind::InvalidInput, "No id provided")),
}
```

If you cannot read this code snippet yet, don't worry; you will soon. That's a `match` block, and the compiler makes sure we cover every use case (whether `id` is empty or not). If we delete the line with `true =>` and try to compile our code, we will get an error.

Listing 1.9   Compiler error for a missing pattern matching

```
error[E0004]: non-exhaustive patterns: `true` not covered
  --> src/main.rs:31:15
   |
31 |          match id.is_empty() {
   |                ^^^^^^^^^^^^^ pattern `true` not covered
   |
   = help: ensure that all possible cases are being handled,
     possibly by adding wildcards or more match arms
   = note: the matched value is of type `bool`
```

The compiler highlights the line and the exact position in our statement, and in addition gives a suggestion for solving the issue at hand. It is designed to produce error messages that are understandable and readable by humans, rather than just exposing the internal parser error.

First making sure the program operates correctly in all use cases might seem tedious in small applications, but once you have to maintain larger systems and add or remove features, you will quickly see how writing Rust can sometimes feel like you are cheating, since so many issues you had to think about in the past will now be covered by the compiler.

It is therefore seldom that you will be able to run newly written Rust code right away. The compiler will be part of your daily routine and help you understand where to improve your code and what you might have forgotten to cover.

You can't jump quickly into Rust as you can, for example, into JavaScript or even Go. You need to become familiar with a set of basic concepts first. In addition, you must learn many aspects of Rust to become a proficient Rust developer. That said, you do not need to know everything to get started; you can learn as you go with the help of the compiler. You see, the Rust compiler is one the strongest arguments for using Rust.

Once you've become proficient, you can use Rust in multiple areas: game development, backend servers, machine learning, and maybe soon Linux kernel development (this is currently an ongoing discussion and trial phase: https://github.com/Rust-for -Linux).

If you develop applications in a larger team, it helps to know that newly trained Rust programmers must pass through the compiler first before they can contribute to the codebase. This will already cover a huge amount of code review and guarantees a baseline of code quality.

1.3 Rust for web services

We covered the main reasons we might choose Rust over other programming languages. Let's look at how we can start writing web services with it. Surprisingly, Rust doesn't cover as much ground when it comes to HTTP as, for example, Go or Node.js. Since Rust is a systems programming language, the Rust community decided to leave efforts around implementing HTTP and other features to the community.

Figure 1.4 shows a typical tech stack of a web service, and to which degree Rust offers help. The bottom two layers (TCP/IP) are covered by the Rust stack. The Rust

The Rust standard library and third-party library coverage of the OSI model

7	Warp | Axum | Rocket	Application	Actix Web	HTTP
6	Hyper	Presentation	actix-server	
5		Session		TLS
4		Transport		TCP
3		Network		IP

Rust standard library   HTTP (server) crates   Web frameworks

**Figure 1.4
Rust covers TCP, but leaves HTTP and larger web framework implementations to the community.**

standard library implements TCP, and we can open a TCP (or User Datagram Protocol, UDP) socket and listen for incoming messages.

However, there is no HTTP implementation. Therefore, if you want to write a pure
HTTP server, you have to either implement it from scratch or use one of the third-
party libraries (like hyper, which is used by curl behind the scenes).

When using a web framework, the choice is already made for you. The web framework Actix Web, for example, uses its own HTTP server implementation, actix-server.
When you use Warp, Axum, or Rocket, they all use Hyper as a web server (opening a
socket, waiting for, and parsing HTTP messages).

We can see in figure 1.4 that TCP is included in the Rust standard library, but
everything above that is enabled by the community. But what does this look like in
code? Let's take an example from Go. The following listing shows an HTTP server
written with Go.

Listing 1.10   A short example of how to write an HTTP server in Go

```go
package main

import (
    "fmt"
    "net/http"
)

func hello(w http.ResponseWriter, req *http.Request) {
    fmt.Fprintf(w, "hello\n")
}


func main() {

    http.HandleFunc("/hello", hello)

    http.ListenAndServe(":8090", nil)
}
```

We can see that Go provides us with an HTTP package. Rust is missing the HTTP
part, and it stops at implementing TCP. We can use Rust to create a TCP server, as
shown in the following listing, but we cannot use it right away to respond with for-
mal HTTP messages.

Listing 1.11   An example TCP server written in Rust

```rust
use std::net::{TcpListener, TcpStream};

fn handle_client(stream: TcpStream) {
    // do something
}

fn main() -> std::io::Result<()> {
    let listener = TcpListener::bind("127.0.0.1:80")?;
```

```
    for stream in listener.incoming() {
        handle_client(stream?);
    }
    Ok(())
}
```

Therefore, it is up to the community to implement HTTP. Luckily, plenty of implementations are out there already. And when choosing a web framework later in the book, you don't need to worry about that part of the stack anymore.

Another big cornerstone of writing web services is asynchronous programming. This gives us the ability to handle multiple requests at once. And it reduces the wait time for responses from the server.

When a web server receives a request, some work has to be done (accessing a database, writing files, and so forth). If a second request comes in before the work is finished, that request would have to wait for the first one. Imagine millions of requests coming in at almost the same time.

Therefore, we need a way to somehow put work in the background and continue accepting requests on our server. This is where asynchronous programming comes in. Other frameworks and languages (like Node.js and Go) do this to some degree automatically in the background for us. With Rust, we have to understand the building blocks of asynchronous programming a bit more granularly to know which frameworks to choose.

A programming language (or the ecosystem around it) has to offer the following concepts so we can create applications that can process work asynchronously:

- *Syntax*—Marks a piece of code as asynchronous
- *Type*—A more complex type that can keep the state of the asynchronous progress
- *Thread scheduler (runtime)*—A way to handle threading or other methods to put work in the background and make progress on it
- *Kernel abstractions*—Use the asynchronous kernel methods in the background

Asynchronous runtimes in Rust

When we talk about the *runtime* here, it is not the same as a Java runtime or Go garbage collection. During compilation, the runtime will be compiled into static code. Each library or framework that facilitates some form of asynchronous code will choose a runtime to build on top of. The work of the runtime is to choose its own way of handling threads and managing work (tasks) behind the scenes.

Therefore, it is possible to end up with multiple runtimes. If you choose a web framework that dictates the Tokio runtime, for example, and has a helper library to do asynchronous HTTP requests, which is built on top of another runtime, then you basically have two runtimes compiled in your binary. Whether or not you run into side effects depends on the design of your application.

What does this look like in Rust? Let's look at listing 1.12 to see how asynchronous fetching of a website looks in Rust. This code can be found in the book's GitHub repository (https://github.com/Rust-Web-Development/code). We don't go into detail here; this is left for chapter 2 and onward, but this should give you a first idea what asynchronous code looks like in Rust. For this snippet to work, you need to add the external crate Reqwest (which is not a typo, and we don't mean the word *request* here) to your project (via the Cargo.toml file).

Listing 1.12   Sending HTTP GET requests asynchronously in Rust

The runtime usage is defined on top of the main function of your application.

We mark the main function as async, so we can use await inside.

We are using the crate Reqwest here to execute an HTTP GET request, which will return the type Future.

```
// ch_01/minimal_reqwest/src/main.rs
// https://github.com/Rust-Web-
        Development/code/tree/main/ch_01/minimal_reqwest

use std::collections::HashMap;

#[tokio::main]
async fn main() -> Result<(), Box<dyn std::error::Error>> {
    let resp = reqwest::get("https://httpbin.org/ip")
        .await?
        .json::<HashMap<String, String>>()
        .await?;
    println!("{:#?}", resp);
    Ok(())
}
```

We use the await keyword to tell the program we want to wait for the future to be in a finished state before we move on in this function.

The keyword Ok returns a result, an empty one in this case.

We print out the content of our response.

We annotate the main function with #[tokio::main]. Tokio is the asynchronous runtime (or thread scheduler) we are using here. Tokio itself is using (through another crate, called Mio) the asynchronous Kernel application programming interface (API) from the operating system we listed earlier.

We can mark a function as async with the standard Rust syntax, and await on a future (http://mng.bz/5mv1) type. A *future* in Rust is a trait, which can be implemented onto types. This trait dictates that the implementation must have a type Output (indicating what the future returns when the computation is complete), and a function called poll (which a runtime can call to do work on the future). When working with web frameworks, you might never touch the actual implementation of a future, but it is important to understand the underlying concept, so compiler messages and framework implementations make sense to you.

In contrast to other languages, in Rust, work by futures is only beginning when handed over to the runtime and actively started. An asynchronous function returns a type of Future, and the caller of the function is responsible for passing this future to a runtime to do something with it.

For the developer, this means adding `.await` to the function call, which indicates to the runtime to execute it. There are also other ways of starting futures (like the Tokio `join!` macro: http://mng.bz/694D) which we will use in chapter 8.

Figure 1.5 shows the building blocks we listed earlier and used in listing 1.12. Chapter 2 will go into more depth about this topic. Rust offers the syntax and type in its standard library and leaves the runtime and kernel abstractions up to the community to implement.

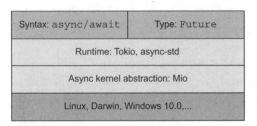

Figure 1.5   Rust provides the syntax and the type for asynchronous programming, but the runtime and kernel abstractions are implemented outside the core language.

Your choice of a runtime is basically taken care of by the web framework you select later. That framework will dictate the runtime that it is dependent on.

Listing 1.13 shows a minimal working web application with the web framework Warp—our later choice for this book. This web framework is built on top of the Tokio runtime, which means we have to also add Tokio to our project (via the Cargo.toml file, shown in listing 1.14).

Listing 1.13   A minimal working HTTP server in Rust with Warp

```
// ch_01/minimal_warp/src/main.rs
// https://github.com/Rust-Web-Development/code/tree/main/ch_01/minimal-warp

use warp::Filter;

#[tokio::main]
async fn main() {
    let hello = warp::get()
        .map(|| format!("Hello, World!"));

    warp::serve(hello)
        .run(([127, 0, 0, 1], 1337))
        .await;
}
```

Listing 1.14   The Cargo.toml file for the minimal Warp example

```
[package]
name = "minimal-warp"
version = "0.1.0"
edition = "2021"
```

```
[dependencies]
tokio = { version = "1.2", features = ["full"] }
warp = "0.3"
```

The syntax might look foreign now, but you can see that everything is abstracted away behind the Warp framework, and the only sign of the Tokio runtime is in the line above the main function. We will talk more about our framework of choice, and how and why we chose it in chapter 2.

You might wonder, if Rust doesn't have a standard runtime to handle asynchronous code, nor does it have HTTP included in the standard library, why would it make sense to write web services with it? It boils down to the language features and the community.

You can argue that no standard HTTP implementation and runtime makes it even more future proof, since the community can always step in and improve something or offer different solutions for different problems. The type safety, speed, and correctness of the language play a crucial part in an environment where you handle asynchronous work in your application and deal with a huge amount of traffic. A fast and safe language will pay off in the long run.

1.4   *Maintainability of Rust applications*

The Rust compiler helps you write sound software, but its other language features help make Rust great for maintenance. For example, it comes with documentation built in. Chapter 5 provides a deeper look at properly documenting your code with built-in tooling. The package manager Cargo has a command to generate documentation from your code comments, which is browsable locally and will be built by default when exporting a library to crates.io. Code embedded in your code documentation will not only show up in pregenerated HTML documents, but also run through the tests as well, so you can make sure you never have outdated code examples.

Next to documenting, modularizing your codebase helps with grouping parts together or extracting reusable code into its own crate. Rust makes this rather easy with the use of the dependency section in the Cargo.toml file to include local libraries, from the official crates.io registry or any other location you wish.

Rust also supports testing by default. You don't need an additional crate or other helper tools to create and run tests. All these built-in and standardized features remove a lot of friction and discussions in your team, and you can focus on writing and implementing code rather than always looking for a new tool to write documentation or tests in.

If you need help later and don't have the expertise on your team, dozens of Discord channels, Reddit forums, and Stack Overflow tags are available to ask for guidance. For example, help for the runtime Tokio and the web framework Warp can be found on the Tokio Discord server (https://discord.com/invite/tokio), which has a channel for each tool. It's a great way to ask for help or read other people's comments to learn more about the tooling at hand.

Summary

- Rust is a systems programming language that produces binaries.
- It comes with a strict compiler with helpful error messages, so you have an easy time spotting mistakes and improvements.
- The tooling around Rust ships with the Rust installation itself or has official recommendations so you save time by not constantly exploring, discussing, and learning new tools.
- You have to pick a runtime when writing asynchronous code (the "how" will be covered in chapter 2), since Rust doesn't include one like Go or Node.js does.
- Web frameworks are built on top of runtimes, so your choice is made by the framework you choose later.
- Rust's speed, safety, and correctness will help you a huge amount when maintaining small to large web services and codebases.
- Documentation and testing are built into the language itself, which makes maintaining your code even easier.

Laying the foundation

2

This chapter covers

- Getting to know the Rust types
- Understanding the Rust ownership system
- Implementing custom behavior in your own types
- Understanding the building blocks of an asynchronous ecosystem
- Choosing third-party libraries to build web services with Rust
- Setting up a basic working web service with Rust

The first chapter provided a pretty good rundown of the features that come with Rust, and the tooling we need to add to be able to create web services with Rust. This chapter elaborates on these points. The first part details how to use the language to create your own types and functions. In the second part, you'll add a web server so you can serve your first response to the user.

As mentioned before, you will fare best if you read chapters 1 to 6 of *The Rust Programming Language* (https://doc.rust-lang.org/book/). This chapter will teach the concepts needed for completing this book, so it might be enough to go through this chapter without any previous knowledge. However, I recommend again to go at least briefly through the first six chapters of *The Rust Programming Language* to have a proper foundation of the language itself.

In this book, we will create an example Q&A web service, where users can ask and answer questions. We are going to build a Representational State Transfer (REST) API and will have a running service, deployed and tested by the end of the book. We will store new questions, update or delete them, and be able to post answers. Later in the book, we will figure out how to authenticate to this web service and how to test properly.

Throughout the book, we focus on the Rust aspects of a web service. Regardless of which web framework you ultimately choose for your own projects, the material presented here should still be applicable in one manner or another. The goal is to educate and show one way of going about an implementation.

It is important to have this in mind: Rust is twofold. You don't need to know the lower-level details of operating systems; however, you benefit from knowing a bit more about how operating systems allocate memory and execute functions. This is also the goal of the book. You shouldn't just learn another syntax but enhance your overall knowledge around systems and web services.

This chapter lays the foundation. Figure 2.1 shows the intent behind the following sections. Once you understand the areas of Rust you will run into repeatedly, you can take your time to learn them thoroughly. The same goes for a web service. If you ever run into performance issues or are not happy with your choice of framework, you'll know your way around in the Rust ecosystem to choose crates that fit your needs better.

To make reading this book a valuable exercise, you should learn these foundations now so you can still benefit from them for many years to come. This is the last chapter of the book that focuses more on fundamentals than code, and we will quickly pick up the pace in the next chapter.

We'll start implementing our web service with structs and have a basic web server running at the end of the chapter, but the goal is to explain the concepts along the way. In the following chapters, we'll assume a basic understanding of the language and ecosystem.

2.1   *Following the Rust playbook*

Rust is a complex language, but you don't have to know all the ins and outs at the beginning, or even during a larger project. The compiler and other tools (Clippy, for example, which we will delve into in chapter 5) will help a great deal to finish up code in a clean and nice way. Therefore, we won't cover every aspect of the language, but you will feel confident in looking up topics yourself when you run into them.

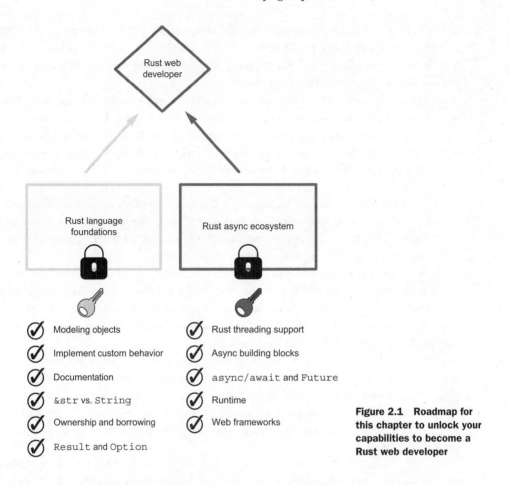

Figure 2.1 Roadmap for this chapter to unlock your capabilities to become a Rust web developer

To work confidently in Rust, you have to get up to speed on these skills:

- Looking up types and behaviors via docs.rs, the official Rust documentation
- Quickly iterating over errors or problems you face
- Understanding how the Rust ownership system works
- Identifying and using macros
- Creating your own types via structs and implementing behavior via `impl`
- Implementing traits and macros on existing types
- Writing functional Rust with options and results

We cover these basics in this chapter, and will practice and go more in depth in the following chapters. It is important to know that even complex problems or challenges you face down the road can be solved by the preceding skills. It just takes experience and the right mindset to overcome them.

Since Rust is a strictly typed language, you need to put in a bit more effort in the beginning of your program. Quickly fetching a JSON file from another endpoint or modeling a simple program can take a bit longer if you are not familiar with existing types and how to handle unknown values you first have to inspect.

2.1.1   Modeling your resources with structs

We want to create a RESTful API, which means we'll provide routes to create, read, update, and delete (CRUD) resources. The first step is therefore to think about which models or types we have to deal with in our web service.

It is wise to start with mapping out your smallest working application. This includes the custom data types you want to implement and their behavior (methods). For our very own application, we need the following:

- Users
- Questions
- Answers

Users can register and log into the system, and then post and view questions and answers to these questions. We will focus on users later in the book, when we talk about authentication and authorization of the application. For now, we'll implement each route without checking for passwords or user IDs.

Figure 2.2 shows what is needed to create and implement our own types in Rust. We'll start by implementing the `Question` type and go through all the quirks we encounter and types we need along the way. You create your own type by using the `struct` keyword and adding fields to it. You then use an `impl` block to add behavior in form of functions.

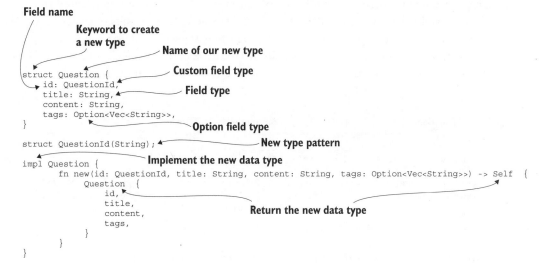

Figure 2.2   Custom types can be created with structs, and adding custom methods is done via the `impl` block.

Let's start by creating our questions and answers and go over the basic life cycle of the creation of a custom type in Rust.

> **Listing 2.1　Creating and implementing our `Question` type**

```
struct Question {
    id: QuestionId,
    title: String,
    content: String,
    tags: Option<Vec<String>>,
}
struct QuestionId(String);

impl Question {
    fn new(
        id: QuestionId,
        title: String,
        content: String,
        tags: Option<Vec<String>>
    ) -> Self {
        Question {
            id,
            title,
            content,
            tags,
        }
    }
}
```

As we create our `Question` type, we use `id` to distinguish between different questions later (we create the ID by hand for now and will move to an autogenerated one later in the book). Each question has a `title`, and the actual question is in the `content`. We also use `tags` to group certain questions together. We will explain what `Option` means in section 2.1.2. Functions look very similar to those in other programming languages. Figure 2.3 shows the function signature in Rust and what each element means.

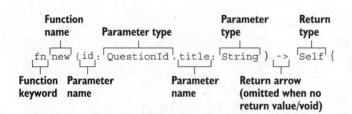

Figure 2.3　The Rust function signature in detail when returning a value

We always need to go through these steps to create custom data in Rust:

1 Create a new struct with `struct Question {…}`.
2 Add fields with their types to the struct.

3 Rust doesn't have a default name for a constructor, so best practice is to have a method called `new`.

4 Add behavior to your custom type with an `impl` block.

5 Return either `Self` or `Question` to instantiate a new object of this type.

We are also using the *New Type pattern* (http://mng.bz/o5Zr), in which we don't simply use a string for our question ID, but encapsulate a string into a struct called `QuestionId`. Every time we pass a parameter or try to create a new question, we need to create a new `QuestionId` instead of just passing a string. Having a custom type conveys a purpose—one the compiler can enforce for us.

For now, this seems unnecessary, but in larger applications, this gives parameters more meaning. You can think of custom types as IDs. You can have functions that take a `Question` ID within an application (like ours) and that also handle `Answer` IDs. Encapsulating primitive types in structs gives them meaning and later flexibility in instantiating them.

2.1.2 Understanding options

Options are important in Rust. They let us make sure we don't have `null` where we would expect a value. Via the `Option` enum, we can always check whether the value provided is present and can handle the case when it is not. Even better, when having an `Option` enum at hand, the compiler makes sure we always cover every case (`Some` or `None`). This also lets us declare not-required fields, so when creating a new question, we don't need to provide a list of tags, but we can if we want to.

Later, when you want to receive data while working with external APIs, marking certain fields as optional is quite helpful. Because Rust is strictly typed, whenever you expect a field on a type to be set but it is not, the compiler will throw an error. Also, by default, all struct fields are required when specified. Therefore, you have to manually make sure that the fields that are not required are marked as `Option<Type>`.

Rust Playground

An important part of the Rust learning journey is to use the tools available to quickly test out ideas. The Rust Playground website (https://play.rust-lang.org/) provides the Rust compiler and the most used crates to quickly iterate over smaller programs. Therefore, you don't always have to create a local Rust project to tinker with a certain topic.

A common way of checking whether `Option` has a value is through the `match` keyword. Listing 2.2, which you can copy and paste and run in the Rust Playground (or click http://mng.bz/neZg), shows how to use a `match` block on an optional value. This example is created out of thin air as a demonstration use case for the `match` block.

Pattern matching in Rust

Novice developers often look at `match` as an alternate keyword for `switch`. However, pattern matching in Rust is much more powerful. Chapter 18 of *The Rust Programming Language* goes into more detail (http://mng.bz/AVYp).

The `match` pattern, for example, also allows the destructuring of structs (http://mng.bz/49na), enums (http://mng.bz/Qnww), and more. This powerful mechanism makes your code more readable and uses Rust's powerful type system to express more meaning in your codebase, which the compiler can enforce.

Listing 2.2 Using `match` to work with `Option` values

```
fn main() {
    struct Book {
        title: String,
        isbn: Option<String>,
    }

    let book = Book {
        title: "Great book".to_string(),
        isbn: Some(String::from("1-123-456"))
    };

    match book.isbn {
        Some(i) => println!(
            "The ISBN of the book: {} is: {}",
            book.title,
            i
        ),
        None => println!("We don't know the ISBN of the book"),
    }
}
```

The standard library also offers a huge variety of methods and traits you can use on an `Option` value (http://mng.bz/Xa7G). For example, `book.isbn.is_some` returns either `true` or `false`, indicating whether it has a value.

2.1.3 *Using documentation to solve errors*

Our simple setup will let us face many basic Rust behaviors and features, so let's try to create a new question (see listing 2.3) in our program with the constructor we implemented previously on the `Question` struct (to debug in the Rust Playground, use http://mng.bz/yaNG). Be aware that this code will not compile and will throw some errors (listing 2.4), which we will fix together right after.

Listing 2.3 Creating an example question and printing it

```
// ch02/src/main.rs

struct Question {
    id: QuestionId,
    title: String,
    content: String,
    tags: Option<Vec<String>>,
}

struct QuestionId(String);

impl Question {
    fn new(
        id: QuestionId,
        title: String,
        content: String,
        tags: Option<Vec<String>>
    ) -> Self {
        Question {
            id,
            title,
            content,
            tags,
        }
    }
}

fn main() {
    let question = Question::new(
        "1",
        "First Question",
        "Content of question",
        ["faq"]
    );
    println!("{}", question);
}
```

Add this snippet at the end of the main.rs file and run it. Notice that we use double colons (::) to call the method new on Question. Rust has two ways of implementing functions onto types:

- Associated functions
- Methods

Associated functions don't take &self as a parameter and are called with two double colons (::). They are roughly equivalent to static functions in other programming languages. Despite being called *associated*, they are not associated to a specific instance. *Methods*, on the other hand, take &self and are called simply via a dot (.). Figure 2.4 shows the differences in implementing and calling each option.

```
impl Question {
    fn new(id: QuestionId, title: String, …) -> Self {
        Question {
            id,
            title,
            content,
            tags,        let q = Question::new(QuestionId("1".to_string()), "title".to_string(), …);
        }
    }

    fn update_title(&self, new_title: String) -> Self {
        Question::new(self.id, new_title, self.content, self.tags)
    }
}                        q.update_title("better_title".to_string());
```

Figure 2.4 An associated function (`new`, at the top) doesn't take an `&self` parameter and is called via double colons (`::`). A method (`update_title`, at the bottom) takes an `&self` parameter and is called via dot notation (`.`). Calling a function from within an `impl` block is possible via the name of the block (`Question::new(…)`, in this case).

We can start our application with the `cargo run` command on the terminal. This, however, will return a long list of errors. This experience won't go away, even after writing Rust for multiple years. The compiler is strict, and you have to start to befriend its sea of red errors.

Rust wants to produce safe and correct code and is therefore picky about what it allows to compile. This has the advantage of teaching you how to write code and gives excellent error messages so you can see where you are wrong.

Listing 2.4 Error messages after trying to compile our code so far

```
error[E0308]: arguments to this function are incorrect
  --> src/main.rs:27:20
   |
27 |        let question = Question::new(
   |                       ^^^^^^^^^^^^^^
28 |            "1",
   |            --- expected struct `QuestionId`, found `&str`
29 |            "First Question",
   |            --------------- expected struct `String`, found `&str`
30 |            "Content of question",
   |            -------------------- expected struct `String`, found `&str`
31 |            ["faq"],
   |            ------- expected enum `Option`, found array `[&str; 1]`
   |
   = note: expected enum `Option<Vec<String>>`
              found array `[&str; 1]`
note: associated function defined here
  --> src/main.rs:11:8
   |
11 |        fn new(
   |           ^^^
12 |            id: QuestionId,
   |            --------------
```

The Rust compiler shows us exactly where and what the problem is.

Putting text between double quotes is somehow not a String but a `&str`.

Instead of an array, the compiler is expecting an enum Option for our tags.

```
13 |          title: String,
   |          -------------
14 |          content: String,
   |          ---------------
15 |          tags: Option<Vec<String>>,
   |          -------------------------
help: try using a conversion method
   |
29 |          "First Question".to_string(),
   |                          ++++++++++++
help: try using a conversion method
   |
30 |          "Content of question".to_string(),
   |                               ++++++++++++

error[E0277]: `Question` doesn't implement `std::fmt::Display`
  --> src/main.rs:33:20
   |
33 |      println!("{}", question);
   |                     ^^^^^^^^ `Question` cannot
       be formatted with the default formatter
   |
   = help: the trait `std::fmt::Display` is not implemented for `Question`
   = note: in format strings you may be able to use `{:?}` (or {:#?}
           for pretty-print) instead
   = note: this error originates in the macro `$crate::format_args_nl`
           (in Nightly builds, run with -Z macro-backtrace for more info)

Some errors have detailed explanations: E0277, E0308.
For more information about an error, try `rustc --explain E0277`.
error: aborting due to 5 previous errors; 1 warning emitted
```

We can't print the question to the console.

You will use these errors to learn more about the language and its features, so you are ready for your journey ahead building a solid web application. You will see that some errors have two issues, and others are just a repeated mistake we made and will go away by fixing the one before.

It is best practice to always start with the first error you see, since this could be the reason the ones afterward appear as well. So let's go over the first issue and see how we could fix it.

Listing 2.5   Our first compiler error

```
  --> src/main.rs:27:20
   |
27 |      let question = Question::new(
   |                     ^^^^^^^^^^^^^
28 |          "1",
   |          --- expected struct `QuestionId`, found `&str`
```

This error shows us two issues. First, we need to pass our custom `QuestionId` type instead of `&str`. And looking at our struct definition from listing 2.3, we need to encapsulate `String` instead of `&str`.

This gives us the chance to open the documentation of &str (https://doc.rust-lang
.org/std/primitive.str.html) and see what we can do to solve this. The first time opening the Rust documentation can be intimidating, but fear not, as it just takes time to
get used to; take a look at figure 2.5.

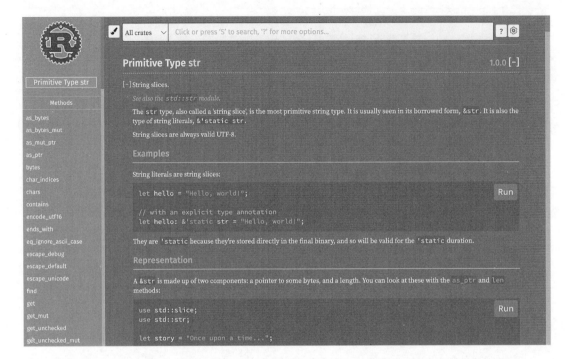

Figure 2.5   Although it's complex, the Rust documentation is fast to navigate and offers tons of information.

The documentation contains a main window and a sidebar on the left. The main window usually introduces the type you are dealing with, and the sidebar offers implementation details as well as the methods and traits implemented on this type. It's
important to go through the following:

- Methods
- Trait implementations
- Auto trait implementations
- Blanket implementations

Browse the docs locally and offline

If you are on a train, airplane, or just want to have the Rust docs locally, you can
install the docs component via rustup:

```
$ rustup component add rust-docs
```

> **(continued)**
>
> Afterward, you can open the docs from the standard library in your default browser:
>
> ```
> $ rustup doc --std
> ```
>
> You can also generate docs from your codebase, which includes all Cargo dependencies as well:
>
> ```
> $ cargo doc --open
> ```
>
> This will also include structs and functions you defined, even if you didn't explicitly create documentation for them.

Before we move on and choose a method to transform our &str into String, we have to understand the difference between these two and why Rust handles them differently.

2.1.4 Handling strings in Rust

The major difference between String (http://mng.bz/M0w7) and &str (https://doc .rust-lang.org/std/primitive.str.html) in Rust is that a string is resizable. A *string* is a collection of bytes, which is implemented as a vector. We can look at the definition in the source code.

Listing 2.6   String definition in the standard library

```
// Source: https://doc.rust-lang.org/src/alloc/string.rs.html#294-296

pub struct String {
    vec: Vec<u8>,
}
```

Strings are created via String::from("popcorn"); and can be altered after they are created. We see that underneath the String is a vector, which means we can remove and insert u8 values in this vector as we wish.

A &str (string literal) is a representation of u8 values (text), which we can't modify. You can see it as a fixed-size window to an underlying string of characters. We will explain the Rust concept of ownership in the next section, but it's already important to understand that if we have String, we "own" this piece of memory and can modify it.

When dealing with &str, we deal with the pointer to the space in memory, and we are allowed to read but not modify it. This makes using &str more memory efficient. Here's a rule of thumb: If you create functions, use &str as a parameter type when you just want to read a string. If you want to own and modify it, use String.

As we see in figure 2.6, both string literals and strings live on the heap but have a different pointer allocated on the stack. You don't need to understand the concept of a heap and stack in detail, but to understand the compiler errors better in the future, becoming familiar with the concept is helpful. The following "Stack vs. heap" sidebar explains the main concepts.

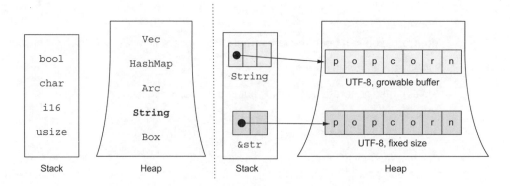

Figure 2.6   Primitive types are stored on the stack in Rust, whereas more complex types are stored on the heap. `String` **and** `&str` **point to more complex data types (collections of UTF-8 values).Whereas** `&str` **has a fat pointer (the memory address and the length field) showing the location on the heap, the** `String` **pointer has not only an address and length field, but also a capacity field.**

Stack vs. heap

Operating systems allocate memory for all the work they do with variables and functions. The operating system has to save functions and call them, and process and reuse data. Two concepts are used for this work: the stack and the heap.

The *stack* is usually controlled by the program, and each thread has its own stack. It stores addresses, register values, and programmatic values (variables, parameters, and return values). Basically, everything with a fixed size (or padded to the correct modulo) can be stored on the stack.

The *heap* is more distinctive (although there can be multiple heaps), and operating on the heap is more expensive. Data doesn't have a fixed size and can be split over multiple blocks, so reading can take more time.

Wait, what is a str?

A `&str` without its ampersand sign is just a `str`, the actual data type we are dealing with. However, a `str` is an immutable sequence of UTF-8 bytes that doesn't have a fixed length. Because its length is unknown, we can handle it behind a pointer (for reference, Stack Overflow provides a great explanation: http://mng.bz/aP9z).

Or to quote the Rust documentation: "The `str` type, also called a 'string slice,' is the most primitive string type. It is usually seen in its borrowed form, `&str`" (https://doc.rust-lang.org/std/primitive.str.html). Section 2.1.5 details *borrowing* in Rust.

A quick summary:

- If you need to own and modify the text, create a `String` type.
- Use `&str` when you need only a view of the underlying text.

- When creating new data types via a struct, you typically create `String` field types.
- When passing strings/text to a function, you usually use `&str`.

2.1.5 *Taking an excursion into moving, borrowing, and ownership*

The simple `String` versus `&str` comparison goes even deeper and touches one of Rust's major concepts: ownership. Simply put, Rust wants to manage memory safely without using a garbage collector or requiring a lot of caution from the developer.

Each computer program is dealing with memory, so either the garbage collector has to clean up and make sure no variable can point to an empty value, or the developer has to think through this process. Rust chooses neither option and introduces a different concept.

The following code listings (2.7 through 2.9) are best run in the Rust Playground: http://mng.bz/gRml. You can try out various combinations to see if you can fix the errors yourself.

Listing 2.7 Assigning `&str` values

```
fn main() {
    let x = "hello";
    let y = x;

    println!("{}", x);
}
```

When we run this program, we see `hello` printed onto the console. Now let's try the same with `String`.

Listing 2.8 Assigning `String` values

```
fn main() {
    let x = String::from("hello");
    let y = x;

    println!("{}", x);
}
```

We get the following error:

```
error[E0382]: borrow of moved value: `x`
 --> src/main.rs:5:20
  |
2 |     let x = String::from("hello");
  |         - move occurs because `x` has type `String`,
  |           which does not implement the `Copy` trait
3 |     let y = x;
  |             - value moved here
4 |
5 |     println!("{}", x);
  |                    ^ value borrowed here after move
```

Why are we getting this error? In listing 2.7, we create a new variable of the type &str: a reference (&) to a string slice (str), https://doc.rust-lang.org/std/primitive.str.html), with the value hello. If we assign this variable to a new one (y = x), we create a new pointer to the same address in memory. Now we have two pointers pointing to the same underlying value.

As shown in figure 2.6, we cannot change the string slice after it is created; it is therefore immutable. We can now print both variables, which are valid and will point to the underlying memory holding the representation of the word *hello*.

Things are changing when we deal with the actual string instead of a reference to one. Listing 2.8 creates a complex type, String. The Rust compiler now enforces the single-ownership principle. When we reassign String with y = x as before, we transfer the ownership from the variable x to y.

By transferring the ownership from x to y, x goes out of scope and Rust internally marks it as uninit (https://doc.rust-lang.org/nomicon/drop-flags.html). Figure 2.7 illustrates this concept. If we try to print the variable x, it doesn't exist anymore since the ownership got transferred to y, and x has no value.

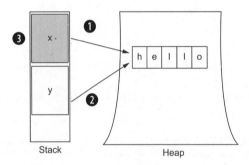

① `let x = String::from("hello");`

② `let y = x;`

③ `//mark x as uninitialized`

Figure 2.7   When reassigning complex types to a new variable, Rust copies the pointer information and gives ownership to the new variable. The old one is not needed anymore and goes out of scope.

Let's explore another area where we have to understand Rust's ownership principle: dealing with functions. Passing a variable to a function hands over the ownership of the underlying data to the function. We have different ways of dealing with this in Rust:

- Moving the ownership to the function and returning a new variable from the function
- Passing a reference of the variable to retain ownership

Listing 2.9 shows one example of modifying a String object through a function. We pass a mutable reference (so we can modify it) to a String to a function. The function is now allowed to access the underlying data and modify it. Once the function completes, we get the ownership back inside main and therefore can print address.

You can play around with various options in this example via this Playground link: http://mng.bz/epBz.

Listing 2.9 Handing over the ownership to a function

```
fn main() {
    let address = String::from("Street 1");        ← Declares a variable and
                                                      assigns a String to it

    let a = add_postal_code(address);        ← Passes an address to the function and assigns
                                                the return value to a variable called a

    println!("{}", a);        ← Prints the
                                 updated address
}

fn add_postal_code(mut address: String) -> String {        ← The function parameter
    address.push_str(", 1234 Kingston");        ←            also has to be declared
    address                                                  as mutable so we can
}                                  The push_str method       modify it (mut address:
                                   alters our String directly. String).
```

Returns the modified String (address)

Let's look at this example in detail. First, new variables are read-only by default, and if we want to change (mutate) them, we must add `mut` to the `let` keyword when creating a new one. We then call the `add_postal_code` function, which will append the postal code to the `String` object we just created.

By passing `address` to the `add_postal_code` function, we move the ownership to this function. When we try to print `address` after this line, we'll get an error as we did in listing 2.8. The function `add_postal_code` expects a mutable `String` object (via the `mut` keyword in the parameter) and adds new characters to it via the `.push_str` function. It then returns the updated `String`, which we assign back to a variable called a.

Instead of coming up with new names for this new variable, we could also use exactly the same name as before, `address`. This is called *variable shadowing* (http://mng.bz/p6ZG) and is a feature of Rust, so you don't have to constantly find new names for variables you want to modify.

Listing 2.10 shows a slightly different approach, one you might come across more frequently in Rust codebases. Instead of passing the value of `address` and losing the ownership, we pass a reference instead. Therefore, we keep the ownership and lend it to the function for the time it requires.

Listing 2.10 Passing a reference

```
fn main() {
    let mut address = String::from("Street 1");        ← Declares a mutable variable
                                                          and assigns a String to it

    add_postal_code(&mut address);        ← Passes a reference to address to
                                             the add_postal_code function

    println!("{}", address);
}

fn add_postal_code(address: &mut String) {        ← The function parameter
    address.push_str(", 1234 Kingston");                expects a mutable
}                                                       reference of a String.
                                          ← The push_str method
                                             alters our String directly.
```

Prints the modified address

The add_postal_code function borrows the ownership for as long as the duration of the function body. The address variable is therefore not going out of scope before we try to print it (as before).

This sums up our excursion to String versus &str and the ownership principles in Rust. One simple error uncovered a lot of inner dynamics of the language. You now understand how to fix our initial error (expecting a QuestionId instead of a &str type) in listing 2.5.

2.1.6   *Using and implementing traits*

The compiler told us that it was expecting a QuestionId instead of a &str type We open the documentation of &str (https://doc.rust-lang.org/std/primitive.str.html) to figure out how to transform it to a value of type String. When scrolling down, we see a trait implementation called ToString. We have to click the [+] next to ToString to get more details (see figure 2.8). We click Read More to navigate to the to_string function definition, which we can use when a type implements the ToString trait (which &str does).

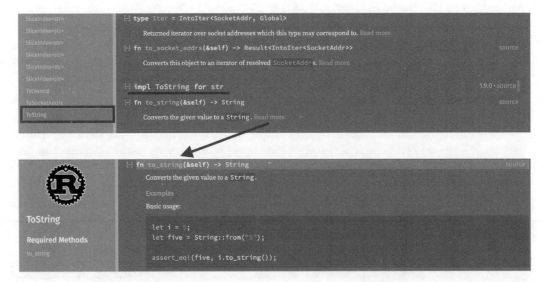

Figure 2.8   The sidebar offers every method available to a certain type, and finding the implementation details requires a bit of digging sometimes.

> ### Traits
> To implement shared behavior, Rust uses *traits*. These roughly translate to *interfaces* in other languages. However, in Rust, you can implement traits on types you didn't define.

(continued)

You can use traits to create behavior that is needed by more than one type in your application. You can also standardize behavior with traits. When turning one type into another, for example, you can use a trait (just like the `ToString` trait in the standard library).

Another advantage of traits is that they enable you to use types in a different context. Rust programs can be generic, accepting every type that behaves a certain way.

Think about a restaurant that accepts all animals that can fit under a table and drink water. Your functions in a Rust program can act similarly. They, for example, can return types with a certain characteristic. As long as your type implements these characteristics, they can be returned.

You will quickly implement traits in Rust when wanting to print out custom structs onto the console, for example (via the `derive` macro—which writes all the manual trait implementation for you during compile time).

It seems we can use `to_string` to convert our `&str` to `String`. The method takes `&self`, which indicates that we call it via a dot on any `&str` we define and returns a `String`. This should help us solve a bunch of our errors. In addition, we try to encapsulate the ID in `QuestionId`, since this is how we defined it in our struct.

Listing 2.11 Turning `&str` into `String`

```
// ch_02/src/main.rs

struct Question {
    id: QuestionId,
    title: String,
    content: String,
    tags: Option<Vec<String>>,
}

struct QuestionId(String);

impl Question {
    fn new(
        id: QuestionId,
        title: String,
        content: String,
        tags: Option<Vec<String>>
    ) -> Self {
      Question {
            id,
            title,
            content,
            tags,
        }
    }
}
```

```
fn main() {
    let question = Question::new(
        QuestionId("1".to_string()),
        "First Question".to_string(),
        "Content of question".to_string(),
        ["faq".to_string()],
    );
    println!("{}", question);
}
```

Executing `cargo run` on the command line shows some progress. We are down to two errors. Let's have a look at the first one again.

Listing 2.12   Error returning an array instead of a vector

```
error[E0308]: mismatched types
  --> src/main.rs:25:9
   |
25 |            ["faq".to_string()],
   |            ^^^^^^^^^^^^^^^^^^^^
   |
              expected enum `Option`,
              found array of 1 element
   |
   = note: expected enum `Option<Vec<String>>`
              found array `[String; 1]`
```

This too looks like two errors in one. The compiler expects an `Option` enum with `Vec` in it; instead it finds an array. We use the documentation again and look for `Option` at docs.rs (https://doc.rust-lang.org/std/option/index.html).

Based on the provided examples, we see that we have to encapsulate our tags in `Some`. And instead of an array, we require in the `Question` struct a vector with strings. In Rust, a vector and an array are not the same, and if you want an array as in other languages, you are probably looking for `Vec` in Rust.

The documentation is helpful here as well, as it shows us two ways of creating vectors in Rust. We can use `Vec::new` and then `.push` to insert elements, or we can use a macro called `vec!`. Use this example to update our code accordingly.

Listing 2.13   Encapsulating and creating a vector

```
fn main() {
    let question = Question::new(
        QuestionId("1".to_string()),
        "First Question".to_string(),
        "Content of question".to_string(),
        Some(vec!("faq".to_string())),
    );
    println!("{}", question);
}
```

Running the program again shows us just one more error.

Listing 2.14   The last error we face is a missing trait implementation

```
error[E0277]: `Question` doesn't implement `std::fmt::Display`
  --> src/main.rs:27:20
   |
27 |        println!("{}", question);
   |                       ^^^^^^^^ `Question` cannot
        be formatted with the default formatter
   |
   = help: the trait `std::fmt::Display` is not implemented for `Question`
   = note: in format strings you may be able to use `{:?}` (or {:#?}
           for pretty-print) instead
   = note: required by `std::fmt::Display::fmt`
   = note: this error originates in a macro
        (in Nightly builds, run with -Z macro-backtrace for more info)

error: aborting due to previous error
```

It seems like we are missing a trait implementation called std::Display. In Rust, you can print out variables via the println! macro and add curly braces ({}) for each variable you want to print:

```
println!("{}", variable_name);
```

This will call the fmt method from the Display trait implementation: http://mng .bz/O6wn. The error also suggests using {:?} instead of the usual curly braces {}. The following "Display vs. debug" sidebar explains the difference.

Display vs. debug

The Display trait is implemented on all primitive types in Rust (http://mng.bz/ YKZN). This trait specifies that an implementation should be provided that displays the data in human-readable form. That is easy for numbers and strings, but what should we do for vectors? Anything can be inside a vector, because Vec<T> is a generic container for data types. For these use cases (complex data structures like vectors), the Rust standard library uses the Debug trait.

The difference for the developer in using either is as follows: When handling strings and numbers, printing is done via two curly braces {}: println!("{}", 3). Whenever you deal with more complex data structures, like structs or JSON values, you can also use {:?}, which calls the Debug trait instead: println!("{:?}", question).

The Debug trait can be derived via the derive macro and put on top of your own structs. Therefore, you don't have to write custom trait implementations and can still print out your own data structures:

```
#[derive(Debug)]
struct Question {
    title: String,
    …
}
```

(continued)

You can also pretty-print something by adding a #: `println!("{:#?}", question)`.
This will allow a multiline representation of the data structure instead of one long string.

Like the `ToString` trait earlier, `Display` is another standard Rust trait implemented on all primitive types in the library. This allows the compiler to know how to display these data types (transforming them to human-readable output). Our custom type is not part of the standard library and therefore does not implement this trait.

How would we go ahead and find out how to implement the trait ourselves? The answer is yet again the Rust documentation. We can search for `Display` (http://mng .bz/G1wq) and click [src] to find the implementation. The comment section shows us an example implementation.

Listing 2.15   Example `Display` trait implementation

```
// https://doc.rust-lang.org/src/core/fmt/mod.rs.html#743-767

/// # Examples
///
/// ```
/// use std::fmt;
///
/// struct Position {
///     longitude: f32,
///     latitude: f32,
/// }
///
/// impl fmt::Display for Position {
///     fn fmt(&self, f: &mut fmt::Formatter<'_>) -> fmt::Result {
///         write!(f, "({}, {})", self.longitude, self.latitude)
///     }
/// }
///
/// assert_eq!("(1.987, 2.983)",
///            format!(
///              "{}",
///              Position {
///                longitude: 1.987, latitude: 2.983,
///              }
///            )
/// );
/// ```
```

With the code example from the Rust documentation (listing 2.14), you can slowly learn how to use the documentation about traits to implement them onto your own types. We will start by copying the basic example into our codebase and try to replace the example struct (in this case, `Position`) with our own: `Question`. Here is a code snippet that implements the `Display` trait for our `Question`, with the changes made in bold:

```
impl std::fmt::Display for Question {
    fn fmt(&self, f: &mut std::fmt::Formatter) -> Result<(), std::fmt::Error>
    {
        write!(
            f,
            "{}, title: {}, content: {}, tags: {:?}",
            self.id, self.title, self.content, self.tags
        )
    }
}
```

When trying to print out a question via the `println!` macro, we invoke the `fmt` function, which we just implemented for our question. This function calls the `write!` macro, which prints text onto the console, and we define what is exactly being written by passing arguments to it.

Two caveats, however: Our `Question` struct has a custom struct called `QuestionId`, which also doesn't implement the `Display` trait by default, and we have a more complex structure for our tags, which is a vector. You can't use the `Display` trait for a more complex structure like a vector and have to use the `Debug` trait instead. The following listing shows our main.rs file with the `Display` and `Debug` traits implemented.

> **Listing 2.16   Implementing the `Display` trait onto our `Question`**

```
...

impl std::fmt::Display for Question {
    fn fmt(&self, f: &mut std::fmt::Formatter)
        -> Result<(), std::fmt::Error> {
        write!(
            f,
            "{}, title: {}, content: {}, tags: {:?}",
            self.id, self.title, self.content, self.tags
        )
    }
}

impl std::fmt::Display for QuestionId {
    fn fmt(&self, f: &mut std::fmt::Formatter)
        -> Result<(), std::fmt::Error> {
        write!(f, "id: {}", self.0)
    }
}

impl std::fmt::Debug for Question {
    fn fmt(&self, f: &mut std::fmt::Formatter<'_>)
        -> Result<(), std::fmt::Error> {
        write!(f, "{:?}", self.tags)
    }
}

...
```

The Debug implementation looks quite similar to the Display trait. Here we use {:?} instead of {} in the write! macro. It would be quite tedious to write all of this code every time we want to implement and display a custom type.

The Rust standard library provides a procedural macro for this called derive, and we can place it on top of our struct definition (via #[derive]). The documentation about the Display trait also tells us an important fact: "Display is similar to Debug, but Display is for user-facing output, and so cannot be derived."

Declarative macros

You can spot macros in Rust by the exclamation point at the end of their names. This indicates a *declarative macro* or *function-like procedural macro* (as opposed to the other macro type, a *procedural macro*). The most famous declarative macro you will use in Rust at the beginning is println!, which prints text onto the console.

Macros take the encapsulated code with them and generate standard Rust code out of it. This happens just before the compiler takes all the Rust code and creates a binary.

You can also create your own macros, although there you enter a new world with almost no rules. Creating your own macros should come after you feel proficient enough in standard Rust and you want to make your life easier.

We therefore go ahead and derive the Debug trait. Afterward, we have to use Debug in our println! macro via {:?} instead of using {}. The updated code is in the following listing. After running the program, you will see the content of our question on the console (ignore the warnings for now).

Listing 2.17   Using the derive macro to implement the Debug trait

```rust
#[derive(Debug)]
struct Question {
    id: QuestionId,
    title: String,
    content: String,
    tags: Option<Vec<String>>,
}

#[derive(Debug)]
struct QuestionId(String);

impl Question {
    fn new(
        id: QuestionId,
        title: String,
        content: String,
        tags: Option<Vec<String>>
    ) -> Self {
        Question {
            id,
            title,
```

```
                content,
                tags,
            }
        }
    }

    fn main() {
        let question = Question::new(
            QuestionId("1".to_string()),
            "First Question".to_string(),
            "Content of question".to_string(),
            Some(vec!("faq".to_string())),
        );
        println!("{:?}", question);
    }
```

There is still room for improvement. We abstracted away the ID of the question behind a `QuestionId` struct, but we still need to know that this struct takes a `String` as an input. We can hide this implementation detail and make it more comfortable for the user to generate an `id` for a question.

Rust provides traits for commonly used functionality. One of them is the `FromStr` trait, which is similar to the `ToString` trait discussed earlier. We can use `FromStr` as follows:

```
let id = QuestionId::from_str("1").unwrap(); // from_str() can fail
```

This simply says, "Create type *X* out of type `&str`." Rust has no implicit casting, just explicit. So we always indicate if we want to change one type to another.

> **Listing 2.18 Implementing the `FromStr` trait on `QuestionId`**

```
use std::io::{Error, ErrorKind};
use std::str::FromStr;

...

impl FromStr for QuestionId {
    type Err = std::io::Error;

    fn from_str(id: &str) -> Result<Self, Self::Err> {
        match id.is_empty() {
            false => Ok(QuestionId(id.to_string())),
            true => Err(
              Error::new(ErrorKind::InvalidInput, "No id provided")
            ),
        }
    }
}

...
```

The signature of the trait allows us to take a `&str` type and return our own type (`QuestionId`) or an error in case the ID is empty. We give the parameter the name `id`, and the type &str (since this is what we will receive). The name (id, in this case) can be anything really. We then match if the id is not empty and return a QuestionId type containing one field, which we transform into a String, as we specified in the struct.

We can then change the way we create the question ID in the main function. Instead of using .to_string, we call ::from_str on the QuestionId. We can see in the implementation of the trait that from_str doesn't take a &self type, and is therefore not a method that we can call via the dot (.) but an associated function that we call via two double colons (::).

Listing 2.19   Using the FromStr trait to create a QuestionId out of a &str

```
...

fn main() {
    let question = Question::new(
        QuestionId::from_str("1").expect("No id provided"),
        "First Question".to_string(),
        "Content of question".to_string(),
        Some(vec!("faq".to_string())),
    );
    println!("{:?}", question);
}
```

2.1.7   *Handling results*

Wait, but why do we have to add .expect after the function? If we look closely, we see that the FromStr trait implementation returns a Result. *Results* are almost like options, and can be one of two variants: either success or error. In the case of success, they encapsulate a value via Ok(value). In the case of an error, they encapsulate the error in Err(error). The Result type is implemented as an enum as well, and looks like this.

Listing 2.20   Result definition in the Rust standard library

```
pub enum Result<T, E> {
    Ok(T),
    Err(E),
}
```

Like Option, Result has a variety of methods and traits implemented. One of these methods is expect, which, based on the documentation, returns the contained Ok value. We can spot that we really return the QuestionId wrapped in an Ok, which means expect is returning the value inside it, or panics with an error message that we specify.

A proper error handling would need a match statement, where we would receive an error from the from_str function and handle it in some shape or form. In our simple example, however, it is enough the way we do it here. Another common method you will find is unwrap, which is nicer to read but panics without an error message specified by you.

Don't use unwrap or expect in production, since they result in panics and crash your application. Always handle error cases with match, or otherwise make sure you catch errors and return them gracefully.

You can easily use the Result enum for your own functions as well. The return signature will look like -> Result<T, E>, where T is your data you want to return, and E is the error (which can be custom or one from the standard library).

Result looks the same as Option; the major difference is the Error variant. Option is used whenever data can be there, but doesn't have to be (the missing data wouldn't cause trouble). Result is used when you really expect data to be there and have to actively manage the case when it isn't.

A simple example is our preceding code. We mark the tags as optional in our Question struct, since we can create a question even without them. However, the ID is needed, and if our QuestionId struct is not able to create one out of a &str, then the creation fails, and we have to return an error to whoever calls this method. With the basic structure and types being implemented, let's add a web server to our application so we can serve the first dummy data to our users.

2.2 Creating our web server

We glanced over which features Rust brings, and doesn't bring, to the table when it comes to building web services. Let's recap the gist of it:

- Rust doesn't come with a runtime that could handle asynchronous background work.
- Rust offers a syntax that expresses asynchronous code blocks.
- Rust includes the Future type for results that have state and a return type.
- Rust implements TCP (and UDP), but not HTTP.
- The chosen web framework comes with HTTP and everything else implemented.
- The runtime is dictated by the web framework we choose.

Our web framework dictates a lot behind the scenes: the runtime, the abstraction over HTTP (plus the HTTP server implementation), and the design around how to pass requests to route handlers. You should therefore feel comfortable with the design decisions that a particular web framework took, and which runtime it is choosing.

To get a feel for the syntax and topics we are going to discuss, listing 2.21 is a preview of the finished example we will have by the end of this chapter. After reading this last part of this chapter, you will understand what this code does. We want to just highlight some areas.

> **Listing 2.21 A minimal Rust HTTP server with Warp**

```
use warp::Filter;

#[tokio::main]
async fn main() {
```

```
let hello = warp::get()
    .map(|| format!("Hello, World!"));

warp::serve(hello)
    .run(([127, 0, 0, 1], 1337))
    .await;
}
```

The third line of the code, #[tokio::main], indicates the runtime we are using. Section 2.2.1 discusses runtimes. But to have a visual in your head, this is how it looks in your Rust source code. Next up, on line 4, is our main function, which we mark as asynchronous. We do so to handle multiple requests at the same time (thanks to the runtime), and inside asynchronous functions, we can use the .await keyword to indicate that the function is asynchronous by nature and doesn't yield a result right away. These are already three (out of four) building blocks of the asynchronous story in Rust.

2.2.1 *Handling multiple requests at once*

When writing server applications, you usually have to serve more than one client at once. Even if not all your connections arrive at exactly the same millisecond, reading from databases or opening files on the hard drive takes time.

Instead of waiting for each process to completely finish and therefore let hundreds, if not thousands, of other requests wait and pile up, you could choose to trigger a process (let's say a database query) and let yourself get notified when it is done. In the meantime, you can start serving other clients.

> **Green threads**
>
> When talking about asynchronous programming, threads are always involved. *Threads* are created (*spawned*) by a process and live inside it. They are usually handled by the operating system (inside the kernel) and are therefore expensive to manage from a user perspective (because of the constant interrupting of the kernel).
>
> Therefore, the concept of a *green thread* (http://mng.bz/nemK) was created. These threads live completely in the user space and are managed by a runtime.

Writing asynchronous applications lets you do exactly this. When looking at our minimal-tcp code from chapter 1 (http://mng.bz/z52a), it is handling stream after stream in a blocking way. We finish processing one stream before we go over to the next one.

In a multithreaded environment, we could put each stream on its own thread, let them compute in the background, and put them back to the foreground and send the answer back to the requesting client. Another design decision uses a single thread, which picks up work whenever possible. The key is that a long-running method can yield back control to a runtime and signal that it needs longer to finish. The runtime is then able to do other computation and checks back to see if this long-running method has finished computing yet.

To process incoming HTTP requests asynchronously, we need a programming language that understands asynchronous concepts and gives us types and syntax to mark code that should be executed asynchronously. And we need a runtime that takes our code and knows how to execute it in a nonblocking way. Figure 2.9 shows the needed ingredients.

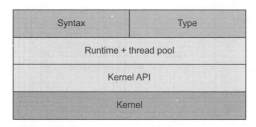

Figure 2.9 **An asynchronous programming environment needs four ingredients (syntax, type, runtime, and kernel abstractions) for it to function.**

To summarize, these are the four ingredients of an asynchronous programming environment:

- Use of the kernel's asynchronous read-and-write API through `epoll/select/poll`. (For further reading, see http://mng.bz/09zx.)
- The capability to offload long-running tasks in the user space and have a mechanism to notify us when the task is done so we can progress with our work. This is a runtime creating and managing the green threads.
- A syntax within the programming language so we can mark asynchronous blocks in our code such that the compiler understands what to do with them.
- A specific type in the standard library for mutually exclusive access and modification. Instead of a type like *number*, which stores a specific value, a type for asynchronous programming needs to store, next to the value, the current state of the long-running operation.

Rust started out having green threads, but later dropped them because of the heavier runtime footprint. Therefore, Rust comes without a runtime or an abstraction over asynchronous kernel APIs. This runs contrary to Node.js and Go, for example, which both come with a native runtime and abstraction over the kernel API.

Rust gives us the syntax and a type. Rust itself understands asynchronous concepts and ships enough ingredients for us to build a runtime and abstract over the kernel API.

2.2.2 *Rust's asynchronous environment*

For Rust to have a smaller footprint, its developers decided not to include any runtime nor abstraction over the kernel async API. This gives the programmer the chance to choose a runtime that fits the needs of a project. This also future-proofs the language in case huge advances in runtimes occur further down the road.

We already saw the major blocks of an async story in figure 2.8. Rust ships with the syntax and a type. Well-tested runtime choices are also available (like Tokio and async-std) and an abstraction over the async kernel API with Mio. Figure 2.10 shows the building blocks derived from the Rust ecosystem.

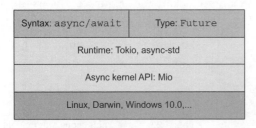

Syntax: `async/await`	Type: `Future`
Runtime: Tokio, async-std	
Async kernel API: Mio	
Linux, Darwin, Windows 10.0,...	

Figure 2.10   The building blocks of the async Rust ecosystem

For its syntax, Rust offers a combination of `async` and `await` as keywords. You mark a function `async` so you can use `await` inside it. A function that you `await` returns a `Future` type, which has the type of value you return in case of a successful execution, and a method called `poll` that executes the long-running process and yields back `Pending` or `Ready`. The `Ready` state can then either have an `Error` or a successful return value.

Often you won't need to understand the ins and outs of the `Future` type. It is helpful in further understanding the underlying system so you can create one when needed, but to start off, it is enough to know why it is there and how it plays with the rest of the ecosystem.

The major decision with every async application in Rust is choosing your runtime. The runtime will already include an abstraction over the kernel API (which in most cases is a library called Mio). But let's have a look at what Rust ships with first, the syntax and the type.

2.2.3   Rust's handling of async/await

On top of the runtime are two building blocks integrated in Rust. The first is the `async/await` syntax. Let's have a look at a code snippet you already saw in chapter 1, which does an asynchronous HTTP call.

Listing 2.22   Example `async` HTTP call

```
use std::collections::HashMap;

#[tokio::main]
async fn main() -> Result<(), Box<dyn std::error::Error>> {
    let resp = reqwest::get("https://httpbin.org/ip")
        .await?
        .json::<HashMap<String, String>>()
        .await?;
    println!("{:#?}", resp);
    Ok(())
}
```

Have in mind that you must add the crates Tokio and Reqwest to your Cargo.toml file for this snippet to work. Many Rust crates split their logic into features, which makes it possible just to include a smaller subset of the functionality, so your application won't include code that you don't need.

```
[dependencies]
reqwest = { version = "0.11", features = ["json"] }
tokio = { version = "1", features = ["full"] }
```

> **Feature flags**
>
> When adding Tokio to your dependencies inside the Cargo.toml file, we have to add feature flags. *Feature flags* allow developers to include just a subset of a crate, which saves time compiling the project and reduces the size of the project.
>
> Not all crates support feature flags, but some do. Be aware that if you include a crate and want to use certain features, the compiler won't notify you that the feature is not included in the Cargo.toml file. The safest bet in the beginning is to include all features of a crate, and after you are done, see if you can reduce the amount of code you pull in by using just certain features.
>
> The naming of the feature flags is not standardized, and it's up to the crate owner to name its features. For Tokio, this means using the feature flag `full`:
>
> ```
> tokio = { version = "1", features = ["full"] }
> ```

The function call `reqwest::get("https://httpbin.org/ip")` returns a future, which wraps the return type. This call returns our current IP address, in the form of an object with a key and a value. In Rust, this can be expressed via a hash map: HashMap<String, String>. The Reqwest crate returns a `Future` by default (https://docs .rs/reqwest/latest/reqwest/#making-a-get-request). If you want a blocking way of making an HTTP request, use the `reqwest::blocking` client: https://docs.rs/reqwest/ latest/reqwest/blocking/index.html.

We expect a hash map wrapped inside a future as a response: Future<Output= HashMap<String, String>>. We then can call `await` on the future, so our runtime picks it up, and tries to execute the functionality inside it. We assume this will take longer, so the runtime will handle the task in the background and fill our content variable when the file is read.

You usually won't come across defining your own futures, at least not in the beginning when working with Rust and web services. It is important to know when using crates or other people's code, that when their functions are marked as `async`, you have to `await` them.

The intent of this syntax is to make writing asynchronous Rust code feel like synchronous, blocking code to the programmer. In the background, Rust is transforming this piece of code into a state machine, where each different `await` represents a state. Once all of the states are ready, the function continues to the last line and returns the result.

With the syntax looking like a blocking, concurrent process, it can be hard to wrap your head around the nature and pitfalls of asynchronous programming. We will go more into depth when we implement our first application. For now, it is enough to understand the ingredients. Let's take a look at the inside of a future to understand what we are dealing with, or what the runtime we are using is dealing with.

2.2.4 Using Rust's Future type

In listing 2.22, we can see that our `await` function is returning something, which we save in the variable `resp`. Here, our `Future` type comes into play. As mentioned, `Future` is a more complex type that has the following signature (listing 2.23). You don't have to understand what it does to its full extent, but the code snippet has two links included so you can dig further. The explanation of the key functionality follows right after the listing.

Listing 2.23 Rust's Future trait

```
// Docs: https://doc.rust-lang.org/std/future/trait.Future.html
// Source code:
// https://doc.rust-lang.org/src/core/future/future.rs.html#36-104

pub trait Future {
    type Output;
    fn poll(self: Pin<&mut Self>, cx: &mut Context<'_>)
        -> Poll<Self::Output>;
}
```

`Future` has an associated type called `Output`, which could be, for example, a file or a string, and a method called `poll`. This method is called frequently to see if the future is ready. The `poll` method returns a type `Poll` that can be either `Pending` or `Ready`. Once ready, `poll` returns the type specified in the second line or an error. Once the future is ready, it returns a result, which then gets assigned to our variable.

You can see that `Future` is a trait. This provides the advantage that you can implement this trait to any type you have in your program.

What is distinct about Rust is that no future is actively being started. In other languages like Go or JavaScript, when assigning a variable to a promise or creating a go routine, each of their runtimes will start executing immediately. In Rust, you have to actively `poll` the future, which is the job of a runtime.

2.2.5 Choosing a runtime

The *runtime* is at the center of your asynchronous web service. Its design and performance play a major part in the underlying performance and security of your application. In Node.js, you have the Google V8 engine to handle the task. Go has its own runtime, which is developed by Google as well.

You don't need to know in detail how a runtime works and how it is executing your asynchronous code. However, it is good to at least have heard the term and the concepts surrounding it. You might run into problems later in your code, and knowledge about how your chosen runtime works could help you solve problems or rewrite your code.

Many criticize Rust for not shipping with a runtime, since it's such a centerpiece in every web service. On the other hand, being able to choose a specific runtime for your needs has the advantage of tailoring your application to your performance and platform requirements.

One of the most popular runtimes, called Tokio, is widely used throughout the industry. It is therefore a first safe bet for your application. We will choose Tokio for our example and later go into detail about how to choose a runtime for your needs.

The runtime is responsible for creating threads, polling our futures, and driving them to completion. It is also responsible for passing on work to the kernel and making sure to use the asynchronous kernel API to not have any bottlenecks there as well. Tokio uses a crate called Mio (https://github.com/tokio-rs/mio) for the asynchronous communication with the operating system kernel. You as a developer will probably never touch the code in Mio, but it is good to know which types of crates and abstraction layers you are pulling into your project when developing web servers with Rust.

As you can see in figure 2.11, a runtime plays a rather large role in a web service. When marking code as `async`, the compiler will hand over the code to the runtime. Then the implementation determines how fast, accurate, and error-free your execution of this task will be.

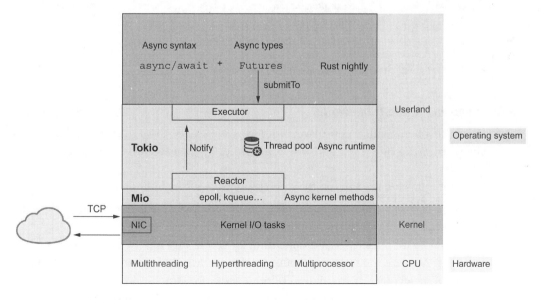

Figure 2.11   The complete asynchronous Rust environment

Let's walk through an example task to see what's happening behind the scenes; see figure 2.12.

1 In our Rust code, we mark a function as async. When we await the return of the function, we tell the runtime during compile time that this is a function that returns a Future type.

2 The runtime takes this piece of code and hands it over to the executor. The executor is responsible for calling the poll method on Future.

3 If it's a network request, the runtime hands it over to Mio, which creates the asynchronous socket in the kernel, and requests some CPU time to finish the task.

4 Once the kernel is done with the work (for example, sending out a request and getting a response), it notifies the waiting process on the socket. The reactor is then responsible for waking up the executor, which continues with the computation with the results returned from the kernel.

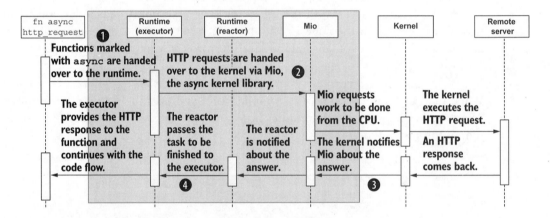

Figure 2.12   Executing async HTTP requests behind the scenes

2.2.6   *Choosing a web framework*

With Rust being still a new playground for web services, you might need more active help from the dev team and the community to solve issues you might have along the way.

The following are the top four web frameworks Rust has to offer:

- *Actix Web* is the most complete, actively used web framework, and packs a lot of features. It can be opinionated at times.

- *Rocket* uses macros to annotate route handlers, and has JSON parsing built in. It is a complete framework with all the features included to write solid web servers.

- *Warp* was one of the first web frameworks for Rust. It is developed close to the Tokio community and offers a lot of freedom. It is the most bare-bones framework, which leaves many design decisions to the developer.

- *Axum* is the newest of the bunch and tries to build as much on top of already existing crates from the Tokio ecosystem, and with design lessons learned from Warp and others.

Actix Web brings its own runtime (but you can also choose to use Tokio). The frameworks Rocket, Warp, and Axum use Tokio.

For the book, we choose Warp. It is small enough to be out of the way, and used enough to be actively managed, with a very active Discord channel as well. Your mileage might vary in your own company or project. It is important to understand where the framework starts and where it ends, what is pure Rust and where your code will be influenced by the framework you are choosing.

Most of the book and code is framework agnostic. Once we set up the server and add our route handlers, we are in pure Rust land again and won't see much of the framework afterward. The book will clearly highlight these pieces, so you know where to plug in your own framework of choice later.

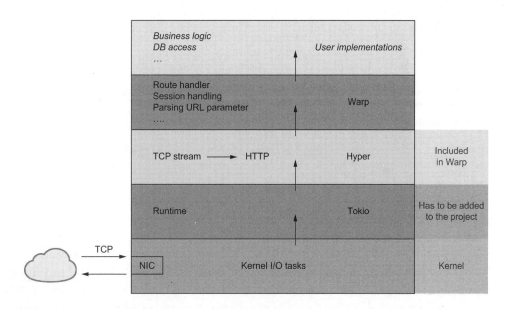

Figure 2.13 When using Warp, you inherit the runtime Tokio and Hyper as the HTTP abstraction and server under the hood.

As you can see in figure 2.13, incoming TCP requests will have to be handed over to the runtime, Tokio, which talks directly to the kernel. The library Hyper will start the HTTP server and accepts these incoming TCP streams. On top of that, Warp will wrap around framework features like passing the HTTP requests to the right route handlers. Listing 2.24 shows this all in action.

Listing 2.24   A minimal Rust HTTP server with Warp

```
use warp::Filter;

#[tokio::main]
async fn main() {
    let hello = warp::path("hello")
        .and(warp::path::param())
        .map(|name: String| format!("Hello, {}!", name));

    warp::serve(hello)
        .run(([127, 0, 0, 1], 1337))
        .await;
}
```

> The .map function is a Warp filter, which takes the (possible) arguments from the previous function and transforms them.

The signature of (.map(||...)) is using a closure (||), which captures the variables in the environment and makes them accessible inside the function (map). In listing 2.24, we don't use any variable inside the map function. If, however, the HTTP GET request had any parameters, we could capture and process them inside map via the closure (||). The Rust book has more details on closures (https://doc.rust-lang.org/book/ch13-01-closures.html).

To close this chapter with a working web server, we will include this example snippet into our codebase. So far, our main function looks like this.

Listing 2.25   Our `main` function to this point

```
fn main() {
    let question = Question::new(
        QuestionId::from_str("1").expect("No id provided"),
        "First Question".to_string(),
        "Content of question".to_string(),
        Some(vec!("faq".to_string())),
    );
    println!("{:?}", question);
}
```

We remove the creation of the new question (we explain how to return JSON in chapter 3), add a runtime and the Warp server to our project, and start the server in the main function. We need to add the two dependencies to our project. The Hyper crate is included in Warp, whereas Tokio has to be added to the project manually. The following listing shows the updated Cargo.toml file.

Listing 2.26   The updated Cargo.toml file with Tokio and Warp added to the project

```
[package]
name = "ch_02"
version = "0.1.0"
edition = "2021"

[dependencies]
tokio = { version = "1.2", features = ["full"] }
warp = "0.3"
```

With the added Tokio dependency, we can annotate our `main` function to use the Tokio runtime, and write asynchronous code inside it, which Warp requires. The next listing shows the updated main.rs file in our ch_02 folder.

Listing 2.27   Starting the Warp server inside our main.rs file

```
use std::str::FromStr;
use std::io::{Error, ErrorKind};

use warp::Filter;

...

#[tokio::main]
async fn main() {
    let question = Question::new(
        QuestionId::from_str("1").expect("No id provided"),
        "First Question".to_string(),
        "Content of question".to_string(),
        Some(vec!("faq".to_string())),
    );
    println!("{:?}", question);

    let hello = warp::get()
        .map(|| format!("Hello, World!"));

    warp::serve(hello)
        .run(([127, 0, 0, 1], 3030))
        .await;
}
```

You can start the server via `cargo run` on the command line (ignore the warnings for now). It still prints the example `question` onto the command line, but also starts the server. You can open a browser and open the address `127.0.0.1:3030`, and you should be greeted with `Hello, World!`.

With the server in place, we can start implementing our REST endpoints, serialize our own structs to return proper JSON to the requesting client, and accept query parameters at our endpoints as well. This and much more waits for us in chapter 3.

Summary

- Always start by mapping out resources via structs and think about the relationships between your types.
- Simplify your life by adding helper methods like `new` onto your types and transforming one type to another.
- Understand the ownership and borrowing principles in Rust and how they affect the way you write code, and which errors the compiler might therefore throw at you.
- Using traits helps you make your custom data types play nicely with the frameworks you are choosing, by adding functionality.

- Using the `derive` macro to implement traits for common use cases saves a lot of self-written code.
- Befriend the Rust documentation, as you will use it often to look up functionalities in types and frameworks. This, in turn, helps you better understand the language.
- Rust ships with the async syntax and types, but we need more to write async applications.
- Runtimes take care of handling multiple computations at the same time and provide an abstraction over the async kernel API at the same time.
- Choose a web framework that is actively maintained, has a large community and support around it, and is maybe used by larger companies (different from the ones you operate under).
- The web framework we choose will abstract over the HTTP implementation, server, and runtime so we can focus on writing business logic for the application.

Part 2

Getting started

This second part of the book covers the business logic and sets up a working web application with various API endpoints. It covers database access, logging, and accessing third-party APIs. We will also clean up after ourselves and split our application into modules. After reading this part, you'll know what your day-to-day will look like developing Rust web applications, and where to look for additional information.

Chapter 3 sets up our first route handler and HTTP GET endpoint. You'll become familiar with the web framework, Warp, and how to funnel an incoming HTTP request to our route handler, how to send back a proper HTTP response, and what to do in case of an error.

Chapter 4 expands on these topics and implements the POST, PUT and DELETE endpoints for our API. You'll learn to accept parameters, parse JSON, and fill in-memory storage with our questions and answers.

After writing so much business logic, it is time to clean up. Chapter 5 details the Rust module system. You'll learn to determine if and when to create sub-crates, or just split logic into its own modules so you can access them throughout your application.

Running web services can fail, users might report problems and bugs will be found. Inspecting has a high priority when developing and running applications in production. Chapter 6 will make sure you have all the tools and skills needed to implement logging, tracing asynchronous behavior and debug your application locally.

Web applications usually don't just open up API endpoints; they also talk to other services and to a database. This is exactly what we do in the last two chapters of Part 2. Chapter 7 replaces our in-memory storage with a PostgreSQL database, and we'll connect to a database and share this connection between our route handlers.

Chapter 8 rounds out part 2 with accessing a third-party API, which gives us a perfect introduction to handling multiple asynchronous calls at once, parsing incoming JSON bodies to our structs, and handling timeouts in these calls.

Create your first route handler

In the first part of this chapter, we will set up a basic web service with all the needed tooling to serve as the baseline for our journey throughout the book. The second part will show how easy it is to implement the handling of cross-origin resource sharing (CORS) in our web server; browsers can reach us even if they are not on the same domain.

This chapter lays the groundwork for working with Warp and sets up our web server, which we will build on in the upcoming chapters. It will teach you how Warp is processing HTTP requests (through its filter system), which later chapters will use to add middleware and pass around state.

From now on, we have to be a bit more opinionated and, as mentioned in chapter 2, we are choosing Warp as our web framework. All the code we are going to talk about can be found in the GitHub repository for this book (https://github.com/Rust-Web-Development/code).

Look at figure 3.1 to remind yourself about the tech stack included in a framework. You will always also choose a runtime and a library that abstracts over the HTTP server. The HTTP library Hyper is already included in Warp, whereas Tokio has to be added to our Cargo.toml file.

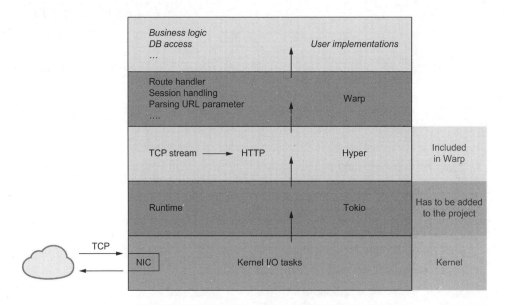

Figure 3.1   The web framework Warp includes Tokio as its runtime and Hyper as a HTTP server library.

Over the course of this book, we will create a Q&A service, which will be used to post questions and give users the chance to answer them. This service can be the start of an internal Q&A website to get information about company products, processes, or codebases.

3.1   Getting to know our web framework: Warp

We choose Warp as our web framework for these four reasons:

- It is small enough to be out of your way, and used enough to be actively maintained, with an active community around it.
- It is based on the Tokio runtime, which is currently the de facto standard runtime in the Rust ecosystem.
- It has an active Discord channel, where questions are frequently answered by the creator and other users.
- It is actively developed, well documented, and updated on GitHub.

Even if you might not like all the design choices Warp makes, these four points are too important to neglect. It is important not to be alone on your journey to develop, deploy, and maintain Rust web services. Having the help of an experienced community is a key enabler in your day-to-day life. We will now look at what you can do with Warp, including which external crates are needed to make it run and how to use its powerful filter system.

3.1.1 What is included in Warp

Remember that Rust doesn't include an HTTP implementation in the standard library; therefore, a web framework needs to either create its own HTTP implementation or use a crate. Warp uses a crate called Hyper for this. *Hyper* is an HTTP server written in Rust, which supports HTTP/1, HTTP/2, and asynchronous concepts, which makes it a perfect foundation for a web framework.

In the first two chapters, you learned that every asynchronous story needs a runtime, and Rust decided against putting one in the standard library. Therefore, Hyper (and therefore Warp) need to build on top of one from the community. They chose Tokio. When working with Warp, you don't need to explicitly include Hyper. However, you need to add Tokio to your dependencies and add it manually to your project.

The reason we don't have to include Hyper is that Warp itself is pulling Hyper into its own codebase and is building on top of the Hyper crate. Tokio, however, is needed as a separate dependency since we have to use the Tokio crate inside our own project to annotate the `main` function (and use other Tokio macros and functions later in the book).

Therefore, every Warp project has at least two dependencies: Warp itself and Tokio. Now that we understand the crates that Warp is built upon, let's focus on how Warp works so you can make sound decisions later, while building your web service.

3.1.2 Warp's filter system

The first two steps for each framework are the same:

1 Start a server on a specific port (`1024` or above).
2 Provide route handler functions to an incoming HTTP request, which matches the path, HTTP method, and parameter specified.

In Warp, *routes* are sets of filters, chained together. Each request tries to match the filter you created, and if it can't, it goes to the next one. We see this process in listing 3.1, where we start a server via Warp (and Warp is using Hyper here under the hood to create and start an HTTP server), and then pass a filter object to the `::serve` method. All the code can be found in the GitHub repository for this project (https://github .com/Rust-Web-Development/code).

> **Listing 3.1   Starting a Warp server with a routes filter object**

```
// import the Filter trait from warp
use warp::Filter;
```

```
#[tokio::main]
async fn main() {
    // create a path Filter
    let hello = warp::path("hello").map(|| format!("Hello, World!"));

    // start the server and pass the route filter to it
    warp::serve(hello).run(([127, 0, 0, 1], 3030)).await;
}
```

Looking at the documentation for ::path() (http://mng.bz/82XP), we see that it is part of the filter module in Warp. When passing the route hi to the ::serve method, Warp can accept incoming HTTP requests on the given IP address and port, and try to match each to the given filters. Here, we are looking for a request on http://127.0.0.1:3030/hello. When you run the server, open a browser, and navigate to this URL, you are greeted with Hello, World! text in your browser window.

Implicitly, Warp assumes that we listen for HTTP GET requests. If we want to explicitly state the HTTP method we are listening to, we can use the method filters in Warp like .get or .post.

This filter system looks innocent in the beginning, but make a mental note: everything you do on the routes is done via filters. Extracting headers, (query) parameters, JSON bodies—this is all done through filters. In chapter 4, we are going to add a local database to our server and share access to this database between the various route handlers. This will also be done through Warp's filter system.

3.2 GET your first JSON response

With the basics covered, we can start to work on our application. With each step, we will dive deeper into the Rust language and its ecosystem. We will now get help from the library called Warp to do the heavy lifting for us, so we can focus on the business logic.

Every time an HTTP request comes in, the framework processes it in a few steps:

1 Check the request path inside the HTTP request.
2 Check the HTTP method (for example, GET, PUT, or POST).
3 Forward the request to a route handler that is responsible for the path and type.
4 Before forwarding the request to the route handler, the request can be passed through middleware, which checks things like authentication headers or adds further information to the request that is handed down to the route handler.

Figure 3.2 illustrates the whole flow. Next to the boxes are the method calls we have to make with Warp to process the requests. A POST, PUT, or DELETE call will look similar, and have only minor changes.

No matter which framework you end up using, all of them follow the same design principles. The actual implementation and how and when you call certain parts might differ, though.

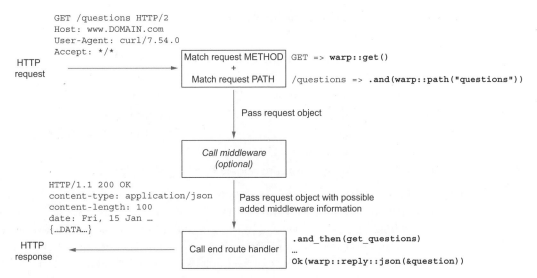

```
GET /questions HTTP/2
Host: www.DOMAIN.com
User-Agent: curl/7.54.0
Accept: */*
```

HTTP
request

Match request METHOD   GET => `warp::get()`
+
Match request PATH   `/questions` => `.and(warp::path("questions"))`

Pass request object

*Call middleware
(optional)*

```
HTTP/1.1 200 OK
content-type: application/json
content-length: 100
date: Fri, 15 Jan …
{…DATA…}
```

Pass request object with possible
added middleware information

HTTP
response

Call end route handler   `.and_then(get_questions)`
                           …
                           `Ok(warp::reply::json(&question))`

Figure 3.2 Workflow of sending, parsing, and answering HTTP GET requests with Warp

3.2.1   Align with your framework's way of thinking

Your first step into implementing your API with a framework is to set up the smallest possible working version. Afterward, you implement the simplest path to see how your framework of choice generally behaves and wants things to be.

Remember that we added Tokio and Warp to our project at the end of chapter 2. The following listing shows the main function again to set the stage for this chapter.

Listing 3.2   The current state of our `main` function

…

```
#[tokio::main]
async fn main() {
    let hello = warp::get()
        .map(|| format!("Hello, World!"));

    warp::serve(hello)
        .run(([127, 0, 0, 1], 3030))
        .await;
}
```

We also added `warp` and `tokio` to our Cargo.toml file under `[dependencies]`.

Listing 3.3   Adding the dependencies to Cargo.toml

…

```
[dependencies]
tokio = { version = "1.2", features = ["full"] }
warp = "0.3"
```

Create a mental or physical list of checkpoints you go through to see if and how your framework is doing the following:

- How does it parse the incoming PATH and HTTP method?
- Can I parse JSON requests directly from the HTTP body?
- How can I parse uniform resource identifier (URI) parameters from the request?
- How can I add middleware such as authentication or logging?
- How do I pass objects like a database connection to the route handlers?
- How do I have to return an HTTP response?
- Does it have a built-in session or cookie handling?

These are the first questions that arise when working with a web framework, so go through the list and see how your framework of choice is supporting these. If one or more are missing, figure out how hard it is to implement this particular part yourself. We will answer all of these in the following chapters with our framework of choice.

A good attitude to have is "I don't know, but let's find out!" Read the example code and make notes on places you don't understand. This might be a lot in the beginning, but you will see that simply having an open mind and reading the framework's documentation can help you quickly learn what the code is all about.

The framework gives you guidance in the beginning on how to accept, parse, and answer HTTP requests. Everything in the middle is up to you—which is a major part of any application. The beauty of a strictly typed language is that you can use and implement the types of the framework to easily extend your own functions and types.

3.2.2   *Handle the success route*

The start of each web application is being able to receive an HTTP GET message and send back an answer. From then on, you can extend and modify this simple working solution. Listing 3.4 shows how to create a route handler we can pass an incoming HTTP request to, and how a route in Warp is created.

The philosophy in this book, as you might have already figured out, is to work with the errors instead of showing a working example right away. This code won't compile, and the *why* is important. We can't serialize a Question yet to answer this request, and the next section will explain how to do it in Rust.

Listing 3.4   Adding our first route handler and deleting printing of the question

```
use warp::Filter;

...

async fn get_questions() -> Result<impl warp::Reply, warp::Rejection> {
    let question = Question::new(
        QuestionId::from_str("1").expect("No id provided"),
        "First Question".to_string(),
        "Content of question".to_string(),
```

Creates our first route handler, which needs to return a reply and rejection for Warp to be able to use it

Creates a new question, which we return to the requesting client

```
        Some(vec!("faq".to_string())),
    );

    Ok(warp::reply::json(
        &question
    ))
}
```

Uses Warp's json reply to return the JSON version of our question

```
#[tokio::main]
async fn main() {
    let get_items = warp::get()
        .and(warp::path("questions"))
        .and(warp::path::end())
        .and_then(get_questions);

    let routes = get_items;

    warp::serve(routes)
        .run(([127, 0; 0, 1], 3030))
        .await;
}
```

Uses Warp's functionality of chaining more than one filter via .and, and therefore creates one big filter and assigns it to get_items

Uses path::end to signal that we listen on exactly /question (and not /question/further/params, for example)

Defines the routes variable, which will come in handy later

Passes the routes filter to Warp's serve method and starts our server

As we discussed earlier, in Warp, the main concept is `Filter`. It is implemented in Warp via a trait, and can parse, mutate, and return data. The more you work with it, the easier it is to understand its usage.

You can chain filters with the `and` keyword. We start with the `get` filter, which filters all HTTP requests with the GET method. Then we add a path, which filters HTTP requests for the parameters after the host URL. So taking listing 3.4 as an example, we filter for all GET requests to `localhost:3030/questions`. We use the `path::end` filter, so we listen exactly to /questions (and not, for example, to /questions/more/deeper). Each request will go through each filter, and if applicable, will call the `.and_then` part, which calls our route handler `get_questions`.

The route handler must have a fixed return signature. It has to return the following:

- A result
- `warp::Reply` for the success part
- `warp::Rejection` for the error

Everything happening in between is up to us. We just have to serve the framework with the right response types. We create a `routes` object, in which we, for now, assign only our combination of filters for an HTTP GET request on the /questions path.

At the end of the `get_questions` function, we call the JSON function from Warp to return our question in JSON format. Now this looks like some magic. How can the compiler know (and the function in this regard) how a JSON structure of our `Question` looks? We can check out the documentation (http://mng.bz/E0wJ) and look at the function signature, shown in the following listing.

```
pub fn json<T>(val: &T) -> Json
where
    T: Serialize,
...
```

This shows that whatever value we pass to the function (`val: &T`) has to be a reference, and it has to implement `Serialize`. The documentation highlights the word *Serialize*, which we can click to end up in the documentation for a library called Serde.

3.2.3   *Get help from Serde*

The *Serde library* bundles serialization and deserialization methods into one framework. It is basically the standard serialization (and deserialization) framework in the Rust ecosystem. It can transform structs to formats like JSON, TOML, or Binary JSON (BSON), and transform them back as well. But first, we need to add Serde to our Cargo.toml.

```
...
[dependencies]
...
serde = { version = "1.0", features = ["derive"] }
```

Instead of writing tedious mapping functionality for each data structure to create the proper JSON format, you just put a macro on top of your struct. The compiler will call the Serde library during compilation and will create the right serialization information for you.

This is exactly what we need to do for our `Question` struct. We use the `derive` macro and add the `Serialize` trait next to the already annotated `Debug` trait and separate it with a comma.

```
use serde::Serialize;

...

#[derive(Debug, Serialize)]
struct Question {
    id: QuestionId(String),
    title: String,
    content: String,
    tags: Option<Vec<String>>,
}

#[derive(Debug, Serialize)]
struct QuestionId(String);

...
```

We have to import the `Serialize` trait via the `use` keyword, and make it available to the file we are using it in. Then, we add it to our struct.

Bear in mind that if you include other custom objects in your struct, they too have to add `Serialize` on top of their struct definition. If the `Question` struct doesn't have a default Rust `std` type like `String`, this too will have to implement the `Serialize` trait.

With the `Serialize` trait added, Warp's JSON function is satisfied. The value we pass to it is a reference to a new question, which implements `Serialize`:

```
async fn get_questions() -> Result<impl warp::Reply, warp::Rejection> {
    let question = Question::new(
        QuestionId::from_str("1").expect("No id provided"),
        "First Question".to_string(),
        "Content of question".to_string(),
        Some(vec!("faq".to_string())),
    );

    Ok(warp::reply::json(
      &question
    ))
}
```

In chapter 4, we will see how this works the other way around. We will see what we need to do to receive JSON data and transform it to our local structs. Hint: It is as easy as adding the `Deserialize` trait from Serde on top of our struct to teach the compiler how to map JSON to our custom data structure.

So far, we assume that we can create a new `Question` and return it to the requesting client. What happens, however, if we can't create a new object or if the path the browser or other server is requesting doesn't exist?

3.2.4 *Handle errors gracefully*

Remember that basically everything in Warp is a filter. If a filter can't map a request to its signature, it will get rejected. The Warp documentation states, "Many of the built-in filters will automatically reject the request with an appropriate rejection." It's important to know that if you have multiple filters, each could return a rejection, so the other filters can pick up the request to see if it fits for them.

If the last filter in the chain can't map the request to its signature, our Warp HTTP server will return this rejection to our requesting client, which results in a 404 error code. This is important to know, because sometimes you might want to handle a failing filter not with 404 but with something else. Figure 3.3 shows how an incoming request is being filtered by our setup paths and how a possible rejection is being recovered.

Therefore, Warp provides us with a `recover` filter, where we can pick up all rejections (how to return a rejection from a function is shown in listing 3.9) from the previous filters and iterate over them in our own error-handling method. This `recover` filter can be added at the end of multiple filter chains. Listing 3.9 shows us how this looks in our `main` function.

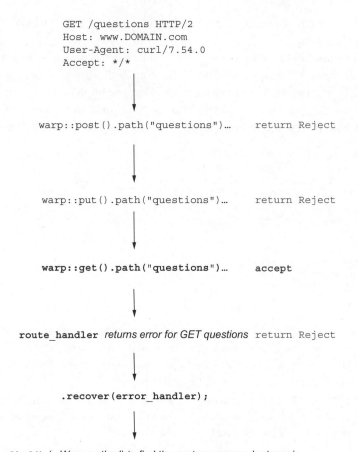

GET /questions HTTP/2
Host: www.DOMAIN.com
User-Agent: curl/7.54.0
Accept: */*

warp::post().path("questions")…   return Reject

warp::put().path("questions")…   return Reject

warp::get().path("questions")…   accept

route_handler *returns error for GET questions* return Reject

.recover(error_handler);

use r.find() *(a Warp method) to find the custom error and return via*
  warp::reply::with_status(String, ErrorStatusCode)

Figure 3.3 As an HTTP request passes through each filter, facing possible rejections along the way, those rejections can be picked up by Warp's recover **method to send out custom HTTP responses.**

But first, we have to do three things to be able to return a custom error in our recover handler:

1 Create our own custom error type.
2 Implement the Reject trait from Warp on this type.
3 Return the custom error in our route handler.

The resulting code looks like this.

Listing 3.8   Adding a custom error and returning it

```
use warp::{Filter, reject::Reject};
…
```

```
#[derive(Debug)]
struct InvalidId;
impl Reject for InvalidId {}

async fn get_questions() -> Result<impl warp::Reply, warp::Rejection> {
    let question = Question::new(
        QuestionId::from_str("1").expect("No id provided"),
        "First Question".to_string(),
        "Content of question".to_string(),
        Some(vec!("faq".to_string())),
    );

    match question.id.0.parse::<i32>() {
        Err(_) => {
            Err(warp::reject::custom(InvalidId))
        },
        Ok(_) => {
            Ok(warp::reply::json(
                &question
            ))
        }
    }
}

...
```

We first create an empty struct for our error type. For Warp to be able to work with this type accordingly, we need to add the `Debug` macro, and implement `Reject` on our just created struct. This allows us some pretty neat error handling later.

In the method itself, we match on the `question_id` (which is a tuple struct that can be accessed via the index, which is `0`) and see if the string can be parsed as a type `i32`. In a later version of the application, you can imagine passing the created object on a more complex validator. For now, it's enough to be sure the ID is a valid number.

If we can't parse the `&str` type to a number, we create a custom error and reject the request via `Err(warp::reject::custom(InvalidId))`. This tells Warp to go to the next `Filter`. We can then use the `recover` filter to fetch every rejection and check which HTTP message we have to send back. We can update our `get_items` route and add the `recover` filter at the end, as shown in the following listing.

Listing 3.9 Using our error handling in the route filter

```
...

#[tokio::main]
async fn main() {
    let get_items = warp::get()
        .and(warp::path("questions"))
        .and(warp::path::end())
        .and_then(get_questions)
        .recover(return_error);
```

```
    let routes = get_items;

    warp::serve(routes)
        .run(([127, 0, 0, 1], 3030))
        .await;
}

...
```

This allows us to do more error handling in the return_error function.

```
use warp::{Filter, reject::Reject, Rejection, Reply, http::StatusCode};

...

async fn return_error(r: Rejection) -> Result<impl Reply, Rejection> {
    if let Some(_InvalidId) = r.find() {
        Ok(warp::reply::with_status(
            "No valid ID presented",
            StatusCode::UNPROCESSABLE_ENTITY,
        ))
    } else {
        Ok(warp::reply::with_status(
            "Route not found",
            StatusCode::NOT_FOUND,
        ))
    }
}

...
```

We can search for specific rejections via r.find. If we find the one we are looking for, we can send back a more specific HTTP code and message. If not, the path was simply not found, and we return a basic 404 Not Found HTTP message.

The whole process is presented again in figure 3.4. An HTTP message comes in and arrives at our server, which we start with warp::serve. The framework looks at the HTTP message and goes through all the created routes (filters) to see if the method and path from the HTTP request matches any of our filters. If it does, it is routed to the function we call at the end of this specific filter (route_handler). Inside the function, we either return warp::Reply or warp::Rejection, and handle the error case in our .recover fallback, where we return a custom error to the requesting party.

You can run the code via cargo run and execute an HTTP request against local-host:3030/questions (as seen in listing 3.11). Either use a third-party app like Postman, or open another terminal window and execute this command.

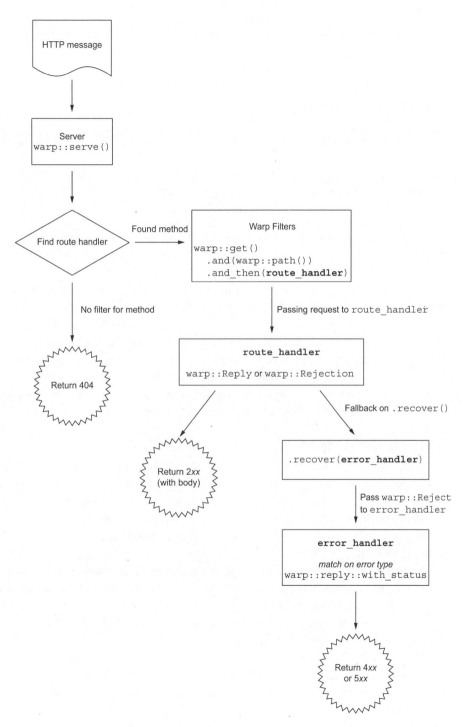

Figure 3.4   Getting an HTTP request, sending it through Warp filters and the route handler, and then returning a proper HTTP message

Listing 3.11   Example curl request to get questions from our server

```
curl localhost:3030/questions
```

You will get a JSON response, shown in the following listing (formatted for the book, in the terminal the response is shown in one line).

Listing 3.12   JSON response from the server

```
{
 "id":"1","title":"First Question",
 "content":"Content of question","tags":["faq"]
}?
```

With this working solution, you can go ahead and try to implement more questions, play around with the code, and change parts. Try to return invalid JSON, for example, or return a different success or error code.

The beauty of Rust is that everything is strictly typed, so looking for features in a library like Warp, understanding which format the return object has to be, and spotting mistakes while refactoring is straightforward and covered by the compiler.

Before we move on to chapter 4 to create the rest of our route handlers and face other interesting topics like sharing data between threads, we'll complete the setup of our web server by enabling CORS. This gives you the chance to put this little server onto another machine or server and run requests against it (we cover this process in chapter 10, but now feels like the right time to properly set up everything).

3.3   *Handling CORS headers*

When developing APIs that are available to the wider public, you need to think about *cross-origin resource sharing* (*CORS*); see http://mng.bz/N5wD. Web browsers have a security mechanism that doesn't allow requests started from domain A against domain B. For your development and production requirements, deploying a website to a server, and trying to send requests from your browser locally or from a different domain, will fail.

For this scenario, CORS was invented. It should soften the stance on the same-origin policy (http://mng.bz/DDwE) and allow browsers to make requests to other domains. How do they do it? Instead of sending, for example, an HTTP PUT request directly, they send a *preflight request* to the server, which is an HTTP OPTIONS request. Figure 3.5 shows what is involved in the preflight request.

This OPTIONS request asks the server if it's OK to send the request, and the server replies with the allowed methods in the header. The browser reads the allowed methods, and if PUT is included, it does a second HTTP request with the actual data in the body.

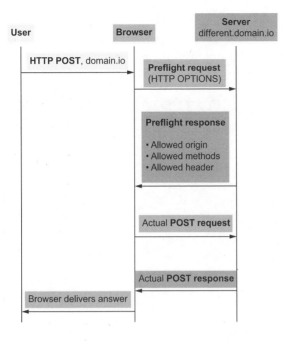

**Figure 3.5   In a CORS workflow, a user
initiates a POST request inside a browser,
and the browser first does a preflight HTTP
OPTIONS request to the server, which has
to respond with allowed domains (origins),
methods, and headers.**

Exceptions exist, however. Since the CORS standard shouldn't break older servers, there are no preflight requests for HTTP requests with the following headers:

- `application/x-www-form-urlencoded`
- `multipart/form-data`
- `text/plain`

And there are none for the following HTTP requests:

- HTTP GET
- HTTP POST
- HTTP HEAD

On our server, we still need to validate every request coming in—but in addition, if we want to open our API to the wider public, we need to send the methods we are accepting and the location we are accepting them from as an answer to any HTTP OPTION request.

Now this is done on an infrastructure level most of the time. With the ever-growing footprint of server applications, it makes sense not to implement CORS on each application but infrastructure-wide in your API gateway, for example.

However, if you run a single instance of your application and want to open your API to the broader public, you have to handle CORS in your application. Thankfully, Warp already supports CORS right out of the box.

3.3.1   *Returning CORS headers on the application level*

Our framework of choice has a cors filter ready for us to use and adjust. In our example, we allow any origin, which should not be done in a production environment. You could specify the origin you allow via the allow_origin filter (http://mng.bz/lRZy).

> **Listing 3.13   Preparing our application to be able to return proper CORS headers**

```
use warp::{
    Filter,
    http::Method,
    reject::Reject,
    Rejection,
    Reply,
    http::StatusCode
};

...

#[tokio::main]
async fn main() {
    let cors = warp::cors()
        .allow_any_origin()
        .allow_header("content-type")
        .allow_methods(
            &[Method::PUT, Method::DELETE, Method::GET, Method::POST]
        );

    let get_items = warp::get()
        .and(warp::path("questions"))
        .and(warp::path::end())
        .and_then(get_questions)
        .recover(return_error);

    let routes = get_items.with(cors);

    warp::serve(routes)
        .run(([127, 0, 0, 1], 3030))
        .await;
}
```

We import http::Method from the Warp framework to use in our allow_methods array. With our knowledge of how CORS works, we know that a browser intercepts a PUT request, for example, and sends an OPTION request first, and expects information about the following:

- Allowed headers
- Allowed methods
- Allowed origin

3.3.2   *Testing CORS responses*

We just set up all of this; now we need to send an OPTION request against our local-host:3030/questions route and fake that we are from a different server.

Listing 3.14   Sending an OPTIONS request via curl

```
curl -X OPTIONS localhost:3030/questions \
     -H "Access-Control-Request-Method: PUT" \
     -H "Access-Control-Request-Headers: content-type" \
     -H "Origin: https://not-origin.io" –verbose
```

We get the following output on the console.

Listing 3.15   Console output from the curl OPTIONS request

```
> OPTIONS /questions/1 HTTP/1.1
> Host: localhost:3030
> User-Agent: curl/7.64.1
> Accept: */*
> Access-Control-Request-Method: PUT
> Access-Control-Request-Headers: content-type
> Origin: https://reqbin.com
>
< HTTP/1.1 200 OK
< access-control-allow-headers: content-type
< access-control-allow-methods: DELETE, PUT
< access-control-allow-origin: https://not-origin.io
< content-length: 0
< date: Fri, 12 Feb 2021 10:15:19 GMT
```

The browser would take this answer as a happy yes and would follow up with the original PUT request from the user. Let's also implement the not-happy path. We'll remove the allowed header from our code, add println! in the error handling, and run curl again.

Listing 3.16   Debugging the type of error we get if CORS fails

```
...

async fn return_error(r: Rejection) -> Result<impl Reply, Rejection> {
    println!("{:?}", r);
    if let Some(InvalidId) = r.find() {
        Ok(warp::reply::with_status(
            "No valid ID presented",
            StatusCode::UNPROCESSABLE_ENTITY,
        ))
    } else {
        Ok(warp::reply::with_status(
            "Route not found",
            StatusCode::NOT_FOUND,
        ))
    }
    ...
}
```

```
...

#[tokio::main]
async fn main() {
    let cors = warp::cors()
        .allow_any_origin()
        .allow_header("not-in-the-request")
        .allow_methods(
          &[Method::PUT, Method::DELETE, Method::GET, Method::POST]
        );
    ...
}
```

On the Rust side, we are getting the console output shown in the following listing.

Listing 3.17   Error response for the curl request from our server

```
   Finished dev [unoptimized + debuginfo] target(s) in 8.63s
    Running `target/debug/practical-rust-book`
Rejection(CorsForbidden(HeaderNotAllowed))
```

And the answer for the curl request looks like the following.

Listing 3.18   Curl error when running the request against our server

```
curl -X OPTIONS localhost:3030/questions \
      -H "Access-Control-Request-Method: PUT" \
      -H "Access-Control-Request-Headers: content-type" \
      -H "Origin: https://not-origin.io" -verbose

*   Trying 127.0.0.1:3030...
* Connected to localhost (127.0.0.1) port 3030 (#0)
> OPTIONS /questions HTTP/1.1
> Host: localhost:3030
> User-Agent: curl/7.79.1
> Accept: */*
> Access-Control-Request-Method: PUT
> Access-Control-Request-Headers: content-type
> Origin: https://not-origin.io
>
* Mark bundle as not supporting multiuse
< HTTP/1.1 403 Forbidden
< content-type: text/plain; charset=utf-8
< content-length: 42
< date: Sat, 30 Apr 2022 20:25:26 GMT
<
* Connection #0 to host localhost left intact
CORS request forbidden: header not allowed?
```

This happens because our cors is not configured yet to allow the wanted Access-Control-Request-Headers: content-type header. We currently don't handle the error case if we reject an OPTION request, so we default to a 404 Not Found message in our `return_error` handler. We see that Warp contains a `CorsForbidden` rejection type, which we can import and use in our error handler.

Listing 3.19 Adding a meaningful error in case CORS is not allowed

```
use warp::{
    Filter,
    http::Method,
    filters::{
        cors::CorsForbidden,
    },
    reject::Reject,
    Rejection,
    Reply,
    http::StatusCode
};

…

async fn return_error(r: Rejection) -> Result<impl Reply, Rejection> {
    if let Some(error) = r.find::<CorsForbidden>() {
        Ok(warp::reply::with_status(
            error.to_string(),
            StatusCode::FORBIDDEN,
        ))
    } else if let Some(InvalidId) = r.find() {
        Ok(warp::reply::with_status(
            "No valid ID presented".to_string(),
            StatusCode::UNPROCESSABLE_ENTITY,
        ))
    } else {
        Ok(warp::reply::with_status(
            "Route not found".to_string(),
            StatusCode::NOT_FOUND,
        ))
    }
}
…
```

With this change, curl returns a proper error message.

Listing 3.20 Proper error response from our server for a header that's not allowed

```
curl -X OPTIONS localhost:3030/questions \
    -H "Access-Control-Request-Method: PUT" \
    -H "Access-Control-Request-Headers: content-type" \
    -H "Origin: https://not-origin.io" —verbose

CORS request forbidden: header not allowed?
```

We can add the proper `content-type` header back to our config and run the code again.

Summary

- It is important to understand which stack is covered by the library you are choosing.
- Usually, you have to include a runtime to support your chosen web framework's asynchronous way of working.
- Every web framework already comes with a web server and types to return proper HTTP messages.
- Try to understand the mindset behind the framework you are choosing and think through a few use cases and how they would be implemented with this mindset.
- Start small and with the happy path, which is the GET route for one particular resource, in most cases.
- Use the Serde library to serialize and deserialize structs you create.
- Immediately start thinking about unsuccessful paths and implement custom error handling afterward.
- When HTTP requests come from a browser and originate from a different domain than the one our server is deployed under, we have to handle OPTION requests, which are part of the CORS workflow.
- The Warp framework has a built-in `cors` filter that can answer the requests appropriately.

Implement a RESTful API

In the previous chapter, we started building our Q&A web service. We created our first custom types, `Question` and `QuestionId`, and started to handle error cases and return them to the user. So far, we've implemented the GET route for /questions and return `404` when any other path or method is requested. This chapter will expand massively on this functionality. We continue to use our GitHub repository for this book (http://mng.bz/BZzJ).

We'll add all missing HTTP methods (POST, PUT, and DELETE) and add the `Answer` type as well. Figure 4.1 gives an overview of which endpoints we plan to implement in this chapter.

API routes

```
GET     /questions (empty body; return JSON)
POST    /questions (JSON body; return HTTP status code)
PUT     /questions/:questionId (JSON body, return HTTP status code)
DELETE  /questions/:questionId (empty body; return HTTP status code)
POST    /answers  (www-url-encoded body; return HTTP status code)
```

Figure 4.1 We implemented the GET route for questions in chapter 3; this chapter covers POST, PUT, and DELETE, as well as adding comments via POST.

We will add in-memory storage, which will be replaced later in the book by a real database. Remember our code examples from chapter 2? We explained a simple asynchronous setup and talked about our runtime handing TCP connections over to different threads.

We therefore have to share data among multiple threads. We have to look at ways to pass data around in our application in a thread-safe manner.

Not every API you are going to build follows the REST model. However, the code you are going to write and the problems you are going to face are the same as those for other design patterns. So even if you choose a different method to receive and answer HTTP requests for your own application, the knowledge in this chapter is still very valuable.

> ### Representational State Transfer
>
> If you design a RESTful service (introduced by Roy Fielding in 2000: http://mng .bz/WM6a), you are ensuring a stateless way of accessing and modifying the data you are providing. A RESTful API is usually a way to GET, UPDATE, CREATE, and DELETE data through HTTP endpoints, which are grouped by resources.
>
> If you, for example, manage questions, you use an HTTP GET request to get a list of questions, and when you pass an ID, you can access just one question. The same goes for UPDATE (via HTTP PATCH or HTTP PUT), CREATE (via HTTP POST), and DELETE (via HTTP DELETE).
>
> This lets you also abstract away your data model inside the database from the representation you offer to your users. You don't even need a question model in your database but can collect the information on the fly and offer it as a question to the requesting user.

This chapter is very web framework heavy since we receive all requests and send out answers with the help of the framework. Everything after that, however, is pure Rust and doesn't depend on the web framework of your choice. We will go through some iterations of the codebase in this chapter. The iteration part (up until section 4.1.3) can be found at http://mng.bz/deWQ.

4.1 GET questions from in-memory

Instead of having the burden of starting with a real database, it is always wise to start with a hash map or array when defining your API. This allows you to change your data models quickly during the development phase, without always having to run database migrations.

Another reason to have an *in-memory database* (a structure in the cache that you initialize at the start of the application) is to run a mock server you want to test against. You can parse a set of data out of a JSON file and read it into a local structure like a vector. In the previous chapter, we returned an example question for an HTTP GET request.

Listing 4.1 Route handler for GET /questions

```
...

async fn get_questions() -> Result<impl Reply, Rejection> {
    let question = Question::new(
        QuestionId::from_str("1").expect("No id provided"),
        "First Question".to_string(),
        "Content of question".to_string(),
        Some(vec!("faq".to_string())),
    );

        match question.id.0.parse::<i32>() {
            Err(_) => {
                Err(warp::reject::custom(InvalidId))
            },
            Ok(_) => {
                Ok(warp::reply::json(
                    &question
                ))
            }
        }
}

...
```

Instead of creating a question on demand and returning it, let's try to create a store of questions that we can return and remove from, alter, and add to later in the chapter.

4.1.1 Setting up a mock database

A common way of creating an in-memory store is by instantiating an array of objects and assigning it to a variable called `store`. You can even think about a more complex store structure that stores our questions, but also users, answers, and so forth. Instead of an array, we choose a hash map, so we can access a question directly by ID and don't have to iterate over a list of questions every time we want to find a specific one.

Listing 4.2 Creating a local store for our questions

```
use std::collections::HashMap;
...
```

```
struct Store {
    questions: HashMap<QuestionId, Question>,
}

...
...
```

Rust's really good documentation provides us with methods we can call on `HashMap`. For example, `insert` lets us add new entries to this map. Therefore, we implement our store with three methods:

- `new`
- `init`
- `add_question`

We can create a new store object that we can access and pass around, `init` the store either with a local JSON file or in our code with a few example questions, and add questions for now to add a larger example base.

In the previous chapter, you learned that Rust doesn't have a standardized way of creating a constructor. Therefore, we use the `new` keyword to create and return a new `Store`.

Listing 4.3   Adding a constructor to our store

```
use std::collections::HashMap;

...

impl Store {
    fn new() -> Self {
        Store {
            questions: HashMap::new(),
        }
    }
}

...
```

`HashMap` is not part of the Rust prelude; therefore, we need to import it from the standard library. To be able to add questions to this newly created hash map, we use the `insert` method. Next, we add a new function inside the `impl Store` block, which makes it available to every new store object via `store.add_question(&question)`.

Listing 4.4   Adding a method to the store to add questions

```
...
impl Store {
    ...

    fn add_question(mut self, question: Question) -> Self {
        self.questions.insert(question.id.clone(), question);
```

```
        self
    }
}
```

...

We expect a question as a parameter, and pass `mut self` (we use `mut` so we can mutate/change `self` by adding questions). The return value is `Self`, which means `Store` in this case.

We add a question in the body via `insert`, which is a `HashMap` method. Our hash map expects a string in the first argument (which we use to insert the `id` of the question) and a question itself in the second one. For the return value, we create a `Store` structure with the just updated `questions` hash map.

Here we clone the `id`, since we will partially transfer its ownership and need to give full ownership of the question to the `store`. If we removed `clone`, we would get the following error:

```
use of partially moved value: `question`
partial move occurs because `question.id` has type `QuestionId`,
which does not implement the `Copy` traitrustcE0382
```

When we try to run the updated version of our code with the added store functionality, we will get back one compiler error. This error shows that it can sometimes be a bit harder to identify the cause of an error:

```
error[E0599]: no method named `insert` found for
struct `HashMap<QuestionId, Question>` in the current scope
  --> src/main.rs:30:24
   |
15 | struct QuestionId(String);
   | --------------------------
   | |
   | doesn't satisfy `QuestionId: Eq`
   | doesn't satisfy `QuestionId: Hash`
...
30 |         self.questions.insert(question.id.clone(), question);
   |                        ^^^^^^ method not found in
   |                        `HashMap<QuestionId, Question>`
   |
   = note: the method `insert` exists but the following trait bounds
     were not satisfied:
           `QuestionId: Eq`
           `QuestionId: Hash`

error: aborting due to previous error
```

The error states that the method was not found in `HashMap`, but if we continue to read the whole error message, we are also told that there is such a method on `HashMap` after all, but *trait bounds* were not satisfied. The error also gives us a list of traits we need to implement for our `QuestionId` struct.

Let's go ahead and fix the error, and then discuss why it appeared in the first place. The following listing shows how to add the traits Eq and Hash to our derive macro.

Listing 4.5   Implementing comparison traits via the `derive` macro

```
...


#[derive(Serialize, Debug, Clone, Eq, Hash)]
struct QuestionId(String);


...
```

But the Rust compiler is still not satisfied. After adding these two traits, we get a new error message:

```
error[E0277]: can't compare `QuestionId` with `QuestionId`
  --> src/main.rs:14:35
   |
14 | #[derive(Serialize, Debug, Clone, Eq, Hash)]
   |                                   ^^ no implementation
   |                                      for `QuestionId == QuestionId`
   |
  ::: /Users/bgruber/.rustup/toolchains/
       stable-x86_64-apple-darwin/lib/rustlib/src/
       rust/library/core/src/cmp.rs:264:15
   |
264 | pub trait Eq: PartialEq<Self> {
    |               --------------- required by this bound in `Eq`
    |
   = help: the trait `PartialEq` is not implemented for `QuestionId`
   = note: this error originates in a derive macro
     (in Nightly builds, run with -Z macro-backtrace for more info)

error: aborting due to previous error
```

Now the compiler explains to us that there is no Eq implementation for QuestionId, and states something about PartialEq. After working with Rust for a longer period of time, these errors don't seem as foreign as they might now, and adding a trait the compiler offers you solves most problems. Later, you will question the error messages more and understand why and when to add something. For now, we'll add the suggested trait.

Listing 4.6   Adding the `PartialEq` trait to the `QuestionId` struct

```
...


#[derive(Serialize, Debug, Clone, PartialEq, Eq, Hash)]
struct QuestionId(String);


...
```

Before we move on, let's find out why we need these three traits in the first place. Using `QuestionId` doesn't work right out of the box when used as an index for our hash map. We have to derive `PartialEq`, `Eq`, and `Hash` for our custom struct. When trying to get a value based on an index, the hash map has to internally compare all the indexes (keys) available and get the one we requested. To do this, Rust compares the hashes of the keys (the one you pass and the ones inside the hash map).

HashMap requires the traits `Eq`, `PartialEq`, and `Hash` for any object used as the HashMap key/index. In our case, since our key/index (`QuestionId`) is of type `String` and already implements these three traits, we just need to declare them as `derived` from the `QuestionId` declaration. The compiler is happy, and `cargo run` will start our server again and answer with the question we added on the /questions path.

4.1.2 Preparing a set of test data

Next comes the `init` method, which we can call and then either read a set of hard-coded example questions or parse a JSON file later to fill our local database structure. This method is added to the `impl` block we started earlier.

> **Listing 4.7 Adding an `init` method to the `Store` and filling it with example questions**

```
...

impl Store {
    ...
    fn init(self) -> Self {
        let question = Question::new(
            QuestionId::from_str("1").expect("Id not set"),
            "How?".to_string(),
            "Please help!".to_string(),
            Some(vec!["general".to_string()])
        );
        self.add_question(question)
    }

    fn add_question(mut self, question: Question) -> Self {
        ...
    }
}

...
```

With the help of the `self` parameter, we can call our internal `add_question` method that we added previously to our database object. We can see that we just need to pass a `Question`; the `self` parameter we use in the `add_question` method is automatically taken from the overall context.

Instead of polluting our codebase with lots of example boilerplate, it is easier to provide an example JSON file that we read and initialize our question structure with. This also makes it more convenient to add and change questions later.

To do this, we provide a questions.json file in the root folder of our project (on the same level as the Cargo.toml file). The structure of our file looks as follows.

```
{
    "1" : {
        "id": "1",
        "title": "How?",
        "content": "Please help!",
        "tags": ["general"]
    }
}
```

To read the data into our application, we use the Serde library we introduced in chapter 3. This time, though, we are using Serde JSON. This library lets us parse a JSON file and automatically parse it in the right structure. We add it in our Cargo.toml file.

```
...

[dependencies]
warp = "0.3"
serde = { version = "1.0", features = ["derive"] }
serde_json = "1.0"
tokio = { version = "1.1.1", features = ["full"] }
```

This also gives us the chance to simplify our codebase quite a bit. Instead of manually adding questions, we parse them from the file and initialize the store with them in one step. Our new `impl` block for the `Store` is shown in the following listing.

```
use serde::{Deserialize, Serialize};
...

impl Store {
    fn new() -> Self {
        Store {
            questions: Self::init(),
        }
    }

    fn add_question(mut self, question: Question) -> Self {
        self.questions.insert(question.id.clone(), question);
        self
    }

    fn init() -> HashMap<QuestionId, Question> {
        let file = include_str!("../questions.json");
        serde_json::from_str(file).expect("can't read questions.json")
```

```
    }
}

#[derive(Deserialize, Serialize, Debug)]
struct Question {
    id: QuestionId,
    title: String,
    content: String,
    tags: Option<Vec<String>>,
}

#[derive(Deserialize, Serialize, Debug, Clone, PartialEq, Eq, Hash)]
struct QuestionId(String);

...
```

We remove add_question from the Store implementation and call init right in the new constructor. Inside init, we change the return value from Self to HashMap. We assign the return value of the init method directly to the questions attribute of Store.

Also, we need to use the Serdes Deserialize trait and implement it via derive on the Question and QuestionId structs. Because we are reading questions from a JSON file, Rust has to know how to deserialize JSON and form it into a Rust question object. The next step is to set up the storage and read from it via our route handlers.

4.1.3 *Reading from the fake database*

The starting point of our Rust application is the main function. There we have the chance to set up the storage before anything else happens. Setting up the storage is straightforward because of our rewrite earlier. All we have to do is call new on the Store struct to return the new storage, which we can assign to a new variable.

Listing 4.11 Creating a new instance of our store before we start the server

```
...

#[tokio::main]
async fn main() {
    let store = Store::new();
    ...
}

...
```

Now we have to pass this newly created object to our route handler. Here we need to adjust to our Warp framework and align with its way of thinking. We discussed the concept of filters earlier, and this is exactly what we need to create. Each HTTP request runs through the filters we set up and adds or modifies the data along the way. To handle state with Warp, we have to create a filter, which holds our store, and pass it to each route we want to access it.

Listing 4.12   Adding a store filter that we can pass to our routes

```
...

#[derive(Clone)]
struct Store {
    questions: HashMap<QuestionId, Question>,
}

...

#[tokio::main]
async fn main() {
    let store = Store::new();
    let store_filter = warp::any().map(move || store.clone());

    ...
    warp::serve(routes)
        .run(([127, 0, 0, 1], 3030))
        .await;
}

...
```

We read this new line as follows:

- With warp::any, the any filter will match any request, so this statement will evaluate any and all requests.
- With .map, we call map on the filter to pass a value to the receiving function.
- Inside map, we use Rust closures. The move keyword indicates to *capture by value*, which means it moves the values into the closure and takes ownership of them.
- We return a clone of our store so every function that applies this Warp filter has access to the store. Usually, we wouldn't need to clone the store here because we have just one route. However, because we will create multiple route handlers that will have all access to the store, we need to clone it.

We can now apply this filter to our route handler.

Listing 4.13   Adding the store to the /questions route and route handler

```
...

#[tokio::main]
async fn main() {
    let store = Store::new();
    let store_filter = warp::any().map(move || store.clone());

    ...

    let get_questions = warp::get()
        .and(warp::path("questions"))
        .and(warp::path::end())
```

```
        .and(store_filter)
        .and_then(get_questions)
        .recover(return_error);

    let routes = get_questions.with(cors);

    warp::serve(routes)
        .run(([127, 0, 0, 1], 3030))
        .await;
}

...
```

We attach the filter with `.and(store_filter)` to our chain of filters. Our Warp framework will now add the store object to our route handler, which means we have to expect one parameter in our get_questions function. We also now read from the store instead of returning our custom question.

This change lets us delete the old creation of a new question for testing purposes, and with it the `impl` block of `Question` and the error handling as well. The next listing shows the updated code in bold, and the deleted code via strike-through.

Listing 4.14   Reading questions from the store in the `get_questions` route handler

```
use std::str::FromStr;
use std::io::{Error, ErrorKind};

...

// Adding the Clone trait which we use in the
// get_questions function further down
#[derive(Deserialize, Serialize, Clone, Debug)]
struct Question {
    id: QuestionId,
    title: String,
    content: String,
    tags: Option<Vec<String>>,
}

impl Question {
    fn new(
        id: QuestionId,
        title: String,
        content: String,
        tags: Option<Vec<String>>
    ) -> Self {
        Question {
            id,
            title,
            content,
            tags,
        }
    }
}
```

```
…

#[derive(Debug)]
struct InvalidId;
impl Reject for InvalidId {}

impl FromStr for QuestionId {
    type Err = std::io::Error;

    fn from_str(id: &str) -> Result<Self, Self::Err> {
        match id.is_empty() {
            false => Ok(QuestionId(id.to_string())),
            true => Err(Error::new(ErrorKind::InvalidInput, "No id pro-
vided")),
        }
    }
}

async fn get_questions(store: Store) -> Result<impl Reply, Rejection> {
    let question = Question::new(
        QuestionId::from_str("1").expect("No id provided"),
        "First Question".to_string(),
        "Content of question".to_string(),
        Some(vec!("faq".to_string())),
    );

    match question.id.0.parse::<i32>() {
        Err(_) => {
            Err(warp::reject::custom(InvalidId))
        },
        Ok(_) => {
            Ok(warp::reply::json(
                &question
            ))
        }
    }

    let res: Vec<Question> = store.questions.values().cloned().collect();

    Ok(warp::reply::json(&res))
}

async fn return_error(r: Rejection) -> Result<impl Reply, Rejection> {
    if let Some(error) = r.find::<CorsForbidden>() {
        Ok(warp::reply::with_status(
            error.to_string(),
            StatusCode::FORBIDDEN,
        ))
    } else if let Some(InvalidId) = r.find() {
        Ok(warp::reply::with_status(
            "No valid ID presented".to_string(),
            StatusCode::UNPROCESSABLE_ENTITY,
        ))
    } else {
        Ok(warp::reply::with_status(
```

```
                "Route not found".to_string(),
                StatusCode::NOT_FOUND,
            ))
        }
    }
}

...
```

We still want to return a list of all questions we currently have for this specific route. We therefore use the method `values` from `HashMap` to discard the hash map keys (`QuestionId`) and clone the hash map values (`Question`). We clone them because our next method, `collect`, requires having ownership over the values and not just a reference.

4.1.4 *Parsing query parameters*

Query parameters are added to give more specification for a route—for example, requesting to read all questions on the platform but limiting the number on each request. So, you could have an HTTP GET call on the following route:

```
localhost:3030/questions?start=1&end=200
```

This indicates that the client or requesting source wants to read the first 200 questions on the platform. This could be a website that wants to display the first set of questions, and when the user scrolls down, it would request the next set:

```
localhost:3030/questions?start=201&end=400
```

We must check in our application for parameters if any are added. We don't create a new route for this, but just add an additional filter.

Listing 4.15 Adding the `query` filter to our route to parse query parameters

```
...

#[tokio::main]
async fn main() {
    let store = Store::new();
    let store_filter = warp::any().map(move || store.clone());

    ...

    let get_questions = warp::get()
        .and(warp::path("questions"))
        .and(warp::path::end())
        .and(warp::query())
        .and(store_filter)
        .and_then(get_questions);

    ...
}

...
```

This is an excellent opportunity to work with the compiler instead of against it. When adding this query filter, we get the following error:

```
error[E0593]: function is expected to take 2 arguments,
but it takes 1 argument
   --> src/main.rs:147:19
    |
79  | async fn get_questions( store: Store) ->
    |     Result<impl warp::Reply, warp::Rejection> {
    | ------------------------------------- takes 1 argument
...
147 |         .and_then(get_questions);
    |          ^^^^^^^^^^^^^ expected function
    |                         that takes 2 arguments
    |
    = note: required because of the requirements
        on the impl of `warp::generic::Func<(_, Store)>` for
        `fn(Store) -> impl Future {get_questions}`
```

The compiler tells us via the line expected function that takes 2 arguments that Warp is adding another parameter to the function call get_questions. We added warp::query to our chain of filters (in listing 4.15), which adds a hash map to the function we call in the last and_then.

After warp::path::end, we add an and with the query filter and afterward add store_filter.clone. That's also the order we must have in mind when adding the parameters to get_questions.

Listing 4.16   Adding the query parameters' HashMap in the route handler

```
...

async fn get_questions(
    params: HashMap<String, String>,
    store: Store
) -> Result<impl warp::Reply, warp::Rejection> {
    let res: Vec<Question> = store.questions.values().cloned().collect();

    Ok(warp::reply::json(&res))
}

...
```

What now? The code will compile and run. We can add console output to see what's inside our HTTP request, so we get an idea of how to handle these new parameters.

Listing 4.17   Debugging the parameters to see the structure

```
...

async fn get_questions(
    params: HashMap<String, String>,
```

```
    store: Store
) -> Result<impl warp::Reply, warp::Rejection> {
    println!("{:?}", params);
    let res: Vec<Question> = store.questions.values().cloned().collect();

    Ok(warp::reply::json(&res))
}
```

...

We put {:?} instead of {} in the println! macro, because HashMap is a complex data structure, and {:?} tells the compiler to use Debug formatting instead of Display. Sending an HTTP GET request like this one

```
curl localhost:3030/questions?start=1&end=200
```

will print the following onto our console (our println! output is in bold):

```
    Finished dev [unoptimized + debuginfo] target(s) in 4.33s
      Running `target/debug/practical-rust-book`
{"start": "1", "end": "200"}
```

We have a hash map with key–value pairs, both as strings. We can definitely work with that. We want to use the values at some point, but it seems like they should be numbers instead of strings. Luckily, Rust provides a built-in parse method that we can use. Let's go over it step-by-step:

1 We need to check whether our parameters' HashMap contains any value.
2 If it does, try to parse the number out of the start String.
3 If it fails, return an error.

We can use match to check if the hash map has a value where we would expect it.

Listing 4.18   Matching on the params to see if we have values in them

...

```
async fn get_questions(
    params: HashMap<String, String>,
    store: Store
) -> Result<impl warp::Reply, warp::Rejection> {

    match params.get("start") {
        Some(start) => println!("{}", start),
        None => println!("No start value"),
    }
    ...
}
```

...

In case of None, we just print out No start value to the console. It seems that we could also do away with the None case altogether and just do something when we have a parameter called start in the hash map. Rust provides us with a shorter version of this match arm in that case, as we see in the following listing.

Listing 4.19 Print out the `start` param to see the structure

```
...

async fn get_questions(
    params: HashMap<String, String>,
    store: Store
) -> Result<impl warp::Reply, warp::Rejection> {

    if let Some(n) = params.get("start") {
        println!("{}", n);
    }
    ...
}

...
```

The short version reads like this: if there is a Some value for the start key in the HashMap, extract the value via Some and create a variable called n. If there is no start key in the HashMap, well then, the if fails and the compiler continues on the line after.

The next step is trying to parse the containing string to a number and return early if that fails for some reason. The HashMap::get function returns Option<&String>, so we have a reference to a string (if the value was present). This type has a parse method implemented that we can use. We also have to specify which type we expect; see the following listing.

Listing 4.20 Trying to parse a params `start` string into a `usize` type

```
...

async fn get_questions(
    params: HashMap<String, String>,
    store: Store
) -> Result<impl warp::Reply, warp::Rejection> {

    if let Some(n) = params.get("start") {
        println!("{:?}", n.parse::<usize>());
    }

    ...
}

...
```

The method `parse` returns `Result`; that's the reason we switch back to the `Debug` display (`{:?}`). Instead of printing the outcome to the console, we add a bit of error handling and assign the start value.

Listing 4.21 Parsing the value to a `usize` type and returning an error if it can't be parsed

```
...

async fn get_questions(
    params: HashMap<String, String>,
    store: Store
) -> Result<impl warp::Reply, warp::Rejection> {

    let mut start = 0;

    if let Some(n) = params.get("start") {
        start = n.parse::<usize>().expect("Could not parse start");
    }

    println!("{}", start);
    ...
}

...
```

We add a mutable `start` variable that defaults to `0`. In our `if` block, we still parse the start entry in the parameters' `HashMap`, but this time we call the `.expect` method on the `Result` object. And just for testing, we print the number to the console.

If the `start` entry can't be parsed to a number, our application fails:

```
Finished dev [unoptimized + debuginfo] target(s) in 7.77s
Running `target/debug/practical-rust-book`
thread 'tokio-runtime-worker' panicked at
    'Could not parse start:
        ParseIntError { kind: InvalidDigit }', src/main.rs:83:34
note: run with `RUST_BACKTRACE=1` environment variable
    to display a backtrace
```

We can see that just adding two parameters to a request can lead to a lot of errors. Either just one is present, or one of them cannot be parsed. To account for the variety of errors, we'll move this logic to its own function, and add our own error type and handling.

4.1.5 Returning custom errors

We would like to return a proper error to the person who made the HTTP request. We already talked about the two possible errors here:

- Cannot parse a number out of the parameter
- Either the start or end parameter is missing

We create an enum that covers both cases.

```
...

#[derive(Debug)]
enum Error {
    ParseError(std::num::ParseIntError),
    MissingParameters,
}

...
```

We derive the Debug implementation on our new Error and add two options for it: ParseError and MissingParameters. As we have seen in the previous error message, when Rust can't parse a number out of the string, we get ParseIntError back. We would like to populate this message back to the user so they know where they might be wrong. We can do this by encapsulating the Error type in parentheses.

Two steps are missing to implement these custom errors in our code:

1 Implement the Display trait so Rust knows how to format the error to a string.
2 Implement Warp's Reject trait on our error so we can return it in a Warp route handler.

Every time we want our custom type to learn new tricks or play nicely with other frameworks, we can implement traits on it. Implementing traits is like learning new behavior or skills in the Rust world. Let's start with the Display trait from the standard library.

```
...

impl std::fmt::Display for Error {
    fn fmt(&self, f: &mut std::fmt::Formatter) -> std::fmt::Result {
        match *self {
            Error::ParseError(ref err) => {
                write!(f, "Cannot parse parameter: {}", err)
            },
            Error::MissingParameters => write!(f, "Missing parameter"),
        }
    }
}

...
```

The Rust documentation tells you exactly how traits from the standard library have to be implemented (http://mng.bz/rnZX). They take self as an argument, which is our custom type, and Formatter from the standard library. We then match on our different enum types and use the `write!` macro to tell the compiler what to print if it comes to it (every time you create a readable output of the error).

Implementing `Reject` from our Warp framework is far easier and just a one-liner, as we see in listing 4.24. The `Reject` trait from Warp is a *marker trait*. They have empty bodies but give the compiler a guarantee that they fulfill certain properties. You can read more about markers via the Rust docs (https://doc.rust-lang.org/std/marker/index.html) and in the official blog post about traits (https://blog.rust-lang.org/2015/05/11/traits.html).

Listing 4.24 Implementing the Warp `Reject` trait for our custom `Error`

```
...

impl Reject for Error {}

...
```

This is enough for Warp to accept our error inside a route handler. Now we have two pieces missing:

- Extracting the parameter logic out in its own function
- Calling the function from within the `get_questions` route handler and letting the error bubble up to our `return_error` function, and handling it there

To give our codebase and data we are handling more meaning, we create a new `Pagination` struct that has two attributes: `start` and `end`. We can use this to return a proper type back to our route handler.

Listing 4.25 Adding a `Pagination` struct to add structure to our receiving query params

```
...

#[derive(Debug)]
struct Pagination {
    start: usize,
    end: usize,
}

...
```

The `#[derive(Debug)]` lets us display this struct in `println!` macros and other scenarios where we want to print out its contents. The next step is to create an `extract_pagination` function to which we pass our parameters' HashMap.

Listing 4.26 Moving the query extraction code to its own function

```
...

fn extract_pagination(
    params: HashMap<String, String>
```

If both parameters are there, we return Result (via return Ok()). We need the return keyword here because we want to return early.

Uses the .contains method on the HashMap to check if both parameters are there

```
) -> Result<Pagination, Error> {
    if params.contains_key("start") && params.contains_key("end") {
        return Ok(Pagination {
            start: params
                .get("start")
                .unwrap()
                .parse::<usize>()
                .map_err(Error::ParseError)?,
            end: params
                .get("end")
                .unwrap()
                .parse::<usize>()
                .map_err(Error::ParseError)?,
        });
    }

    Err(Error::MissingParameters)
}
...
```

Creates a new Pagination object and sets the start and end number

The .get method on HashMap returns an option, because it can't be sure that the key exists. We can do the unsafe .unwrap here, because we already checked if both parameters are in the HashMap a few lines earlier. We parse the containing &str value to a usize integer type. This returns Result, which we unwrap or return an error if it fails via .map_err and the question mark at the end of the line.

If not, the if clause isn't being executed and we go right down to Err, where we return our custom MissingParameters error, which we access from the Error enum with the double colons (::).

We can now call in this method or the get_questions route handler and replace the previous code with it.

Listing 4.27   Returning different questions based on the passing params

```
...
async fn get_questions(
    params: HashMap<String, String>,
    store: Store,
) -> Result<impl warp::Reply, warp::Rejection> {
    if !params.is_empty() {
        let pagination = extract_pagination(params)?;
        let res: Vec<Question> = store.questions.values().cloned().collect();
        let res = &res[pagination.start..pagination.end];
        Ok(warp::reply::json(&res))
    } else {
        let res: Vec<Question> = store.questions.values().cloned().collect();
        Ok(warp::reply::json(&res))
    }
}
...
```

We first check if our parameters' HashMap is not empty, and then pass it over to the extract_pagination function. This will either return a Pagination object or return our custom Error early via the question mark (?) at the end. Afterward, we use the start and end parameters to take a slice out of our Vec to return the questions specified by the user.

If the parameters are invalid, we can handle the error in the return_error function that we created in chapter 3. We add another else if block and look for our custom error in the Rejection filter.

```
use warp::{Filter, reject::Reject, Reply, Rejection, http::StatusCode};

...

async fn return_error(r: Rejection) -> Result<impl Reply, Rejection> {
    if let Some(error) = r.find::<Error>() {
        Ok(warp::reply::with_status(
            error.to_string(),
            StatusCode::RANGE_NOT_SATISFIABLE,
        ))
    } else if let Some(error) = r.find::<CorsForbidden>() {
        Ok(warp::reply::with_status(
            error.to_string(),
            StatusCode::FORBIDDEN,
        ))
    } else {
        Ok(warp::reply::with_status(
            "Route not found".to_string(),
            StatusCode::NOT_FOUND,
        ))
    }
}

...
```

But what happens if we specify an end parameter that is greater than the length of our vector? And what happens if start is 20 and end is 10? We would need to handle these options as well to make our application even more foolproof. This exercise is up to you to implement; nothing new is coming your way that we haven't covered yet.

When starting our application via cargo run, we should get the exact output as before. But under the hood, we made massive improvements:

- Reading from a local JSON file
- Removing a good chunk of code
- Passing state to our route handlers
- Adding custom error handling

Next, we will update our in-memory storage with a PUT and POST request that we add a JSON structure to. A few more challenges remain ahead, so let's dive right into it.

4.2   POST, PUT, and DELETE questions

We have a few new steps to go through to be able to update our storage:

- Opening a route for an HTTP PUT request that has a parameter in it
- Opening a route for an HTTP POST request

- Accepting and reading JSON from the body of the PUT and POST request
- Updating our in-memory storage in a thread-safe manner

The first three are framework specific, and we have to learn how Warp is expecting us to create routes for this situation. The last one is Rust specific. We already set up our storage, but since we have multiple requests coming in at the same time, one write operation can take a longer time, while another request to update the store comes in.

Let's start at the end here and make sure you understand how and why we need to adjust our local state (`Store`) so it can work and operate in an asynchronous environment. After that, we will add the missing route handlers and open new API endpoints on our server.

4.2.1 *Updating our data in a thread-safe way*

When operating an asynchronous web server, we have to be aware that thousands (or more) requests can come in at the same second, and every request wants to write or read data. We have a single data structure that provides us with the state in our application. But what happens when two or more requests want to write to the same structure or read from it?

We must give store access to each request separately and notify each request to wait until the previous read or write is done on the `Store`. In this case, two processes (or more) want to update the same data structure. We need to put other processes on a waiting list so just one process at a time can alter our data.

In addition, you learned in chapter 3 that Rust has a unique view of ownership. Just one instance or process can have ownership over a particular variable or object. This is to prevent race conditions and null pointers, where data is referenced that is not there anymore. It seems we have to wait for one request to finish, for it to be able to return the ownership of the `Store` to the next one. This runs completely counter to the asynchronous mindset.

We are facing two problems:

- Preventing two or more processes from altering data at the same time
- Giving each route handler ownership over the data store if needed so it can be mutated

Before we can even think about having waiting lists on our `Store` to alter data, we first have to make sure Rust can share the ownership of a state. So, let's tackle the second problem first.

In the preceding chapter, we explained how Rust transfers ownership when passing variables around in our code. Figure 4.2 shows how, when passing a complex value (like `String`) to another variable, the compiler marks it as `uninit` (https://doc.rust-lang.org/nomicon/drop-flags.html). Rust makes sure just one pointer on the stack has ownership over this structure on the heap. And just this one pointer is allowed to modify it.

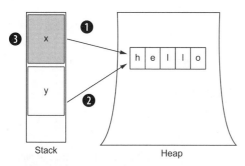

❶ `let x = String::from("hello");`

❷ `let y = x;`

❸ `//mark x as uninitialized`

Figure 4.2 Reassigning a complex data type like `String` to another variable requires internally moving ownership over to the new variable and dropping the old one.

This ownership concept is a problem for us right now. Rust's safety measurements are preventing us from simply sharing data among functions and threads, because whenever we pass a value to a new function, we transfer the ownership of this value, and have to wait until we get it back. Two options come to mind:

- Create a copy of our store for each route handler.
- Wait until one route handler is finished to give back the ownership of the store and pass it on to the next one.

However, neither addresses the underlying issue in an appropriate way. The first one would pollute our memory quite a lot, and we would still not be able to mutate the data inside the store. The second option would work counter to our asynchronous approach.

Lucky for us, Rust comes equipped to deal with these problems. Specifically, it provides the following:

- `Rc<T>`
- `Arc<T>`

The `Rc` or `Arc` type will place the underlying data structure `T` on the heap and create a pointer on the stack. Then you can make a copy of that pointer that references the same data. The difference between these two is that `Rc` works only on single-threaded systems, and `Arc` is there for multithreaded, enabling you to share data among multiple threads. Figure 4.3 shows the concept of cloning an `Arc` and how it works internally.

The `Arc` type is *atomically reference counted*. It is like a container, which moves the wrapped data in it onto the heap and creates a pointer to it on the stack. When cloning an `Arc`, you clone the pointer that points to the same data structure on the heap, and internally, `Arc` increments its count. When the internal count reaches 0 (when all variables pointing to the variables go out of scope), `Arc` drops the value. This makes it safe to share complex data on the heap among different variables.

We are using multithreading (via Tokio), which means we need to use `Arc<T>` and wrap our data store in it. But this is just one part of the solution. Reading to the same

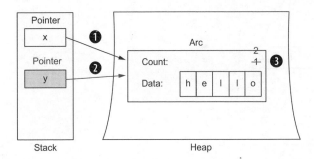

① `let x = Arc::new(String::from("hello"));`

② `let y = Arc::clone(&x);`

③ `//increment Arc counter + 1`

Figure 4.3 Instead of dropping the value x, Rust increments the `Arc` count. Whenever x or y are going out of scope, Rust decreases the count until it is at 0, and then calls `.drop` to remove the value from the heap.

`Store` is fine, but we also want the chance to mutate it. An HTTP POST request on one thread can add questions, and an HTTP PUT request on another thread can try to alter an existing question.

Therefore, we need to look for solutions. Rust also has us covered in this scenario. We can use either of these two types:

- `Mutex`
- `RwLock`

Both make sure that a reader or writer has unique access to the underlying data. They lock the data as soon as a writer or reader wants access and unlock it for the next reader or writer when the previous one is finished. The difference is that `Mutex` blocks for either a writer or reader, whereas `RwLock` allows many readers simultaneously but just one writer at a time.

We have to be cautious, however. Both types are part of the `std::sync` module, which focuses on synchronous tasks, and so are not well suited for our async environment. Implementations of the `RwLock` type can be used for an async environment, so we need to add these to our project.

We are already using Tokio, which comes with `RwLock` (http://mng.bz/Vy95). First, we encapsulate our questions in `Arc`, so we can place the data onto the heap and can have multiple pointers to it. In addition, we wrap our questions structure in `RwLock`, so we prevent multiple writes at the same time.

Listing 4.29 Making our `HashMap` thread safe

```
...

use std::sync::Arc;
use tokio::sync::RwLock;

...
```

```
#[derive(Clone)]
struct Store {
    questions: Arc<RwLock<HashMap<QuestionId, Question>>>,
}

impl Store {
    fn new() -> Self {
        Store {
            questions: Arc::new(RwLock::new(Self::init())),
        }
    }

    ...

}
...
```

We have to update the way we read questions from our `Store` in the `get_questions` function as well.

> **Listing 4.30 Adjusting our way of reading the store**

```
...
async fn get_questions(
    params: HashMap<String, String>,
    store: Store,
) -> Result<impl warp::Reply, warp::Rejection> {
    if !params.is_empty() {
        let pagination = extract_pagination(params)?;
        let res: Vec<Question> = store
            .questions
            .read()
            .await
            .values()
            .cloned()
            .collect();
        let res = &res[pagination.start..pagination.end];
        Ok(warp::reply::json(&res))
    } else {
        let res: Vec<Question> =
        store.questions.read().await.values().cloned().collect();
        Ok(warp::reply::json(&res))
    }
}...
```

A simple read on the `questions` is enough to request reading from `RwLock`. We have to `.await` the `read` function, because it could be that a lock is in place because another process is currently accessing the same data. With the updated wrapping of our `Store` structure in mind, we are creating two new functions: updating and inserting questions.

4.2.2   Adding a question

We solved our problem of handling state in a thread-safe manner. Now we can go ahead and implement the rest of our API routes and explore how we parse bodies from an HTTP request and read parameters from a URL. The first route we will add accepts HTTP POST requests to the /questions path. Figure 4.4 shows our progress so far and what we expect from the POST endpoint we are now implementing.

API routes

```
GET     /questions (empty body; return JSON)
POST    /questions (JSON body; return HTTP status code)
PUT     /questions/:questionId (JSON body, return HTTP status code)
DELETE  /questions/:questionId (empty body; return HTTP status code)
POST    /answers  (www-url-encoded body; return HTTP status code)
```

Figure 4.4   We expect new questions in the body of the HTTP POST request on the /questions path.

Listing 4.31 shows our add_question route handler. We expect the store to be passed to our function, and a question. We then can use the RwLock we implemented on the Store, and use write to request write access to it. As with read before, we .await the write function. Whenever we get access, we can insert a new question in the underlying hash map.

> **Listing 4.31   Adding a route handler for adding a question to the store**

```
...

async fn add_question(
    store: Store,
    question: Question
) -> Result<impl warp::Reply, warp::Rejection> {
    store.questions.write().await.insert(question.id.clone(), question);

    Ok(warp::reply::with_status(
        "Question added",
        StatusCode::OK,
    ))
}

...
```

The insert method takes two arguments: the index for the hash map and the value we want to store next to it. We can spot Rust's ownership principles here as well: we access the ID of the question in the first parameter, and therefore pass the ownership of the question to the insert method of the hash map. This would be fine if we weren't using the question anywhere else again. But the second argument takes the question and stores it in the hash map.

Therefore, we clone the question_id in the first parameter to create a copy, and then give ownership of the initial question from the function parameters to the insert method.

Listing 4.32   Adding the POST route for /questions

```
...

#[tokio::main]
async fn main() {
    ...

    let get_questions = warp::get()
        .and(warp::path("questions"))
        .and(warp::path::end())
        .and(warp::query())
        .and(store_filter.clone())
        .and_then(get_questions);

    let add_question = warp::post()
        .and(warp::path("questions"))
        .and(warp::path::end())
        .and(store_filter.clone())
        .and(warp::body::json())
        .and_then(add_question);

    let routes = get_questions
        .or(add_question)
        .with(cors)
        .recover(return_error);

    warp::serve(routes)
        .run(([127, 0, 0, 1], 3030))
        .await;
}
```

Creates a new variable and uses warp::post this time to filter HTTP POST requests

We still listen on the same root path, /questions.

Closes the path definition

Adds our store to this route so we can pass it to the route handler later

Extracts the JSON body, which is getting added to the parameters as well

Calls add_question with store and the json body as the parameters

We added two new routes to our route variable. Be aware that we removed the individual recover after the end of the get_questions filter, and added it the end of the routes, because now we try different routes before recovering Not Found paths. You can check via the following curl command if the add_question route handlers fails:

```
$ curl --location --request POST 'localhost:3030/questions' \
    --header 'Content-Type: application/json' \
    --data-raw '{
    "title": "New question",
    "content": "How does this work again?"
  }'
Request body deserialize error: missing field `id` at line 4 column 1?
```

4.2.3   *Updating a question*

As in the previous section, we expect JSON to be sent in the HTTP request. Instead of a POST, however, we require the PUT method. The other difference is that the route we are opening up is also expecting an ID for the question. This is a best practice in the REST mindset, where we access the exact resource we want via the URL and pass the updated data in the body. Our web framework Warp has to be able to parse the URL parameter and hand it over the route handler, so we can later use this for indexing the hash map and updating the value next to it. Figure 4.5 shows our progress until now and what still lies ahead.

API routes

```
GET    /questions (empty body; return JSON)
POST   /questions (JSON body; return HTTP status code)
PUT    /questions/:questionId (JSON body, return HTTP status code)
DELETE /questions/:questionId (empty body; return HTTP status code)
POST   /answers  (www-url-encoded body; return HTTP status code)
```

Figure 4.5   The PUT method adds a URL parameter that we need to parse via Warp and add to our route handler.

First, let's go through the code of update_question. In addition to passing the Store to the function, we also add the question_id and a question. This simple-looking addition adds a new error case: what if we don't have the question the user is requesting? We have to handle the case that the hash map can't find the question. The following listing shows both our route handler update_question and the new error we are adding to the Error enum—and therefore also to our implementation of the Display trait.

Listing 4.33   Updating a question and returning 404 if it cannot be found

```
...

#[derive(Debug)]
enum Error {
    ParseError(std::num::ParseIntError),
    MissingParameters,
    QuestionNotFound,
}

impl std::fmt::Display for Error {
    fn fmt(&self, f: &mut std::fmt::Formatter) -> std::fmt::Result {
        match *self {
            Error::ParseError(ref err) => {
                write!(f, "Cannot parse parameter: {}", err)
            },
            Error::MissingParameters => write!(f, "Missing parameter"),
            Error::QuestionNotFound => write!(f, "Question not found"),
        }
    }
}
```

```
async fn update_question(
    id: String,
    store: Store,
    question: Question
) -> Result<impl warp::Reply, warp::Rejection> {
    match store.questions.write().await.get_mut(&QuestionId(id)) {
        Some(q) => *q = question,
        None => return Err(warp::reject::custom(Error::QuestionNotFound)),
    }

    Ok(warp::reply::with_status(
        "Question updated",
        StatusCode::OK,
    ))
}

...
```

Instead of just writing to the HashMap object as in the add_question route handler, we are requesting a mutable reference to the question we are trying to access, so we can alter the content inside it. We are using the match block to check if the HashMap object has a question to the ID we are passing.

The match arm lets us unwrap a possible question and overwrite it via *q = question. If there is no question, we abort early and return our custom error QuestionNot-Found. We could alter our return_error function that catches all the errors on our routes, but we use our default 404 case for now. This is a great exercise for you to go through to see how to handle such a case.

Adding this route handler to our server is shown in the following listing. It all looks similar to the previous add_question one, with one small difference: we add a new param filter from the Warp framework to specify our PUT path.

Listing 4.34 Adding the PUT route for /questions/:questionID

```
...

#[tokio::main]
async fn main() {
    ...

    let get_questions = warp::get()
        .and(warp::path("questions"))
        .and(warp::path::end())
        .and(store_filter.clone())
        .and_then(get_questions);

    let add_question = warp::post()
        .and(warp::path("questions"))
        .and(warp::path::end())
        .and(store_filter.clone())
        .and(warp::body::json())
        .and_then(add_question);
```

We still listen on the same root path, /questions.

Creates a new variable and uses warp::put this time to filter HTTP PUT requests

```
let update_question = warp::put()
    .and(warp::path("questions"))
    .and(warp::path::param::<String>())
    .and(warp::path::end())
    .and(store_filter.clone())
    .and(warp::body::json())
    .and_then(update_question);

let routes = get_questions
    .or(add_question)
    .or(update_question)
    .with(cors)
    .recover(return_error);

warp::serve(routes)
    .run(([127, 0, 0, 1], 3030))
    .await;
}
```

Closes the path definition

Adds a String parameter, so the filter is getting triggered for /questions/1234, for example

Adds our store to this route so we can pass it to the route handler later

Extracts the JSON body, which is getting added to the parameters as well

Calls update_question with store and the json body as the parameters

The Warp framework offers us additional filters. Before we end the construction of the path with warp::path::end, we add a new filter: warp::path::param::<String>. This allows us to just listen to requests on paths like app.ourdomain.io/questions/42. If we execute a PUT request on this path but forget the ID, our server will return a 404 because there is no Warp path that listens on this HTTP method and this path:

```
$ curl --location --request PUT 'localhost:3030/questions' \
--header 'Content-Type: application/json' \
--data-raw '{
    "id": 1,
    "title": "NEW TITLE",
    "content": "OLD CONTENT"
}'
Route not found?
```

But what happens when we send a question to either the POST or PUT route handler that is missing some fields or doesn't look like a question at all?

4.2.4   *Handling malformed requests*

We see the beauty of our strictly typed programming language when parsing the JSON from the HTTP POST or PUT body. This happens automatically, and all we have to do is check for `BodyDeserizalizeError` in the `return_error` method to return an appropriate error back to the client.

Listing 4.35   Adding an error when the question in the PUT body can't be read

```
use warp::{
    filters::{body::BodyDeserializeError, cors::CorsForbidden},
    http::Method,
```

```
        http::StatusCode,
        reject::Reject,
        Filter, Rejection, Reply,
    };…

async fn return_error(r: Rejection) -> Result<impl Reply, Rejection> {
    if let Some(error) = r.find::<Error>() {
        Ok(warp::reply::with_status(
            error.to_string(),
            StatusCode::RANGE_NOT_SATISFIABLE,
        ))
    } else if let Some(error) = r.find::<CorsForbidden>() {
        Ok(warp::reply::with_status(
            error.to_string(),
            StatusCode::FORBIDDEN,
        ))
    } else if let Some(error) = r.find::<BodyDeserializeError>() {
        Ok(warp::reply::with_status(
            error.to_string(),
            StatusCode::UNPROCESSABLE_ENTITY,
        ))
    } else {
        Ok(warp::reply::with_status(
            "Route not found".to_string(),
            StatusCode::NOT_FOUND,
        ))
    }
}
…
```

We are importing `BodyDeserializeError` from Warp and check in the `return_error` function whether the `Rejection` contains this type of error. If yes, we return the error message as a `String` object and add a `StatusCode` to the response.

If we are adding a question that misses the `content` field, for example, our application throws an error:

```
$ curl --location --request POST 'localhost:3030/questions' \
    --header 'Content-Type: application/json' \
    --data-raw '{
    "id": "5",
    "title": "NEW TITLE"
  }'
Request body deserialize error: missing field `content` at line 4 column 1?
```

This is a great exercise to take even further. We could imagine catching the error and returning a message that is nicer to read and interpret. This is up to you to explore and play around with.

4.2.5　*Removing questions from the storage*

Our last missing piece for a CRUD application is the *delete* part—at least when it comes to our questions resource. We can start again by imagining what our route handler would look like and what information we need in order to delete a question from our storage. Then, we move to Warp and see which filters we need in order to extract the information out of the request. Figure 4.6 shows that DELETE is our last endpoint for the /questions route.

API routes

```
GET     /questions (empty body; return JSON)
POST    /questions (JSON body; return HTTP status code)
PUT     /questions/:questionId (JSON body, return HTTP status code)
DELETE  /questions/:questionId (empty body; return HTTP status code)
POST    /answers  (www-url-encoded body; return HTTP status code)
```

Figure 4.6　The last method to fully implement the questions resource is HTTP DELETE.

This time around, we don't need any question being passed to our function. We simply need an ID, and with that, we can try to remove the question from the state. The following listing shows our implementation. We pass the ID as a `String` object and the store object and return either `200` if successful or `404` if we can't find the question.

Listing 4.36　Adding a route handler to delete the question

```
...
async fn delete_question(
    id: String,
    store: Store,
) -> Result<impl warp::Reply, warp::Rejection> {
    match store.questions.write().await.remove(&QuestionId(id)) {
        Some(_) => {
            return Ok(
                warp::reply::with_status(
                    "Question deleted",
                    StatusCode::OK
                )
            )
        },
        None => return Err(warp::reject::custom(Error::QuestionNotFound)),
    }
}
...
```

As within the `update_question` function, we need to match by accessing the `HashMap` via the index, because we might not be able to find the question. We can use `.remove` to pass the question ID, and if we find something, simply return `Ok` with the right status code and message, and signal via the underscore (_) that we don't need the return value from the `match` block.

And to complete the implementation, we add a new route to our server, which looks oddly familiar to the `update_question` route—except we don't parse the body this time.

Listing 4.37 Adding a path for deleting a question

```
...
#[tokio::main]
async fn main() {
    let store = Store::new();
    let store_filter = warp::any().map(move || store.clone());

    ...
    let update_question = warp::put()
        .and(warp::path("questions"))
        .and(warp::path::param::<String>())
        .and(warp::path::end())
        .and(store_filter.clone())
        .and(warp::body::json())
        .and_then(update_question);

    let delete_question = warp::delete()
        .and(warp::path("questions"))
        .and(warp::path::param::<String>())
        .and(warp::path::end())
        .and(store_filter.clone())
        .and_then(delete_question);

    let routes = get_questions
        .or(update_question)
        .or(add_question)
        .or(add_answer)
        .or(delete_question)
        .with(cors)
        .recover(return_error);
    ...
}

...
```

This completes our questions resource. We can now add, update, and delete questions, as well as request all the questions available in our application. It is up to you to go even more granular: how about requesting a single question via an ID? We saw how we can pass an URL parameter and parse it (in the update question example), but instead of updating the question in the hash map, we need to return it.

We are not quite finished yet. So far, we just handled JSON bodies in our HTTP requests, but the web is more complex, and we want to look at another common format of passing information via HTTP.

4.3   *POST answers via url-form-encoded*

We already saw how to handle the URL parameter (passing the question ID on the /questions/:question_id route) and what a JSON body looks like and how to parse it with Warp. A typical web application has to handle another common interaction format: application/x-www-form-urlencoded. As seen in figure 4.7, this is the last endpoint we are going to implement.

API routes

```
GET    /questions (empty body; return JSON)
POST   /questions (JSON body; return HTTP status code)
PUT    /questions/:questionId (JSON body, return HTTP status code)
DELETE /questions/:questionId (empty body; return HTTP status code)
POST   /answers  (www-url-encoded body; return HTTP status code)
```

Figure 4.7   The last route we are implementing: adding answers via POST and a www-url-encoded body

We are using a new resource for this example: answers. We already know how to create new types and how to implement route handlers, so this time we can focus on how to parse this new format via Warp.

4.3.1   *Difference between url-form-encoded and JSON*

Both url-form-encoded and JSON have their pros and cons. The choice comes down to preference, and if you have to work in an environment where either of them is already used and you have to create a new application or service that works with already existing systems.

An example POST request looks like this:

```
POST /test HTTP/1.1
Host: foo.example
Content-Type: application/x-www-form-urlencoded
Content-Length: 27

field1=value1&field2=value2
```

We see that the values being passed are a combination of keys and values, with &s in between to separate them.

An example POST curl for an application/x-www-form-urlencoded request looks as follows:

```
$ curl --location --request POST 'localhost:3030/questions' \
--header 'Content-Type: application/x-www-form-urlencoded' \
--data-urlencode 'id=1' \
--data-urlencode 'title=First question' \
--data-urlencode 'content=This is the question I had.'
```

A POST request with a JSON body looks like this (the differences are marked bold):

```
$ curl --location --request POST 'localhost:3030/questions' \
--header 'Content-Type: application/json' \
--data-raw '{
    "id": "1",
    "title": "New question",
    "content": "How and why?"
}'
```

Whatever you use comes down to preference. Sending JSON especially can be an advantage when data is getting more complex.

A server application now has to know on which endpoint it is expecting these query parameters, so it can look for them accordingly. They have to be parsed separately from the URI parameters, which we saw with the question ID example and are also different from the query params we passed in section 4.1.4. Our web framework Warp luckily supports this right out of the box.

4.3.2 *Adding answers via url-form-encoded*

First, we need to add a new struct called Answer, where we specify our requirements for what an answer in our system should look like. We also add a new answers structure in our Store. This has the same signature as the questions attribute: a HashMap to store the answers, wrapped inside a read-write lock to guarantee data integrity, and this construct wrapped in an Arc to be able to pass the structure between threads.

We saw in the preceding section that we are getting key–value pairs passed in the HTTP body, which in the Rust world is a HashMap with a String as the key and value type. The following listing shows the creation of the Answer struct, adding it to the store and implementing the add_answers route handler.

> **Listing 4.38 Adding answers to our project**

```
...

#[derive(Deserialize, Serialize, Debug, Clone, PartialEq, Eq, Hash)]
struct AnswerId(String);

#[derive(Serialize, Deserialize, Debug, Clone)]
struct Answer {
    id: AnswerId,
    content: String,
    question_id: QuestionId,
}

...

#[derive(Clone)]
struct Store {
    questions: Arc<RwLock<HashMap<QuestionId, Question>>>,
    answers: Arc<RwLock<HashMap<AnswerId, Answer>>>,
}
```

```
impl Store {
    fn new() -> Self {
        Store {
            questions: Arc::new(RwLock::new(Self::init())),
            answers: Arc::new(RwLock::new(HashMap::new())),
        }
    }

    fn init() -> HashMap<String, Question> {
        let file = include_str!("../questions.json");
        serde_json::from_str(file).expect("can't read questions.json")
    }
}

...


async fn add_answer(
    store: Store,
    params: HashMap<String, String>,
) -> Result<impl warp::Reply, warp::Rejection> {
    let answer = Answer {
        id: AnswerId("1".to_string()),
        content: params.get("content").unwrap().to_string(),
        question_id: QuestionId(
            params.get("questionId").unwrap().to_string()
        ),
    };

    store.answers.write().await.insert(answer.id.clone(), answer);

    Ok(warp::reply::with_status("Answer added", StatusCode::OK))
}
...
```

This function doesn't scale very well since we are implementing the ID by hand. We will improve upon this later in the book, but for now it is a nice exercise for you to find a way to generate unique IDs when creating new answers.

The important piece is reading from the parameters from the hash map. We see the use of unwrap here, which is not production-ready code. If we can't find a parameter, the Rust application will panic and crash. We can think about using match here instead and returning each error case for a missing parameter separately. To finish this up, we create a new route path and attach it to a route handler in our main function.

Listing 4.39　Adding a route handler to add an answer via a url-form body

```
#[tokio::main]
async fn main() {
    let store = Store::new();
    let store_filter = warp::any().map(move || store.clone());

    ...
```

```
let add_answer = warp::post()
    .and(warp::path("answers"))
    .and(warp::path::end())
    .and(store_filter.clone())
    .and(warp::body::form())
    .and_then(add_answer);

let routes = get_questions
    .or(update_question)
    .or(add_question)
    .or(add_answer)
    .or(delete_question)
    .with(cors)
    .recover(return_error);

warp::serve(routes)
    .run(([127, 0, 0, 1], 3030))
    .await;
}
```

The only new filter we are using is `warp::body::form`. This works like `warp::body::json`, which we used in the `add_question` handler. It does all the hard work for us behind the scenes, and adds `HashMap<String, String>` to our parameters in the `add_answer` function.

This chapter is already quite long. We didn't cover every edge case, and some design decisions can also be made differently. Therefore, it is up to you to sharpen your skills and try to implement the following exercises:

- Create a random, unique ID instead of the one by hand.
- Add error handling if the fields that we require are not present.
- Check whether a question exists that we want to post an answer to.
- Change the route for answers, and use /questions/:questionId/answers instead.

Summary

- Starting with a local `HashMap` object first as your in-memory storage lets you iterate more quickly over design concepts before adding a real database.
- We can use the Serde JSON library to parse external JSON files and map them onto our custom data types.
- Hash maps work great as in-memory storage solutions, but remember that the keys you use *must* implement the tree traits (`PartialEq`, `Eq`, and `Hash`) to be able to compare against each other.
- To be able to pass around state, we have to create a filter that returns a copy of the object we want to pass to more than one route handler.
- Each type of data you receive via HTTP can be parsed via filters in Warp, and you can use either `json`, `query`, `param`, or `form` from the framework.
- When adding more filters to extract data on our path, Warp automatically adds parameters in the function we are calling at the end.

- It is always helpful to create custom data types for each type of data we receive and parse from the HTTP body or from the path parameters.
- We have to implement traits on our custom errors to be able to return them via Warp.
- Warp includes HTTP status code types that we can use to return proper HTTP responses.

Clean up your codebase

This chapter covers

- Grouping your functions into modules
- Splitting your modules into files
- Creating a practical folder structure within your Rust project
- Understanding the difference between doc comments and hidden comments
- Adding example code in your comments and testing it
- Using Clippy to lint your code
- Using Cargo to format and compile your codebase

Rust comes equipped with a large set of tools that makes it easy to organize, structure, test, and comment it. The ecosystem values good documentation style, which is the reason Rust has a built-in commenting system that generates code documentation on the fly, and even tests the code in your comments so your documentation is never out-of-date.

A widely supported linter called Clippy is the de facto standard in the Rust world. It comes with many preset rules and helps point out best practices or missing implementations. In addition, Rust's package manager Cargo helps autoformat your code based on predefined rules.

In the preceding chapter, we built out API routes for our Q&A applications, extracted information out of URL parameters, and most importantly, added our own structures and error implementations and handling. We added all this into the main.rs file, which grew with every route handler we added.

Clearly, this file does too much. Even for a large application, the main.rs file should just connect all the pieces and start the server instead of owning any real implementation logic. In addition, we added a lot of custom code that could use some explanations. We could use Rust's built-in capabilities of splitting code and documenting it.

We start off this chapter by looking at the module system to see how to split your code and how to make it public or private. Later, we'll add comments, write code examples in doc comments, and lint and format our code.

5.1   Modularizing your code

So far, we put every line of code in the main.rs file of our project. This can work well for a small mock server you want to run and maintain in your service architecture, because it is easier to maintain, and not a lot will change after the initial creation.

A larger and more actively maintained project, however, is better served by grouping logical components together and moving them into their own folders and files. This makes it easier to work on multiple parts of the application at the same time, as well as to focus on parts of the code that change often versus the parts that don't.

Rust differentiates between applications and libraries. If you create a new application via `cargo new APP_NAME`, it will create a main.rs file for you. A new library project is created by using `--lib` and would create a lib.rs file instead of main.rs.

The main difference is that a library crate won't create an executable (binary). It is meant to provide a public interface to an underlying functionality. A binary crate, on the other hand, where the main.rs file holds the code that starts your application, will create a binary that you can use to execute and start the application. In our case, this is the start of our web server. Everything else—route handlers, errors, and parsing parameters—can be moved into their own logical units and files.

5.1.1   Using Rust's built-in mod system

Rust uses *modules* to group code together. The `mod` keyword indicates a new module, which has to have a name. Let's see how we group our errors and error handling together.

> **Listing 5.1   Introducing an error module to group our error handling inside main.rs**

```
...

mod error {
    #[derive(Debug)]
```

```
    enum Error {
        ParseError(std::num::ParseIntError),
        MissingParameters,
        QuestionNotFound,
    }

    impl std::fmt::Display for Error {
        fn fmt(&self, f: &mut std::fmt::Formatter) -> std::fmt::Result {
            match *self {
                Error::ParseError(ref err) => {
                    write!(f, "Cannot parse parameter: {}", err)
                },
                Error::MissingParameters => write!(f, "Missing parameter"),
                Error::QuestionNotFound => write!(f, "Question not found"),
            }
        }
    }

    impl Reject for Error {}

}
...
```

A Rust naming convention dictates using snake_case when naming modules: lower-case letters with an underscore to separate words. Therefore, we named our module error instead of Error.

That seems rather easy, and it is. However, our code stops compiling, and we get a few errors (the important pieces are highlighted in bold, and clipped duplicates are indicated via ...):

```
$ cargo build
   Compiling ch_04 v0.1.0
     (/Users/gruberbastian/CodingIsFun/RWD/code/ch_04/final)
error[E0433]: failed to resolve:
   use of undeclared type `Error`
   --> src/main.rs:110:26
    |
110 |                   .map_err(Error::ParseError)?,
    |                            ^^^^^ use of undeclared type `Error`

error[E0433]: failed to resolve: use of undeclared type `Error`
   --> src/main.rs:115:26
    |

...

error[E0405]: cannot find trait `Reject` in this scope
  --> src/main.rs:76:10
    |
76 |     impl Reject for Error {}
   |          ^^^^^^ not found in this scope
    |
```

```
help: consider importing one of these items
     |
60   |     use crate::Reject;
     |
60   |     use warp::reject::Reject;
     |

 ...

error[E0412]: cannot find type `Error` in this scope
  --> src/main.rs:80:35
     |
80   |         if let Some(error) = r.find::<Error>() {
     |                                       ^^^^^ not found in this scope
     |
help: consider importing one of these items
     |
1    | use core::fmt::Error;
     |
1    | use serde::__private::doc::Error;
     |
1    | use serde::__private::fmt::Error;
     |
1    | use serde::de::Error;
     |
       and 9 other candidates

 ...
Some errors have detailed explanations: E0405, E0412, E0433.
For more information about an error, try `rustc --explain E0405`.
warning: `ch_04` (bin "ch_04") generated 1 warning
error: could not compile `ch_04` due to 8 previous errors; 1 warning emitted
```

These two compiler-errors teach us a lot about the module system in Rust:

- Inside the error module, we can't access the `Reject` trait from Warp, but even so we imported it in the same file (error in in line 76).
- The rest of the application can't find the `Error` enum anymore, since it's now moved into its own module (error in lines 110 and 80).

The first one (`Reject: not found in this scope`) indicates that the modules are operating in a new, separate scope. Everything we need inside them, we have to import.

Listing 5.2   Moving the Warp `Reject` trait from the main.rs imports into our error module

```
 ...

use warp::{
    filters::{body::BodyDeserializeError, cors::CorsForbidden},
    http::Method,
    http::StatusCode,
    reject::Reject,
    Filter, Rejection, Reply,
};
```

```
...

mod error {
    use warp::reject::Reject;

    #[derive(Debug)]
    enum Error {
        ParseError(std::num::ParseIntError),
        MissingParameters,
        QuestionNotFound,
    }

    ...

}

...
```

We remove the import of `Reject` from the beginning of the main.rs file and move it into our `error` module. Since we don't use `Reject` anywhere else, the compiler error disappears, and we are left with a bunch more, which have all the same source.

By moving the `Error` enum behind a module, the rest of the code can't find it anymore. We need to make sure to update the path to the enum in the rest of the code. The `extract_pagination` function is a perfect example to work through the process of updating the code to our new module. We start by changing the error return value from `Error` to `error::Error`. This is how we access an entity behind a module: by writing down the module name and using the double-colon (`::`) to access the enum behind it.

> Listing 5.3 Adding the namespace to import the `Error` enum from the new error module

```
fn extract_pagination(
    params: HashMap<String, String>
) -> Result<Pagination, error::Error> {
    ...

    Err(Error::MissingParameters)
}
```

This, however, brings up a new error:

```
enum `Error` is private
private enumrustcE0603

// https://doc.rust-lang.org/error-index.html#E0603
```

It tells us that the `Error` enum is private. All types and functions in Rust are private by default, and if we want to expose them, we have to use the `pub` keyword.

```
...

mod error {
    use warp::reject::Reject;

    #[derive(Debug)]
    pub enum Error {
        ParseError(std::num::ParseIntError),
        MissingParameters,
        QuestionNotFound,
    }

    ...

}

...
```

One logical piece is still outside our error module: the return_error function, which would make sense to also include in this module.

```
...

mod error {
    use warp::{
        filters::{
            body::BodyDeserializeError,
            cors::CorsForbidden,
        },
        reject::Reject,
        Rejection,
        Reply,
        http::StatusCode,
    };

    ...

    async fn return_error(r: Rejection) -> Result<impl Reply, Rejection> {
        if let Some(error) = r.find::<Error>() {
            Ok(warp::reply::with_status(
                error.to_string(),
                StatusCode::RANGE_NOT_SATISFIABLE,
            ))
        } else if let Some(error) = r.find::<CorsForbidden>() {
            Ok(warp::reply::with_status(
                error.to_string(),
                StatusCode::FORBIDDEN,
            ))
        } else if let Some(error) = r.find::<BodyDeserializeError>() {
            Ok(warp::reply::with_status(
                error.to_string(),
```

```
            StatusCode::UNPROCESSABLE_ENTITY,
        ))
    } else {
        Ok(warp::reply::with_status(
            "Route not found".to_string(),
            StatusCode::NOT_FOUND,
        ))
    }
}
}

...
```

That's all: the compiler error disappears, and we can move on to the next. We simply have to add error:: in front of every Error enum usage in our code to solve the remaining compiler errors.

We move the use of StatusCode, Reply, Rejection, and the two Warp filters we were using uniquely for this function also inside the module and remove them from the overall imports at the beginning of the main.rs file (with the exception of Status-Code, which we also use in our route handler functions).

We need to fix two errors after doing this:

- Make our return_error function public.
- Call error::return_error in our routes building instead of plain return_error.

Listing 5.6   Making the `return_error` function public for other modules to access it

```
...

mod error {
    ...

    pub async fn return_error(r: Rejection)
        -> Result<impl Reply, Rejection> {
        println!("{:?}", r);
        if let Some(error) = r.find::<Error>() {
            Ok(warp::reply::with_status(
                error.to_string(),
                StatusCode::UNPROCESSABLE_ENTITY
            ))

        ...

        }
    }

}

...


#[tokio::main]
async fn main() {
```

```
    let store = Store::new();
    let store_filter = warp::any().map(move || store.clone());

    ...

    let routes = get_questions
        .or(update_question)
        .or(add_question)
        .or(add_answer)
        .or(delete_question)
        .with(cors)
        .recover(error::return_error);

    warp::serve(routes)
        .run(([127, 0, 0, 1], 3030))
        .await;
}
```

We accomplished the first step of simplifying and grouping our code. Everything to do with errors goes into its own module from now on. This also has the advantage of seeing which types we need to import from other libraries or our application. It seems that the error module is application code agnostic, which leads to the revelation that this piece of code can be a library, maintained by another team or imported in more than one micro service, for example.

5.1.2   *Practical folder structure for different use cases*

The next step is to move code out of the main.rs file and into its own folder or single file. Which direction you go depends on the complexity of code you want to group together. You can have a folder called error, with files for each error type and functionality. Or you can have a single file called error.rs that contains the group of code we just put together into a module. Let's go down the latter route first and create a file called error.rs that lives on the same level as main.rs.

Listing 5.7   Moving the error module from main.rs into a newly created error.rs file

```
mod error {
  use warp::{
      filters::{
          body::BodyDeserializeError,
          cors::CorsForbidden,
      },
      reject::Reject,
      Rejection,
      Reply,
      http::StatusCode,
  };

  #[derive(Debug)]
  pub enum Error {
      ParseError(std::num::ParseIntError),
```

```
        MissingParameters,
        QuestionNotFound,
    }

    ...
}
```

Notice that the code listing shows the content of error.rs this time. But inside the file is nothing new. Once we exclude this module from the main.rs file, however, we run into a bunch of new compiler errors—which makes sense. The compiler cannot find the error implementation anymore. To reference code from another file, we have to use the mod keyword.

Listing 5.8   Adding the error module to our dependency tree by adding it to main.rs

```
...
use std::sync::Arc;
use tokio::sync::RwLock;

mod error;

...
```

Since our code lives in another file and everything is private by default in Rust, we need to add pub in front of our module definition.

Listing 5.9   Making the error module accessible for other modules via the pub keyword

```
pub mod error {

    ...

}
```

We can see the downside of this decision rather quickly when updating our code. To return an Error enum from a function, now we now need two different error references first.

Listing 5.10   The current structure requires two modules with the same name

```
...

fn extract_pagination(
    params: HashMap<String, String>
) -> Result<Pagination, error::error::Error> {
    ...
}

...
```

The use of mod {} creates a distinct scope, even if it's the only module in the file. That scope makes the extra error:: necessary. We therefore get rid of the module declaration inside error.rs.

Listing 5.11 Removing the redundant mod keyword in errors.rs

```
use warp::{
    filters::{
        body::BodyDeserializeError,
        cors::CorsForbidden,
    },
    reject::Reject,
    Rejection,
    Reply,
    http::StatusCode,
};

...

pub async fn return_error(r: Rejection) -> Result<impl Reply, Rejection> {
    println!("{:?}", r);
    if let Some(error) = r.find::<Error>() {
        Ok(warp::reply::with_status(
            error.to_string(),
            StatusCode::UNPROCESSABLE_ENTITY
        ))
    } else if let Some(error) = r.find::<CorsForbidden>() {
        Ok(warp::reply::with_status(
            error.to_string(),
            StatusCode::FORBIDDEN
        ))
    } else if let Some(error) = r.find::<BodyDeserializeError>() {
        Ok(warp::reply::with_status(
            error.to_string(),
            StatusCode::UNPROCESSABLE_ENTITY
        ))
    } else {
        Ok(warp::reply::with_status(
            "Route not found".to_string(),
            StatusCode::NOT_FOUND,
        ))
    }
}
```

And without changing anything in main.rs, our code works. So why do we use mod instead of use when working with our own files? The mod keyword tells our compiler the path to a module, and it stores it for future use. The use keyword uses the module and tells the compiler this: a module is available, and here is the path to it so I can use it in this file.

It becomes clearer when we continue moving bits and pieces from the main.rs file into new folders and files. Have a look at this book's GitHub repository (https://github .com/Rust-Web-Development/code) to see the full code, since this would take too many pages to show here. We will, however, show how the mod system works with different files and folders.

We move our store logic into its own file, and as we did with error, declare it inside main.rs via mod store. We could choose to move every model or type into its own file, under the folder types. We also go on and move out the route handlers into a folder called routes and have a file for the answer and question handlers each. The structure looks like this:

```
$ tree .
.
├── Cargo.lock
├── Cargo.toml
├── questions.json
└── src
    ├── error.rs
    ├── main.rs
    ├── routes
    │   ├── answer.rs
    │   ├── mod.rs
    │   └── question.rs
    └── types
        ├── answer.rs
        ├── mod.rs
        ├── pagination.rs
        └── question.rs

3 directories, 12 files
```

Based on that example, we can explain how Rust is communicating and exposing the logic inside the various files. We use the mod keyword to include the modules in the main.rs file.

Listing 5.12   Adding the modules to the source tree by adding them to the main.rs file

```
use warp::{
    Filter,
    http::Method,
};

mod error;
mod store;
mod types;
mod routes;

#[tokio::main]
async fn main() {
    let store = store::Store::new();
    let store_filter = warp::any().map(move || store.clone());

    ...
}
```

We include `error` and `store` based on the filename we gave the files that the logic is stored in, and it is on the same hierarchy level as the main.rs file. Therefore, we don't need a special `pub mod {}` inside error.rs or store.rs. Figure 5.1 gives an overview of how we connect the different files through mod.rs files and `mod` imports.

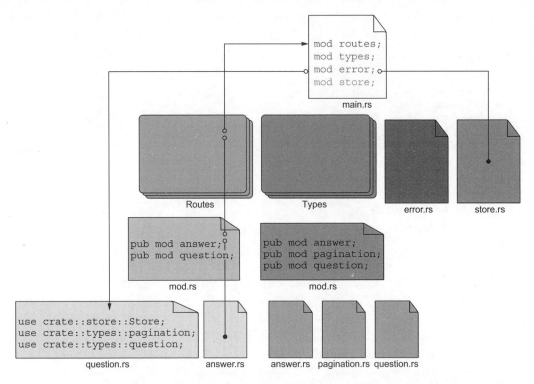

Figure 5.1   We connect all our submodules (files) via the main.rs file and expose modules (files) inside folders via a mod.rs file, in which `pub mod FILENAME;` is making it available throughout the application.

The types and routes are different, though. We created folders that contain multiple files. We create a mod.rs file in the folders and expose the modules (files) inside them via the `pub mod` keyword.

Listing 5.13   src/routes/mod.rs

```
pub mod question;
pub mod answer;
```

And we do the same with our types.

Listing 5.14   src/types/mod.rs

```
pub mod question;
pub mod answer;
pub mod pagination;
```

We access one module from another via the use keyword and use the project hierarchy (folder structure) to access them. Look at the answer.rs file and how we import the Store.

Listing 5.15 src/routes/answer.rs

```
use std::collections::HashMap;
use warp::http::StatusCode;

use crate::store::Store;

...
```

We use the use crate::... combination to access modules in our own crate. This is possible because we imported all submodules inside the main.rs file via mod store, and so forth. To summarize:

- The main.rs file has to import all the other modules via the mod keyword.
- Files in folders need to be exposed via a mod.rs file and use the pub mod keywords to make them available to the other modules (including main.rs).
- Submodules can then import functionality from other modules via the use crate:: keyword combination.

5.1.3 Creating libraries and sub-crates

Once your codebase is growing, it can be helpful to split independent functionality into libraries that live next to your application in the same repository. We saw earlier that our error implementation is application agnostic and might also be useful for other applications in the future.

Where should code live?
You can choose to have one big file of code, split code into multiple files, create folders for these files, or create whole new crates for subfunctionality in your codebase. Each decision has upsides and downsides. Using sub-crates can make workflows harder.

A rule of thumb can be your team size. How many people need to work on a certain functionality? How often does this functionality change? And do you need this piece of code you want to split out of a larger file in more than one project?

If you need the code in more than one project, it's best to use a sub-crate and live also with the downsides of having it in a different Git repository where you have to be aware to always keep it in sync and update it through a separate Git flow. If you don't need this piece of code in a different project, folders and separate files are the best way of going about it in the beginning.

Remember that books serve a teaching purpose, and a choice shown here might not be the best in a real-world scenario. Since we can't develop a large and complex enough application in one or two chapters, splitting out code in a sub-crate rarely makes sense other than to show what you would do if you have to.

We are currently developing a Rust binary (created with `cargo new` at the beginning of the book). But Cargo also offers a way to create a library, which would create a lib.rs file instead of main.rs. Section 5.2 will show more differences between a library and a binary crate. Figure 5.2 shows how we add the new library to the rest of the codebase.

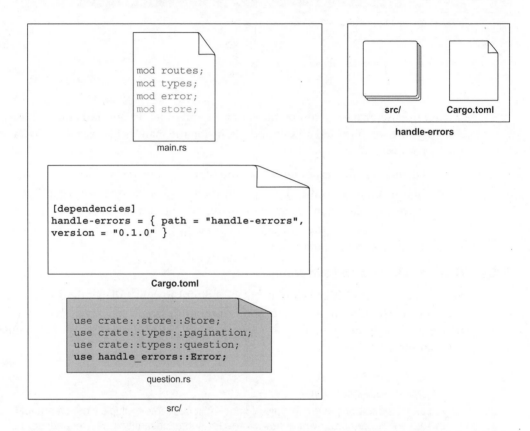

Figure 5.2 After creating a new library in our application folder, we can add it to the Cargo dependencies and specify a local path; afterward, we use it as any other external library in our files.

Let's navigate to the root folder of our project and create a new library:

```
$ cargo new handle-errors --lib
```

We then move all the code in error.rs into PROJECT_NAME/handle-errors/src/lib.rs.

Listing 5.16   handle-errors/src/lib.rs

```
use warp::{
    filters::{body::BodyDeserializeError, cors::CorsForbidden},
    http::StatusCode,
```

```
    reject::Reject,
    Rejection, Reply,
};

#[derive(Debug)]
pub enum Error {
    ParseError(std::num::ParseIntError),
    MissingParameters,
    QuestionNotFound,
}

...
```

After we delete error.rs, we get a few errors. That is to be expected, since our code is relying on this module. We have to go through a couple of steps:

1. Let the Rust compiler know where to find the new error code.
2. Import the error code from the new location instead of the old one.

We use our Cargo.toml file to import external libraries into our project. Even though handle-errors lives in the same repository, it is still an external library that we need to explicitly include. Instead of fetching the code from a Git repository somewhere from the internet or crates.io, we specify a local path for it.

Listing 5.17 ./Cargo.toml of the project

```
...

[dependencies]
warp = "0.3"
serde = { version = "1.0", features = ["derive"] }
serde_json = "1.0"
tokio = { version = "1.1.1", features = ["full"] }
# We can omit the version number for local imports
handle-errors = { path = "handle-errors" }
```

The handle-errors crate also has Warp as dependency, as we use `Filter` and `Status-Code`, for example, from the crate.

Listing 5.18 The handle-errors Cargo.toml with Warp as a dependency

```
[package]
name = "handle-errors"
version = "0.1.0"
edition = "2021"

[dependencies]
warp = "0.3"
```

This allows us to remove the `mod errors;` line in our main.rs file and import the functionality directly in each file where we need it.

```
use warp::{http::Method, Filter};
use handle_errors::return_error;

mod routes;
mod store;
mod types;

#[tokio::main]
async fn main() {
    …

    let routes = get_questions
        .or(update_question)
        .or(add_question)
        .or(add_answer)
        .or(delete_question)
        .with(cors)
        .recover(return_error);

    warp::serve(routes).run(([127, 0, 0, 1], 3030)).await;
}
```

The same goes for our other files. Go through the codebase and remove the old usage of error. Import the needed pieces instead, as in the following code listing, for pagination.rs.

```
use std::collections::HashMap;
use handle_errors::Error;

…

pub fn extract_pagination(params: HashMap<String, String>)
    -> Result<Pagination, Error> {
        if params.contains_key("start") && params.contains_key("end") {
            return Ok(Pagination {
                start: params
                    .get("start")
                    .unwrap()
                    .parse::<usize>()
                    .map_err(Error::ParseError)?,
                end: params
                    .get("end")
                    .unwrap()
                    .parse::<usize>()
                    .map_err(Error::ParseError)?,
            });
        }

        Err(Error::MissingParameters)
}
```

Creating smaller libraries within an application can further help modularize your codebase. You can then decide to completely exclude this library from the code and offer it as a separate standalone library inside your company or the wider world. Excluding code like this can help you prevent having to always increase version numbers for a larger codebase containing code that will either never change again or not for a long time.

5.2 Documenting your code

Documentation is a first citizen in Rust. This means that Rust has a built-in system for publishing and providing documentation. It also differentiates between *public comments*, which make it into the documentation, and *private comments*, which stay in the codebase.

Since documentation is built into the language and the tooling, every crate in the Rust ecosystem has rather good documentation. Even if you don't put any comments into your codebase, Cargo can generate base documentation listing all traits, functions, and third-party libraries included in your code.

Adding more help is not only great when building libraries, but also when documenting real-life applications. Even simple functions can seem strange after a few months or years out in the field, and comments help us understand each component better.

An example of good documentation can be found for `std::env::args` in the standard library (http://mng.bz/xMaB). Rust doc comments are compatible with Markdown as well, so you can use links, highlight code, and insert headers.

5.2.1 Using doc comments and private comments

Rust differentiates between doc comments and comments that won't be published as follows:

- `///`—One-line doc comment
- `/** ... */`—Block doc comment
- `//!` and `/*! ... */`—Apply doc comment to the previous block instead of the one underneath
- `//`—One-line comment (not being published)
- `/* ... */`—Block comment (not being published)

With this knowledge, let's go ahead and use them in our code. We pick the `Pagination` type as a start.

Listing 5.21 Documenting src/types/pagination.rs

```
...

/// Pagination struct that is getting extracted
/// from query params
#[derive(Debug)]
```

```rust
pub struct Pagination {
    /// The index of the first item that has to be returned
    pub start: usize,
    /// The index of the last item that has to be returned
    pub end: usize,
}


/// Extract query parameters from the `/questions` route
/// # Example query
/// GET requests to this route can have a pagination attached so we just
/// return the questions we need
/// `/questions?start=1&end=10`
pub fn extract_pagination(params: HashMap<String, String>)
    -> Result<Pagination, Error> {
        // Could be improved in the future
        if params.contains_key("start") && params.contains_key("end") {
            return Ok(Pagination {
                // Takes the "start" parameter in the query
                // and tries to convert it to a number
                start: params
                    .get("start")
                    .unwrap()
                    .parse::<usize>()
                    .map_err(Error::ParseError)?,
                // Takes the "end" parameter in the query
                // and tries to convert it to a number
                end: params
                    .get("end")
                    .unwrap()
                    .parse::<usize>()
                    .map_err(Error::ParseError)?,
            });
        }

        Err(Error::MissingParameters)
}
```

It is good practice to introduce each function, method, or other piece of functionality in your code from a high-level, business perspective. You then can use an examples section to show how this piece of code would be used and describe it in more detail. If you have a struct, put doc comments on top of its values. Even if its use is obvious now, the added comments will make it easier to do the following:

- Go through your code later in the project phase
- Read through your produced documentation

Rust does a few things automatically. A Cargo command called doc creates documentation of your codebase. This command will create a new folder structure inside your project (/target/doc/project_name), and if you publish your Rust projects to https://crates.io, the documentation will automatically be built from the source code and published at the website https://docs.rs.

Using $ cargo doc --open will open the generated documentation in your browser so you can navigate through your project's documentation locally. Figure 5.3 shows the view as the finished documents are opening in the browser.

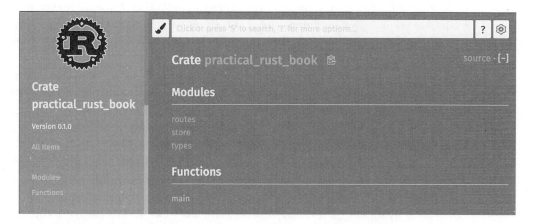

Figure 5.3 **The Cargo command** `cargo doc` **produces documentation for our Rust application.**

Navigating to Types and then Pagination will show us the two pieces of logic we have in our pagination.rs file: a struct called Pagination and a function called extract_pagination. Figure 5.4 shows the result of our added doc comments for our function.

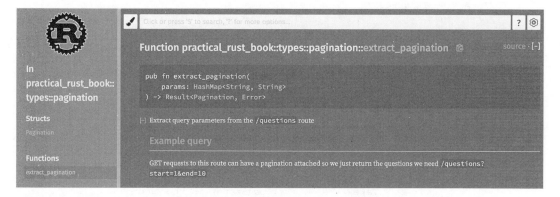

Figure 5.4 **Every function and struct is listed in the documentation, and benefits from added doc comments by the programmer.**

5.2.2   Adding code in your comments

When introducing your application to a wider audience or finishing up a pull request on your team, it is helpful to explain what the newly added feature is doing and how it can be used. Many people use READMEs for this or add example code in the comment section of your file.

Rust highly encourages adding example code to your comments. It will be highlighted via Markdown in your published documentation, but a great feature is that the code in your comments will be run in your tests as well. This way, Rust makes sure that example code is never outdated, and if you change a function signature or body, you have to update the example in the comments as well. You can do so by surrounding your code with triple backticks: ```.

There is a caveat, though: currently, code in doc comments is run only if you create a library instead of an application (binary). We created our application with a standard cargo new command, which results in cargo new --bin. When you want to create a library (and create a lib.rs file instead of main.rs), you have to type cargo new --lib.

The original idea behind that is that libraries are exposed to outside usage and have a limited scope and a well-defined API. This issue is currently being worked on, so that code in doc comments will also be run when creating a Rust binary.

Adding examples in your code is nevertheless helpful. We can add an example usage of extract_pagination in our doc comments as follows.

Listing 5.22   Adding an example usage for `extract_pagination`

```rust
/// Extract query parameters from the `/questions` route
/// # Example query
/// GET requests to this route can have a pagination attached so we just
/// return the questions we need
/// `/questions?start=1&end=10`
/// # Example usage
/// ```rust
/// let mut query = HashMap::new();
/// query.insert("start".to_string(), "1".to_string());
/// query.insert("end".to_string(), "10".to_string());
/// let p = types::pagination::extract_pagination(query).unwrap();
/// assert_eq!(p.start, 1);
/// assert_eq!(p.end, 10);
/// ```
pub fn extract_pagination(params: HashMap<String, String>)
    -> Result<Pagination, Error> {
        // Could be improved in the future
        if params.contains_key("start") && params.contains_key("end") {
            return Ok(Pagination {
                // Takes the "start" parameter in the query
                // and tries to convert it to a number
                start: params
                    .get("start")
                    .unwrap()
                    .parse::<usize>()
                    .map_err(Error::ParseError)?,
                // Takes the "end" parameter in the query
                // and tries to convert it to a number
```

```
                    end: params
                        .get("end")
                        .unwrap()
                        .parse::<usize>()
                        .map_err(Error::ParseError)?,
            });
        }

        Err(Error::MissingParameters)
    }
```

When running the `cargo doc --open` command again, we are presented with an added section with a code example that has also syntax highlighting (figure 5.5).

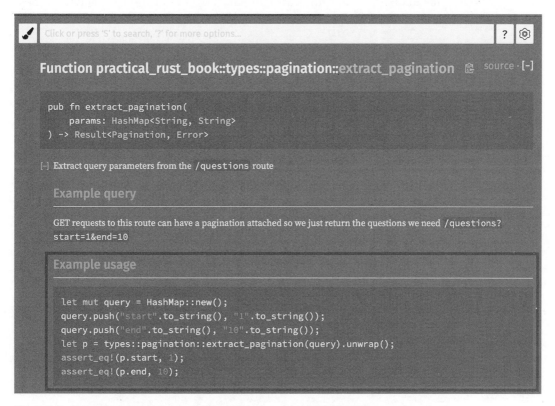

Figure 5.5 Using Markdown lets us add headers and syntax highlighting to our code examples.

The addition to automatically generate documentation around your project is a huge boost in the future-proofing of your codebase. You don't need to worry about outdated tools, having a different style of documentation in each project, or worry about manually compiling and publishing documentation yourself.

The next step in creating a solid codebase is making sure you are using best practices around naming, structuring, and formatting your code. So let's jump right into it.

5.3   *Linting and formatting your codebase*

Rust also shines when it comes to tooling for linting your codebase. If you come from a language that doesn't have a standard tool or rules, it can be frustrating to either enforce your rules to existing or new projects, or to standardize the tooling across a team or company. Rust offers two standard tools to help with that.

The first is Clippy, and the second is Rustfmt. Both are managed under the official Rust Language umbrella and therefore gain support throughout the community. Let's take a look at how these two helpers create a pleasant environment for us.

5.3.1   *Installing and using Clippy*

Clippy is maintained around the Rust core and lives under the Rust GitHub repository. You have to install Clippy via `rustup`:

```
$ rustup component add clippy
```

This tool can also later be added in your continuous integration (CI) pipeline as a separate step. For now, we focus on locally linting and formatting our codebase. After installing Clippy, you can run it:

```
$ cargo clippy
```

You have two options for including linting rules:

- Creating a clippy.toml or .clippy.toml file in your project folder (at the same level as the Cargo.toml file)
- Adding rules at the top of your main.rs or lib.rs file

Let's go through a workflow. We use the method of adding rules to our main.rs file, right at the top.

Listing 5.23   Adding Clippy rules to our main.rs file

```
#![warn(
    clippy::all,
)]

use warp::{
    Filter,
    http::Method,
};

mod error;
mod store;
mod types;
mod routes;
```

```
#[tokio::main]
async fn main() {
    let store = store::Store::new();
    let store_filter = warp::any().map(move || store.clone());

    ...

}
```

Now we can run Clippy and see if we have room for improvement in our code. The tool sometimes has a quirk, requiring you to run cargo clean before running cargo clippy. To test an example, change to the src/routes/question.rs file to check for the parameters, as in the following snippet (highlighted in bold):

...

```
pub async fn get_questions(
    params: HashMap<String, String>,
    store: Store,
) -> Result<impl warp::Reply, warp::Rejection> {
    if params.len() > 0 {
        let pagination = extract_pagination(params)?;
        let res: Vec<Question> =
      store.questions.read().values().cloned().collect();
        let res = &res[pagination.start..pagination.end];
        Ok(warp::reply::json(&res))
    } else {
        let res: Vec<Question> =
      store.questions.read().values().cloned().collect();
        Ok(warp::reply::json(&res))
    }
}
```

...

Now when we run cargo clippy, we get a warning:

```
$ cargo clean
$ cargo clippy

...


warning: length comparison to zero
  --> src/routes/question.rs:13:8
   |
13 |       if params.len() > 0 {
   |          ^^^^^^^^^^^^^^^^ help: using `!is_empty`
   |                              is clearer and
   |                              more explicit: `!params.is_empty()`
note: the lint level is defined here
  --> src/main.rs:2:5
   |
2  |       clippy::all,
   |       ^^^^^^^^^^^
```

```
    = note: `#[warn(clippy::len_zero)]` implied by `#[warn(clippy::all)]`
    = help: for further information visit
      https://rust-lang.github.io/rust-clippy/master/index.html#len_zero

warning: 1 warning emitted

    Finished dev [unoptimized + debuginfo] target(s) in 36.06s
```

It tells us that we should use is_empty instead of checking on .len() > 0 in our questions.rs file. It even tells us which linting rule it triggered and where to find more information. After opening the provided website (http://mng.bz/AVBW), we get the following information:

```
What it does
Checks for getting the length of something via .len()
just to compare to zero, and suggests using .is_empty() where applicable.

Why is this bad
Some structures can answer .is_empty() much faster than
calculating their length. So it is good to get into the habit of
using .is_empty(), and having it is cheap.
Besides, it makes the intent clearer than a
manual comparison in some contexts.
```

We'll go ahead and change this part of our code (highlighted in bold) and run cargo clippy again:

```
...

pub async fn get_questions(
    params: HashMap<String, String>,
    store: Store
) -> Result<impl warp::Reply, warp::Rejection> {
  if !params.is_empty() {

    ...

}

...
```

Clippy is now happy with our codebase, as it doesn't return any more warnings:

```
$ cargo clippy
    Finished dev [unoptimized + debuginfo] target(s) in 0.18s
```

If you don't want to go through the list of all possible linting rules (http://mng.bz/Zp0Z), you can add collections of linting rules:

- `clippy::all`—All lints that are on by default (`correctness`, `suspicious`, `style`, `complexity`, `perf`).
- `clippy::correctness`—Code that is outright wrong or useless.
- `clippy::suspicious`—Code that is most likely wrong or useless.
- `clippy::style`—Code that should be written in a more idiomatic way.
- `clippy::complexity`—Code that does something simple but in a complex way.
- `clippy::perf`—Code that can be written to run faster.
- `clippy::pedantic`—Lints that are rather strict or have occasional false positives.
- `clippy::nursery`—New lints that are still under development.
- `clippy::cargo`—Lints for the Cargo manifest.

Playing around with strict rules can help you learn the language even better. Rust is a complex language under the hood, and getting really proficient takes time. Having Clippy's guidance can give you a huge boost in confidence when writing idiomatic Rust.

5.3.2 *Formatting your code with Rustfmt*

Another tool with a slightly different focus is Rustfmt, which can be installed (just like Clippy) via `rustup`:

```
$ rustup component add rustfmt
```

Rustfmt focuses on formatting your code. You can indicate, for example, how many blank lines you want to enforce between items and the width of comments. All of this is adjustable via a rustfmt.toml file in your project folder (which has to be on the same level as the Cargo.toml file). A list of all options can be found on a filterable website: https://rust-lang.github.io/rustfmt.

We can navigate on the terminal to our project folder and run the following command to automatically format our code based on the standard format settings:

```
$ cargo fmt
```

Summary

- Splitting your code into smaller pieces can be done via modules and the `mod` keyword.
- Moving these modules into files is helpful to separate your codebase.
- Rust automatically assumes the filename as the module name, which means you don't have to add another `mod MODULENAME {}` to each new file, and can use the filename instead by default.
- Having a mod.rs file in folder lets you expose submodules to the main.rs file.
- All modules have to be imported into the main.rs file so they can be imported and used in other files via the `use` keyword.

- Rust has private comments (//) and doc comments (///), and automatically publishes documentation of your project via `cargo doc`.
- Rust offers Clippy as an officially supported linting tool.
- You can import either a collection or individual rules for it.
- The Rustfmt tool formats your codebase to fit a certain style, which can be adjusted through a TOML file.

Logging, tracing, and debugging

This chapter covers

- Using logging, tracing, and debugging in your web service
- Understanding logging options in Rust
- Using external crates to improve your logging experience
- Using the tracing crate in your web service
- Setting up a debugging environment for your Rust web service
- Debugging a web service written in Rust

The first five chapters of the book covered implementing a web service in Rust, why and how to implement asynchronous concepts, and the splitting of our Rust code into modules and libraries. This alone helps to read and understand the code and makes future changes fast to implement. You also learned how to use the rigid nature of the compiler to help spot errors and improve your code.

This chapter covers the instrumentation of your web service. By this, we mean tracing information and diagnosing errors. Even during development, you most probably start to log information to the console to introspect HTTP calls or errors inside functions. This behavior, however, can be expanded and more streamlined. This is covered by logging and tracing your application.

The Rust compiler finds most of the errors before your application can even be compiled, but it can't account for all possible bugs. In some cases, your Rust code will look fine, but still won't behave the way you want it to behave. In addition, the compiler doesn't know about the business case of your web service. When running a web service, you want to know when an HTTP request comes in, what it looked like, and how the web service responded. And to go deeper into that, you might want to log every login or registration attempt, error cases (when you can't read from a database, for example), and other information you need for a better understanding about your running application(s). The whole flow of an incoming request until the outgoing response is shown in figure 6.1.

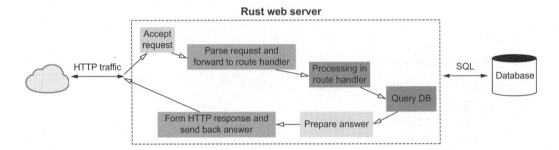

Figure 6.1   A running web service has many points of failure. Each step should produce enough logs for later investigation.

In this chapter, we first cover logging to the console or to a file in Rust, and then move on to tracing—what it means and how to use it to instrument your running application and spot errors in asynchronous code. The last part of this chapter covers debugging. Sometimes during development, you'll wonder why certain variables are set or not set, or why loops don't yield the outcome you were hoping for, and so forth. Debugging your Rust application can help you know exactly when and how certain code pieces are executed and with which values.

6.1   Logging in your Rust application

A running web service gets HTTP requests, sends out information, fetches data from a database, and does computations. All the inner workings of your web service are meant to be logged and stored somewhere. Different situations require a different introspection level.

Let's say you are getting a high number of new sign-ups on your application, and you want to check the legitimacy of these requests. Is it a robot who is exploiting your service? Another case could be hundreds of new support tickets from users complaining that they can't log in to your application anymore. What can you do to figure out what is happening in your system?

The first step would be to go through your logs. And now the questions become, Did you log at the right moments in your user journey? Did you store the logs somewhere so they are easy retrievable?

---

stdout vs. stderr

When an application is started, it connects different input and output streams. These are communication channels between the application and its environment.

In the early days, these were actual, physical devices, but UNIX abstracted this away and was able to connect by default to the terminal the application was started in. This means you can type in commands via the terminal to the application through `stdin` (standard input), and the application can send out diagnostics through standard output (`stdout`) and standard error (`stderr`).

Printing something on the console via `println!` in Rust connects to `stdout`, whereas logging libraries send information to `stderr`. These will both end up on the terminal by default, but you can change the location for `stderr`, for example, to be directed to a file or a remote server. Rust also has an `eprintln!` macro (https://doc.rust-lang .org/std/macro.eprintln.html) that writes to `stderr` and should be used for only error and progress messages.

Which one you use is up to you, but best practices are to use `stderr` for diagnostics, and `stdout` for general output.

Logging is different from simply printing out text on a terminal:

- Logging should have more information and a fixed structure.
- `println!` uses `stdout` as an output stream in your application.
- Logging generally sends output to `stderr` (a standard adopted by libraries, although you can log to `stdout` as well).
- You can choose to log to the terminal, a file, or a server.
- Logging has different levels (from info to critical).
- If you target machines with your logs (to process log information, for example), using JSON as your logging format is preferred.
- If you mostly use your logs for humans to consume, standard text separated by commas or spaces is the way to go.

Logging in Rust is handled via the *facade pattern*. This pattern is part of the *Gang of Four* book, which covers design patterns in software architecture. (See *Design Patterns: Elements of Reusable Object-Oriented Software* by Erich Gamma et al., Addison-Wesley Professional, 1994.) To quote the book:

> *It shields clients from subsystem components, thereby reducing the number of objects that clients deal with and making the subsystem easier to use.*

In practice, this means that you will call the functions exposed by the facade crate/object, which internally will call the actual logic from another crate. The advantage is that if you want to change the logging logic, you can just swap out logging crates and keep the actual code untouched.

When logging in Rust, you'll mostly use the facade crate called log. In your Rust code, you will therefore always import two libraries. The facade (log) and the actual logging implementation (another logging crate that fits your needs). In figure 6.2, env-logger is using the log crate as a facade.

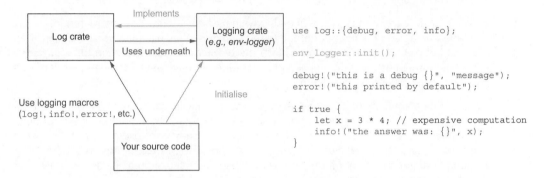

Figure 6.2   When using a crate for logging, chances are high that you will use the logging macros from a crate called log.

With Rust, you have different levels for your logs. Not all logging libraries support all of them. An example list of logging levels (also available through the log crate at https://docs.rs/log/0.4.16/log/#macros) is as follows:

- debug—Used for debugging during development
- info—Information purposes only
- warning—Indicates not mission-critical problems
- error—A typical error such as a closed database connection
- trace—Used in one-off debugging or builds, indicates fine-grained logging
- critical—Indicates mission-critical errors that should be addressed immediately

In code, these look like the following listing.

Listing 6.1   Log levels

```
use log::{info, warn, error, debug}

info!("User {} logged in", user.id);
warn!("User {} logged in {} times", user.id, login_count);
err!("Failed to load User {} from DB", user.id);
debug!(
        "User {} access controls: {}, {}",
        user.id, user.admin, user.supervisor
);
```

Using different levels in your logs helps reveal useful information. At some point, you'll collect logs and want to know whether you have an error or not. You might want to start your web service by saying, "Just show me the errors; I don't care about debug or info logs," and thus those logs will not be executed at runtime. You usually do this by setting environment variables and telling the logging crate, and therefore the compiler, to include only the logs with certain levels (`warn`, `info`, or `error`, for example). This cleans up your logs and helps you avoid having to remove lines of log-code by hand before deploying it to production.

In addition to putting simple text into the `stderr` stream, you can log your information in JSON format so it's easier to parse from another service. We will see over the course of this chapter how libraries can help us create more structure in our logs. With this knowledge, let's start implementing our first logging mechanism so we can iterate and improve over it.

6.1.1   Implementing logging in your web service

As we saw in figure 6.2, we need two new crates. We will start with the env_logger crate as our actual logger implementation, and then look at a few others later. We also need the logging facade log, with which we call the logging macros. We add these two to our Cargo.toml file, as shown in the following listing.

> **Listing 6.2   Adding logger dependencies to Cargo.toml**

```
[package]
name = "practical-rust-book"
version = "0.1.0"
edition = "2021"

[dependencies]
warp = "0.3"
serde = { version = "1.0", features = ["derive"] }
serde_json = "1.0"
tokio = { version = "1.1.1", features = ["full"] }
# We can omit the version number for local imports
handle-errors = { path = "handle-errors" }
log = "0.4"
env_logger = "0.9"
```

We will start to get a feeling for logging by adding a few logging macros to our `main` function in main.rs and looking at our terminal output. The next listing shows the main.rs file and what we need to do to get started.

> **Listing 6.3   Adding the first logs to our application in main.rs**

```
#![warn(clippy::all)]

use warp::{http::Method, Filter};
use handle_errors::return_error;
```

```
mod routes;
mod store;
mod types;

#[tokio::main]
async fn main() {
    env_logger::init();

    log::error!("This is an error!");
    log::info!("This is info!");
    log::warn!("This is a warning!");

    let store = store::Store::new();
    let store_filter = warp::any().map(move || store.clone());

    let cors = warp::cors()
        .allow_any_origin()
        .allow_header("content-type")
        .allow_methods(&[Method::PUT, Method::DELETE, Method::GET,
    Method::POST]);

    ...

}
```

Figure 6.2 showed us that we need to initialize the actual logging implementation, and then we can use the facade crate log to do the actual logging. When we run our application via `cargo run`, we see the following on our terminal.

Listing 6.4   Terminal output with the first logs

```
Finished dev [unoptimized + debuginfo] target(s) in 10.31s
  Running `target/debug/practical-rust-book`
[2021-06-26T11:01:49Z ERROR practical_rust_book] This is an error!
```

That's odd. We see the `log:error!` output, but the `log::info!` and `log::warn!` seem to be hidden or are not being triggered. Whenever we don't understand something, it's good practice to try to figure out the problem based on some of our own research, explain our reasoning to ourselves, and then go look for the answer in the documentation. You gain knowledge faster by thinking about a possible solution to a problem and being proven wrong, than by just reading the answer.

Let's go through these steps:

1 The info and warning macros are printed just beneath the error, so the compiler should have gone over them and printed something to the console. So maybe by default, env-logger is not logging every level to the console when running a Rust program?

2 It could be that logging every level is too noisy in production, and env-logger is preventing noisy logging by defaulting to printing only error logs.

3   We go to the Rust docs for this crate (http://mng.bz/RvaP) and read up on it.
We can find the following quote:

> *Log levels are controlled on a per module basis, and by default all logging is
> disabled except for the error level. Logging is controlled via the RUST_LOG
> environment variable.*

This makes sense! Now we know that we have to pass the RUST_LOG environment variable to the cargo run command. Let's try again. We can see the results in the following listing.

Listing 6.5   Running the application with the `RUST_LOG` environment variable

```
> RUST_LOG=info cargo run
    Finished dev [unoptimized + debuginfo] target(s) in 0.09s
    Running `target/debug/practical-rust-book`
[2021-06-26T11:10:45Z ERROR practical_rust_book] This is an error!
[2021-06-26T11:10:45Z INFO  practical_rust_book] This is info!
[2021-06-26T11:10:45Z WARN  practical_rust_book] This is a warning!
[2021-06-26T11:10:45Z INFO  warp::server] Server::run; addr=127.0.0.1:3030
[2021-06-26T11:10:45Z INFO  warp::server] listening on http://127.0.0.1:3030
```

This looks much better. By prepending RUST_LOG=info to the cargo run command, we pass the log level we want to log to our application. The env-logger crate is now printing out every log with the level info, warn, or error.

But hold on, what are the last two lines? We are getting two more info logs that seem to come from the Warp crate. Digging through the source code of Warp (http://mng.bz/2rGX), we can see that the web framework is using a library called Tracing to print info logs to the console as well. The following listing shows this part of the code.

Listing 6.6   Warp source code logging via `tracing::info`

```
...
{
    /// Run this `Server` forever on the current thread.
    pub async fn run(self, addr: impl Into<SocketAddr>) {
        let (addr, fut) = self.bind_ephemeral(addr);
        let span = tracing::info_span!("Server::run", ?addr);
        tracing::info!(parent: &span, "listening on http://{}", addr);

        fut.instrument(span).await;
    }
...
}
```

By passing the RUST_LOG environment variable to cargo run, we also activated the inner logging mechanism from Warp. In section 6.2, we will have a look at this Tracing library and why we want to use this going forward. For now, however, let's build more understanding around logging.

We can try another trick, and pass debug as the log level when starting our server. We then send some HTTP requests to it and see what happens:

```
$ RUST_LOG=debug cargo run
```

Depending on your setup, you can use an app like Postman to send HTTP requests, or can use the command-line tool curl:

```
curl --location --request GET 'localhost:3030/questions'
```

After starting the web server with debug, and sending the first HTTP GET request, we can see the following output on the command line.

Listing 6.7 Debug output from our web server with an incoming HTTP request

```
$ RUST_LOG=debug cargo run
    Finished dev [unoptimized + debuginfo] target(s) in 0.09s
     Running `target/debug/practical-rust-book`
[2021-06-26T11:18:34Z ERROR practical_rust_book] This is an error!
[2021-06-26T11:18:34Z INFO  practical_rust_book] This is info!
[2021-06-26T11:18:34Z WARN  practical_rust_book] This is a warning!
[2021-06-26T11:18:34Z INFO  warp::server] Server::run; addr=127.0.0.1:3030
[2021-06-26T11:18:34Z INFO  warp::server] listening on http://127.0.0.1:3030
[2021-06-26T11:18:52Z DEBUG hyper::proto::h1::io] parsed 6 headers
[2021-06-26T11:18:52Z DEBUG hyper::proto::h1::conn] incoming body is empty
[2021-06-26T11:18:52Z DEBUG warp::filters::query] route was called
    without a query string, defaulting to empty
[2021-06-26T11:18:52Z DEBUG hyper::proto::h1::io] flushed 213 bytes
```

I marked the newly added logs in bold (the last four lines of listing 6.7 with DEBUG). We saw in earlier chapters that Rust doesn't come with HTTP implemented, and therefore Warp is using other abstraction layers. Under the hood, it is using a crate called Hyper that serves as the HTTP server, so Warp can focus on the web framework tooling.

By enabling debug, we also triggered logs from the underlying Hyper crate, and Warp also has an additional debug log for the incoming query. When you are writing your web server and you hit a wall or expect a different route or outcome from your incoming HTTP requests, it is worth enabling debug logs when starting your application to get more insight about what is coming in and going out.

Let's try another trick. At the beginning of the chapter, you learned about logging crates by default to stderr, which is the terminal the program is started in. We can try to redirect the output to a file by using common UNIX knowledge. As explained, each program opens three streams (stdin, stdout, stderr), and these streams have numbers assigned to them as well: 0, 1, and 2. We can therefore try to pipe stream 2 to a file:

```
$ RUST_LOG=info cargo run 2>logs.txt
```

Starting our server like this seems to break things, or it doesn't print anything to the console anymore. Let's see if we at least have a new file called logs.txt. It turns out we do, as the following listing shows.

Listing 6.8 Redirecting `stderr` to a log file

```
$ cat logs.txt
    Finished dev [unoptimized + debuginfo] target(s) in 0.10s
     Running `target/debug/practical-rust-book`
[2021-06-26T11:34:20Z ERROR practical_rust_book] This is an error!
[2021-06-26T11:34:20Z INFO  practical_rust_book] This is info!
[2021-06-26T11:34:20Z WARN  practical_rust_book] This is a warning!
[2021-06-26T11:34:20Z INFO  warp::server] Server::run; addr=127.0.0.1:3030
[2021-06-26T11:34:20Z INFO  warp::server] listening on http://127.0.0.1:3030
```

We also have the Cargo output in our log file. This is not ideal but a start. We see that we already reach a limit of what we can do with env-logger. There is no built-in way to log to a file or another output stream. Next to the option to log to a file, we don't always want to start our compiled binary with environment variables attached to it, but through a config file (or code) that we can set up and adjust more easily.

We can see the facade pattern in action right now, when trying to switch to a different logging library. We can try the log4rs crate next, which gives us the option to log to a file and configure the log level via a config file.

So go ahead and add this library to your Cargo.toml file as in listing 6.9. We also removed the env-logger crate, but you can keep it in there if you like for future comparison between the two.

Listing 6.9 Adding log4rs to our Cargo.toml

```
[package]
name = "practical-rust-book"
version = "0.1.0"
edition = "2021"

[dependencies]
warp = "0.3"
serde = { version = "1.0", features = ["derive"] }
serde_json = "1.0"
tokio = { version = "1.1.1", features = ["full"] }
# We can omit the version number for local imports
handle-errors = { path = "handle-errors" }
log = "0.4"
log4rs = "1.0"
```

This library requires a config file, and the location has to be passed to the `init` function when starting the logger. The next listing shows an example config.

Listing 6.10 Our example log4rs.yaml config that we place in the root directory

```
refresh_rate: 30 seconds
appenders:
  stdout:
    kind: console
  file:
    kind: file
    path: "stderr.log"
    encoder:
      pattern: "{d} - {m}{n}"
root:
  level: info
  appenders:
    - stdout
    - file
```

This crate gives you the option to have *rolling log files*, which means new logs will be appended to the log file, and if it grows too big, new ones will be created. Going through the config, we have three major options:

- refresh_rate—When you want to change the config during production without restarting the server.
- appenders—You can set our outputs here; we log to stdout and to a file.
- root—Setting up your logger with the log level and the combination of appenders you want to log to.

In our code, we need to initialize log4rs, but otherwise don't have to change anything. That's the beauty of a facade pattern: all your actual logs can stay the same, while in the background we swapped our logging library for a different one.

Listing 6.11 Initializing log4rs in main.rs

```
...

#[tokio::main]
async fn main() {
    log4rs::init_file("log4rs.yaml", Default::default()).unwrap();

    log::error!("This is an error!");
    log::info!("This is info!");
    log::warn!("This is a warning!");


    ...
}
```

With log4rs::init_file("log4rs.yaml"…) we set up our new logger and specify the location of the config file we want to use. Start your server with cargo run (no RUST_LOG environment variable this time) and see what happens.

Listing 6.12 Terminal output after swapping out the logger

```
$ cargo run
    Finished dev [unoptimized + debuginfo] target(s) in 0.11s
     Running `target/debug/practical-rust-book`
2021-06-27T06:50:17.034119+02:00 ERROR practical_rust_book -
    This is an error!
2021-06-27T06:50:17.034166+02:00 INFO practical_rust_book - This is  info!
2021-06-27T06:50:17.034209+02:00 WARN practical_rust_book -
    This is a warning!
2021-06-27T06:50:17.034650+02:00 INFO warp::server -
    Server::run; addr=127.0.0.1:3030
2021-06-27T06:50:17.034717+02:00 INFO warp::server -
    listening on http://127.0.0.1:3030
```

Our logs look a bit different, but our logs and log levels are still working as before. In addition, you can now find a stderr.log file in the root directory of your project with the same logs you see on the console. That's because we use two appenders in log4rs (stdout and the file).

Now try something wild and change the log level to debug in the log4rs.yaml file, wait 30 seconds, and send over an HTTP request to your server. You will see that now the application also shows debug logs, without you having to restart your application or anything. Listing 6.13 shows the content of the file after booting the application with the info log level, changing it to debug during runtime (via the config file) and sending an HTTP GET request to the /questions endpoint after waiting 30 seconds.

Listing 6.13 The newly shown logs when changing the log level

```
2021-06-27T06:57:47.749489+02:00 - This is an error!
2021-06-27T06:57:47.749586+02:00 - This is info!
2021-06-27T06:57:47.749638+02:00 - This is a warning!
2021-06-27T06:57:47.750219+02:00 - Server::run; addr=127.0.0.1:3030
2021-06-27T06:57:47.750287+02:00 - listening on http://127.0.0.1:3030
2021-06-27T06:58:27.326621+02:00 - parsed 6 headers
2021-06-27T06:58:27.326719+02:00 - incoming body is empty
2021-06-27T06:58:27.326905+02:00 - route was called without
    a query string, defaulting to empty
2021-06-27T06:58:27.327225+02:00 - flushed 213 bytes
```

This setup is already much more comfortable. But we are not quite done yet. Now that we know how logging works, let's get more specific and try to follow up on each HTTP request. Change the log level back to info in your log4rs.yaml file and continue with the next section.

6.1.2 *Logging incoming HTTP requests*

We saw earlier that Warp is already doing some internal logging. Let's find out if there is more to it than just internal code. Maybe Warp is exposing a logging API for us. Based on the README.md file in the GitHub repository, Warp is supposed to expose logs through its `Filter` mechanism. We check out the docs on docs.rs and look at the Filters subsection (http://mng.bz/19Yg). And in the list, we find Logger Filters, which link to the "Module `warp::filters::log`" page (http://mng.bz/PoyP). It provides two functions: `log` and `custom`. The `custom` function has an example, shown in the following listing.

Listing 6.14   Warp's custom log example from docs.rs

```
use warp::Filter;

let log = warp::log::custom(|info| {
    // Use a log macro, or slog, or println, or whatever!
    eprintln!(
        "{} {} {}",
        info.method(),
        info.path(),
        info.status(),
    );
});
let route = warp::any()
    .map(warp::reply)
    .with(log);
```

That's neat. It seems we don't have to add the logging function to every route but can add it to the end of our route object. We can integrate this code example in our main.rs file and see where it takes us.

Listing 6.15   Adding custom logs to our main.rs file

```
...

#[tokio::main]
async fn main() {
    log4rs::init_file("log4rs.yaml", Default::default()).unwrap();

    log::error!("This is an error!");
    log::info!("This is info!");
    log::warn!("This is a warning!");

    let log = warp::log::custom(|info| {
        eprintln!(
            "{} {} {}",
            info.method(),
            info.path(),
            info.status(),
        );
    });

    ...

    let routes = get_questions
        .or(update_question)
```

```
        .or(add_question)
        .or(add_answer)
        .or(delete_question)
        .with(cors)
        .with(log)
        .recover(return_error);

    warp::serve(routes).run(([127, 0, 0, 1], 3030)).await;
}
```

The log function itself uses eprintln! instead of println!. We talked earlier about stdout versus stderr. The println! macro sends output directly to stdout, whereas eprintln! prints text to stderr. Logging libraries and collectors are used to collecting logs from the stderr stream, so the example (and we, in the future) will use stderr for our logging.

We add the log filter via with(log) to our routes objects and restart our application. We can then send an HTTP GET request to the /questions endpoint and monitor the logs if we see any changes. The following listing shows the new response (in bold) when we start the server and send an HTTP GET request to the application.

Listing 6.16 The log created when adding the custom log filter to the routes object

```
$ cargo run
    Compiling practical-rust-book v0.1.0 (/Users/bgruber/CodingIsFun/Manning/
      practical-rust-book/ch_06)
      Finished dev [unoptimized + debuginfo] target(s) in 11.46s
      Running `target/debug/practical-rust-book`
2021-06-27T07:21:07.919400+02:00 ERROR practical_rust_book -
    This is an error!
2021-06-27T07:21:07.919968+02:00 INFO practical_rust_book -
    This is info!
2021-06-27T07:21:07.920012+02:00 WARN practical_rust_book -
    This is a warning!
2021-06-27T07:21:07.920465+02:00 INFO warp::server -
    Server::run; addr=127.0.0.1:3030
2021-06-27T07:21:07.920530+02:00 INFO warp::server -
    listening on http://127.0.0.1:3030
GET /questions 200 OK
```

We get exactly what we expected. We logged the method, the path, and the status we respond with. We accessed this information through the info struct, implemented in Warp. We can go through the docs (http://mng.bz/JVov) to see what else we can access through this object.

We might find interesting the elapsed time for the request, the request headers sent to our server, and the remote address where the request came from. Let's try adding this to our code.

Listing 6.17   Adding more information to our log filter

```
...

#[tokio::main]
async fn main() {
    log4rs::init_file("log4rs.yaml", Default::default()).unwrap();

    log::error!("This is an error!");
    log::info!("This is info!");
    log::warn!("This is a warning!");

    let log = warp::log::custom(|info| {
        eprintln!(
            "{} {} {} {:?} from {} with {:?}",
            info.method(),
            info.path(),
            info.status(),
            info.elapsed(),
            info.remote_addr().unwrap(),
            info.request_headers()
        );
    });

    ...

}
```

We access the time it took for the whole request and response via the `elapsed`
method, where the request came from via `remote_addr`, and the headers sent via
`request_headers`. We can `eprintln!` the values via Debug (`{:?}`) and not via `Display`
(`{}`) because the values contain vectors (except `remote_addr`, which implements the
`Display` trait), and types don't implement the `Display` trait by default. In a more
sophisticated approach, you can build a standalone function to parse the information
out of the request and access specific information (such as the host of the request)
and implement the `Display` trait for it.

We will, however, use a different end solution, and it's a great exercise for you to
implement by yourself. The result looks like this:

```
$ cargo run
   Compiling practical-rust-book v0.1.0

   ...

GET /questions 200 OK 207.958µs from 127.0.0.1:61729 with
  {"host": "localhost:3030", "user-agent": "curl/7.64.1", "accept": "*/*"}
```

This brings us one step closer to our final implementation, which is covered in section 6.2. You know now that we can log in Rust, can log via the open streams of the
running application (`stdout` and `stderr`), and can use the default `stderr` (printing
to the terminal) or redirect the stream to a file—or do both.

We also explored the option to log every incoming HTTP request and get the time it took to complete and where it came from. All these building blocks will be useful for our final implementation.

6.1.3 Creating structured logs

So far, we've been concerned about the "how" and "where" to log, but not the "what." To generate useful logs, we must think ahead and imagine a situation where we need these bits of information to solve a problem or to collect enough evidence to support an assumption we have about the behavior of our system.

Imagine that a user of our service is trying to query the first 50 questions, but the answer is always 0; no questions are being returned. The user opens a bug ticket and emails it to us. We then have to figure out what happened and why. The user probably leaves us some information in the ticket, like this:

- The user ID
- The time they queried the website
- The response they received (`200`, but empty, for example)

What would we do to investigate this issue? In a large production system, you usually are part of a more complex architecture, and every service running in it sends logs directly to a centralized logging instance, or the instance collects the logs from each service (and reads its `stderr` output or generated log file).

Logs must contain the right amount of information and might need to be parsed by another service. We therefore have to think about the structure and the form of the logs more carefully. These requirements might come from yourself if you are setting up the infrastructure, or you must follow them when implementing a new service in an existing ecosystem.

The first step is to transform our text to the console and in the file into JSON so it's easier for the log collector to parse the information. This is easily done via our log4rs logger config file. The updated file is shown in the following listing.

Listing 6.18 Updated log4rs config so we can store logs in JSON

```
refresh_rate: 30 seconds
appenders:
  stdout:
    kind: console
    encoder:
      kind: json
  file:
    kind: file
    path: "stderr.log"
    encoder:
      kind: json

root:
  level: info
```

```
appenders:
  - stdout
  - file
```

We add a new encoder to the stdout appender, with the type json. For the file
appender, we remove the pattern encoder and replace it with the same json encoder
from earlier. Restarting our application with cargo run shows that our logs are now
printed in JSON on terminal output. (The following is formatted for better readability; on your machine, the output is printed in one long line.)

Listing 6.19   Logs are now printed and stored in JSON

```
$ cargo run
    Finished dev [unoptimized + debuginfo] target(s) in 0.32s
     Running `target/debug/practical-rust-book`
{"time":"2021-06-27T20:38:08.689498+02:00",
    "message":"This is an error!",
    "module_path":"practical_rust_book",
    "file":"src/main.rs",
    "line":15,
    "level":"ERROR",
    "target":"practical_rust_book",
    "thread":"main",
    "thread_id":4571676160,"mdc":{}
}
{"time":"2021-06-27T20:38:08.690124+02:00",
    "message":"This is info!",
    "module_path":"practical_rust_book",
    "file":"src/main.rs",
    "line":16,
    "level":"INFO",
    "target":"practical_rust_book",
    "thread":"main",
    "thread_id":4571676160,"mdc":{}
}
{"time":"2021-06-27T20:38:08.690203+02:00",
    "message":"This is a warning!",
    "module_path":"practical_rust_book",
    "file":"src/main.rs",
    "line":17,
    "level":"WARN",
    "target":"practical_rust_book",
    "thread":"main",
    "thread_id":4571676160,"mdc":{}
}
{"time":"2021-06-27T20:38:08.690749+02:00",
    "message":"Server::run; addr=127.0.0.1:3030",
    "module_path":"warp::server",
    "file":"/Users/bgruber/.cargo/registry/src/
        github.com-1ecc6299db9ec823/warp-0.3.1/src/server.rs",
    "line":133,
    "level":"INFO",
    "target":"warp::server",
```

```
        "thread":"main",
        "thread_id":4571676160,"mdc":{}
}
{"time":"2021-06-27T20:38:08.690866+02:00",
        "message":"listening on http://127.0.0.1:3030 ",
        "module_path":"warp::server",
        "file":"/Users/bgruber/.cargo/registry/src/
                github.com-1ecc6299db9ec823/warp-0.3.1/src/server.rs",
        "line":134,
        "level":"INFO",
        "target":"warp::server",
        "thread":"main",
        "thread_id":4571676160,"mdc":{}
}
```

The same information is also stored in the log file in the root directory of our application. That's a first good step. But what happens when we send over our HTTP GET request to the server? The following listing shows the result (formatted here for print purposes, but appears as one long line on your machine).

Listing 6.20 HTTP GET log is not being formatted to JSON

```
$ cargo run
        Finished dev [unoptimized + debuginfo] target(s) in 0.58s
        Running `target/debug/practical-rust-book`
…

{"time":"2021-06-28T08:42:30.059163+02:00",
        "message":"listening on http://127.0.0.1:3030 ",
        "module_path":"warp::server",
        "file":"/Users/bgruber/.cargo/registry/src/
                github.com-1ecc6299db9ec823/warp-0.3.1/src/server.rs",
        "line":134,
        "level":"INFO",
        "target":"warp::server",
        "thread":"main",
        "thread_id":4477177344,"mdc":{}
}
GET /questions 200 OK 254.528µs from 127.0.0.1:51439
        with {"host": "localhost:3030",
            "user-agent": "curl/7.64.1", "accept": "*/*"
        }
```

It seems it's the old format instead of JSON. And looking into our log file, we also can't see the HTTP GET log anywhere. That's because we use the Warp log directly with `eprintln!` instead of the `info!` macro from the `log` crate. So instead of doing this:

```
let log = warp::log::custom(|info| {
    eprintln!(
        "{} {} {} {:?} from {} with {:?}",
        info.method(),
        info.path(),
        info.status(),
```

```
            info.elapsed(),
            info.remote_addr().unwrap(),
            info.request_headers()
        );
});
we can try to use the log::info! macro instead:
let log = warp::log::custom(|info| {
    log::info!(
        "{} {} {} {:?} from {} with {:?}",
        info.method(),
        info.path(),
        info.status(),
        info.elapsed(),
        info.remote_addr().unwrap(),
        info.request_headers()
    );
});
```

After the change, the log output from the incoming HTTP request is also in JSON (formatted here to fit, but one long line on your machine):

```
{"time":"2021-06-28T08:44:38.495573+02:00",
    "message":"GET /questions 200 OK 300.494µs
        from 127.0.0.1:51531 with
            {\"host\": \"localhost:3030\",
             \"user-agent\": \"curl/7.64.1\",
             \"accept\": \"*/*\"}",
"module_path":"practical_rust_book",
"file":"src/main.rs",
"line":20,
"level":"INFO",
"target":"practical_rust_book",
"thread":"tokio-runtime-worker","thread_id":123145515622400,"mdc":{}
}
```

We can see that your custom structure we pass to log::info! is being put in the message structure of the log4rs output. Next, we want to follow the whole request from start to finish, so we can later follow up on problems or inspect any malicious activity.

We need to go through each route handler or any other function call and add logs as we see fit. Later, we'll see how to make this more automatic and without creating too much noise in our code.

We started querying the GET /questions route; let's follow through and go to routes/questions.rs and add more logs along the way, as we see in the next listing.

> **Listing 6.21 Adding logs to the get_questions route handler**

```
...

pub async fn get_questions(
    params: HashMap<String, String>,
    store: Store,
) -> Result<impl warp::Reply, warp::Rejection> {
```

```
log::info!("Start querying questions");
if !params.is_empty() {
    let pagination = extract_pagination(params)?;
    log::info!("Pagination set {:?}", &pagination);
    let res: Vec<Question> =
store.questions.read().await.values().cloned().collect();
    let res = &res[pagination.start..pagination.end];
    Ok(warp::reply::json(&res))
} else {
    log::info!("No pagination used");
    let res: Vec<Question> =
store.questions.read().await.values().cloned().collect();
    Ok(warp::reply::json(&res))
}
}
```

...

Now every time we query the /questions route, we get three log statements (shortened for better readability):

```
{"time":"2021-09-07T12:45:51.100961113+02:00","message":"…}
{"time":"2021-09-07T12:45:51.101065002+02:00","message":"No pagination…}
{"time":"2021-09-07T12:45:51.101155267+02:00","message":"GET /questions …}
```

This is just one request, however. Imagine a web server that is getting hit with many hundreds of requests a minute. The logs would be quite noisy, making it is harder to figure out which log belongs to which request. We can add another parameter, a request ID, so we can later filter the logs by a specific ID.

The crate Uuid is great for creating all sorts of unique IDs. We just need simple ID generation, so first we add the crate with the feature flag v4 to our Cargo.toml.

Listing 6.22   Updated Cargo.toml with Uuid package included

...

```
[dependencies]
warp = "0.3"
serde = { version = "1.0", features = ["derive"] }
serde_json = "1.0"
tokio = { version = "1.1.1", features = ["full"] }
# We can omit the version number for local imports
handle-errors = { path = "handle-errors" }
log = "0.4"
env_logger = "0.8"
log4rs = "1.0"
uuid = { version = "0.8", features = ["v4"] }
```

And with that, we can create a new Warp filter (remember, we always need to create filters when we want to pass information down a route) and create a unique ID. The next listing shows the added code for the main.rs file.

```
...

#[tokio::main]
async fn main() {
    log4rs::init_file("log4rs.yaml", Default::default()).unwrap();

    let log = warp::log::custom(|info| {
        log::info!(
            "{} {} {} {:?} from {} with {:?}",
            info.method(),
            info.path(),
            info.status(),
            info.elapsed(),
            info.remote_addr().unwrap(),
            info.request_headers()
        );
    });

    let store = store::Store::new();
    let store_filter = warp::any().map(move || store.clone());

    let id_filter = warp::any().map(|| uuid::Uuid::new_v4().to_string());

    let cors = warp::cors()
     .allow_any_origin()
     .allow_header("content-type")
     .allow_methods(&[
         Method::PUT,
         Method::DELETE,
         Method::GET,
         Method::POST
     ]);

    let get_questions = warp::get()
     .and(warp::path("questions"))
     .and(warp::path::end())
     .and(warp::query())
     .and(store_filter.clone())
     .and(id_filter)
     .and_then(routes::question::get_questions);

...
```

The next listing shows how we use this added parameter in the get_questions route handler, to print out the request_id for each incoming /questions request.

```
...

pub async fn get_questions(
    params: HashMap<String, String>,
    store: Store,
```

```
        id: String,
) -> Result<impl warp::Reply, warp::Rejection> {
    log::info!("{} Start querying questions", id);
    if !params.is_empty() {
        let pagination = extract_pagination(params)?;
        log::info!("{} Pagination set {:?}", id, &pagination);
        let res: Vec<Question> =
      store.questions.read().await.values().cloned().collect();
        let res = &res[pagination.start..pagination.end];

        Ok(warp::reply::json(&res))
    } else {
        log::info!("{} No pagination used", id);
        let res: Vec<Question> =
      store.questions.read().await.values().cloned().collect();

        Ok(warp::reply::json(&res))
    }
}

...
```

Restarting (and recompiling) the server shows us the new ID for each request against the localhost:3030/questions route (shortened for readability):

```
...
{"time":"2021-09-07T13:26:01.279131716+02:00",
    "message":"5da2bc97-e960-4984-be8a-d75be4728119 …}
{"time":"2021-09-07T13:26:01.279234525+02:00",
    "message":"5da2bc97-e960-4984-be8a-d75be4728119 No pagination used….}
{"time":"2021-09-07T13:26:01.279325632+02:00",
    "message":"Request Id: 5da2bc97-e960-4984-be8a-d75be4728119 GET ….}
```

We could even clean up the code a bit and create a global `Context` struct, where we add our store and the `unique_id` generation. However, the path we went down is not the right one.

For smaller applications, this might be fine, but we are trying to stitch something together that is better served by addressing the elephant in the room: logging of asynchronous applications and following requests throughout the stack is cumbersome when using pure logging libraries. Whenever you feel like you must pull too many rabbits out of a hat to get something done, it is wise to take a step back and see if you can take another angle.

Tracing vs. logging

The concept of tracing is not really standardized, but here in our context, tracing offers a way to follow a request from start to finish, with us being able to put an ID onto the request and follow it through each stage of the process. This allows us to see more detail around an error.

(continued)

For example, imagine a user who tries to log in to your application but receives an error message from the system. The user is sure to have used the right password, since nothing has changed in the past few months, and now you are getting a support email with the stated problem.

The first step is to get the email of the user and the date of the login attempt. With this information, you can go through your logs and follow this request through your stack to see where the problem occurred. You can put logs (or events) in your codebase with this workflow in mind, so you don't forget to write logs at the right moment in time.

And in this case, that angle is using the Tracing crate. It is meant to instrument applications and follow calls through the stack. It offers first-class support for futures and asynchronous applications and offers a variety of customizations that all come in handy when instrumenting web applications.

This doesn't mean everything we did was for nothing. We set up an understanding of logging, the problems it can solve, and how to address logging in a Rust application. It could be that the application you are building is small enough, or structured logging with log4rs, for example, is doing the job.

6.2   *Tracing in asynchronous applications*

We saw that we had to jump through quite a lot of hoops to create logs that can be traced to one specific request. The Tracing crate wants to tackle this problem by offering a different mindset for the simple logging procedure we used before.

The knowledge built in the first part of this chapter helps us understand what tracing is trying to offer, and which functionalities we need to look for when replacing the logging crates in our application so far. We used log4rs as the logger implementation, with the log crate as our abstraction. With Tracing, we can remove both crates and rely solely on Tracing to implement everything. What we have to do is to remove our logging crates from the previous solution and add Tracing and tracing-subscriber to our Cargo.toml file.

Listing 6.25   Updated Cargo.toml file with tracing crates

```
[package]
name = "practical-rust-book"
version = "0.1.0"
edition = "2021"

[dependencies]
warp = "0.3"
serde = { version = "1.0", features = ["derive"] }
serde_json = "1.0"
tokio = { version = "1.1.1", features = ["full"] }
```

```
# We can omit the version number for local imports
handle-errors = { path = "handle-errors" }
log = "0.4"
env_logger = "0.8"
log4rs = "1.0"
uuid = { version = "0.8", features = ["v4"] }
tracing = { version = "0.1", features = ["log"] }
tracing-subscriber = { version = "0.3", features = ["env-filter"] }
```

Adding tracing-subscriber seems foreign now; why would we need two different crates again? Let's dive into the Tracing library and see how it wants to solve our logging-in-asynchronous-applications problem.

6.2.1   Introducing the Tracing crate

The Tracing crate introduces three main concepts to conquer the challenges we are facing when logging in large, asynchronous applications:

- Spans
- Events
- Subscribers

A *span* is a period, with a start and an end. Most of the time, the start is the request, and the end is the sending out of the HTTP response. You can manually create spans or use the default built-in behavior in Warp, which does it for you. You can also have nested spans. For example, you can open a span when fetching data from the database, and that span is embedded in a bigger span that can be the HTTP request life cycle itself. This can help distinguish between logs later and help find the one you are looking for faster or easier.

Since we are dealing mostly with asynchronous functions, Tracing offers a macro called instrument (see figure 6.3), which opens and closes spans for us. We annotate our async functions with this macro, and everything else is done in the

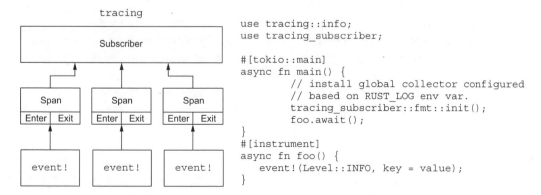

Figure 6.3   A basic tracing workflow consists of three elements: events, which write the logs; spans, which define a period in time and have a start and an end; and a subscriber, which collects all the logs.

background. You should avoid using manual spans in async functions, since the `.await` on them can yield a not-ready state, and the span would exit, leading to incorrect log entries.

Next, we have *events*. These are your logs, which are happening inside spans. An event can be anything you want it to be: the return of results for a database query, the start and end of decrypting a password, or its success or failure, for example. We can therefore replace our previous `info!` macros, for example, with `event!` macros.

And finally, *subscribers*. We know from our previous logging crates that we have to initialize the default logger in our `main` function. The same is true for Tracing. Each application needs a global subscriber that can collect all the events happening in your codebase and decide what to do with them.

By default, the tracing-subscriber crate comes with the `fmt` subscriber, which is meant to format and log events to the console. If you want other subscribers (for example, for logging to a file), you need a different flavor of subscriber, which there are plenty of.

6.2.2   *Integrating tracing in our application*

After removing our previous logging crates and adding the two tracing crates as in listing 6.25, we can move to our main.rs file to set up the subscriber and activate the tracing filter from Warp. If you have a larger codebase and decided very late in the journey to switch out your previous logging crates with Tracing, fear not.

Tracing does a good job in offering the same macros that log offers, so when replacing logging crates with Tracing, you don't have to go through your whole codebase right away. You can use the same macros you used before, and piece by piece replace them with the advised Tracing macros.

To recap, next to a global subscriber, which collects all the logs in your application, Tracing has the concepts of spans and events. A span is a moment in time, in which events can happen. Each event is then collected by a subscriber, which will store all the events and, depending on the settings, send them to a file or `stdout`, in the format you specify (JSON, for example).

Our web framework Warp supports the Tracing library rather well and helps us create these spans in which we can create events. If you have a larger codebase and want to move from a simple logging implementation to tracing, you can do so by just swapping out your logger implementation (such as env_logger, for example) with Tracing. The `info!`, `error!`, and other macros will work right out of the box.

The first step is to set up a subscriber, and call `init` on it. This will set the global log collector with your configurations. Each span created later will report back to this subscriber. Since we are still in the context of the Warp web framework, we must follow the given mindset, which means working with filters to create spans. The following listing shows our main.rs file, in which we swapped out our previous logging crate, log4rs, with Tracing.

Listing 6.26 Using Tracing instead of log4rs in main.rs, and removing `id_filter`

```
#![warn(clippy::all)]

use warp::{http::Method, Filter};
use handle_errors::return_error;
use tracing_subscriber::fmt::format::FmtSpan;

mod routes;
mod store;
mod types;

#[tokio::main]
async fn main() {
    let log_filter = std::env::var("RUST_LOG")
        .unwrap_or_else(|_|
            "practical_rust_book=info,warp=error".to_owned()
        );

    let store = store::Store::new();
    let store_filter = warp::any().map(move || store.clone());

    let id_filter = warp::any().map(|| uuid::Uuid::new_v4().to_string());

    tracing_subscriber::fmt()
        // Use the filter we built above to determine which traces to record.
        .with_env_filter(log_filter)
        // Record an event when each span closes.
        // This can be used to time our
        // routes' durations!
        .with_span_events(FmtSpan::CLOSE)
        .init();

    let cors = warp::cors()
        .allow_any_origin()
        .allow_header("content-type")
        .allow_methods(&[
        Method::PUT,
        Method::DELETE,
        Method::GET,
        Method::POST]
    );

    let get_questions = warp::get()
        .and(warp::path("questions"))
        .and(warp::path::end())
        .and(warp::query())
        .and(store_filter.clone())
        .and(id_filter)
        .and_then(routes::question::get_questions)
        .with(warp::trace(|info| {
            tracing::info_span!(
                "get_questions request",
                method = %info.method(),
                path = %info.path(),
```

Step 1: Add the log level.

Step 2: Set the tracing subscriber.

```
              id = %uuid::Uuid::new_v4(),
        )})
    );
```

◁──┐ **Step 3: Set**
   up logging for
   custom events.

...

```
    let routes = get_questions
        .or(update_question)
        .or(add_question)
        .or(add_answer)
        .or(delete_question)
        .with(cors)
        .with(warp::trace::request())
        .recover(return_error);

    warp::serve(routes).run(([127, 0, 0, 1], 3030)).await;
}
```

Step 4: Set
up logging for
incoming requests.

First (1) we need to remove the old log4rs config, since we are moving completely to tracing. In the first lines of the `main` function, we add the log level for the application. We can pass it via an environment variable called `RUST_LOG`, but if this is not set, we fall back to a default one.

The default one we pass is twofold: we pass one for our server implementation, which is indicated by the application name (which we set in the Cargo.toml file), and one for our Warp web framework. As we learned, Warp is also using tracing internally, and we can tell Warp to log `errors`, `debug`, or `info` events as well (we currently want to log only `errors`).

Next up (2), we set the tracing subscriber. This subscriber receives all the internal log and tracing events and decides what to do with it. Here, we set the `fmt` subscriber, which according to the documentation (http://mng.bz/wyMQ) is doing the following:

The `FmtSubscriber` formats and records tracing events as line-oriented logs.

There are more subscriber variants, but we'll get to that a bit later. Next, we pass the filter we created to the subscriber, so it knows which events to log (`info`, `debug`, `error`, etc.). We can also use a config called `with_span_events` (`FmtSpan::CLOSE`), which indicates that our subscriber will also log the closing of spans. By calling `init`, we activate the subscriber and can from now on log events in our application.

For the routes themselves (3), we can have two overarching tracing logs. Since Warp is developed close to Tokio (so is Tracing), we take advantage of the synergy in the ecosystem. We can use the `warp::trace` filter (http://mng.bz/qon2) to log custom events or each incoming request. In our example server, we do both. If you use another web framework in your own project, you might want to check the tracing support and how to enable it (if available). All major web frameworks use Tracing or support it through middleware.

We attach a `warp::trace` filter to the `get_questions` route, and inside the closure we use `tracing::info_span!` (which is a shortcut to calling `tracing::span` with the log level INFO) and pass custom data we want to log. For this to work, we need to add the ampersand (&) to the variables we want to log.

This indicates that we want to use the Display trait to print the data (we could also use a question mark [?], which would trigger the Debug macro to print the data to the console). The ampersand and question mark symbols are specific to the Tracing crate (http://mng.bz/7Zwy) and have nothing to do with Rust macros.

Last (4), but not least, we add the warp::trace::request filter to our routes. This will log every incoming request as well. For this to happen, we need to add the Debug trait to our Store, so Tracing can print out the store parameter. The following listing shows deriving the Debug trait.

Listing 6.27 Adding the Debug trait to the Store struct in src/store.rs

```
...

#[derive(Debug, Clone)]
pub struct Store {
    pub questions: Arc<RwLock<HashMap<QuestionId, Question>>>,
    pub answers: Arc<RwLock<HashMap<AnswerId, Answer>>>,
}

...
```

With this setup in place, we can move on to replace our previous logging mechanisms in the get_questions route handler. The following listing shows the updated code snippets.

Listing 6.28 Replacing log::info with tracing::event in routes/question.rs

```
use std::collections::HashMap;

use warp::http::StatusCode;
use tracing::{instrument, info};

use handle_errors::Error;
use crate::store::Store;
use crate::types::pagination::extract_pagination;
use crate::types::question::{Question, QuestionId};

#[instrument]
pub async fn get_questions(
    params: HashMap<String, String>,
    store: Store,
) -> Result<impl warp::Reply, warp::Rejection> {
    info!("querying questions");
    if !params.is_empty() {
        let pagination = extract_pagination(params)?;
        info!(pagination = true);
        let res: Vec<Question> =
      store.questions.read().await.values().cloned().collect();
```

```
        let res = &res[pagination.start..pagination.end];
        Ok(warp::reply::json(&res))
    } else {
        info!(pagination = false);
        let res: Vec<Question> =
    store.questions.read().await.values().cloned().collect();
        Ok(warp::reply::json(&res))
    }
}
...
```

We start by importing the instrument, event, and level from the Tracing library. We use the `instrument` macro (https://tracing.rs/tracing/attr.instrument.html) to automatically open and close a span when the function is called. All tracing events inside this function will then be automatically assigned to this span.

When we rerun our application with the added tracing crate and macros, and query the /questions route, we see the following logs on our console (shortened for readability):

```
Oct 13 14:00:06.384  INFO get_questions request{method=GET ....
Oct 13 14:00:06.386  INFO get_questions request{method=GET path=/...
Oct 13 14:00:06.386  INFO get_questions request{method=GET path=/questions...
Oct 13 14:00:06.387  INFO get_questions request{method=GET path=/questions...
```

If we were to remove the `instrument` macro (#[instrument]) on top of our get_ questions function, the logs would look like this (shortened for readability):

```
Oct 13 14:03:04.774  INFO get_questions request{method=GET path...
Oct 13 14:03:04.775  INFO get_questions request{method=GET path...
Oct 13 14:03:04.775  INFO get_questions request{method=GET path...
```

Instead of four log entries, we just get three. The macro opens a span for us when entering and closes it when leaving the function. It also logs the closing of the function span. In addition, we are missing all the details about which parameters were passed and returned from this function. Whether to use `instrument` depends on how much information you would like to log. Have in mind: when using the `instrument` macro, you are already getting quite a bit of information for free.

6.3   *Debugging Rust applications*

In the first two sections, you learned how to use logging mechanisms to get an introspective into our Rust application. The logs can reveal a deeper logical problem in your codebase that you want to dig into. Debugging a Rust application can reveal a problem that is hard to log or figure out via tests.

Debugger (LLDB and GDB)

A *debugger* is a tool that will run another piece of code in a controlled environment so it can be inspected and interacted with. When using a debugger, you can set breakpoints in your actual written code and then start your application with it.

Once you hit a specified breakpoint, the application will stop, and the debugger is able to show deeper analyses about the state of the application at this certain point. You can see information such as "what is currently stored in variable *x*."

We have two debuggers to choose from: Low Level Debugger (LLDB) and GNU Debugger (GDB). *LLDB* is part of Low Level Virtual Machine (LLVM), which is a set of compiler tools, and *GDB* is part of the GNU project. The one you choose depends a bit on yourself. If you use the command line, you can use GDB, and if you use an IDE like Visual Studio Code, LLDB is an easy choice.

From a birds-eye-view, debuggers work like this:

- A debugger itself is a program that runs the actual application (our Rust web service) inside it.
- Via breakpoints, a debugger can stop the execution of the program on a line-by-line basis.
- Once the process is interrupted (or stopped), the debugger can give an overview of the current state of the application at this point in time.
- The developer can then look at the state and figure out if a variable was set correctly or the calling function was returning the expected data.

Figure 6.4 visualizes the relationship between your Rust binary, the debugger, and the break points (Kernel interrupts) you are setting.

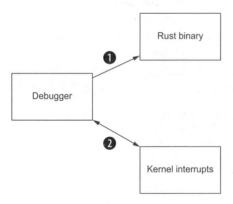

1 A debugger is an application that will execute the given binary and attach itself to the process.

2 A debugger uses **PTRACE** kernel events to step through the execution process of the running binary.

Figure 6.4   Birds-eye view of the debugging setup. A debugger attaches itself to the process of our Rust application, and uses kernel interrupt events to step in, pause the process, and display the state.

6.3.1   *Using GDB on the command line*

A debugger doesn't come with the Rust installation. It is an independent tool that can be installed in multiple ways and depends on your operating system. Rust comes with a command-line tool called rust-gdb, which is described in the source code (http://mng.bz/m282) as follows:

```
# Run GDB with the additional arguments that load the pretty printers
# Set the environment variable `RUST_GDB` to overwrite the call to a
# different/specific command (defaults to `gdb`).
RUST_GDB="${RUST_GDB:-gdb}"
PYTHONPATH="$PYTHONPATH:$GDB_PYTHON_MODULE_DIRECTORY" exec ${RUST_GDB} \
  --directory="$GDB_PYTHON_MODULE_DIRECTORY" \
  -iex "add-auto-load-safe-path $GDB_PYTHON_MODULE_DIRECTORY" \
  "$@"
```

The tool ships with the default Rust installation. If you don't have GDB installed yet on your system, you'll see this error (or a similar one):

```
$ rust-gdb

/…/.rustup/toolchains/stable-x86_64-apple-darwin/bin/rust-gdb:
    line 21: exec: gdb: not found
```

To install GDB on an Intel-based macOS, you can use brew:

```
brew install gdb
```

On Arch, for example, you can do it as follows:

```
pacman -S gdb
```

If you are on an ARM-based machine (like Apple computers with an Apple M1 chip and upward), you are out of luck. GDB is not supported as of writing this book, and you have to use LLDB (https://lldb.llvm.org), which is the default debugger on macOS.

Afterward, you can use the command-line tool to set breakpoints and start the debugging process. Explaining exactly how GDB works would exceed the size of the book. The most important commands and a basic workflow look like this:

> **We first build our application via cargo build.**   **We can use the just built binary to run within GDB via rust-gdb. The name of your application can be viewed/changed in the Cargo.toml file.**

```
$ cargo build   ◁─┘
$ rust-gdb target/debug/NAME_OF_YOUR_APPLICATIONS   ◁─┘
```

We can also specify files in folders.

```
(gdb) b main:11
(gdb) b src/routes/question.rs:11   ◁─┘
(gdb) r   ◁─
...
```

The "r" command runs the application and stops at the first breakpoint we set.

Starts the debugger interface, where we can interact with our application. The command "b" sets a breakpoint, and main:11 specifies the file and the line number we want to set it to.

```
(gdb) c          ◁────┐
...                    │
(gdb) p store    ◁──┐  │
...                 │  │
```

> After hitting a breakpoint, we can either do more (like printing out variables) or simply enter "c" for "continue the process."

> The "p" command stands for print, which lets us print variables.

This workflow works well for the most basic run-through of your application. If you like a more visual experience, you can use an IDE like Visual Studio Code, which has a built-in debugger interface.

6.3.2 Debugging our web service with LLDB

Let's go through an example debugging session to see how it compares to spot a problem via println! or dgb!. Debugging can look scary at first and quite uncomfortable. However, you will see that, as when looking at source code, your eyes will adjust to the environment, and you can use the tool in multiple scenarios.

In our first example session, we want to see whether a POST request is sending the right content to our web service. We can scatter a few println! macros around and hope to catch the point in the code where we can inspect the right data, or we can fire up our LLDB debugger and set a few breakpoints. The following listing shows the command-line interactions and output, and following right after is the explanation of each step. Note that step 6 is not in listing 6.29. It includes opening another terminal window and executing a curl command, which is explained following the listing.

> **Listing 6.29   Starting our web service via LLDB and using breakpoints**

Step 1
```
$ cargo build
    Finished dev [unoptimized + debuginfo] target(s) in 0.04s
```

Step 2
```
$ lldb target/debug/practical-rust-book
(lldb) target create "target/debug/practical-rust-book"
Current executable set to '/target/debug/practical-rust-book' (arm64).
```
Step 3
```
(lldb) b add_question
Breakpoint 1: where = practical-rust-… + 48 at question.rs:58:48,
    address = 0x0000000100102f54
```
Step 4
```
(lldb) breakpoint list
Current breakpoints:
1: name = 'add_question', locations = 1
  1.1: where = practical-rust-… 48 at question.rs:58:48,
    address = practical-rust-book[0x0000000100102f54],
    unresolved, hit count = 0
```

Step 5
```
(lldb) r
Process 96335 launched: '…./target/debug/practical-rust-book' (arm64)
2022-05-02T17:37:44.327462Z  INFO get_questions request
    {method=POST path=/questions id=8feb7e42-cc15-4bde-a34e-97878c2d3cc4}:
    practical_rust_book: close time.busy=61.0µs time.idle=89.6µs
```
Step 7
```
Process 96335 stopped
* thread #11, name = 'tokio-runtime-worker', stop reason = breakpoint 1.1
    frame #0: 0x0000000100102f54 practical-rust-book`practical_rust_book
```

```
                ::routes::question::add_question::hd2aa84941d704842
                (store=Store @ 0x000000017125cee0,
                    question=Question @ 0x000000017125cf28
                ) at question.rs:58:48
     55             pub async fn add_question(
     56                 store: Store,
     57                 question: Question,
  -> 58             ) -> Result<impl warp::Reply, warp::Rejection> {
     59                 store
     60                     .questions
     61                     .write()
        Target 0: (practical-rust-book) stopped.
```

Step 8 ⇢ `(lldb) frame variable`

```
        (practical_rust_book::store::Store) store = {
        ...

            title = {
              vec = {
                buf = {
                  ptr = (pointer = "question title",
                  _marker = core::marker::PhantomData<unsigned char>
                      @ 0x000000017125cf40)
                  cap = 9
                  alloc = {}
                }
                len = 9
              }
            }
            content = {
              vec = {
                buf = {
                  ptr = (pointer = "question content", _
                  marker = core::marker::PhantomData<unsigned char>
                      @ 0x000000017125cf58)
                  cap = 19
                  alloc = {}
                }
                len = 19
              }
            }
            tags = {}
        }
        (lldb) process continue        ⟵┘ Step 9
```

The flow is as follows:

1 Crate a binary that we can load in LLDB via `cargo build`.

2 At the command line, open the binary via LLDB.

3 Set breakpoints via the b command followed by the function name (add_
   question) we want to break at.

4 Show all the breakpoints via the `breakpoint list` command.

5 Run the program via r.

6 Open another terminal and execute the following `curl`:

```
$ curl --location --request POST 'localhost:3030/questions' \
      --header 'Content-Type: application/json' \
      --data-raw '{
      "id": "10",
      "title": "question title",
      "content": "question content"
}'
```

7 Inspect the breakpoint in the LLDB command-line tool.

8 View the current variable stack via `frame variable`.

9 Use `process continue` to tell LLDB to proceed with running the binary—until the next possible breakpoint.

Not all the features LLDB has to offer are currently supported by Rust. To get a clear overview, check out the "Rustc Dev Guide" (http://mng.bz/5md1) for an up-to-date view about the state of debugging in Rust.

For example, it is not easy to inspect the store and see what's inside of it via the command-line tool. If you have a visual code editor (like Visual Studio Code) on your machine, it might be more comfortable to use the editor with LLDB installed as a plugin to navigate through the debugging process. The next section, 6.3.3, describes how.

6.3.3 *Using Visual Studio Code and LLDB*

To be able to use Visual Studio Code as a Rust debugger, you need to install an extension called CodeLLDB. As of this writing, this extension is the one with the dragon symbol to its left. You can use the search bar to look for and install the extension. After the extension is installed, you can add a red point next to the line number in your files/code.

This will set a breakpoint on the line, and later, when starting the debugger via the user interface (UI), it will stop right there, and you can inspect the variables and the current stack of your application. Figure 6.5 shows a running debugging session in Visual Studio Code.

The advantage of using the debugger with this UI is that you can visually see right away your location in the code, and on the left side, you can navigate through your current set variables and see the call stack if needed.

The advantage of using an IDE like Visual Studio Code is that you can click the Step Over button (see figure 6.6) after hitting a breakpoint to jump to the next step in the code.

When you first run your application via the debugger in Visual Studio Code, you need to create a launch.json file (listing 6.30). Visual Studio Code will create one for you, but if you use a more complex setup later (like passing ENV variables to your application), this is the file to look for and adjust. It will be created in the root of your application folder under the folder .vscode.

Figure 6.5   A running debugging session in Visual Studio Code. We set a breakpoint on line 25 and started the debugging session by clicking the green arrow symbol at the top left.

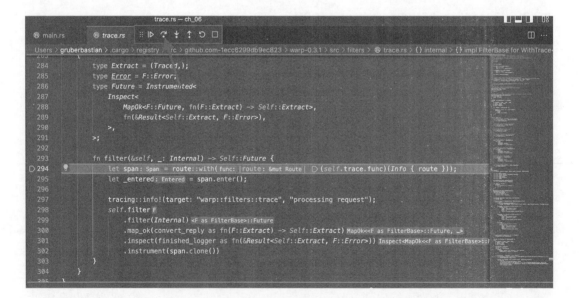

Figure 6.6   The Step Over button highlights each following step in the code, and even brings up internal crates if the next function being called is inside a third-party library. This way, you get an inside tour of each request you want to follow.

Listing 6.30   An example launch.json file

```json
{
    "configurations": [
        {
            "type": "lldb",
            "request": "launch",
            "name": "Debug executable 'practical-rust-book'",
            "cargo": {
                "args": [
                    "build",
                    "--bin=practical-rust-book",
                    "--package=practical-rust-book"
                ],
                "filter": {
                    "name": "practical-rust-book",
                    "kind": "bin"
                }
            },
            "args": [],
            "cwd": "${workspaceFolder}"
        },
        {
            "type": "lldb",
            "request": "launch",
            "name": "Debug unit tests in executable 'practical-rust-book'",
            "cargo": {
                "args": [
                    "test",
                    "--no-run",
                    "--bin=practical-rust-book",
                    "--package=practical-rust-book"
                ],
                "filter": {
                    "name": "practical-rust-book",
                    "kind": "bin"
                }
            },
            "args": [],
            "cwd": "${workspaceFolder}"
        }
    ]
}
```

With this launch.json file, we are using LLDB within Visual Studio Code, instead of GDB as we did in section 6.3.1 via the command line. LLDB is well supported within Visual Studio Code, and the IDE will use it as a default debugger for your Rust application. Most help and tricks you will find on the internet will also use LLDB when dealing with Visual Studio Code. It is thereby advised to follow along, at least until you are more familiar with debuggers and the workflow in general.

Summary

- Logging is crucial in production so you can introspect reported bugs or spot malicious behavior.
- The log crate uses the facade pattern, which means you use the log crate as the API and a logging crate for the actual implementation. This gives you the advantage of be able to change the logging crate later while still keeping the same log functions in your code.
- Rust has a variety of logging crates that offer logging to files, to the console, or other output streams.
- A crate called Tracing is better suited for asynchronous applications. This gives you better abstraction layers and the ability to follow through function calls even if they are called in random order.
- Debugging is a good way to find bugs or to be able to dig deeper into problems.
- You have the option of using a command-line interface or an IDE like Visual Studio Code to debug your Rust code.

Add a database
to your application

This chapter covers

- Setting up a local database
- Choosing a SQL crate suitable for your needs
- Adding a database connection to our web service
- Mapping our structs to tables
- Extending our code to run queries within the code
- Running database migrations
- Switching to a new database management system

In the previous chapter, we added the ability to log metrics about our applications. Next to the extraction of code into several modules, this makes for an already solid web service. We try to go through the steps as you would do at the start of writing a new web service.

Chapters 1 to 6 provided a solid foundation, which we will build out in the remaining chapters. We will move more and more toward a production-grade application, and one step almost all web services have to face at some point is talking to a database.

Handling the nitty-gritty database internals is not the focus of this book, so what we are going to do is set up an example database so we can store and retrieve data from it. The important part is understanding how to connect to a database with Rust, where you should abstract the interaction with the database, and how it affects your code.

The step toward using a database comes with major questions you have to answer for yourself:

- Do you want an object-relational mapping (ORM) tool or do you want to write Structured Query Language (SQL) commands directly?
- Should this crate work in a synchronous or asynchronous way?
- Do you have the need for migration scripts, and does the crate you chose support it?
- Do you need additional safety around your queries (type checking)?
- Do you need connection pooling, support for transactions, and batch processing?

This chapter will answer these questions and prepare you for a solid start to using Rust to work with databases. But first things first: we have to set up a database.

7.1   *Setting up our example database*

For the book, we are using PostgreSQL (version 14.4). The crate we will be choosing later, however, also works with other databases, and the actual code will essentially be the same regardless of the database. Well, everything up until the SQL we will write. Depending on your database, your SQL code might look a bit different.

Your mileage might also be very dependent on your operating system. For Linux users, you can use your package manager to install PostgreSQL. For developers working with macOS, the package manager Homebrew makes it easy to install PostgreSQL. Please reference the Download page to install the latest version for your operating system (www.postgresql.org/download/).

Setting up PostgreSQL locally is always slightly changing. This book can't account for the many Linux distributions, or Windows and macOS changes. Therefore, I recommend either using PostgreSQL inside a Docker container, or setting it up locally using the exhaustive PostgreSQL documentation: http://mng.bz/69BD.

Generally, you want to make sure that you have the following:

- PostgreSQL installed
- The PostgreSQL server running
- The PSQL CLI tool installed (this usually comes with the basic PostgreSQL install)
- A location/file for the database set up
- A database called PostgreSQL (`postgres`)

Afterward, you can create your own user to create new databases with. This is done via the command-line utility PSQL.

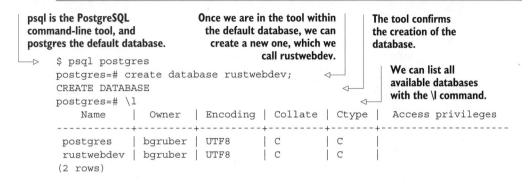

Listing 7.1   Creating the example database via PSQL

psql is the PostgreSQL command-line tool, and postgres the default database.

Once we are in the tool within the default database, we can create a new one, which we call rustwebdev.

The tool confirms the creation of the database.

We can list all available databases with the \l command.

```
$ psql postgres
postgres=# create database rustwebdev;
CREATE DATABASE
postgres=# \l
     Name    |  Owner   | Encoding | Collate | Ctype | Access privileges
-------------+----------+----------+---------+-------+--------------------
 postgres    | bgruber  | UTF8     | C       | C     |
 rustwebdev  | bgruber  | UTF8     | C       | C     |
(2 rows)
```

This is the manual way of creating our database. When we deploy our application in a later chapter, we have to make sure to also include the creation of the database in our build script or Docker file.

7.2   Creating our first tables

Now that we have a running database server and created a database, the next step is to create tables for our actual data. Later in the chapter, we will use migrations to create tables in a more automated way, but as with everything else, doing it by hand first is the better way of learning. Once you have done something by hand, you see the up- and downsides of solutions trying to do this in a more automated way.

Still inside PSQL, we can connect to our newly created database and create the tables we might need. We start with a table for our questions. As a reminder, listing 7.2 shows the Question struct from our web service. We need to transform the QuestionId from String to i32, to accommodate the PostgreSQL structure in listing 7.4.

Listing 7.2   Question struct

```rust
use serde::{Deserialize, Serialize};

#[derive(Deserialize, Serialize, Debug, Clone)]
pub struct Question {
    pub id: QuestionId,
    pub title: String,
    pub content: String,
    pub tags: Option<Vec<String>>,
}
#[derive(Deserialize, Serialize, Debug, Clone, PartialEq, Eq, Hash)]
pub struct QuestionId(pub i32);
```

This change will also have an impact on our route creation in main.rs, where we pass the parameters as i32 instead of String, as shown in the following listing.

```
...

let update_question = warp::put()
        .and(warp::path("questions"))
        .and(warp::path::param::<i32>())
        .and(warp::path::end())
        .and(store_filter.clone())
        .and(warp::body::json())
        .and_then(routes::question::update_question);

    let delete_question = warp::delete()
        .and(warp::path("questions"))
        .and(warp::path::param::<i32>())
        .and(warp::path::end())
        .and(store_filter.clone())
        .and_then(routes::question::delete_question);

...
```

We have `Strings`, `i32`, and a `vector` (or array in the PostgreSQL world) of `Strings` in our `Question` struct. The SQL to create a corresponding table looks like the following listing. You can copy and paste or type the SQL as shown directly in PSQL and press Enter.

```
CREATE TABLE IF NOT EXISTS questions (
    id serial PRIMARY KEY,          ◄───┤ We let PostgreSQL
    title VARCHAR (255) NOT NULL,        │ create the IDs for us.
    content TEXT NOT NULL,
    tags TEXT [],
    created_on TIMESTAMP NOT NULL DEFAULT NOW()  ◄───┤ It's always wise to have a
);                                                    │ timestamp attached to entries,
                                                      │ and we tell PostgreSQL to
                                                      │ create one for us by default.
```

As a reminder, our `Answer` struct is shown again in the following listing.

```
use serde::{Deserialize, Serialize};

use crate::types::question::QuestionId;

#[derive(Serialize, Deserialize, Debug, Clone)]
pub struct Answer {
    pub id: AnswerId,
    pub content: String,
    pub question_id: QuestionId,
}

#[derive(Deserialize, Serialize, Debug, Clone, PartialEq, Eq, Hash)]
pub struct AnswerId(pub i32);
```

Possible SQL for creating the corresponding table is in the following listing.

Listing 7.6 SQL to create an `answers` table

```
CREATE TABLE IF NOT EXISTS answers (
    id serial PRIMARY KEY,
    content TEXT NOT NULL,
    created_on TIMESTAMP NOT NULL DEFAULT NOW(),
    corresponding_question integer REFERENCES questions
);
```

We can check if the tables were created with the \dt command:

```
rustwebdev=# \dt
          List of relations
 Schema |   Name    | Type  |  Owner
--------+-----------+-------+---------
 public | answers   | table | bgruber
 public | questions | table | bgruber
(2 rows)
```

Now that we've tested creating the table, let's see if we can delete (drop) it as well. This can be done via the DROP [TABLE_NAME]; command:

```
rustwebdev=# \dt
          List of relations
 Schema |   Name    | Type  |  Owner
--------+-----------+-------+---------
 public | answers   | table | bgruber
 public | questions | table | bgruber
(2 rows)

rustwebdev=# drop table answers, questions;
DROP TABLE
rustwebdev=# \dt
Did not find any relations.
```

We went through the process of creating tables manually and became familiar with our database of choice. Now it's time to put the experience in code. We first choose a crate and then decide if we need an ORM crate or prefer plain SQL in our codebase.

7.3 Working with a database crate

In this book, we choose to write SQL directly and don't use an ORM crate. It's a preference, and you or your team might decide otherwise. Our reasons are that code you learn stays cleaner that way. It might be more verbose, but if you learn a new language, it is good that the crates you are using don't interfere too much yet with the solution you write.

ORM vs. pure SQL

ORM is a technique to translate SQL queries into everyday-looking code. The Rust crate Diesel (https://diesel.rs/) is a library that will translate code to SQL queries behind the scenes. So instead of writing, for example,

```
SELECT * from questions
```

you would have code that looks like this:

```
questions_table.load_all();
```

This makes it a bit easier to read and digest from a developer perspective. You could potentially also save a lot of boilerplate code and make the queries feel more natural in your codebase than having a string that contains SQL.

Another area is application security. ORMs tend to handle security concerns like SQL injection better than handwritten SQL from the developer. When it comes to sanitizing user input, ORMs are usually equipped with enough tooling so the developer doesn't have to think about special characters, and the ORM itself is formatting so it ends up sanitized in the database.

The downside is that the database structure is getting too close to your Rust code, which means structs can get annotated with the ORM macros. It makes it harder to separate database logic from your types in your code.

It is easy to reason about SQL, since the language is old and proven, and help exists throughout the internet. If something breaks, you typically know where to look. If you have an ORM, you have to trust that the underlying code translates your queries into reasonable SQL and does the right thing.

After you have written the same piece of code multiple times, or if you realize abstracting away the SQL would make your code more readable and more easily maintainable, that's the point where you can choose something else.

> **NOTE** If you decide to use an ORM, Diesel is a valid choice and has a great tutorial for getting started. After reading this chapter, you can go through its "Getting Started" guide (https://diesel.rs/guides/getting-started) and try to convert our choice of SQLx into using Diesel as an ORM.

Depending on your professional level, sometimes the choice of a crate is answered by the question "What is the majority using?" This shouldn't be the guiding light throughout your career, but to get started and get reasonable help, the first step is to follow the herd, and then later deviate from a given path if necessary. Figure 7.1 shows an example abstraction with the use of SQLx, the Rust crate we are going to use for our SQL queries in our codebase.

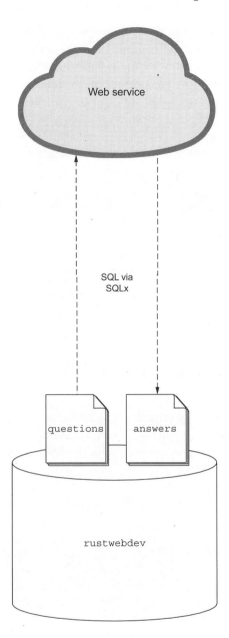

Figure 7.1 Our `rustwebdev` database and the `questions` and `answers` tables are interacting via SQLx and SQL with our web service.

In the Rust ecosystem, SQLx is a good choice to get started with for several reasons:

- It is asynchronous.
- The PostgreSQL driver is written in Rust.
- It supports multiple database engines (MySQL, PostgreSQL, SQLite).
- It works with different runtimes (Tokio, async-std, Actix Web).
- It is widely used in the community.

It also has a big drawback. Since SQLx doesn't provide its own abstraction over SQL, it can't verify correct SQL that easily. It does the compile-time checks of your SQL queries via macros and by connecting to your development database. Depending on your use case, you might not want to connect to a database every time you compile your code.

7.3.1   Adding SQLx into our project

Heading over to the GitHub page of SQLx (https://github.com/launchbadge/sqlx), it tells us to add the following requirement to our Cargo.toml file.

> **Listing 7.7   Adding the SQLx dependencies to our Cargo.toml**

```
[package]
name = "practical-rust-book"
version = "0.1.0"                          We add tokio, migrate, and postgres
edition = "2021"                           features to the crate, so we can run
                                           on top of our runtime and later run
[dependencies]                             migrations within the codebase.
...
// Formatted for print purposes; this has to be on one line
// or it won't compile
sqlx = {
    version = "0.5",
    features = [ "runtime-tokio-rustls", "migrate", "postgres" ]
}
```

Before we jump into the code, let's remember to re-create the tables we need initially by hand. In later sections of this chapter, we will use a command-line tool to run migrations that will do this for us. As a reminder, you can open the PSQL tool via the command line and create the tables from there:

```
$ psql rustwebdev
psql (14.1)
Type "help" for help.

rustwebdev=# CREATE TABLE IF NOT EXISTS questions (
    id serial PRIMARY KEY,
    title VARCHAR (255) NOT NULL,
    content TEXT NOT NULL,
    tags TEXT [],
    created_on TIMESTAMP NOT NULL DEFAULT NOW()
);
CREATE TABLE
rustwebdev=# CREATE TABLE IF NOT EXISTS answers (
    id serial PRIMARY KEY,
    content TEXT NOT NULL,
    created_on TIMESTAMP NOT NULL DEFAULT NOW(),
    corresponding_question integer REFERENCES questions
);
CREATE TABLE
rustwebdev=# \dt
```

```
          List of relations
 Schema |   Name    | Type  | Owner
--------+-----------+-------+---------
 public | answers   | table | bgruber
 public | questions | table | bgruber
(2 rows)
```

Now we can think through our places in the codebase where we interface or where we might want to update or fetch data from the database.

7.3.2 Connecting Store to our database

We have multiple options for how and where to put the interface to the database. We could do it directly in the route handlers, we could attach it to our `Store` object (which holds our `questions` and `answers` as well as reading the example JSON file so far), or we could create our own database object to handle the queries and mutations.

The same goes for the creation of the connection pool. Is it better done inside main.rs and then passed down to the object or route handler, or should we create the connection during the creation of the `Store` (or `Database`) object?

> **How to abstract away database access in a (large) codebase**
>
> When it comes to databases, the complexity of the code might seem to increase. However, a database access is nothing more, from an architecture perspective, than any other module added to your Rust application. If you have a larger application to work with, you can split each domain or area of your business logic in a folder (like users, questions, or answers) and structure the code separately in files as we did in this small example in this book (routes, types, store).
>
> The complexity arises from where, when, and how to connect to the database. One way of doing it in larger applications is creating a `Context` object. This context gets filled with information (like `user_id` from the request and `database_url`) and is passed down to each route handler. The route handler then either connects to the database via the URL in the context, or the context is already holding an open database connection the route handler can use to execute the SQL query.
>
> Therefore, even in larger Rust applications, the way to add a database won't change. It's more a question of where you bundle information and how to pass it down. We will see in chapter 10, when we deploy the book's source code, how to parameterize our codebase and use some of these concepts.

In this example, we will put the database connection directly into our `Store` object and perform the queries through it. Therefore, calling the route handler will still, internally, call `Store`, but instead of reading and writing from a vector in the RAM, we will talk to our PostgreSQL instance.

We also create the connection pool to our database inside `Store`. We could choose to do this on a higher level inside main.rs, and then pass it down to when creating a new `Store` object. It really depends on your mindset and size of your application. We will run into quite a few problems or tradeoffs later. Take the following considerations into account:

- What if we add answers, users, comments, and other types of data to our web service; will one `Store` object be enough to handle it all?
- Should we therefore decide to move the SQL queries into the route handler itself?
- What if the SQL queries become quite complex and large; maybe that's too much noise inside the route handler itself?

Here's a rule of thumb: when you want to change one part of the system, you don't want to accidentally change another part, or even read and consume another part that you're not interested in. Changing a route handler shouldn't even touch the SQL at all.

It could therefore be wise to create a folder for each data type (questions, answers, users, and so forth) that contains files called mod.rs, methods.rs, and store.rs. This would split the files by data type and by concern. For now, we are happy with one large store.rs file and will split it later, once we introduce users and authentication.

With SQLx added to our dependencies, we can now use it inside our codebase. We will start to look into store.rs: how we initialize the connection to our PostgreSQL database, and what changes we have to make to query questions from the database instead of the JSON file.

Listing 7.8 Updating store.rs to replace the JSON file with a database connection

```
use tokio::sync::RwLock;
use std::collections::HashMap;
use std::sync::Arc;
use sqlx::postgres::{PgPoolOptions, PgPool, PgRow};
use sqlx::Row;

use crate::types::{
    answer::Answer,
    question::{Question, QuestionId},
};

#[derive(Debug, Clone)]
pub struct Store {
    pub connection: PgPool,
}

impl Store {
    pub async fn new(db_url: &str) -> Self {
        let db_pool = match PgPoolOptions::new()
        .max_connections(5)
        .connect(db_url).await {
            Ok(pool) => pool,
            Err(e) => panic!("Couldn't establish DB connection: {}", e),
        };
```

We remove reading from the local JSON file and therefore don't need these three imports anymore.

We also remove questions and answers from the Store fields and simply have the connection pool there for now.

In case we can't establish a database connection, we let the application fail.

```
        Store {
            connection: db_pool,
        }
    }

    fn init() -> HashMap<QuestionId, Question> {
        let file = include_str!("../questions.json");
        serde_json::from_str(file).expect("can't read questions.json")
    }
```

...

Listing 7.8 shows us a lot of changes. But don't worry, it's all straightforward. First, we switch our mindset from a file-based/local-storage mindset to a database mindset. We remove our `questions` and `answers` fields from the `Store` struct and replace them with a `connection` field, which holds the connection pool for our PostgreSQL database.

> ### Connection pools
>
> *Connection pools* is a database term that basically means you have more than one database connection open at the same time. Because we operate in an asynchronous environment, we might want to have more than one database query running at the same time. Instead of opening just one connection and creating potentially a long queue of requests waiting for the database to become free to use, we let a fixed number of connections be open, and the database crate will handle giving out free connections to incoming requests.
>
> Another advantage of using connection pools is that they limit the number of connections to avoid overwhelming the database server.

We take the example code from the SQLx GitHub repository page (https://github .com/launchbadge/sqlx) and create a new connection pool, which we store in the `connection` field in our `Store` object. This gives us the ability to create a new store and pass it down to the route handlers, which themselves can use a connection from the pool and to database queries if they need to. Figure 7.2 demonstrates this concept.

We also see that now we expect a `&str` type when creating a new `Store`. We first go with the simplest solution possible (passing down the database URL in the main.rs file), and later in the book, we will see how to use configuration files to do this in a better way. Listing 7.9 shows the updated line inside our main.rs file.

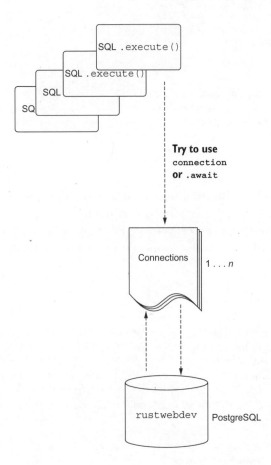

Figure 7.2   Connection pools allow us to keep more than one connection to the database open so we can process more database operations at the same time.

Listing 7.9   Passing down the database URL inside main.rs

...

```
#[tokio::main]
async fn main() -> Result<(), sqlx::Error>{
    let log_filter = std::env::var("RUST_LOG").unwrap_or_else(|_| {
        "handle_errors=warn,practical_rust_book=warn,warp=warn".to_owned()
    });

    // if you need to add a username and password,
    // the connection would look like:
    // "postgres://username:password@localhost:5432/rustwebdev"
    let store =
        store::Store::new("postgres://localhost:5432/rustwebdev").await;
    let store_filter = warp::any().map(move || store.clone());

...

}
```

Our database runs on localhost, and the PostgreSQL server uses the standard port (5432). We created a database with the name rustwebdev earlier. We also have to put an await behind the new function, because opening the database connection is asynchronous and can fail.

7.4 Reimplementing our route handlers

Now that we've implemented SQLx into our codebase and adjusted our Store to use the database connection and offer a pool of connection, we can focus on our route handlers. Instead of adding the database query directly in the handler, we for now extend the Store implementation and add each database query as an associated function.

Figure 7.3 shows the importance of our abstractions. We switch out the local data structure and replace it with a database, and the rest of the application stays untouched.

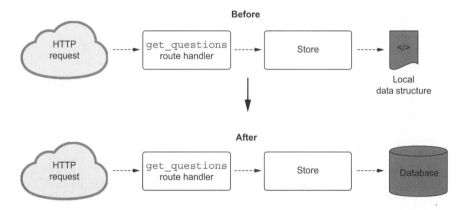

Figure 7.3 Replacing the local Vec<Questions> and Vec<Answers> storage objects with a PostgreSQL database

This works well for the purpose of the book. We have just two types (Question and Answer), and therefore one global store module is enough to house every SQL query we want to make inside our application. But what about a larger-scale application? You have multiple options:

- You can have different folders for each domain of your application, and replicate the structure inside each (types, routes, store.rs), and therefore reduce the number of lines in your store.rs file.
- You can create a Context type, which holds information you need throughout your application and route handlers (like user_id and db_connection_pool) for each database you use. You can create this Context in your main.rs file and pass it down to each route handler. This would make each route handler a bit "dumber" and therefore easier to test and change.

We, for example, pass down a `Store` object, which holds the connection. This solution makes it a bit tighter together and harder to change and test. One reason we are doing it like this is that we have just one piece of information we want to pass down to each route handler, which is the database connection. The interesting part with this approach is to see how even a seemingly little change has far-reaching consequences throughout the codebase.

7.4.1   Adding the database to get_questions

Now is the time to go through our route handlers and see how we have to update them to make them work with the database queries. First up is `get_questions`. The following listing shows the `get_questions` route handler as it currently stands.

Listing 7.10   The `get_questions` route handler inside /route/questions.rs so far

```
...

pub async fn get_questions(
    params: HashMap<String, String>,
    store: Store,
) -> Result<impl warp::Reply, warp::Rejection> {
    if !params.is_empty() {
        let pagination = extract_pagination(params)?;
        let res: Vec<Question> =
    store.questions.read().await.values().cloned().collect();
        let res = &res[pagination.start..pagination.end];
        Ok(warp::reply::json(&res))
    } else {
        let res: Vec<Question> =
            store.questions.read().await.values().cloned().collect();
        Ok(warp::reply::json(&res))
    }
}

...
```

We are already reading the questions from the store, but we assume they are locked behind a local data structure, behind an `Arc` inside a `HashMap`. Depending on the parameters (using pagination or not when querying questions), we return a different slice of the result. We are going to change that behavior quite a lot.

But first, let's create a `get_questions` method inside our `Store`, so we can separate the database logic from the business logic. We will go back to the route handler after we are confident of querying questions from the database.

Listing 7.11   The newly created `get_questions` method inside store.rs

```
use sqlx::postgres::{PgPoolOptions, PgPool, PgRow};
use sqlx::Row;

use handle_errors::Error;
```

```
use crate::types::{
    question::{Question, QuestionId},
};

#[derive(Debug, Clone)]
pub struct Store {
    pub connection: PgPool,
}

impl Store {
    pub async fn new(db_url: &str) -> Self {
        let db_pool = match PgPoolOptions::new()
        .max_connections(5)
        .connect(db_url).await {
            Ok(pool) => pool,
            Err(_) => panic!("Couldn't establish DB connection!"),
        };

        Store {
            connection: db_pool,
        }
    }

    pub async fn get_questions(
        &self,
        limit: Option<u32>,
        offset: u32
    ) -> Result<Vec<Question>, sqlx::Error> {
        match sqlx::query("SELECT * from questions LIMIT $1 OFFSET $2")
            .bind(limit)
            .bind(offset)
            .map(|row: PgRow| Question {
                id: QuestionId(row.get("id")),
                title: row.get("title"),
                content: row.get("content"),
                tags: row.get("tags"),
            })
            .fetch_all(&self.connection)
            .await {
                Ok(questions) => Ok(questions),
                Err(e) => {
                    tracing::event!(tracing::Level::ERROR, "{:?}", e);
                    Err(Error::DatabaseQueryError)
                }
            }
    }

    ...

}
```

We pass a limit and offset parameter to the function, which indicates if pagination is wanted by the client, and return a vector of questions and a sqlx error type in case something goes wrong.

We write plain SQL via the query function and add the dollar sign ($) and a number for the variables we pass to the query.

The bind method replaces a $ + number pair in the SQL query with the variable we specify here.

The second bind is our offset variable.

If we want to return a question (or all of them) from the query, we use map to go over each returned PostgreSQL row we receive and create a Question out of it.

The fetch_all method executes our SQL statement and returns all the added questions back to us.

We have the chance to start from scratch, and we are going to deal with all the ramifications of our decisions later. We create a new method called get_questions, and we know from the route handler that this method can get parameters that indicate pagination. In the PostgreSQL world, this is done via parameters called offset and limit.

Pagination in databases

It is usually not that straightforward to implement pagination behavior. It highly depends on your use case. With larger datasets, for example, a cursor could be an optimal choice. For the use case of this book, we want to focus on interacting with the database and don't care about performance. If you implement this behavior in your own project, I recommend studying the material from your database and the type of options it offers.

An offset indicates where to start querying, and a limit gives us the number of results we want. If we have 100 questions in the database, an offset of 50 would signal that we want to start returning from question 50 onward, and a limit of 10 would return 10 questions from this position on. We therefore use the type u32 for the limit and also for the offset parameter.

The method returns either a list of questions or the SQLx error. We are executing a query with sqlx with the query method and write plain SQL inside it. The only exception is integrating our values into the SQL query itself. The SQLx crate uses the dollar sign ($) and a number (1) in combination with the .bind method to assign a variable to the placeholders marked with the $ sign:

```
sqlx::query("SELECT * from questions LIMIT $1 OFFSET $2")
    .bind(limit)
    .bind(offset)
```

PostgreSQL can use default parameters for both. If we pass None as a limit, PostgreSQL will ignore it, and if we pass 0 as an offset, it will do the same. So instead of writing two versions of the same function (one where we expect these parameters and one where we don't), we will use the Rust Default trait later. That's also the reason the limit parameter is an Option that can hold a number or None. If we don't pass a number, limit will be None, and PostgreSQL will ignore it for us.

The query returns a Result, which we use match on and either return the resulting Vec full of questions, or an error. To get the result, however, we have to do two things first. We need to .map over the resulting rows (of the type PgRow) and create Questions out of it, and then use .fetch_all where we pass our database connection to actually execute the query:

```
pub async fn get_questions(
    &self,
    limit: Option<i32>,
    offset: i32
) -> Result<Vec<Question>, sqlx::Error> {
        match sqlx::query("SELECT * from questions LIMIT $1 OFFSET $2")
            .bind(limit)
            .bind(offset)
            .map(|row: PgRow| Question {
                id: QuestionId(row.get("id")),
```

```
            title: row.get("title"),
            content: row.get("content"),
            tags: row.get("tags"),
            })
        .fetch_all(&self.connection)
        .await {
            Ok(questions) => Ok(questions),
            Err(e) => Err(e),
        }
}
```

This rather simple function has two implications for the rest of our codebase:

- We have a new error type (`sqlx::Error`) that we cannot handle yet inside our Error crate.
- We expect `limit` and `offset` parameters, which we (a) called differently until now, and (b) must find a way to create default values for them if the client isn't passing them on to us.

We need to add SQLx as a dependency to the Cargo.toml file of handle-errors.

Listing 7.12 Adding sqlx to the handle-errors crate

```
[package]
name = "handle-errors"
version = "0.1.0"
edition = "2021"


[dependencies]
warp = "0.3"
sqlx = { version = "0.5" }
```

Then we extend our error crate so we can support `sqlx::Error` in our codebase. We are going to extend the enum in handle-errors/src/lib.rs.

Listing 7.13 Extending the `Error` enum and `Display` trait for the `sqlx::Error` type

```
use warp::{
    filters::{body::BodyDeserializeError, cors::CorsForbidden},
    http::StatusCode,
    reject::Reject,
    Rejection, Reply,
};

use sqlx::error::Error as SqlxError;          ◁── Imports the sqlx Error and
                                                  renames it so there is no
                                                  confusion with our own
                                                  Error enum

#[derive(Debug)]
pub enum Error {
    ParseError(std::num::ParseIntError),
    MissingParameters,                        ◁── Adds a new error
    QuestionNotFound,                             type to our enum,
    DatabaseQueryError(SqlxError),            ◁── which can hold the
}                                                 actual sqlx error
```

```rust
impl std::fmt::Display for Error {
    fn fmt(&self, f: &mut std::fmt::Formatter) -> std::fmt::Result {
        match &*self {
            Error::ParseError(ref err) => {
                write!(f, "Cannot parse parameter: {}", err)
            },
            Error::MissingParameters => write!(f, "Missing parameter"),
            Error::QuestionNotFound => write!(f, "Question not found"),
            Error::DatabaseQueryError => {
                write!(f, "Query could not be executed", e)    ◁────────┐
            },
        }
    }
}
```

> To be able to print the new error type, we need to implement the Display trait for it as well.

...

Next up is our pagination type. We have to rewrite quite a lot to accommodate the changes inside store.rs. The next listing shows the updated pagination.rs file and highlights our changes.

Listing 7.14   Updating pagination.rs with the `Default` trait and renaming

```rust
use std::collections::HashMap;

use handle_errors::Error;

/// Pagination struct which is getting extract
/// from query params
#[derive(Default, Debug)]
pub struct Pagination {
    /// The index of the last item which has to be returned
    pub limit: Option<u32>,    ◁────────┐
    /// The index of the first item which has to be returned
    pub offset: u32,    ◁────────┐
}

/// Extract query parameters from the `/questions` route
/// # Example query
/// GET requests to this route can have a pagination attached so we just
/// return the questions we need
/// `/questions?start=1&end=10`
/// # Example usage
/// ```rust
/// use std::collections::HashMap;
///
/// let mut query = HashMap::new();
/// query.insert("limit".to_string(), "1".to_string());
/// query.insert("offset".to_string(), "10".to_string());
/// let p = pagination::extract_pagination(query).unwrap();
/// assert_eq!(p.limit, Some(1));
/// assert_eq!(p.offset, 10);
/// ```
```

> We rename the first Pagination field to limit, which can be either None or a number. If we pass None, PostgreSQL will ignore it by default, and we save ourselves a few if statements because of that.

> The second parameter is offset, and if we pass 0, PostgreSQL will ignore it. Same with the limit field; we can save ourselves a few if statements because of that.

```
pub fn extract_pagination(
    params: HashMap<String, String>
) -> Result<Pagination, Error> {
    // Could be improved in the future
    if params.contains_key("limit") && params.contains_key("offset") {
        return Ok(Pagination {
            // Takes the "limit" parameter in the query
            // and tries to convert it to a number
            limit: Some(params
                .get("limit")
                .unwrap()
                .parse::<u32>()
                .map_err(Error::ParseError)?),
            // Takes the "offset" parameter in the query
            // and tries to convert it to a number
            offset: params
                .get("offset")
                .unwrap()
                .parse::<u32>()
                .map_err(Error::ParseError)?,

        });
    }

    Err(Error::MissingParameters)
}
```

Parse will turn a &str into a u32.

First, we rename start and end to limit and offset. This is also the order the SQL expects when querying PostgreSQL. The database also dictates our types for both fields. The limit field is changed from usize to Option<u32>. The Option is so that we can default back to None, which is ignored by PostgreSQL (http://mng.bz/o56r). And offset is type u32, which we can default back to 0 if not specified, which tells PostgreSQL to return all available records.

Rust has a handy trait called Default, which we can call so it creates the specific type with default values. We are going to use this feature, so we don't have to write two separate functions (one with parameters and one without). Instead, if the client doesn't pass the limit and offset parameters, we create the Pagination object with default values, which will get ignored by our database. If we get valid parameters, we create the Pagination object with these instead.

Our extract_pagination function has also changed slightly. We wrap the limit in Some, and change the casting from usize to u32 since our SQL expects a u32 number.

With all these changes in place, we can finally rewrite our get_questions route handler to use our new logic. The following listing shows the updated code.

> **Listing 7.15 Updated `get_questions` route handler in routes/questions.rs**

```
use types::pagination::Pagination;
use tracing::{event, instrument, Level};
use crate::types::pagination::Pagination;
...
```

```
#[instrument]
pub async fn get_questions(
    params: HashMap<String, String>,
    store: Store,
) -> Result<impl warp::Reply, warp::Rejection> {
    event!(target: "practical_rust_book", Level::INFO, "querying questions");
    let mut pagination = Pagination::default();

    if !params.is_empty() {
        event!(Level::INFO, pagination = true);
        pagination = extract_pagination(params)?;
        let res: Vec<Question> = store.questions.read().await.values()
            .cloned().collect();
        let res = &res[pagination.start..pagination.end];
        Ok(warp::reply::json(&res))
    } else {}

    info!(pagination = false);
    let res: Vec<Question> = match store
        .get_questions(pagination.limit, pagination.offset)
        .await {
            Ok(res) => res,
            Err(e) => {
                return Err(warp::reject::custom(
                    Error::DatabaseQueryError(e)
                ))
            },
    };

    Ok(warp::reply::json(&res))
}

...
```

Creates a mutable variable with the default parameter for Pagination

In case the pagination object is not empty, we override our mutable variable from above and replace it with the given Pagination from the client.

In case of an error, we simply pass the error up to our error handler in the handle-error crate.

We mostly deleted old code. To start, we instantiate the Pagination object with our default parameters, and in case the function is getting valid parameters from the request, we update the object with real values. Afterward, we call the get_questions function from the store, which will query the database for us and return, in case of success, a Vec object full of questions. In case of an error, we use our updated error handling and return a database error. All the major changes we made going from our local in-memory storage to a PostgreSQL database are documented in figure 7.4.

Before	After
Store initializes questions Vec from a JSON file.	Store creates a PostgreSQL connection pool.
Store holds questions and answers behind a mutex.	Store uses the connection pool to query the database tables directly.
get_questions route handler requests a read/write.	get_questions calls a Store function that queries the database.
The pagination struct has the fields start and end.	The pagination struct uses the PostgreSQL terms limit and offset.

Figure 7.4   Brief overview of the changes in the codebase so far

So, onward. Let's implement the `add_question` route handler so we can add questions to our database.

7.4.2   Reimplementing the add_question route handler

As with the previous route handler, we start with the `Store` implementation and then go on to the `add_question` route handler itself. We will see that even such a little change will have consequences for the rest of our codebase.

The following code snippet reminds us of the details of our `questions` table:

```
CREATE TABLE IF NOT EXISTS questions (
    id serial PRIMARY KEY,
    title VARCHAR (255) NOT NULL,
    content TEXT NOT NULL,
    tags TEXT [],
    created_on TIMESTAMP NOT NULL DEFAULT NOW()
);
```

We don't create and increment the `id` in our codebase but let the database do the job. To remind us as well of our `Question` struct:

```
pub struct Question {
    pub id: QuestionId,
    pub title: String,
    pub content: String,
    pub tags: Option<Vec<String>>,
}
```

This impacts our design decision when passing down a `Question` object to the function that creates a question in the database. The Rust compiler checks whether all required fields are part of the object, and if not, it raises an error. A common pattern in this regard is creating a new type called `NewQuestion` (as shown in figure 7.5), which is meant to be used when someone creates a new object without having all the needed information to start with. We therefore extend our question.rs file in the types folder.

> **Listing 7.16   Adding `NewQuestion` to /types/question.rs**

```
...


#[derive(Deserialize, Serialize, Debug, Clone)]
pub struct NewQuestion {
    pub title: String,
    pub content: String,
    pub tags: Option<Vec<String>>,
}
```

We will use this as a parameter in our `add_question` function inside store.rs. Therefore, neither the client nor we have to generate an `id` and fulfill the compiler checks.

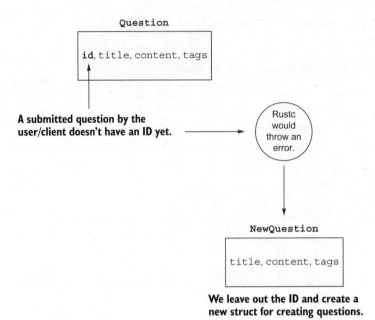

Figure 7.5   **We create a new question type for the creation of a question, which doesn't have an ID yet.**

Once we return or use the information inside our application, we fall back to the full Question type. The following listing shows the associated function in Store.

Listing 7.17   Adding the add_question function to store.rs

```rust
use crate::types::question::NewQuestion;
...

pub async fn add_question(
    &self,
    new_question: NewQuestion
) -> Result<Question, sqlx::Error> {
    match sqlx::query(
        "INSERT INTO questions (title, content, tags)
        VALUES ($1, $2, $3)
        RETURNING id, title, content, tags"
    )
    .bind(new_question.title)
    .bind(new_question.content)
    .bind(new_question.tags)
    .map(|row: PgRow| Question {
        id: QuestionId(row.get("id")),
        title: row.get("title"),
        content: row.get("content"),
        tags: row.get("tags"),
    })
```

```
    .fetch_one(&self.connection)
    .await
    {
        Ok(question) => Ok(question),
        Err(e) => Err(e),
    }
}

...
```

We pass NewQuestion to our function. The return signature is the same as with get_questions. We also repeat the pattern that we match on the Result of the sqlx::query, which looks a bit different now.

We specifically insert title, content, and tags (leaving id and creation_date to the database to fill this out for us), add three $+number signs that will be replaced by our bind variables during execution, and we also return something from the SQL itself.

The requesting client might be interested in the id that we created. Therefore, we return all the fields needed from the SQL query and can map the results to a Question type afterward and return the ID, if successful, from the add_question function.

With that in place, we can rewrite our add_question route handler, which is shown next.

Listing 7.18 Updating the `add_question` route handler in routes/question.rs

```
use crate::types::question::NewQuestion;
...

pub async fn add_question(
    store: Store,
    new_question: NewQuestion,
) -> Result<impl warp::Reply, warp::Rejection> {
    if let Err(e) = store.add_question(new_question).await {
        return Err(warp::reject::custom(Error::DatabaseQueryError(e)));
    }

    Ok(warp::reply::with_status("Question added", StatusCode::OK))
}

...
```

It could be called an antipattern to just wrap the database function inside another function and return it. In this case, though, we have an overarching pattern. We add route handlers to our routes object for Warp, and these route handlers return proper HTTP return codes.

We abstract the access to the database behind Store, so changing a route handler won't interfere (even by accident) with our SQL and other logic we need to make it work. To round it up, we present the last two question route handlers.

7.4.3 Adjusting the update and delete questions handler

The last two routes for our questions API are updating and deleting a question. We have everything in place now to add the needed functions inside store.rs and adjust the route handlers accordingly. We will reuse the patterns from the previous routes to store and route handler functions, and just adjust the SQL to fit our needs. The following listing shows the update_question store function to update a question entry in the database.

Listing 7.19 Updating a question in the database in store.rs

```
...

pub async fn update_question(
    &self,
    question: Question,
    question_id: i32
) -> Result<Question, sqlx::Error> {
    match sqlx::query(
        "UPDATE questions
        SET title = $1, content = $2, tags = $3
        WHERE id = $4
        RETURNING id, title, content, tags"
    )
    .bind(question.title)
    .bind(question.content)
    .bind(question.tags)
    .bind(question_id)
    .map(|row: PgRow| Question {
        id: QuestionId(row.get("id")),
        title: row.get("title"),
        content: row.get("content"),
        tags: row.get("tags"),
    })
    .fetch_one(&self.connection)
    .await {
        Ok(question) => Ok(question),
        Err(e) => Err(e),
    }
}
```

We are facing another design decision with the parameters of this function. We know that in our API, we expect an id parameter that specifies the to-be-updated question, and a body with the JSON of the updated question. We can pass this directly down to the route handler and the store function. Alternatively, we can choose to omit the ID and just pass the question around, which has the ID already included.

I decided to pass the id down to the last function, because there might be a case where a mismatch between the id and the id inside the question is wanted. In the SQL, we return the id, title, content, and tags of the question, so we can pass the question back up to the route handler, which can return it from there to the querying client.

The next listing shows the route handler for /questions/{id}.

Listing 7.20 `update_question` **inside routes/question.rs**

...

```
                                        Changes the type of
                                        the id for a question
pub async fn update_question(            from String to i32
    id: i32,                  ←─┘
    store: Store,
    question: Question,
) -> Result<impl warp::Reply, warp::Rejection> {
    let res = match store.update_question(question, id).await {
        Ok(res) => res,
        Err(e) => return
            Err(warp::reject::custom(Error::DatabaseQueryError(e))),
    };

    Ok(warp::reply::json(&res))
}
```

We call the `update_question` function inside `Store`, and return either an error or the resulting updated question. To delete a question, we can even save more lines of code and consider another way of executing our SQL via SQLx. The following listing shows the `Store` function accordingly.

Listing 7.21 `delete_question` **in store.rs**

...

```
pub async fn delete_question(
    &self,
    question_id: i32
) -> Result<bool, sqlx::Error> {
    match sqlx::query("DELETE FROM questions WHERE id = $1")
    .bind(question_id)
    .execute(&self.connection)
    .await {
        Ok(_) => Ok(true),
        Err(e) => Err(e),
    }
}
```

Here we pass the ID down to the function and use it for our WHERE clause in the SQL command. Instead of using `fetch_one`, we simply use `execute` from the SQLx library, since we can't return a row we just deleted. The following listing shows the route handler for deleting a question.

Listing 7.22 `delete_question` **route handler in routes/question.rs**

...

```
pub async fn delete_question(
    id: i32,
```

```
    store: Store,
) -> Result<impl warp::Reply, warp::Rejection> {
    if let Err(e) = store.delete_question(id).await {
        return Err(warp::reject::custom(Error::DatabaseQueryError(e)));
    }

    Ok(warp::reply::with_status(
        format!("Question {} deleted", id),
        StatusCode::OK)
    )
}
```

Another small change: we use the if-let pattern. Since we don't return any valuable information from the store function, we simply want to check if the function failed, and if not, we return 200 back to the client.

7.4.4   *Updating the add_answer route*

Last but not least, we have to make the same changes for our answers as well. First, we use the same pattern as we did with NewQuestion (a Question without an id), and use this NewAnswer for our add_answer route handler to parse the form-body from the incoming HTTP request. The following listing shows the src/types/answers.rs file with the added NewAnswer struct.

> **Listing 7.23   Adding the NewAnswer type to our answers module**

```
// ch_07/src/types/answers.rs

use serde::{Deserialize, Serialize};

use crate::types::question::QuestionId;

#[derive(Serialize, Deserialize, Debug, Clone)]
pub struct Answer {
    pub id: AnswerId,
    pub content: String,
    pub question_id: QuestionId,
}

#[derive(Deserialize, Serialize, Debug, Clone, PartialEq, Eq, Hash)]
pub struct AnswerId(pub i32);

#[derive(Deserialize, Serialize, Debug, Clone)]
pub struct NewAnswer {
    pub content: String,
    pub question_id: QuestionId,
}
```

And the next listing shows the updated route handler add_answer, where we expect NewAnswer as a parameter and pass it down to the store function.

```
// ch_07/src/routes/answer.rs

use warp::http::StatusCode;

use crate::store::Store;
use crate::types::answer::NewAnswer;

pub async fn add_answer(
    store: Store,
    new_answer: NewAnswer,
) -> Result<impl warp::Reply, warp::Rejection> {
    match store.add_answer(new_answer).await {
        Ok(_) => Ok(warp::reply::with_status(
            "Answer added",
            StatusCode::OK)
        ),
        Err(e) => Err(warp::reject::custom(e)),
    }
}
```

The only missing piece is the store function, shown here.

```
// ch_07/src/store.rs

use crate::types::{
    answer::{Answer, NewAnswer, AnswerId},
    question::{Question, QuestionId, NewQuestion},
};
...

    pub async fn add_answer(
        &self,
        new_answer: NewAnswer
    ) -> Result<Answer, Error> {
        match sqlx::query(
            "INSERT INTO answers (content, question_id) VALUES ($1, $2)"
        )
        .bind(new_answer.content)
        .bind(new_answer.question_id.0)
        .map(|row: PgRow| Answer {
                id: AnswerId(row.get("id")),
                content: row.get("content"),
                question_id: QuestionId(row.get("question_id")),
        })
        .fetch_one(&self.connection)
        .await {
            Ok(answer) => Ok(answer),
            Err(e) => {
                tracing::event!(tracing::Level::ERROR, "{:?}", e);
                 Err(Error::DatabaseQueryError(e))
            },
        }
    }
```

We can test the implementation by starting our application via `cargo run`, and start curl via your command line:

```
curl localhost:3030/questions
```

If everything worked, your result should be empty now. Since we query our database and didn't add any questions, we can't receive anything. We can see, however, that we omitted the `limit` and `offset` parameters, and the code still works.

7.5   *Error handling and tracing database interactions*

One important piece to understand is that we introduced a whole new layer of complexity and point of failure. The API might fail now for many reasons:

- The database is down.
- The SQL is wrong or outdated and fails.
- We return the wrong data for whatever reason.
- We try to insert data that is not valid (wrong ID, question not found, and so forth).

So far, we populate the database errors back to the user, which is not ideal at all, and I would say even an antipattern. We don't want to lose the errors either, however. The best way going forward could be to log the errors somewhere and return a 4*xx* or 5*xx* error back to the user in case something is off. Figure 7.6 is demonstrating this concept.

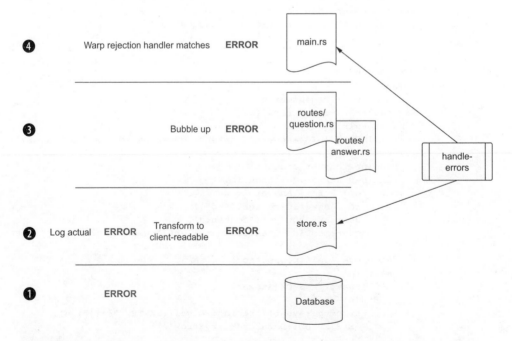

Figure 7.6   We log the actual error via the Tracing library and return a client-appropriate error from the store up to the Warp error handler we implemented in the handle-errors crate.

The first change we are going to make is moving DatabaseQueryError to Store, where we won't return any specific information of the error. This information stays inside our logging mechanism; therefore, we are also going to add a tracing event in an error case. The following listing shows the adjusted store.rs.

Listing 7.26 Returning `DatabaseQueryError` inside store.rs

```rust
use sqlx::postgres::{PgPoolOptions, PgPool, PgRow};
use sqlx::Row;

use handle_errors::Error;

...

    pub async fn get_questions(
        self,
        limit: Option<i32>,
        offset: i32
    ) -> Result<Vec<Question>, Error> {
        ...

            .await {
                Ok(questions) => Ok(questions),
                Err(e) => {
                    tracing::event!(tracing::Level::ERROR, "{:?}", e);
                    Err(Error::DatabaseQueryError)
                }
            }
    }

    pub async fn add_question(
        self,
        new_question: NewQuestion
    ) -> Result<Question, Error> {

            ...
            .await {
                Ok(question) => Ok(question),
                Err(e) => {
                    tracing::event!(tracing::Level::ERROR, "{:?}", e);
                    Err(Error::DatabaseQueryError)
                },
            }
    }

    pub async fn update_question(
        self,
        question: Question,
        id: i32
    ) -> Result<Question, Error> {
            ...

            .await {
                Ok(question) => Ok(question),
```

```
                Err(e) => {
                    tracing::event!(tracing::Level::ERROR, "{:?}", e);
                    Err(Error::DatabaseQueryError)
                },
            }
        }

        pub async fn delete_question(self, id: i32) -> Result<bool, Error> {
            ...

            .await {
                Ok(_) => Ok(true),
                Err(e) => {
                    tracing::event!(tracing::Level::ERROR, "{:?}", e);
                    Err(Error::DatabaseQueryError)
                },
            }
        }

        pub async fn add_answer(
            self,
            new_answer: NewAnswer
        ) -> Result<Answer, Error> {
                ...

                Ok(answer) => Ok(answer),
                Err(error) => {
                    tracing::event!(tracing::Level::ERROR, "{:?}", e);
                    Err(Error::DatabaseQueryError)
                },
            }
        }
    }
```

We are also going to remove SQLx from the handle-error crate again. You can, of course, decide otherwise, and handle SQLx errors inside the handle-error crate and implement the logging there. This choice comes down to the size and complexity of your application. Listing 7.28 shows the updated lib.rs file inside handle-errors. But first, we'll add the Tracing library to our dependencies in the handle-errors crate (listing 7.27).

> **Listing 7.27   Adding the Tracing library to the handle-errors dependencies**

```
[package]
name = "handle-errors"
version = "0.1.0"
edition = "2021"

[dependencies]
warp = "0.3"
tracing = { version = "0.1", features = ["log"] }
```

Now we can use the library throughout our crate.

Listing 7.28 Removing SQLx dependencies from handle-errors

```
use warp::{
    filters::{body::BodyDeserializeError, cors::CorsForbidden},
    http::StatusCode,
    reject::Reject,
    Rejection, Reply,
};
use sqlx::error::Error as SqlxError;
use tracing::{event, Level, instrument};

#[derive(Debug)]
pub enum Error {
    ParseError(std::num::ParseIntError),
    MissingParameters,
    QuestionNotFound,
    DatabaseQueryError(SqlxError),
    DatabaseQueryError,

}

impl std::fmt::Display for Error {
    fn fmt(&self, f: &mut std::fmt::Formatter) -> std::fmt::Result {
        match &*self {
            Error::ParseError(ref err) => {
                write!(f, "Cannot parse parameter: {}", err)
            },
            Error::MissingParameters => write!(f, "Missing parameter"),
            Error::QuestionNotFound => write!(f, "Question not found"),
            Error::DatabaseQueryError(_) => write!(f, "Cannot update, invalid
    data."),
            Error::DatabaseQueryError => {
                write!(f, "Cannot update, invalid data.")
            },
        }
    }
}

impl Reject for Error {}

#[instrument]
pub async fn return_error(r: Rejection) -> Result<impl Reply, Rejection> {
    if let Some(crate::Error::DatabaseQueryError) = r.find() {
        event!(
            Level::ERROR,
            code = error.as_database_er-
    ror().unwrap().code().unwrap().parse::<i32>().unwrap(),
            db_message = error.as_database_error().unwrap().message(),
            constraint = error.as_database_error().unwrap().con-
    straint().unwrap()
        );
        event!(Level::ERROR, "Database query error");
        Ok(warp::reply::with_status(
            crate::Error::DatabaseQueryError.to_string(),
            "Invalid entity".to_string(),
```

```
                StatusCode::UNPROCESSABLE_ENTITY,
        ))
    } else if let Some(error) = r.find::<CorsForbidden>() {
        event!(Level::ERROR, "CORS forbidden error: {}", error);
        Ok(warp::reply::with_status(
            error.to_string(),
            StatusCode::FORBIDDEN,
        ))
    } else if let Some(error) = r.find::<BodyDeserializeError>() {
        event!(Level::ERROR, "Cannot deserizalize request body: {}", error);
        Ok(warp::reply::with_status(
            error.to_string(),
            StatusCode::UNPROCESSABLE_ENTITY,
        ))
    } else if let Some(error) = r.find::<Error>() {
        event!(Level::ERROR, "{}", error);
        Ok(warp::reply::with_status(
            error.to_string(),
            StatusCode::UNPROCESSABLE_ENTITY,
        ))
    } else {
        event!(Level::WARN, "Requested route was not found");
        Ok(warp::reply::with_status(
            "Route not found".to_string(),
            StatusCode::NOT_FOUND,
        ))
    }
}
```

We took the chance to clean up some older pieces of code we don't rely on anymore
(QuestionNotFoundError, for example). This design decision gives us the opportunity
to remove anything in relation to the underlying error inside our route handlers.
They simply populate the error and pass it on to the upper layer. The following listing
shows the removal of the Error::DatabaseQueryError inside routes/question.rs.

Listing 7.29   Remove Error::DatabaseQueryError from /routes/question.rs

```
use std::collections::HashMap;

use warp::http::StatusCode;
use tracing::{instrument, event, Level};

use handle_errors::Error;

use crate::store::Store;
use crate::types::pagination::{Pagination, extract_pagination};
use crate::types::question::{Question, NewQuestion};

#[instrument]
pub async fn get_questions(
    params: HashMap<String, String>,
    store: Store,
) -> Result<impl warp::Reply, warp::Rejection> {
```

```
        event!(target: "practical_rust_book", Level::INFO, "querying questions");
        let mut pagination = Pagination::default();

        if !params.is_empty() {
            event!(Level::INFO, pagination = true);
            pagination = extract_pagination(params)?;
        }

        match store.get_questions(pagination.limit, pagination.offset).await {
            Ok(res) => Ok(warp::reply::json(&res)),
            Err(e) => Err(warp::reject::custom(e)),
        }
}

pub async fn update_question(
    id: i32,
    store: Store,
    question: Question,
) -> Result<impl warp::Reply, warp::Rejection> {
    match store.update_question(question, id).await {
        Ok(res) => Ok(warp::reply::json(&res)),
        Err(e) => Err(warp::reject::custom(e)),
    }
}


pub async fn delete_question(
    id: i32,
    store: Store,
) -> Result<impl warp::Reply, warp::Rejection> {
    match store.delete_question(id).await {
        Ok(_) => Ok(warp::reply::with_status(
            format!("Question {} deleted", id),
            StatusCode::OK
        )),
        Err(e) => Err(warp::reject::custom(e)),
    }
}

pub async fn add_question(
    store: Store,
    new_question: NewQuestion,
) -> Result<impl warp::Reply, warp::Rejection> {
    match store.add_question(new_question).await {
        Ok(_) => Ok(warp::reply::with_status(
            "Question added",
            StatusCode::OK
        )),
        Err(e) => Err(warp::reject::custom(e)),
    }
}
```

The same is going to take place inside our answer route handler. We can see that our route handlers really don't do much. In this case, feel free to move the store logic up into the handlers themselves. However, in slightly more complex web services, the route handler is doing more than just passing data up and down, and if we ever want to replace PostgreSQL with another database, or add caching, we won't have to touch the route handlers at all.

When trying to add an answer to a nonexistent question, we get the following output on the command line (formatted for print purposes):

```
$ cargo run
    Compiling practical-rust-book v0.1.0
      (/Users/bgruber/CodingIsFun/Manning/code/ch_07)
     Finished dev [unoptimized + debuginfo] target(s) in 11.82s
      Running `target/debug/practical-rust-book`
Feb 01 13:39:07.065 ERROR practical_rust_book::store:
    code=23503
    db_message="insert or update on table \"answers\"
        violates foreign key constraint
        \"answers_corresponding_question_fkey\""
        constraint="answers_corresponding_question_fkey"
Feb 01 13:39:07.066 ERROR warp::filters::trace:
    unable to process request (internal error)
    status=500
    error=Rejection(
        [DatabaseQueryError, MethodNotAllowed,
         MethodNotAllowed,MethodNotAllowed]
    )
Feb 01 13:39:07.066 ERROR handle_errors: Database query error
```

And the client receives a 422 HTTP error response with the following message:

```
Cannot update, invalid data.
```

Now we've separated the information we keep inside our system from the HTTP response and HTTP code we send back to the requesting client, without losing any information. Internally and externally, we can make many adjustments:

- Change the message based on the SQL error code.
- Change the HTTP error code based on the SQL error code.
- Log more or less information internally.

The codebase now has a good size to play around with and adjust based on your needs. Having such a small codebase is also a great playground for future exploration. If you want to try out new functionality on a crate that you need for your day-to-day job, having a large enough codebase to do so can save you a huge amount of time.

7.6 *Integrating SQL migrations*

So far, we set up the tables by hand before using SQLx to update and delete rows from them. In a real-world scenario, the layout of your data changes, and you can't possibly expect new developers to go through the manual process of creating tables by hand just so they can run your application.

For these use cases, it is advised to use *migrations*. These are files that have a time-stamp attached to their filename. They include SQL queries that alter the layout of your tables or create them from scratch. Next to your database, a migration tool will create a separate table just to keep track of which migration was run last, to know which ones still have to be processed.

Let's say you start your application with questions and answers, but later you want to add comments and maybe add users to the questions. You can either choose to alter the table by hand and adjust the code, or you write migration files to do it for you.

When another developer joins the team or you deploy your application at some point to a new cloud provider, all previous migrations will be run until the last one— from the initial setup of your table until the last one, updating and adding users and comments.

The SQLx crate offers us two ways of running migrations. It has a CLI tool that can create and run them, and at the same time, in the base SQLx crate is a macro called `migrate!` that runs the files in the migrations folder for us.

You could use SQLx CLI (https://crates.io/crates/sqlx-cli) in your Docker or any other build environment when you deploy your application to be sure the database tables are up-to-date and match the current structs in your codebase. Or you create the migration files by hand (be aware of the order) and use the macro to run them before you start your server.

In our example, we are going to use both, just to get a feel for each way. We are going to install SQLx CLI via `cargo install`:

```
$ cargo install sqlx-cli
```

We can now create our first migration:

```
$ sqlx migrate add -r questions_table
```

This will create a new folder called migrations in our root directory, with two empty files, called 20220509150516_questions_table.up.sql and 20220509150516_questions_table.down.sql. The timestamp before the name will depend on when you execute the command. The filename not only has the `questions_table` in the title, but also the key-words up and down. When creating migrations, we not only want to create or alter a table, but also to be able to revert a SQL command.

In the *_questions_table.up.sql file, we create the `questions` table:

```
CREATE TABLE IF NOT EXISTS questions (
    id serial PRIMARY KEY,
    title VARCHAR (255) NOT NULL,
    content TEXT NOT NULL,
    tags TEXT [],
    created_on TIMESTAMP NOT NULL DEFAULT NOW()
);
```

And in the *_questions_table.down.sql file, we do the reverse, dropping the questions table:

```
DROP TABLE IF EXISTS questions;
```

We try dropping our previous questions and answers tables first to see if the migration works. Log into PSQL and drop the questions table:

```
$ psql rustwebdev
rustwebdev=# drop table answers, questions;
DROP TABLE
rustwebdev=#
```

Now from the command line, we can run the first migration:

```
$ sqlx migrate run --database-url postgresql://localhost:5432/rustwebdev
Applied 20220116194720/migrate questions table (5.37987ms)
```

It worked! We can do the same for answers:

```
$ sqlx migrate add -r answers_table
```

Go to the newly created *_answers_table.up.sql file and add the SQL statement:

```
CREATE TABLE IF NOT EXISTS answers (
    id serial PRIMARY KEY,
    content TEXT NOT NULL,
    created_on TIMESTAMP NOT NULL DEFAULT NOW(),
    corresponding_question integer REFERENCES questions
);
```

And the *_answers.down.sql file drops the answers table:

```
DROP TABLE IF EXISTS answers;
```

And runs them:

```
$ sqlx migrate run --database-url postgresql://localhost:5432/rustwebdev
Applied 20220116194720/migrate answers table (5.37987ms)
```

Logging into PSQL shows us the created questions and answers tables, plus an internal _sqlx_migrations table to keep track of the already run migrations:

```
$ psql rustwebdev
psql (14.1)
Type "help" for help.

rustwebdev=# \dt
            List of relations
 Schema |       Name       | Type  |  Owner
--------+------------------+-------+---------
 public | _sqlx_migrations | table | bgruber
```

```
public | answers        | table | bgruber
public | questions      | table | bgruber
(3 rows)
```

We can now try to revert our changes. Each revert will trigger the latest migration and try to run the *.down.sql script:

```
$ sqlx migrate revert --database-url "postgresql://localhost:5432/rustwebdev"

Applied 20220514145724/revert answers table (5.696291ms)

$ sqlx migrate revert --database-url "postgresql://localhost:5432/rustwebdev"

Applied 20220509150516/revert questions table (2.82ms)
```

You might have a setup script in your build pipeline where you can trigger command-line tools. But we can also trigger these migrations directly from within our codebase, via the migrate! macro from the SQLx crate. We choose to run the migrations before we start the server in our codebase and fail early if we can't accomplish them. The advantage here is that other developers have no options but to run the migrations, whereas a setup bash script, for example, can be easily forgotten to be run. The following listing shows the updated main.rs file.

Listing 7.30 Executing migrations via our codebase

```
...

#[tokio::main]
async fn main() {
    let log_filter = std::env::var("RUST_LOG").unwrap_or_else(|_| {
        "handle_errors=warn,practical_rust_book=info,warp=error".to_owned()
    });

    let store = store::Store::new("postgres://localhost:5432/rustwebdev").await;

    sqlx::migrate!()
        .run(&store.clone().connection)
        .await
        .expect("Cannot run migration");

    let store_filter = warp::any().map(move || store.clone());

    ...

}
```

You can go ahead and try deleting the created tables and rerun your server. Make sure to also always drop the migrations table, because SQLx will check this table first if all migrations are up-to-date. If you delete all created tables but the migrations table, you will get an error.

7.7   *Case study: Switching database management systems*

Say you develop your application and figure out that the current database management system (DBMS) doesn't fulfill your needs anymore (let's say you started with MySQL and now want to move to PostgreSQL). How hard would it be to switch out the DBMS, and how would it affect your code?

We can account for changes and make them easier through abstractions as we already did:

- Just the store object should host information about how to connect to the database and have the database-related information.
- Every other part of the application should use exposed store functions.
- For example, the route handlers shouldn't know or touch anything database related. They should run the exposed functions from a store object.

Now, switching from MySQL to PostgreSQL has no impact on our business logic. However, keep in mind the following implications:

- The SQL queries might change slightly when using a different DBMS.
- Your database crate has to support connecting and querying your new database server (be it PostgreSQL, MySQL, or SQLite, for example).
- Not all database types might be supported by your new management system of choice (when moving from PostgreSQL to SQLite, for example, arrays are no longer supported).

With the choice of SQLx earlier in the chapter, switching databases requires a few steps. To demonstrate a possible change, and to break a few things, we are choosing SQLite after having used PostgreSQL so far in the book. First, we need to add the new DBMS as a feature to our Cargo.toml import.

> **Listing 7.31   Adding SQLite as a feature for the SQLx database crate**

```
[package]
name = "practical-rust-book"
version = "0.1.0"
edition = "2021"

[dependencies]
...
tracing-subscriber = "0.2"
// Formatted for print purposes
// This has to be all one line
sqlx = { version = "0.5",
    features = [ "runtime-tokio-rustls", "migrate", "sqlite" ] }
```

Next, we go to our store.rs file and replace our previous sqlx::postgres import with sqlx::sqlite, and change the .map functions to return SqliteRow instead of a PgRow. We also have to change the connection type in the Store struct from PqPool to SqlitePool, and return SqlitePoolOptions from the new function.

Listing 7.32   Replacing PostgreSQL with SQLite in store.rs

```rust
use sqlx::sqlite::{SqlitePool, SqlitePoolOptions, SqliteRow};
use sqlx::postgres::{PgPool, PgPoolOptions, PgRow};
use sqlx::Row;

...

#[derive(Debug, Clone)]
pub struct Store {
    pub connection: SqlitePool,
}

impl Store {
    pub async fn new(db_url: &str) -> Self {
        let db_pool = match SqlitePoolOptions::new()
        .max_connections(5)
        .connect(db_url).await {
            Ok(pool) => pool,
            Err(e) => panic!("Couldn't establish DB connection: {}", e),
        };

        Store {
            connection: db_pool,
        }
    }

    pub async fn get_questions(
        &self,
        limit: Option<u32>,
        offset: u32
    ) -> Result<Vec<Question>, Error> {
        match sqlx::query("SELECT * from questions LIMIT $1 OFFSET $2")
            .bind(limit)
            .bind(offset)
            .map(|row: SqliteRow| Question {
                id: QuestionId(row.get("id")),
                title: row.get("title"),
                content: row.get("content"),
                tags: row.get("tags"),
            })
            .fetch_all(&self.connection)
            .await {
                Ok(questions) => Ok(questions),
                Err(e) => {
                    tracing::event!(tracing::Level::ERROR, "{:?}", e);
                    Err(Error::DatabaseQueryError)
                }
            }
    }
}

...
```

However, not all is good. The compiler throws the following error:

```
error[E0277]: the trait bound `Vec<std::string::String>: Type<Sqlite>`
is not satisfied
  --> src/store.rs:83:27
   |
83 |                   tags: row.get("tags"),
   |                         ^^^ the trait `Type<Sqlite>` is not
   |                             implemented for `Vec<std::string::String>`
```

SQLite doesn't implement arrays, so we would have to work around that constraint (by storing a JSON string and parsing it into a `Vec` after fetching it from the database, for example). The missing array type also impacts our migration files. We can't use the same SQL or the same structs we used with PostgreSQL. We have to either simplify our models (and remove the `tags`, for example) or adjust our SQL. The only other change we have to make is adjusting our database URL inside main.rs.

Listing 7.33   Updating the SQL URL in main.rs to switch from PostgreSQL to SQLite

```
...

#[tokio::main]
async fn main() {
    let log_filter = std::env::var("RUST_LOG").unwrap_or_else(|_| {
        "handle_errors=warn,practical_rust_book=warn,warp=warn".to_owned()
    });

    let store = store::Store::new("sqlite:rustwebdev.db").await;

    sqlx::migrate!()
        .run(&store.clone().connection)
        .await
        .expect("Cannot migrate DB");

...
```

That is basically it. We don't touch any business logic or route handlers, and all we have to do is create a local rustwebdev.db file and start our server again.

Summary

- You have to decide whether you prefer an ORM to handle your database queries or would rather write your SQL yourself.
- The de facto crate to handle your SQL queries is SQLx in the Rust ecosystem.
- Adding a database to your web service opens many design decisions about your codebase.
- It is generally advised to separate the data layer from the other business logic.
- With smaller applications, it could make sense to query the database directly from the route handlers.
- With SQLx, you write plain SQL yourself and pass the resulting data around in your application.

- You use the `bind` function to add local values to your SQL query.
- Use `fetch/fetch_one/fetch_all` when data will be returned a query, and execute when no data will be returned.
- You are adding a whole new layer of complexity, so don't forget to properly instrument/trace the internal interactions with your database and codebase to spot errors.
- It is best to create, drop, and alter your tables via migrations.
- You can run migrations from your codebase or via a command-line tool.
- Switching out the DBMS doesn't affect our business logic, but depending on the new system you are choosing (SQLite or MySQL, for example), you have to adapt to the supported database types.

Integrate third-party APIs

8

This chapter covers

- Sending HTTP requests from your codebase
- Authenticating at third-party APIs
- Modeling structs for JSON responses
- Sending multiple requests at once
- Handling timeouts and retries
- Integrating external HTTP calls in your route handlers

There is rarely a web service that doesn't need to communicate with either third-party APIs or internally with other microservices. For this book, we are making HTTP requests to external APIs to demonstrate how that affects your codebase. It is up to you, after having a basic understanding of how to use HTTP crates in conjunction with Tokio, to find another crate able to talk the protocol of your choosing.

Use cases for sending HTTP requests can be as follows:

- Shortening shared URLs in questions and answers
- Verifying addresses when creating new accounts
- Showing stock data when adding stock symbols in the questions/answers

- Sending out emails or text messages when someone answers your question
- Sending account creation emails

And these are just examples from our tiny application we built so far. Being able to send HTTP requests is important when you want to move toward using Rust in production. Another interesting use case is handling multiple HTTP requests at once. We will use our runtime of choice (Tokio) to `join!` various network requests and execute them in a bundle.

> **NOTE** The +join! macro allows a runtime to run multiple async operations on the same thread concurrently (but not in parallel). If one of these async operations blocks the thread, others will also stop making progress (for reference, see http://mng.bz/ne5g).

When integrating external requests into your route handler, it is crucial to execute them as fast as possible, and to provide clear logging and HTTP responses to the user. Like the database addition in chapter 7, external HTTP requests add a new layer of complexity and points of failure. Therefore, using Tracing here is important as well. Another aspect you have to think about is to authenticate for third-party API services. Often this means creating an account and copying the API token from the website into your environment file.

Since Rust is a systems programming language, you have different levels of abstractions when choosing to send HTTP (or even TCP) requests. You can either choose to implement everything by yourself again (on top of the TCP abstraction in the library) or choose Hyper, which offers HTTP abstractions but no comfortable way of handling the response from a request. The following listing shows a GET implementation via Hyper, where we simply print the results onto the command line.

Listing 8.1   HTTP GET implementation via Hyper

```rust
use hyper::{body::HttpBody as _, Client};
use tokio::io::{self, AsyncWriteExt as _};

type Result<T> =
    std::result::Result<T, Box<dyn std::error::Error + Send + Sync>>;

#[tokio::main]
async fn main() -> Result<()> {
    let client = Client::new();

    let mut res = client.get("http://www.google.com".parse::<hyper::Uri>()
        .unwrap()).await?;

    println!("Response: {}", res.status());
    println!("Headers: {:#?}\n", res.headers());

    while let Some(next) = res.data().await {
        let chunk = next?;
```

```
        io::stdout().write_all(&chunk).await?;
    }

    println!("\n\nDone!");

    Ok(())
}
```

If you want to run this example at home, don't forget to add Hyper and Tokio to your dependencies:

```
[dependencies]
hyper = { version = "0.14", features = ["full"] }
tokio = { version = "1", features = ["full"] }
```

In some cases, you might want to have a more lightweight implementation and don't need all the bells and whistles. Another crate is Reqwest, which is built on top of Hyper and offers more layers of abstraction. Listing 8.2 shows an example HTTP GET request.

> **NOTE**   Check with your web framework of choice; maybe it already integrates an HTTP client or supports a crate other than Reqwest. The Actix Web framework, for example, advises using the Actix Web Client (awc); see https://crates.io/crates/awc.

Listing 8.2   Example HTTP GET with Reqwest

```
#[tokio::main]
async fn main() -> Result<(), Box<dyn std::error::Error>> {
    let client = reqwest::Client::new();
    let res = client.post("http://httpbin.org/post")
        .body("the exact body is sent")
        .send()
        .await?
        .text()
        .await?;

    println!("{:?}", res);

    Ok(())
}
```

We can see that Reqwest offers us functions like text (http://mng.bz/vXyJ) that we can call on top of the result. In most cases when working with the Tokio runtime, Reqwest is the crate of choice when it comes to sending HTTP requests. For completion's sake, the dependencies you need to run this example are the following:

```
[dependencies]
reqwest = { version = "0.11", features = ["json"] }
tokio = { version = "1", features = ["full"] }
```

Many crates offer *features*, which enable the user to get a more lightweight version into their own codebase. Instead of pulling the whole crate into your project, you can choose to opt in or out of certain features. This can also be the cause for some headaches—for example, when you want to work with JSON in your HTTP workflow but forget to import the JSON feature set from Reqwest.

8.1 Preparing the codebase

We are going to use Reqwest as our HTTP client crate. As with every new crate in the async Rust ecosystem, we have to check whether an HTTP client is supported by our runtime. We can choose a synchronous HTTP client, of course, and in some instances this might be sufficient. But in our case, we might have to send out multiple HTTP requests per minute, and doing this asynchronously gives us a nice performance boost.

> ### What if an async crate is using a different runtime?
> If you don't want to choose Reqwest but rather a crate that depends on another runtime, what would be the consequences? The Tokio runtime, after being started, creates a new operating system thread. Then it uses internal logic to spawn new tasks and does the work needed. If you now use a crate with a different runtime, this new runtime will also need an operating system thread to do the work it needs to do (like sending out HTTP requests through the kernel, for example).
>
> This means your application will be heavier in terms of operating system resources, and harder to debug because you have to monitor multiple operating system threads to get an idea about possible bottlenecks or other issues. Therefore, even if you dislike handling the available HTTP crate that supports your current runtime, keep in mind that the cost of runtime complexity is probably higher than the cognitive load of maintaining code you slightly dislike.

8.1.1 Picking an API

For our use case, a question-and-answer service, we can choose various third-party APIs to enhance our service. We might use third-party APIs to display stock-ticker symbols next to mentioned companies, display nutrition information next to mentioned food, or block swear words when the site has to be especially kid friendly. It really depends on your use case.

For this book, we use the Bad Words API, which runs a profanity check for given text. We picked it because it opens a lot more questions and nuances, which you can implement in your own time after reading the book to further enhance your Rust skills. For example:

- Should we permanently overwrite the content of questions and answers by blocking out profane words, or do we store two versions of the text?
- Do we block out profane words just when returning the content to the requesting client and store the original in our database?

- Do we block these words based on a website setting that we need to check locally or per request?
- Do different countries consider different words profane?

We will go through one workflow. As mentioned, thinking about more options for your own implementation is an interesting exercise to challenge your solution design.

Without being affiliated in any way, we picked the Bad Words API (http://mng .bz/49ma) from a company called *APILayer*. This is one of the fastest and easiest APIs I found to use in this context; it is free for our test scenario, and the documentation is sufficient. Please don't see this as a general recommendation for this service, but of course feel free to explore the website and do your own research.

When opening the documentation for the API (http://mng.bz/XaGG), we can get clear requirements for what the endpoint expects (a header, for example, with the API key):

```
curl --request POST \
--url 'https://api.apilayer.com/bad_words?censor_character=*' \
--header 'apikey: xxxxxxx' \
--data-raw '{body}'
```

We can also see what we are going to receive (JSON with various key–value pairs):

```
{
  "bad_words_list": [
    {
      "deviations": 0,
      "end": 16,
      "info": 2,
      "original": "shitty",
      "replacedLen": 6,
      "start": 10,
      "word": "shitty"
    }
  ],
  "bad_words_total": 1,
  "censored_content": "this is a ****** sentence",
  "content": "this is a shitty sentence"
}
```

Your next steps depend highly on the complexity of the API endpoint. Sometimes you even want to move all of the logic out to a separate microservice and do the querying and manipulating of the data there, before returning it back to the route handler.

As with any documentation, it might be out-of-date. Therefore, it is best not to blindly trust the website but check the exact responses from the API for yourself. A quick way of verifying the endpoint results is using either curl (https://curl.se/docs/ manual.html) on the command line, or an application like Postman (www.postman .com), as seen in figure 8.1, which also provides the option to store a set of requests so you can easily repeat them in the future.

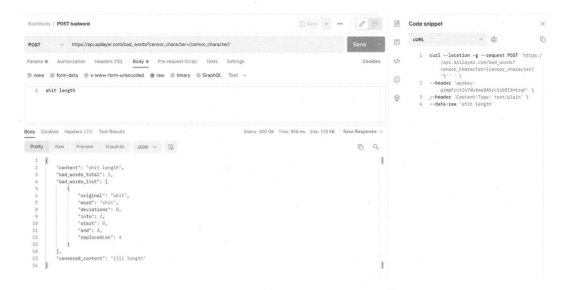

Figure 8.1   An application like Postman lets you collect and save HTTP requests so you can easily refire them and therefore quickly test endpoints and workflows.

8.1.2   *Getting to know our HTTP crate*

After we have a sense of the various responses we can get, it is time to query the endpoint with Rust code and see how to iterate over the first implementation for a solid solution. If this is the first time you are trying out a new crate, my recommendation is to create a new Cargo project on your local hard drive and integrate just the needed crates to play around with the code examples provided by the crate's Git repository.

If it's not an overly complex crate, you can use the Rust Playground website to try out a few things. The reason is the following: when using a new crate, if you don't get the response you expect, you won't know immediately whether the problem is in your code or you are using the crate incorrectly.

An additional complexity occurs when using Rust. When adding a new code example, you might have to fight a bit with the borrow checker and the ownership model. You want to first test the easiest path, make sure it works, and then implement it in your codebase. If you are already used to the library, feel free to skip this step and integrate the needed code immediately in the actual codebase.

> **Life hack when using crates**
>
> When using crates, it is helpful to first try the happy path (the best possible scenario). This requires removing every line of code not needed for the solution to work. I've learned that it is helpful to have a folder on your hard drive, named after the crate, and then implement a few examples either as separate Rust projects or as one larger

(continued)

one. The advantage is that if you "quickly" want to try out a new feature or a different way of doing things, you can do it in your private codebase first.

The Rust Playground helps with this, as you can save playgrounds and bookmark them. If you then encounter a problem in your codebase, you can jump to your smaller example codebases and test certain crate APIs or features and see whether they work.

This is the small downside of using Rust: it demands almost perfect code before compilation. Adding new complexity often has side effects related to ownership principles that need to be solved first. This costs time, and if you want to iterate faster over a possible solution, smaller helper projects let you know faster whether certain workflows are possible.

However, it might be a good idea to create the smallest possible Rust project with just the crates needed to make the request and try multiple scenarios. Once it works in this little project, you can move the code over to your actual codebase. You already saw an example HTTP POST request in this chapter's introduction.

We can adjust the example to use the actual API endpoint and figure out how to add the parameters needed for the call. After subscribing to the API (for free), you can visit the documentation website (http://mng.bz/XaGG) to display the example HTTP call and see the API key you have to send with the HTTP POST request. This will result in the example code in listing 8.3.

NOTE Adding the API key directly into source code is an absolute no-go. However, teaching material has to make certain sacrifices. Chapter 10 shows how to properly handle secrets via environment variables and files. Introducing these concepts here would cloud out the points I want to make. So please bear with me and know not to copy this code into a production environment.

Listing 8.3   Sending a POST to our API endpoint

Creates a new client that will allow us to send out HTTP requests

The post method will use HTTP POST behind the scenes and accepts a &str as the URL.

```
#[tokio::main]
async fn main() -> Result<(), Box<dyn std::error::Error>> {
    let client = reqwest::Client::new();
    let res = client
        .post("https://api.apilayer.com/bad_words?censor_character=*")
        .header("apikey", "xxxxx")
        .body("a list with shit words")
        .send()
        .await?
        .text()
        .await?;
```

The result of send is just the headers of the response. To get the body, we need .text, which is also asynchronous.

The send method is asynchronous and can return an error, so we add .await and a "?" behind it.

Adds the authorization header manually and as a key–value pair

The body contains our content we want to check for profane words.

```
    println!("{}", res);

    Ok(())
}
```

A first cargo run returns the following (formatted for print purposes):

```
$ cargo run
{"content": "a list with shit words", "bad_words_total": 1,
"bad_words_list": [{"original": "shit", "word": "shit", "deviations": 0,
"info": 2, "start": 12, "end": 16, "replacedLen": 4}], "censored_content":
"a list with **** words"}
```

This was a success. With this simple example working, we can play around with different parameters and get to know the crate before we include it in our codebase. A good place to start, as always, is reading the documentation: https://docs.rs/reqwest/latest/reqwest/. After we feel comfortable handling a few use cases, we can move on to integrate the solution in our codebase.

8.1.3   Adding an example HTTP call with Reqwest

First, we need to add the crate to the Cargo.toml file. We are going to include the JSON feature set, because we want to deserialize the response from JSON to a local struct.

> **Listing 8.4   Adding Reqwest to Cargo.toml**

```
[package]
name = "practical-rust-book"
version = "0.1.0"
edition = "2021"

[dependencies]
...

log4rs = "1.0"
uuid = { version = "0.8", features = ["v4"] }
tracing = { version = "0.1", features = ["log"] }
tracing-subscriber = "0.2"
sqlx = { version = "0.5", features = [ "runtime-tokio-rustls", "migrate",
"postgres" ] }
reqwest = { version = "0.11", features = ["json"] }
```

Next, we can start thinking about where such a request to an external API might happen. We want to censor, or have the option to mark, profane words. This can either happen before we store questions or answers to the database, or we run the check before we display the questions and answers, so the frontend has the ability to hide these words in case the user is under 18 (or whatever age you decide).

For a first test, we want to integrate the call to the Bad Words API when we are saving new questions to the database. For now, we simply overwrite the bad words and replace them with a symbol. I mention again that this is a great exercise to think through to store both the original sentence and the censored sentence.

Therefore, the very next step is to copy and paste the example from our helper project into the `add_question` route handler and see if we can get the exact same result as previously. Listing 8.5 shows the updated piece of code. Be aware that we have our API key hardcoded in our question.rs file. We change this in chapter 10, when we prepare our codebase to be deployed to production and read this API key from an environment file.

> **Listing 8.5   Adding the HTTP call to routes/question.rs**

```
...

pub async fn add_question(
    store: Store,
    new_question: NewQuestion,
) -> Result<impl warp::Reply, warp::Rejection> {
    let client = reqwest::Client::new();
    let res = client
        .post("https://api.apilayer.com/bad_words?censor_character=*")
        .header("apikey", "xxxxx")
        .body("a list with shit words")
        .send()
        .await?
        .text()
        .await?;

    println!("{}", res);

    match store.add_question(new_question).await {
        Ok(_) => Ok(warp::reply::with_status(
            "Question added",
            StatusCode::OK
        )),
        Err(e) => Err(warp::reject::custom(e)),
    }
}
```

But before we can even run the code, the compiler throws us an error message:

```
error[E0277]: the trait bound `reqwest::Error: warp::reject::Reject`
is not satisfied
   --> src/routes/question.rs:161:15
    |
161 |          .await?
    |               ^ the trait `warp::reject::Reject` is not
    |                 implemented for `reqwest::Error`
    |
    = note: required because of the requirements on the impl of
`From<reqwest::Error>` for `Rejection`
    = note: required because of the requirements on the impl of
`FromResidual<Result<Infallible, reqwest::Error>>` for `Result<_,
Rejection>`
```

This is the reason I mentioned earlier to start from a simple codebase: because these error messages let us think, "Hmm, maybe I misunderstood how this crate behaves or maybe I have a typo somewhere." But this is not the case. This error comes up because we return a `warp::Reject` error from the route handlers, but the `try!` block (for which the `?` is a shortcut) is returning a Reqwest error.

We have seen this before in earlier chapters, and this was the whole reason around creating the handle-errors crate to combine errors and convert them to Warp errors so we can answer incoming HTTP requests with proper Warp HTTP errors. Therefore, we have to think about how to handle the case that Reqwest returns an error and how we want to communicate this internally to our logs and externally to the user.

8.1.4   *Handling errors for external API requests*

The error message we get from the compiler is the following:

```
the trait `warp::reject::Reject` is not implemented for `reqwest::Error`
```

We somehow have to try to implement `Reject` for the `reqwest::Error` type. We have to know, however, that we don't own `reqwest::Error`. And by Rust's design, we are not allowed to implement a trait for a type we don't own. That's very important to remember and understand, because it has design implications for the solutions you create.

However, we can wrap the `reqwest::Error` in our already created `Error` enum, which we already do for other error types. We put our focus on the handle-errors crate we created during our journey through this book for now. We have to add Reqwest to its dependencies so we can encapsulate the error from the crate in our own `Error` enum.

Listing 8.6   Adding Reqwest to the error-handling crate

```
[package]
name = "handle-errors"
version = "0.1.0"
edition = "2021"

[dependencies]
warp = "0.3"
tracing = { version = "0.1", features = ["log"] }
reqwest = "0.11"
```

Next, we open lib.rs and extend the error handling with a possible `reqwest` API error. The following listing shows the extended code for handle-errors.

Listing 8.7   Extend handle-errors/src/lib.rs with a possible `reqwest::Error`

```
...

use tracing::{event, Level, instrument};
use reqwest::Error as ReqwestError;
```

```
#[derive(Debug)]
pub enum Error {
    ParseError(std::num::ParseIntError),
    MissingParameters,
    DatabaseQueryError,
    ExternalAPIError(ReqwestError),          ◁──┐  Adds a new
}                                                  enum variant

impl std::fmt::Display for Error {
    fn fmt(&self, f: &mut std::fmt::Formatter) -> std::fmt::Result {
        match &*self {
            Error::ParseError(ref err) => {
                write!(f, "Cannot parse parameter: {}", err)
            },
            Error::MissingParameters => write!(f, "Missing parameter"),
            Error::DatabaseQueryError => {
                write!(f, "Cannot update, invalid data.")
            },
            Error::ExternalAPIError(err) => {
                write!(f, "Cannot execute: {}", err)        ◁──┐  To be able to log or
            },                                                     print the error, we
        }                                                          need to also implement
    }                                                              the Display trait for
}                                                                  this new variant.

impl Reject for Error {}

#[instrument]
pub async fn return_error(r: Rejection) -> Result<impl Reply, Rejection> {
    if let Some(crate::Error::DatabaseQueryError) = r.find() {
        event!(Level::ERROR, "Database query error");
        Ok(warp::reply::with_status(
            crate::Error::DatabaseQueryError.to_string(),
            StatusCode::UNPROCESSABLE_ENTITY,
        ))
    } else if let Some(crate::Error::ExternalAPIError(e)) = r.find() {     ◁──┐
        event!(Level::ERROR, "{}", e);                                          Extends the if/else
        Ok(warp::reply::with_status(                                            block, where we check
            "Internal Server Error".to_string(),                               for our new error, and
            StatusCode::INTERNAL_SERVER_ERROR,                                  if we find it, logs the
        ))                                                                      details and returns
    } else if let Some(error) = r.find::<CorsForbidden>() {                     500 to the client
        event!(Level::ERROR, "CORS forbidden error: {}", error);
        Ok(warp::reply::with_status(
            error.to_string(),
            StatusCode::FORBIDDEN,
        ))

    ...
```

We extend the handle-error crate exactly as we did before with `DatabaseQueryError` and others. In this case, we also expect a parameter that holds the actual error message, so we know exactly what went wrong.

With this in place, we can focus again on our route handler and see how to transform the thrown error message by Request to our internal error type. As you may remember, we are getting an error because Request by default returns an internal `reqwest::Error` type, but our route handlers are returning `warp::Reject` in case of an error. Now we can't implement the `Reject` trait onto a type we don't own, so we implemented our own `Error` enum, and we return a variation of the enum in our route handler, which in turn has the `Reject` trait implemented so Warp and the compiler are satisfied.

This means we somehow have to transform `reqwest::Error` into our own enum `Error`. Luckily with Rust, we can use a method called `.map_err` on a `Result` type, which can take an error and return something else (http://mng.bz/yagG).

Listing 8.8   Example usage of `.map_err` from the Rust docs

```rust
fn stringify(x: u32) -> String { format!("error code: {}", x) }

let x: Result<u32, u32> = Ok(2);
assert_eq!(x.map_err(stringify), Ok(2));

let x: Result<u32, u32> = Err(13);
assert_eq!(x.map_err(stringify), Err("error code: 13".to_string()));
```

The following listing shows how we can apply this thinking to our added piece of code.

Listing 8.9   Using `.map_error` in our routes/question.rs route handler

```rust
...

pub async fn add_question(
    store: Store,
    new_question: NewQuestion,
) -> Result<impl warp::Reply, warp::Rejection> {
    let client = reqwest::Client::new();
    let res = client
        .post("https://api.apilayer.com/bad_words?censor_character=*")
        .header("apikey", "xxxxx")
        .body("a list with shit words")
        .send()
        .await
        .map_err(|e| handle_errors::Error::ExternalAPIError(e))?      ◁─┐
        .text()
        .await
        .map_err(|e| handle_errors::Error::ExternalAPIError(e))?;

    println!("{}", res);

    match store.add_question(new_question).await {
        Ok(_) => Ok(warp::reply::with_status(
            "Question added",
            StatusCode::OK
        )),
```

Uses map_err to transform reqwest::Error into our own internal Error enum variant so we can return warp::Rejection from this route handler

```
            Err(e) => Err(warp::reject::custom(e)),
        }
    }
}
```

Instead of using the question mark operator behind .await, we add a .map_error method to wrap reqwest::Error into our own error type, and return this one early (via the ? operator). If the request doesn't fail, we move on (by printing the result to the command line for now).

Let's test this. We can, for example, mistype the API key, and therefore the call should fail. We run the server application via cargo run and send an example POST request:

```
$ curl --location --request POST 'localhost:3030/questions' \
    --header 'Content-Type: application/json' \
    --data-raw '{
    "title": "NEW ass  TITLE",
    "content": "OLD CONTENT shit"
  }'
```

When executing this command, we should see a fail response. But instead we get this:

```
Question added?
```

This is a success message from line 92 in the same file:

```
    ...

match store.add_question(new_question).await {
        Ok(_) => Ok(warp::reply::with_status(
            "Question added",
            StatusCode::OK
        )),
        Err(e) => Err(warp::reject::custom(e)),
    }
}

    ...
```

This suggests that even if we make this API request fail (by mistyping the API key), we still save the question in the database. So, what is our problem here? How would we investigate this behavior? As always, we first go the documentation of the crate we are using and check which error we should get: http://mng.bz/M047. Because we are calling the .send method, we check the documentation for this method first. We can see an Errors section, shown in figure 8.2.

It states nothing about 400 or 500 errors from the corresponding server or any business logic like that. For us, this means that the crate won't throw an error if a call fails, but the error is in the response. Digging further in the documentation, we find that the Response type has an error_for_status method implemented. This means

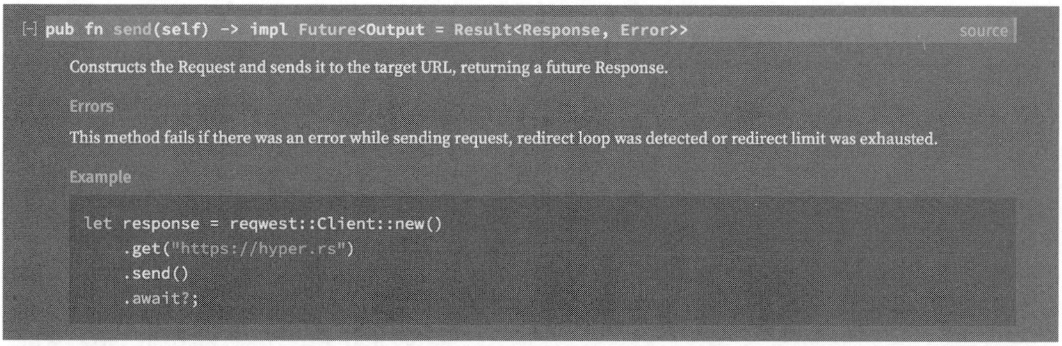

```
[-] pub fn send(self) -> impl Future<Output = Result<Response, Error>>                    source

    Constructs the Request and sends it to the target URL, returning a future Response.

    Errors

    This method fails if there was an error while sending request, redirect loop was detected or redirect limit was exhausted.

    Example

    let response = reqwest::Client::new()
        .get("https://hyper.rs")
        .send()
        .await?;
```

Figure 8.2 The documentation for the send method of the Reqwest crate, which states when this method throws an error

that if the client itself doesn't have an error, we get the possible error (like a 400) from the API via this method. Figure 8.3 shows the documentation for this method.

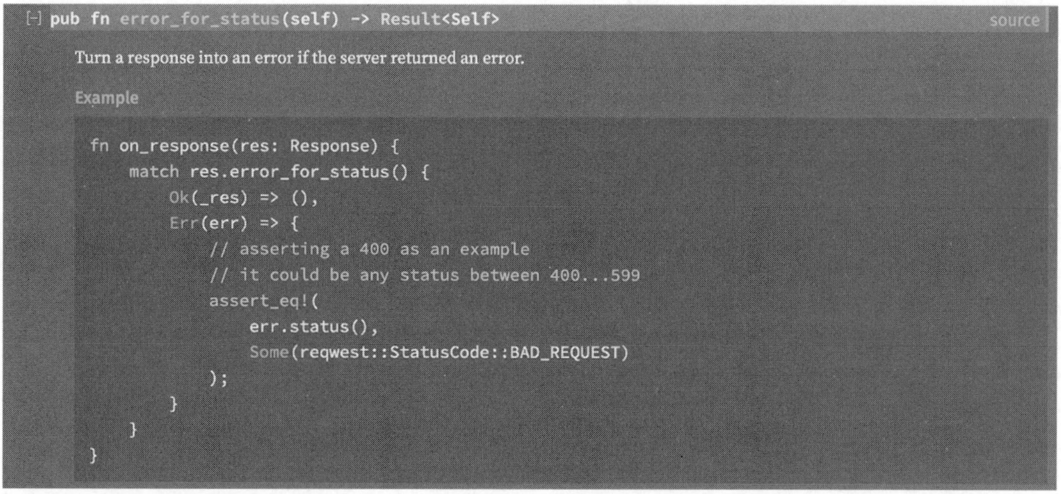

```
[-] pub fn error_for_status(self) -> Result<Self>                                         source

    Turn a response into an error if the server returned an error.

    Example

    fn on_response(res: Response) {
        match res.error_for_status() {
            Ok(_res) => (),
            Err(err) => {
                // asserting a 400 as an example
                // it could be any status between 400...599
                assert_eq!(
                    err.status(),
                    Some(reqwest::StatusCode::BAD_REQUEST)
                );
            }
        }
    }
```

Figure 8.3 The documentation for error_for_status seems to return the possible API error we want.

We can therefore change our example code in the add_question route handler to see the outcome of using this method.

Listing 8.10 Using extended error handling to properly catch API errors

```
...

pub async fn add_question(
    store: Store,
```

```
        new_question: NewQuestion,
) -> Result<impl warp::Reply, warp::Rejection> {
    let client = reqwest::Client::new();
    let res = client
        .post("https://api.apilayer.com/bad_words?censor_character=*")
        .header("apikey", "xxxxx")
        .body("a list with shit words")
        .send()
        .await
        .map_err(|e| handle_errors::Error::ExternalAPIError(e))?;

    match res.error_for_status() {
        Ok(res) => {
            let res = res.text()
                .await
                .map_err(|e| handle_errors::Error::ExternalAPIError(e))?;

            println!("{}", res);

            match store.add_question(new_question).await {
                Ok(_) => Ok(warp::reply::with_status(
                    "Question added",
                    StatusCode::OK
                )),
                Err(e) => Err(warp::reject::custom(e)),
            }
        },
        Err(err) => {
            Err(warp::reject::custom(
                handle_errors::Error::ExternalAPIError(err)
            )),
        }
    }
}
```

> **If Reqwest doesn't return an error, it is still possible that the external API returned a non-200 HTTP status code, which we check via the error_for_status method.**

Even if the error handling is not perfect (and not fine-tuned in general), we can see the magic of the Rust type system and error handling in this example. Compiling and running the code via `cargo run` lets us fire up curl again to test the implementation:

```
$ curl --location --request POST 'localhost:3030/questions' \
    --header 'Content-Type: application/json' \
    --data-raw '{
    "title": "NEW ass  TITLE",
    "content": "OLD CONTENT shit"
  }'
```

Remember, we currently already prefill the body of our HTTP POST request in our code, which means curl is just hitting the endpoint and the body won't be used yet. We mistyped the API key on purpose to let it fail. We are getting two different errors: one for the requesting client (our curl) and one for our internal logger (via the event! macro in the handle-error crate).

Listing 8.11 The curl request now returns a proper internal server error for the user

```
$ curl --location --request POST 'localhost:3030/questions' \
    --header 'Content-Type: application/json' \
    --data-raw '{
    "title": "NEW ass  TITLE",
    "content": "OLD fuck CONTENT shit"
 }'
INTERNAL ERVER ERROR
```

And the next listing shows the error messages we see in the terminal after we start the server and try to process the curl request.

Listing 8.12 Internal error messages indicating a wrong API key being set

```
$ cargo run
   Compiling practical-rust-book v0.1.0
     (/Users/bgruber/CodingIsFun/Manning/code/ch_08)
   Finished dev [unoptimized + debuginfo] target(s) in 5.90s
     Running `target/debug/practical-rust-book`
Mar 07 14:55:50.026 ERROR warp::filters::trace: unable to process request
(internal error) status=500 error=Rejection([MethodNotAllowed,
ExternalAPIError(reqwest::Error { kind: Status(401), url: Url { scheme:
"https", username: "", password: None, host:
Some(Domain("api.apilayer.com")), port: None, path: "/bad_words", query:
Some("censor_character=*"), fragment: None } }), MethodNotAllowed,
MethodNotAllowed])
Mar 07 14:55:50.027 ERROR handle_errors: HTTP status client error (401
Unauthorized) for url
(https://api.apilayer.com/bad_words?censor_character=*)
```

This gives you an idea of why different error messages (internal and external) make so much sense. We don't want to tell the client that we can't authenticate at a particular service, and therefore just blame us (500) that we currently can't handle the request. Internally, however, we need more information. For our logs, we write out as many details as needed to fix the error fast.

We are now able to send an example HTTP request to an external API and have the error handling in place to differentiate between internal and external errors. We figured out when and why an HTTP crate would throw an error, and this error is different from an unreachable API. For this, we have to look into the response ourselves. Figure 8.4 visualizes the different errors and where they can happen.

To get more context around our requests and errors, and to make it easier to work with both, it is a good idea to create a struct for a possible response and error. Basically, strictly type our interactions with the API to make it easier in the future to work with.

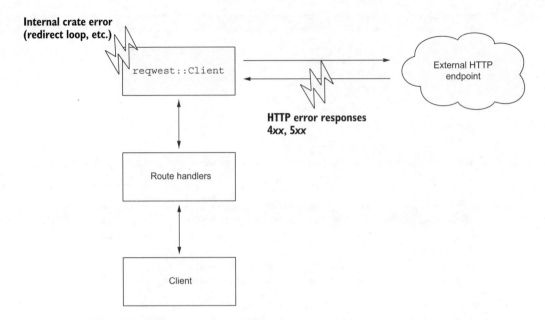

Figure 8.4   We have to handle two errors in our flow: an internal crate error and nonsuccess (4xx,5xx) HTTP responses from the web service.

8.2   *Deserializing JSON responses to structs*

For now, we simply printed out errors and responses to the command line in the terminal. To work properly with an external API, we need to have typed responses. We can create BadWordsError and a BadWordsResponse structs. This gives us three advantages:

- Newcomers to the code can read which fields are part of the response to better understand the code in general.
- We can parse the response and error as a JSON and form proper types, which lets us use the compiler to type-check during coding.
- We can implement behavior on top of the created structs so we can extend and hide behavior behind them (functions like get_bad_words_list, for example).

So how would we start to type out responses from an external API? As with everything, we check the API documentation (http://mng.bz/XaGG). What we can't expect from documentation, sadly, is that it is complete or up-to-date, but it gives us a preliminary idea what a response looks like.

As I already mentioned, a good approach is to send out a curl to the external API and see what comes back. This is a prototyping approach, and with enough information gathered, you can start to create structs.

8.2.1 Gathering API response information

A fast and easy way to get an initial idea about a possible structure is to copy and paste the response from the API documentation in the online Transform tool (https://transform.tools/json-to-rust-serde), which is shown in figure 8.5.

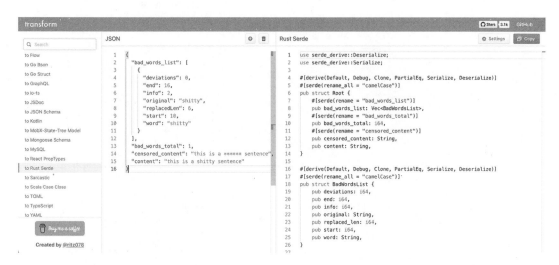

Figure 8.5 The online Transform tool can create Rust structs out of a given JSON.

The result can be a guiding light. You don't have to deserialize every JSON element, just the ones you need. Your struct can, for example, have just two fields (`censored_content` and `content`), and you can still deserialize the returning JSON and map it to your new type. A second way is to print out the result as a string (which we already do currently in our codebase) and go through the fields you see there and construct a type matching what you received.

If you still have your helper project at hand, with the minimal Rust example using Request, you can open it up and add another dependency, namely Serde JSON. This gives you a generic `Value` enum that you can use to parse generic JSON out of a response without having to create your own type first. The following listing shows the extended example code, which you can use to play through some invalid HTTP requests and check which response you will get back.

Listing 8.13 Extension of the minimal Reqwest example

```
use serde_json::json;          ◁——  Imports the json!
                                     macro from serde_json
#[tokio::main]
async fn main() -> Result<(), Box<dyn std::error::Error>> {
    let client = reqwest::Client::new();
    let res = client
        .post("https://api.apilayer.com/bad_words?censor_character=*")
        .header("apikey", "API_KEY")
```

```
        .body("a list with shit words")
        .send()
        .await?;

    let status_code = res.status();
    let message = res.text().await?;

    let response = json!({
        "StatusCode": status_code.as_str(),
        "Message": message
    });

    println!("{:#?}", response);

    Ok(())
}
```

Uses the macro when
transforming the
response into JSON

An example output could look like this (if the API key is wrong, for example):

```
$ cargo run
   Compiling req v0.1.0 (/Users/bgruber/CodingIsFun/Rust/helpers/req)
    Finished dev [unoptimized + debuginfo] target(s) in 2.33s
     Running `target/debug/req`
Object({
    "StatusCode": String(
        "401",
    ),
    "Message": String(
        "{\"message\":\"Invalid authentication credentials\"}",
    ),
})
```

We get our example error code out of the response, and later we can parse the error as a JSON structure and pretty-print it (via #) to the console. But Reqwest errors are even more functional. We can check whether it was a success via res.is_success (http://mng.bz/aPAz) or if it was a client (http://mng.bz/gR8l) or server (http://mng.bz/ep8z) error. This information is helpful when we later make our error handling a bit more sophisticated.

8.2.2 Creating types for our API responses

Whichever method you choose, a possible structure will look like the ones in the next listing.

Listing 8.14 `BadWordResponse` and `BadWord` types for the API response

```
#[derive(Deserialize, Serialize, Debug, Clone)]
struct BadWord {
    original: String,
    word: String,
    deviations: i64,
    info: i64,
```

```
    #[serde(rename = "replacedLen")]
    replaced_len: i64,
}

#[derive(Deserialize, Serialize, Debug, Clone)]
struct BadWordsResponse {
    content: String,
    bad_words_total: i64,
    bad_words_list: Vec<BadWord>,
    censored_content: String,
}
```

This covers the success path. However, we also have a case where we get an error. Until now, we just covered the case of the Reqwest client itself throwing an error, but not the API giving us non 200 responses back. The crate we are using lets us check if we get an error back via the `response.status` function call, and assess via `.is_client_error` or `.is_server_error` if we have a 4*xx* or 5*xx* error code on our hands. The next listing shows our updated question routes file and the `add_question` route handler.

Listing 8.15   Updated routes/question.rs file and route handler

```
use serde::{Deserialize, Serialize};
...


#[derive(Deserialize, Serialize, Debug, Clone)]
pub struct APIResponse {
    message: String
}

#[derive(Deserialize, Serialize, Debug, Clone)]
struct BadWord {
    original: String,
    word: String,
    deviations: i64,
    info: i64,
    #[serde(rename = "replacedLen")]
    replaced_len: i64,
}

#[derive(Deserialize, Serialize, Debug, Clone)]
struct BadWordsResponse {
    content: String,
    bad_words_total: i64,
    bad_words_list: Vec<BadWord>,
    censored_content: String,
}

...


pub async fn add_question(
    store: Store,
    new_question: NewQuestion,
) -> Result<impl warp::Reply, warp::Rejection> {
```

```
let client = reqwest::Client::new();
let res = client
    .post("https://api.apilayer.com/bad_words?censor_character=*")
    .header("apikey", "API_KEY")
    .body(new_question.content)
    .send()
    .await
    .map_err(|e| handle_errors::Error::ExternalAPIError(e))?;
```

Checks whether the response status was successful

The status also indicates whether it was a client or server error.

```
if !res.status().is_success() {
    if res.status().is_client_error() {
        let err = transform_error(res).await;
        return Err(handle_errors::Error::ClientError(err));
    } else {
        let err = transform_error(res).await;
        return Err(handle_errors::Error::ServerError(err));
    }
}
```

The APILayer API doesn't return a nice error, so we create our own.

Returns a client or server error with our APILayerError encapsulated

```
match res.error_for_status() {
    Ok(res) => {
        let res = res.text()
            .await
            .map_err(|e| handle_errors::Error::ExternalAPIError(e))?;

        println!("{}", res);

        match store.add_question(new_question).await {
            Ok(question) => Ok(warp::reply::with_status("Question added",
                StatusCode::OK)),
            Err(e) => Err(warp::reject::custom(e)),
        }
    },
    Err(err) => Err(warp::reject::custom(handle_errors::Error::Exter-
        nalAPIError(err))),
}
```

```
let res = res.json::<BadWordsResponse>()
    .await
    .map_err(|e| handle_errors::Error::ExternalAPIError(e))?;

let content = res.censored_content;

let question = NewQuestion {
    title: new_question.title,
    content,
    tags: new_question.tags,
};
```

While we are at it, we return a proper question back to the client instead of just a string and HTTP code

```
match store.add_question(question).await {
    Ok(question) => Ok(warp::reply::json(&question)),
    Err(e) => Err(warp::reject::custom(e)),
}
```

```
async fn transform_error(
    res: reqwest::Response
) -> handle_errors::APILayerError {
    handle_errors::APILayerError {
        status: res.status().as_u16(),
        message: res.json::<APIResponse>().await.unwrap().message,
    }
}
```

Takes a response (which
we know is an error at this
point) and adds a status
code to the message

We use the integrated status check of the Reqwest response, and in case of an error, we read the status code and the message body, and create our own `APILayerError`—which we will see in listing 8.16. We then return either a client or a server error, based on the status code of the HTTP response.

Externally, this has no impact on the message we will send back to the client, which is 500—Internal Server Error. But internally, we can send the added information to our logs, so we can filter for certain types of errors during production. Listing 8.15 shows the added types and the passing back of the error to the client. Internally, we have to handle the different error types. Therefore, we add another two error cases to our `Error` enum in the handle-error crate. The following listing shows the extended lib.rs file in the handle-errors crate.

Listing 8.16 Extending the handle-errors crate with external API error cases

```
...



#[derive(Debug)]
pub enum Error {
    ParseError(std::num::ParseIntError),
    MissingParameters,
    DatabaseQueryError,
    ExternalAPIError(ReqwestError),
    ClientError(APILayerError),
    ServerError(APILayerError)
}

#[derive(Debug, Clone)]
pub struct APILayerError {
    pub status: u16,
    pub message: String,
}

impl std::fmt::Display for APILayerError {
    fn fmt(&self, f: &mut std::fmt::Formatter) -> std::fmt::Result {
        write!(f, "Status: {}, Message: {}", self.status, self.message)
    }
}

impl std::fmt::Display for Error {
    fn fmt(&self, f: &mut std::fmt::Formatter) -> std::fmt::Result {
        match &*self {
```

In case the HTTP client
(Reqwest) returns an error,
we create a ClientError
enum variant

In case the external API returns a
4xx or 5xx HTTP status code, we
have a ServerError variant.

We want to type out the error we expect
here so we create a new Error type, which
we will return from the helper function.

We want to log or print out the error, so
we implement the Display trait by hand.

```
        Error::ParseError(ref err) => {
            write!(f, "Cannot parse parameter: {}", err)
        },
        Error::MissingParameters => write!(f, "Missing parameter"),
        Error::DatabaseQueryError => {
            write!(f, "Cannot update, invalid data.")
        },
        Error::ExternalAPIError(err) => {
            write!(f, "External API error: {}", err)
        },
        Error::ClientError(err) => {
            write!(f, "External Client error: {}", err)
        },
        Error::ServerError(err) => {
            write!(f, "External Server error: {}", err)
        },
    }
  }
}

impl Reject for Error {}
impl Reject for APILayerError {}

#[instrument]
pub async fn return_error(r: Rejection) -> Result<impl Reply, Rejection> {
    …

    else if let Some(crate::Error::ExternalAPIError(e)) = r.find() {
        event!(Level::ERROR, "{}", e);
        Ok(warp::reply::with_status(
            "Internal Server Error".to_string(),
            StatusCode::INTERNAL_SERVER_ERROR,
        ))
    } else if let Some(crate::Error::ClientError(e)) = r.find() {
        event!(Level::ERROR, "{}", e);
        Ok(warp::reply::with_status(
            "Internal Server Error".to_string(),
            StatusCode::INTERNAL_SERVER_ERROR,
        ))
    } else if let Some(crate::Error::ServerError(e)) = r.find() {
        event!(Level::ERROR, "{}", e);
        Ok(warp::reply::with_status(
            "Internal Server Error".to_string(),
            StatusCode::INTERNAL_SERVER_ERROR,
        ))
    } else if let Some(error) = r.find::<CorsForbidden>() {
        event!(Level::ERROR, "CORS forbidden error: {}", error);
        Ok(warp::reply::with_status(
            error.to_string(),
            StatusCode::FORBIDDEN,
        ))
    …

}
```

With this logic in place, we finally can move on to send real data to the API, and refactor the code even further, so we don't have to duplicate the logic of sending and receiving data in each route handler.

Even if you don't completely agree with the way we pass errors up and down, the basic principle when handling errors in Rust is the same: creating structs for the API responses and differentiating between internal and external errors. Internally, we can look at more details, but to the client, we send out a predefined error code and message so as not to reveal any internal logic or sensitive data.

8.3 Sending questions and answers to the API

With the basic functionality in place, now we can extract the pieces of code we want to reuse in each route handler. We will develop the easy solution: sending the content of the title and the answer/question to the API, and if they contain any profane words, we overwrite the content with the one from the API. As mentioned earlier, we could also have two entries per content (the original and a sanitized one), or other combinations. We first refactor the add_question route handler, and then go on to others that also deal with new content (update_question and add_answer).

8.3.1 Refactoring the add_question route handler

The current solution is to make one HTTP request and process the result or the possible error case. When we store a new question, we have a title and the content. Therefore, we can either choose to merge these two as one content body and send it to the API, or make two requests.

If we do it in one go, we save a few resources and possible error cases. On the other hand, we have to somehow find a way to merge and split the title and body before and after the request. That's the reason that our first solution is to take out the external HTTP part of the route handler, strip out the created structs for the APILayer call as well, and create a new helper file with the functionality and error handling.

We then can call the external API from various places without duplicating the code. We will look at methods of handling multiple HTTP calls and timeouts in the next section. We will first move out all the pieces of code we need to make the external HTTP call, and create a new file, profanity.rs, for it. The following listing shows the result.

Listing 8.17 Doing external HTTP calls in src/profanity.rs

```
use serde::{Deserialize, Serialize};

#[derive(Deserialize, Serialize, Debug, Clone)]
pub struct APIResponse {
    message: String
}
```

```rust
#[derive(Deserialize, Serialize, Debug, Clone)]
struct BadWord {
    original: String,
    word: String,
    deviations: i64,
    info: i64,
    #[serde(rename = "replacedLen")]
    replaced_len: i64,
}

#[derive(Deserialize, Serialize, Debug, Clone)]
struct BadWordsResponse {
    content: String,
    bad_words_total: i64,
    bad_words_list: Vec<BadWord>,
    censored_content: String,
}

pub async fn check_profanity(
    content: String
) -> Result<String, handle_errors::Error> {
    let client = reqwest::Client::new();
    let res = client
        .post("https://api.apilayer.com/bad_words?censor_character=*")
        .header("apikey", "API_KEY")
        .body(content)
        .send()
        .await
        .map_err(|e| handle_errors::Error::ExternalAPIError(e))?;

    if !res.status().is_success() {
        if res.status().is_client_error() {
            let err = transform_error(res).await;
            return Err(handle_errors::Error::ClientError(err));
        } else {
            let err = transform_error(res).await;
            return Err(handle_errors::Error::ServerError(err));
        }
    }

    match res.json::<BadWordsResponse>()
        .await {
            Ok(res) => Ok(res.censored_content),
            Err(e) => Err(handle_errors::Error::ExternalAPIError(e)),
        }
}

async fn transform_error(
    res: reqwest::Response
) -> handle_errors::APILayerError {
    handle_errors::APILayerError {
        status: res.status().as_u16(),
        message: res.json::<APIResponse>().await.unwrap().message,
    }
}
```

As we covered previously in the book, we need the line mod profanity; in main.rs so we can access the public function inside the file throughout our codebase.

Listing 8.18   Adding the new module to our main.rs file

```
#![warn(clippy::all)]

...

mod routes;          |  We have to add the profnatity module
mod store;           |  in the main.rs so we can access it in
mod profanity;   ◁──┘  other modules/files in our codebase.
mod types;

#[tokio::main]
async fn main() {
    let log_filter = std::env::var("RUST_LOG")

...
```

Back to our route handler. We can now replace all the extracted code with just the function call, where we pass the title and content of the new question to the profanity check function and handle the result. The next listing shows the updated code.

Listing 8.19   The updated add_question route handler

```
...

use crate::profanity::check_profanity;   ◁──  Imports our created
                                              check_profanity function,
...                                           which we exported to its
                                              own file

pub async fn add_question(
    store: Store,                                Calls the function,
    new_question: NewQuestion,                   awaits the Future,
) -> Result<impl warp::Reply, warp::Rejection> { and matches on the
    let title = match check_profanity(new_question.title).await {  ◁──  returning Result
        Ok(res) => res,
        Err(e) => return Err(warp::reject::custom(e)),
    };

    let content = match check_profanity(new_question.content).await {  ◁──
        Ok(res) => res,
        Err(e) => return Err(warp::reject::custom(e)),       We do this a second
    };                                                       time: first was the title;
                                                             now we are checking for
    let question = NewQuestion {                             profane words in the
        title,                                               question itself.
        content,
        tags: new_question.tags,
    };
```

```
match store.add_question(question).await {
    Ok(_) => Ok(warp::reply::with_status(
        "Question added",
        StatusCode::OK
    )),
    Err(e) => Err(warp::reject::custom(e)),
}
}
```

We call the function (and therefore the API) twice for each new question: once for the title and once for the content. If both calls return a valid response, we create an updated new question, where we overwrite the content with possible censored content and store it in the database.

We can test the new code by starting the server via `cargo run`, and send the following `curl` via the command line:

```
$ curl --location --request POST 'localhost:3030/questions' \
--header 'Content-Type: application/json' \
--data-raw '{
    "title": "NEW shit TITLE",
    "content": "OLD shit CONTENT"
}'
```

If you press Enter, you can check whether the censored question was saved in our PostgreSQL database:

```
$ psql rustwebdev
psql (14.2)
Type "help" for help.

rustwebdev=# select * from questions;
 id |     title      |              content               | tags |
created_on
----+----------------+------------------------------------+------+------------
----------------
  1 | NEW **** TITLE | OLD **** CONTENT |      | 2022-03-15 08:52:44.327796
(1 row)

rustwebdev=#
```

And it worked! The profane words are censored via the * symbol. You can, of course, adjust how you want to store and display the censored words by replacing the response from the API with your own symbols or letters.

8.3.2   *Making profanity checks for updating questions*

The only times a client can add content to our database is either by updating questions or adding answers. The difference between the `update_question` and `add_question` route handler is that updating a question requires an `id`, and we can use the `Question` struct; with the `add_question` function, we needed the `NewQuestion` type since we don't have an ID just yet. The following listing shows the updated `update_question` route handler.

Listing 8.20 **Adding the profanity check to** `update_question`

```
...

pub async fn update_question(
    id: i32,
    store: Store,
    question: Question,
) -> Result<impl warp::Reply, warp::Rejection> {
    let title = match check_profanity(question.title).await {
        Ok(res) => res,
        Err(e) => return Err(warp::reject::custom(e)),
    };

    let content = match check_profanity(question.content).await {
        Ok(res) => res,
        Err(e) => return Err(warp::reject::custom(e)),
    };

    let question = Question {
        id: question.id,
        title,
        content,
        tags: question.tags,
    };

    match store.update_question(question, id).await {
        Ok(res) => Ok(warp::reply::json(&res)),
        Err(e) => Err(warp::reject::custom(e)),
    }
}

...
```

You can test the implementation with this example `curl`:

```
$ curl --location --request PUT 'localhost:3030/questions/1' \
--header 'Content-Type: application/json' \
--data-raw '{
    "id": 1,
    "title": "NEW TITLE",
    "content": "OLD ass CONTENT"
}'
```

8.3.3 *Updating the add_answer route handler*

The last place to add to the profanity filter is the `add_answer` route handler. This time around, we don't have a title to worry about, so all we do is check the content of the given answer. The next listing shows the updated code.

Listing 8.21   Updated `add_answer` **route handler in src/routes/answer.rs**

```
use std::collections::HashMap;
use warp::http::StatusCode;

use crate::store::Store;
use crate::types::answer::NewAnswer;
use crate::profanity::check_profanity;

pub async fn add_answer(
    store: Store,
    new_answer: NewAnswer,
) -> Result<impl warp::Reply, warp::Rejection> {
    let content = match
        check_profanity(params.get("content").unwrap().to_string()).await {
            Ok(res) => res,
            Err(e) => return Err(warp::reject::custom(e)),
        };

    let answer = NewAnswer {
        content,
        question_id: new_answer.question_id,
    };

    match store.add_answer(answer).await {
        Ok(_) => Ok(warp::reply::with_status(
            "Answer added",
            StatusCode::OK
        )),
        Err(e) => Err(warp::reject::custom(e)),
    }
}
```

And with that in place, we are done updating all the relevant route handlers. Now, whenever we add content to our database, we run it through this profanity check first. If the API finds any words on the blocklist, it returns a censored version of the passed string.

8.4   *Handling timeouts and multiple requests at once*

After having implemented the success and failure paths, we can think about other cases our service has to cover. What if a delay occurs in the API response from the external server: how long until our HTTP call times out, and we are getting an internal error because of it?

What would happen next? The timeout happens, and we return an error to the user. What should the user do, try again? We can maybe already cover this case before responding with an error. We could implement a certain number of retries before falling back to a 500 server error.

Another use case you will run into when developing web services in Rust is the need (for either performance or usability reasons) to run multiple HTTP calls concurrently or in parallel. You can use `tokio::join!` (to run futures concurrently on the same thread), or spawn a new task via `tokio::spawn` and run the calls in parallel.

8.4.1   *Implementing a retry for external HTTP calls*

Various strategies exist for retrying an HTTP call. The most common use case in this scenario is *exponential backoff*. Instead of just retrying after a fixed amount of time, the timeout increases for each failed retry until finally giving up and returning an error.

Our chosen HTTP client Reqwest does not have this feature built in, so we have to use a third-party library that extends our chosen crate. The one we are going to use in this book context is called `reqwest_retry` (http://mng.bz/p6oG). Another caveat is that Reqwest doesn't really have the concept of built-in middleware, which this retry crate requires. Therefore, we need yet another crate that adds middleware around Reqwest, and afterward, we can use `reqwest_retry`. Here is example code:

The retry mechanism is middleware, which is based on the reqwest_ middleware crate.

Imports our newly added crate to add support for middleware to our reqwest HTTP client

```
use reqwest_middleware::{ClientBuilder, ClientWithMiddleware};
use reqwest_retry::{RetryTransientMiddleware, policies::ExponentialBackoff};

async fn run_retries() {

    let retry_policy = ExponentialBackoff::builder().build_with_max_retries(3);
    let client = ClientBuilder::new(reqwest::Client::new())
        .with(RetryTransientMiddleware::new_with_policy(retry_policy))
        .build();

    client
        .get("https:/ /truelayer.com")
        .header("foo", "bar")
        .send()
        .await
        .unwrap();
}
```

Replaces the old client building from the standard reqwest crate with the new method and client from the reqwest_middleware crate

Creates a new retry policy with the number of retries we want to do in case of a failure

I highlighted the important pieces in bold. Instead of using `ClientBuilder` from our Reqwest crate, we build the client via `reqwest_middleware`. This crate is a wrapper around Reqwest and extends it.

> **NOTE** Be sure that you need exponential backoff or other middleware in your HTTP requests. The added complexity might not be worth the tradeoff in your project. This book uses it as an example of how it can be done.

The beauty of our profanity abstraction is that we can change the HTTP client framework in just one spot, and no other changes throughout the code are needed. If we therefore choose to implement a retry method, we have to add the needed crates in our Cargo.toml file, as seen in the next listing.

> **Listing 8.22   Adding the middleware and retry crates to our project via Cargo.toml**

```
[package]
name = "practical-rust-book"
```

```
version = "0.1.0"
edition = "2021"

[dependencies]
…
reqwest = { version = "0.11", features = ["json"] }
reqwest-middleware = "0.1.1"
reqwest-retry = "0.1.1"
```

Afterward, we can replace building the Reqwest client with the exposed method in the just added middleware crate.

Listing 8.23   Using the middleware in profanity.rs

```
use serde::{Deserialize, Serialize};
use reqwest_middleware::ClientBuilder
use reqwest_retry::{RetryTransientMiddleware, policies::ExponentialBackoff};

…

pub async fn check_profanity(
    content: String
) -> Result<String, handle_errors::Error> {
    let retry_policy = ExponentialBackoff::builder().build_with_max_retries(3);
    let client = ClientBuilder::new(reqwest::Client::new())
        .with(RetryTransientMiddleware::new_with_policy(retry_policy))
        .build();

    let res = client
        .post("https://api.apilayer.com/bad_words?censor_character=*")
        .header("apikey", "API_KEY")
        .body(content)
        .send()
        .await
        .map_err(|e| handle_errors::Error::ExternalAPIError(e))?;

    …
}
```

However, these changes have an impact on our error handling. Now, when calling `.post` on the `client`, we actually receive a different error—namely, `reqwest_middleware::Error` instead of a `reqwest::Error`.

We can extend the handling-errors crate as shown in listing 8.24. Remember to also add `reqwest_middleware` to Cargo.toml inside the handling-errors crate:

```
[package]
name = "handle-errors"
version = "0.1.0"
edition = "2021"

[dependencies]
warp = "0.3"
tracing = { version = "0.1", features = ["log"] }
```

```
reqwest = "0.11"
reqwest-middleware = "0.1.1"
```

Now we can access the error in the lib.rs file inside handling-errors.

Listing 8.24 Extending handling-errors to accompany the added middleware crate

```
use warp::{
    filters::{body::BodyDeserializeError, cors::CorsForbidden},
    http::StatusCode,
    reject::Reject,
    Rejection, Reply,
};
use tracing::{event, Level, instrument};
use reqwest::Error as ReqwestError;
use reqwest_middleware::Error as MiddlewareReqwestError;


#[derive(Debug)]
pub enum Error {
    ParseError(std::num::ParseIntError),
    MissingParameters,
    DatabaseQueryError,
    ReqwestAPIError(ReqwestError),
    MiddlewareReqwestAPIError(MiddlewareReqwestError),
    ClientError(APILayerError),
    ServerError(APILayerError)
}

...

impl std::fmt::Display for Error {
    fn fmt(&self, f: &mut std::fmt::Formatter) -> std::fmt::Result {
        match &*self {
            Error::ParseError(ref err) => {
                write!(f, "Cannot parse parameter: {}", err)
            },
            Error::MissingParameters => write!(f, "Missing parameter"),
            Error::DatabaseQueryError => {
                write!(f, "Cannot update, invalid data.")
            },
            Error::ReqwestAPIError(err) => {
                write!(f, "External API error: {}", err)
            },
            Error::MiddlewareReqwestAPIError(err) => {
                Write!(f, "External API error: {}", err)
            },
            Error::ClientError(err) => {
                write!(f, "External Client error: {}", err)
            },
            Error::ServerError(err) => {
                Write!(f, "External Server error: {}", err)
            },
        }
```

```
        }
    }

    ...


#[instrument]
pub async fn return_error(r: Rejection) -> Result<impl Reply, Rejection> {
    if let Some(crate::Error::DatabaseQueryError) = r.find() {
        event!(Level::ERROR, "Database query error");
        Ok(warp::reply::with_status(
            crate::Error::DatabaseQueryError.to_string(),
            StatusCode::UNPROCESSABLE_ENTITY,
        ))
    } else if let Some(crate::Error::ReqwestAPIError(e)) = r.find() {
        event!(Level::ERROR, "{}", e);
        Ok(warp::reply::with_status(
            "Internal Server Error".to_string(),
            StatusCode::INTERNAL_SERVER_ERROR,
        ))
    } else if let Some(crate::Error::MiddlewareReqwestAPIError(e)) = r.find() {
        event!(Level::ERROR, "{}", e);
        Ok(warp::reply::with_status(
            "Internal Server Error".to_string(),
            StatusCode::INTERNAL_SERVER_ERROR,
        ))
    }

    ...

    }
}
```

And back in our profanity.rs file, we change the errors as shown here.

Listing 8.25   Updating the errors to reflect the changes in the handle-errors crate

```
use serde::{Deserialize, Serialize};
use reqwest_middleware::ClientBuilder;
use reqwest_retry::{RetryTransientMiddleware, policies::ExponentialBackoff};

...


pub async fn check_profanity(
    content: String
) -> Result<String, handle_errors::Error> {
    let retry_policy =
     ExponentialBackoff::builder().build_with_max_retries(3);
    let client = ClientBuilder::new(reqwest::Client::new())
        .with(RetryTransientMiddleware::new_with_policy(retry_policy))
        .build();

    let res = client
        .post("https://api.apilayer.com/bad_words?censor_character=*")
        .header("apikey", "API_KEY")
        .body(content)
```

```
        .send()
        .await
        .map_err(|e| handle_errors::Error::MiddlewareReqwestAPIError(e))?;

    ...

match res.json::<BadWordsResponse>()
    .await {
        Ok(res) => Ok(res.censored_content),
        Err(e) => Err(handle_errors::Error::ReqwestAPIError(e)),
    }
}
```

We can test the functionality by running the server via `cargo run` and go offline via turning off the Wi-Fi or unplugging the Ethernet cable.

8.4.2 *Executing futures concurrently or in parallel*

The other use case you will run into when developing web services, which we talked about earlier, is executing HTTP calls in parallel or concurrently. In plain English, *concurrency* means making progress on more than one task at the same time.

Although this can have the effect of starting and pausing tasks, while finishing them, *parallelism* means that more resources are being created or used to work simultaneously on the given tasks.

In our context, `tokio::spawn` is literally creating another task, either on the same thread or a new thread is created. This allows for parallel execution of the given work. When using `tokio::join!`, Tokio will execute the futures (HTTP calls) concurrently on the same thread, and makes progress on both of them at the same time (by context switching, for example).

You have to evaluate, based on your needs, whether this actually gives you a performance boost, and if so, which one is better. Listing 8.26 shows the route handler update_question with the usage of `tokio::spawn`, and listing 8.27 uses `tokio::join!`.

Listing 8.26 Using `tokio::spawn` inside the `update_question` route handler

...

```
pub async fn update_question(
    id: i32,
    store: Store,
    question: Question,
) -> Result<impl warp::Reply, warp::Rejection> {
    let title = tokio::spawn(check_profanity(question.title));
    let content = tokio::spawn(check_profanity(question.content));

    let (title, content) = (title.await.unwrap(), content.await.unwrap());
```

Uses tokio::spawn to wrap our asynchronous function that returns a future, without awaiting it yet

We can now run both in parallel, returning a tuple that contains the Result for the title and one for the content check.

Does the same for the question content check

Checks if both HTTP calls were successful

```
 ⮑ if title.is_err() {
        return Err(warp::reject::custom(title.unwrap_err()));
    }

 ⮑ if content.is_err() {
        return Err(warp::reject::custom(content.unwrap_err()));
    }

    let question = Question {
        id: question.id,
        title: title.unwrap(),            We have to unwrap
        content: content.unwrap(),        the Result here again.
        tags: question.tags,
    };

    match store.update_question(question, id).await {
        Ok(res) => Ok(warp::reply::json(&res)),
        Err(e) => Err(warp::reject::custom(e)),
    }
}

...
```

Listing 8.27   Using `tokio::join!` inside the `update_question` route handler

```
...

pub async fn update_question(
    id: i32,
    store: Store,
    question: Question,
) -> Result<impl warp::Reply, warp::Rejection> {        Instead of the
    let title = check_profanity(question.title);        spawn, we don't
    let content = check_profanity(question.content);     have to wrap the
                                                         function calls
    let (title, content) = tokio::join!(title, content); ⮜ separately. We
                                                          just call them
    if title.is_err() {                                   inside the join!
        return Err(warp::reject::custom(title.unwrap_err())); macro without
    }                                                      any await.

    if content.is_err() {
        return Err(warp::reject::custom(content.unwrap_err()));
    }

    let question = Question {
        id: question.id,
        title: title.unwrap(),
        content: content.unwrap(),
        tags: question.tags,
    };

    match store.update_question(question, id).await {
        Ok(res) => Ok(warp::reply::json(&res)),
```

```
      Err(e) => Err(warp::reject::custom(e)),
   }
}
```

...

This chapter highlighted the process of adding a simple HTTP client to our codebase through adding proper error handling and then refining the execution behavior. The beauty of Rust is in the details here. By adding a new crate, the compiler spotted a different return type and made sure we handled the case properly.

The strictly typed nature helped us create our own types, handling errors and spotting problems way before they potentially reached us in production. The rich ecosystem lets us extend a crate's functionality and spared us from writing this retry code all by ourselves.

Summary

- Choosing an HTTP client depends partly on the runtime you chose for your project.
- You can choose from various levels of abstraction when adding an HTTP client, depending on your needs.
- Going with a widely used crate gives you the advantage of a richer ecosystem around the crate and more help on the internet.
- Error handling is crucial when implementing HTTP calls to other services.
- You don't want to expose internal errors to clients.
- You also don't want to lose details when logging errors.
- Rust gives you the option of handling errors internally and externally at the same time with different details.
- Creating structs for responses and errors from your third-party API service helps future developers but also makes your codebase easier to study and extend, and prevents possible mistakes in the future.
- Adding default retries of failed HTTP calls helps prevent the user from sending the same request multiple times a second.
- The Tokio runtime exposes methods and macros to bundle futures to be able to work concurrently or in parallel (via join! or spawn).

Part 3

Bring it into production

This last part is all about rounding up our previous work and making it ready for production. This means adding a mechanism for authenticating users, so the public can't just access or tamper with our data. We'll also have a look at what it means to parameterize our application. Hardcoding variables like port numbers and URLs is not future-proof and makes it hard to adjust our application dynamically for various environments. The last chapter of part 3, and the book, is about testing.

Chapter 9 starts with stateless and stateful authentication and how to implement authentication middleware in our application. This gives us the chance to restrict API endpoints and resources to certain users.

With chapter 10, the business logic coding ends, and we talk about deployments. We first have to start to think about how to get all the hardcoded variables out of our application and into config or environment files. Then we'll read them into our application and compile a Rust codebase for multiple architectures, as well as set it up inside a Docker container.

The final chapter, 11, is about testing. We'll unit-test part of the application and do deeper integration tests for whole workflows. This chapter also covers how to set up a mock server, and how to spin it up and wind it down from a different process.

Add authentication
and authorization

This chapter covers

- Understanding the difference between authentication and authorization
- Adding authentication to your web service
- Adapting existing API endpoints to handle authentication
- Using various forms of authentication for your web service
- Using cookies with Warp
- Adding authorization middleware for your routes

Parts 1 and 2 covered the basics of a web service: everything you need to know to add routes, a database, and external APIs, and to observe a running application via logs. Part 3 will help you do everything necessary to ship a Rust web service to production. The three chapters in this last part cover authentication and authorization, deployment, and testing.

You'll need everything you learned so far for this chapter. Adding authentication basically means adding a registration and user route to the API, adding a user table to the database, and adding user IDs to the questions and answers. This means extending the API and migrating the database—tasks you learned in the previous chapters.

Every topic so far can be handled slightly differently. You can name your routes differently, group modules in your own way, or choose a different database structure or abstraction. The aim of this book is to give you concrete working examples, and that's true in this third part even more so than in parts 1 and 2. In terms of authentication, you'll need to decide whether you want to use cookies, which encryption standard you want to use for your passwords, whether you want to use passwords at all, and more. Therefore, we go through the changes you have to make regardless of your actual implementation choice (as seen in figures 9.1 and 9.2).

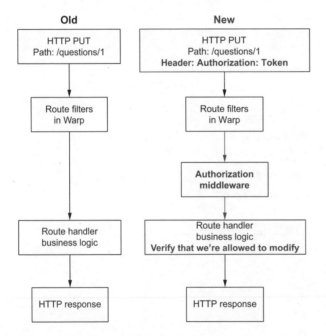

Figure 9.1   Changes to our current application to add authorization

Creating a user table, adding user IDs, and adding a check for your routes if the user has the right privileges to access the endpoint are all universal. Changing a hash algorithm for your password or adjusting the authorization middleware are details left to the environment, project, or engineer to decide.

9.1   *Adding authentication to our web service*

Almost every web service you provide will have some form of authentication method. This is to limit the access and therefore the data that the service is providing. In a consumer-facing service, you want to provide registration, login, and logout endpoints

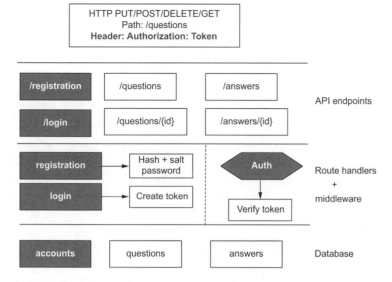

Figure 9.2   Adding new endpoints, route handlers, and middleware to our existing application

so a user can verify itself but also destroy the token by logging out. On your end, it is also helpful to be able to de-authenticate a user in case a breach occurs or a contract with the user ends. Figure 9.3 shows the registration and login path we implement in our application.

If you operate a microservice in a wider company network, you might not need this form of authentication. Section 9.2 is probably more interesting to you, because it cov-

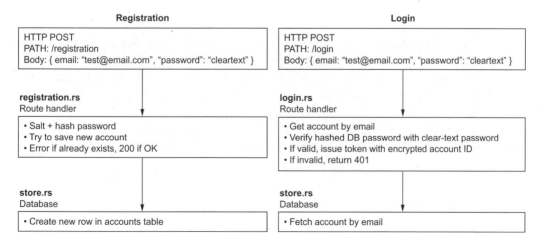

Figure 9.3   Authentication flow

ers the question of how to secure endpoints by validating a token or key. In this section, however, we have to decide multiple open issues:

- Which user information do we need to store?
- How does a user want to authenticate to our service?
- How long should an authentication token be valid?
- Which encryption method should we use for the password and the token?

Note that we don't go in the direction of managing user profiles (for example, deleting a user or updating certain information like an address). Based on our journey through the book so far, it should be clear how to add endpoints and internal logic in order to add or delete elements from a database. Here, we focus instead on creating users and validating them against our endpoints.

9.1.1 *Creating the user concept*

First things first: the idea of a user has to exist in our application before we can create new ones. As mentioned earlier, we don't require a whole lot in the beginning. An email and password are fine for the start. This allows us to uniquely identify and check against a hashed password. Note here as well that we could go down the road of not needing a password at all but sending out login links via email instead. We covered how to use third-party libraries, so this exercise is up to you to implement. The following listing shows a possible user struct.

Listing 9.1   User struct

```
struct User {
    email: String,
    password: String,
}
```

We could have two issues with the name User. PostgreSQL has a default table called user that holds the users of the database. It is also a reserved keyword (http://mng .bz/O6Xn). Additionally, the term *user* is not really clear. Maybe we have multiple types of users, like admin or developer.

What we could do instead is create accounts. An *account* can have different roles (maybe multiple at the same time) and is generic enough to grow and clear enough for us to exactly understand its position in the wider application.

Therefore, we can start with a new type for our web service, called Account. We will create a new file under the path src/types called account.rs.

Listing 9.2   The new Account type in src/types/account.rs

```
use serde::{Deserialize, Serialize};

#[derive(Serialize, Deserialize, Debug, Clone)]
pub struct Account {
    pub email: String,
```

```
    pub password: String,
}
```

We need to expose this module (listing 9.3). We can already access the modules listed in the mod.rs file through the line `mod types` in main.rs.

Listing 9.3 Exposing the account module in src/types/mod.rs

```
pub mod answer;
pub mod pagination;
pub mod question;
pub mod account;
```

With the account in place, let's think through if we have everything. We want to offer a registration route where a new user can put in an email and password. We'll then check whether the email is already in our system, and if not, add a new entry in our accounts database table.

Further, when creating a new question or answer, we want to assign this question or answer to a specific user. We could add the email to the created question or answer to have an association between the two. Common practice is to use an ID. When changing details about the user, we don't have to go through all entries and update the same data; we can keep the ID associated with the question or answer, and simply change just the email in the accounts table.

If we think back about our question type, we ended up having two: `NewQuestion`, *without* the ID, and `Question` *with* the ID. The reason is that when creating a new type of some sort, it doesn't exist yet in the database and therefore doesn't have an ID. Once it is created, we take the ID from the database. We could use the same pattern when creating an account. The following listing shows a possible version of the account.rs file.

Listing 9.4 Adding an ID to the account

```
use serde::{Deserialize, Serialize};

#[derive(Serialize, Deserialize, Debug, Clone)]
pub struct Account {
    pub id: AccountId,
    pub email: String,
    pub password: String,
}

#[derive(Deserialize, Serialize, Debug, Clone, PartialEq, Eq, Hash)]
pub struct AccountId(pub i32);

#[derive(Deserialize, Serialize, Debug, Clone)]
pub struct NewAccount {
    pub email: String,
    pub password: String,
}
```

This, however, will get quite noisy fast. How can we trust or know whether the type we are dealing with is following this pattern? Another solution is to use `Option` for the ID field. The next listing shows the end result for the account.rs file.

Listing 9.5   Using `Option` for the ID field in src/types/account.rs

```rust
use serde::{Deserialize, Serialize};

#[derive(Serialize, Deserialize, Debug, Clone)]
pub struct Account {
    pub id: Option<AccountId>,
    pub email: String,
    pub password: String,
}

#[derive(Deserialize, Serialize, Debug, Clone, PartialEq, Eq, Hash)]
pub struct AccountId(pub i32);
```

This also saves us some code. Next up is creating a table in our database. We can use the migration from chapter 7. We also have to think about extending our previous tables (questions and answers), so they are able to hold an account ID.

9.1.2   *Migrating the database*

We already have the SQLx CLI tool installed in chapter 7. As a reminder, this was the command we used:

```
$ cargo install sqlx-cli
```

With the CLI tool from SQLx in place, we can create a new migration (a file in the migrations folder that holds the SQL to be executed), where we create a new accounts table. We create a new migration with the following command (the `-r` parameter creates up and down migration files for us to fill in):

```
$ sqlx migrate add -r create_accounts_table
```

Be aware that you have to run this command in the root folder of your project. Under the hood, this command will check for an existing folder called migrations, and if it doesn't exist, will create one. Afterward, it creates a file with the name you gave after the add command, and prefixes it with a timestamp:

```
❭ l migrations/
.rw-r--r--   31 gruberbastian 23 May 20:42 -N
20220509150516_questions_table.down.sql
.rw-r--r-- 197 gruberbastian 23 May 20:42 -N
20220509150516_questions_table.up.sql
.rw-r--r--   30 gruberbastian 23 May 20:42 -N
20220514145724_answers_table.down.sql
.rw-r--r-- 199 gruberbastian 23 May 20:42 -N
20220514145724_answers_table.up.sql
```

```
.rw-r--r--  34 gruberbastian 23 May 20:48 -N
20220523174842_create_accounts_table.down.sql
.rw-r--r--  32 gruberbastian 23 May 20:48 -N
20220523174842_create_accounts_table.up.sql
```

We created two files:

- One *up* file for creating the accounts table
- One reversion file, *down*, for deleting it again

We open the up file first and add the needed SQL to create a new table with an ID, email, and password field, as shown in the following listing.

Listing 9.6   Creating migrations in migrations/**_create_accounts_table.up.sql

```
CREATE TABLE IF NOT EXISTS accounts (
    id serial NOT NULL,
    email VARCHAR(255) NOT NULL PRIMARY KEY,
    password VARCHAR(255) NOT NULL
);
```

The next listing shows the reversion, which drops the `accounts` table again.

Listing 9.7   Reverting the migration in **_create_accounts_table.down.sql

```
DROP TABLE IF EXISTS accounts;
```

These migration files will be executed after we start our server. As you may remember, line 19 in main.rs holds the logic to execute the migrations (highlighted in bold):

```
...

async fn main() -> Result<(), sqlx::Error> {
    ...

    let store =
        store::Store::new("postgres://localhost:5432/rustwebdev").await?;

    sqlx::migrate!().run(&store.clone().connection).await?;

    . .
```

After executing `cargo run` on the command line, we can check via PSQL if the table was created:

```
$ psql rustwebdev
psql (14.2)
Type "help" for help.
```

```
rustwebdev=# \dt
                    List of relations
 Schema |       Name        | Type  |     Owner
--------+-------------------+-------+---------------
 public | _sqlx_migrations  | table | gruberbastian
 public | accounts          | table | gruberbastian
 public | answers           | table | gruberbastian
 public | questions         | table | gruberbastian
(4 rows)

rustwebdev=#
```

With the table in place and our account type implemented, we can go over the plan for our registration-login-logout life cycle. First up will be the creation of a new account. We already know that a user needs to provide a password. This fact alone leads to multiple choices—for example, how should we store this password? Definitely not in plain text. Therefore, we have to think about a hashing algorithm to prevent anyone from ever seeing the password being used.

9.1.3 Adding the registration endpoint

Before we can think about how to handle passwords, we need to add a new API endpoint for the registration process. This endpoint will expect an email and password, and returns, for now, a 200 HTTP response. We can think later about automatically logging in the user after registration and sending back a form of token or cookie so the client can continue being logged in.

In a production environment, you also can send out emails, provide verification links, and so forth. For now, however, we focus purely on accepting data, hashing the password before storing it, and then sending back an HTTP response.

For starters, we add a new file in the src/routes folder, named authentication.rs. There we store our logic for the registration, login, and logout routes. The following listing shows our first attempt in adding an account to the database.

Listing 9.8 Adding the registration route in src/routes/authentication.rs

```
use warp::http::StatusCode;

use crate::store::Store;
use crate::types::account::Account;

pub async fn register(
    store: Store,
    account: Account,
) -> Result<impl warp::Reply, warp::Rejection> {
    match store.add_account(account).await {
        Ok(_) => {
            Ok(warp::reply::with_status("Account added", StatusCode::OK))
        },
        Err(e) => Err(warp::reject::custom(e)),
    }
}
```

Two details are still missing. First, we need to add a new function to our store, add_account, which will hold the SQL to add a new account to the accounts table in our PostgreSQL database. And second, we need to add the route to our routes object in main.rs. The following listing shows the add_account function in the store.rs file.

> **Listing 9.9 Extending our `Store` object with the `add_account` function**

```
...


use crate::types::{
    answer::Answer,
    question::{NewQuestion, Question, QuestionId},
    account::Account,
};


...


    pub async fn add_account(self, account: Account) -> Result<bool, Error> {
        match sqlx::query("INSERT INTO accounts (email, password)
            VALUES ($1, $2)")
            .bind(account.email)
            .bind(account.password)
            .execute(&self.connection)
            .await
        {
        Ok(_) => Ok(true),
        Err(error) => {
            tracing::event!(
                tracing::Level::ERROR,
                code = error
                    .as_database_error()
                    .unwrap()
                    .code()
                    .unwrap()
                    .parse::<i32>()
                    .unwrap(),
                db_message = error
                    .as_database_error()
                    .unwrap()
                    .message(),
                constraint = error
                    .as_database_error()
                    .unwrap()
                    .constraint()
                    .unwrap()
            );
            Err(Error::DatabaseQueryError)
        }
        }
    }

...
```

This is basically a copy of the add_answer logic. We take the account parameter and create an INSERT SQL query to our accounts table. Next is adding the route to the routes object, as shown in the following listing.

Listing 9.10　Adding register to the routes object in main.rs

```
...

#[tokio::main]
async fn main() -> Result<(), sqlx::Error> {
    ...

    let add_answer = warp::post()
        .and(warp::path("answers"))
        .and(warp::path::end())
        .and(store_filter.clone())
        .and(warp::body::form())
        .and_then(routes::answer::add_answer);

    let registration = warp::post()
        .and(warp::path("registration"))
        .and(warp::path::end())
        .and(store_filter.clone())
        .and(warp::body::json())
        .and_then(routes::authentication::register);

    let routes = get_questions
        .or(update_question)
        .or(add_question)
        .or(delete_question)
        .or(add_answer)
        .or(registration)
        .with(cors)
        .with(warp::trace::request())
        .recover(return_error);

    warp::serve(routes).run(([127, 0, 0, 1], 3030)).await;

    Ok(())
}
```

We have the option to expect either a JSON body or parameters in the URL. It is up to the API design to answer this question. We go for a JSON body for now, but feel free to decide otherwise in your application. Running our first test is a success. Well, sort of. After running the application via cargo run, we can send this example curl via the command line:

```
curl --location --request POST 'localhost:3030/registration' \
--header 'Content-Type: application/json' \
--data-raw '{
    "email": "example@email.com",
    "password": "cleartext"
}'
```

We can save this new user in the database, but we already see some drawbacks. The very first one is the password. We are not hashing the password but storing it in plain text. That's not good. A second optimization would be to check for a valid email address. Later, we also have to think about how the password is sent over the wire (from the client to our servers) and what we could do to encrypt that transfer.

9.1.4   *Hashing the password*

The first step is to make sure that we never store any plain-text password, and that we make it impossible for even our engineers who work on the software directly to decrypt the passwords from the database. A common way to prevent clear-text storing of passwords is using hashes instead. Various hash algorithms are out there, and depending on your use case and hardware, you can choose different ones. The "Password Storage Cheat Sheet" (http://mng.bz/YKzN) has a great overview.

Hashing alone is not enough, though. If an intruder breaks into your system and copies the account database, they can compare the password hashes with a list of hashes of already cracked passwords. It won't take them long to compare and find the clear-text password to the corresponding hash.

That's the reason you also have to *salt* your password. This means adding a random generated sequence in front of (or after) your password, before you hash it. This makes it nearly impossible for nonauthorized people to figure out the password behind the hash.

We extend our registration logic and add the hashing of the password before storing it in the database. This makes every password hash unique, and the same password stored a second time will have a different hash. We import two new crates for our solution:

- rand—To generate random characters of a certain length for our salt.
- rust-argon2—This is the hashing algorithm we are choosing for our passwords (http://mng.bz/epYv).

The following listing shows the updated Cargo.toml file.

> **Listing 9.11   Adding rand and rust-argon2 to our project**

```
[package]
name = "practical-rust-book"
version = "0.1.0"
edition = "2021"

[dependencies]
warp = "0.3"
serde = { version = "1.0", features = ["derive"] }
serde_json = "1.0"
tokio = { version = "1.1.1", features = ["full"] }
handle-errors = { path = "handle-errors", version = "0.1.0" }
log = "0.4"
env_logger = "0.8"
```

```
log4rs = "1.0"
uuid = { version = "0.8", features = ["v4"] }
tracing = { version = "0.1", features = ["log"] }
tracing-subscriber = "0.2"
sqlx = { version = "0.5", features = [ "runtime-tokio-rustls", "migrate",
"postgres", "uuid" ] }
reqwest = { version = "0.11", features = ["json"] }
reqwest-middleware = "0.1.1"
reqwest-retry = "0.1.1"
rand = "0.8"
rust-argon2 = "1.0"
paseto = "2.0"
```

The following listing shows the updated authentication.rs file in the routes folder.

Listing 9.12   Extending authentication.rs with the hash logic

```
use warp::http::StatusCode;
use argon2::{self, Config};          ←  Imports the implementation of
use rand::Rng;                            the argon2 hashing algorithm
                              ←  The rand crate
use crate::store::Store;               helps us create a
use crate::types::account::Account;    random salt.

pub async fn register(
    store: Store,
    account: Account,
) -> Result<impl warp::Reply, warp::Rejection> {
    let hashed_password = hash_password(account.password.as_bytes());   ←

    let account = Account {
        id: account.id,
        email: account.email,
        password: hashed_password,
    };

    match store.add_account(account).await {
        Ok(_) => Ok(warp::reply::with_status("Account added", StatusCode::OK)),
        Err(e) => Err(warp::reject::custom(e)),
    }
}

pub fn hash_password(password: &[u8]) -> String {        ←
    let salt = rand::thread_rng().gen::<[u8; 32]>();     ←
    let config = Config::default();
    argon2::hash_encoded(password, &salt, &config).unwrap()   ←
}
```

Takes the password as a byte array and passes it to the newly created hash function

Instead of the password from the user (plain text), we use the hashed (and salted) version of it for the database.

The hash function returns a string, the hashed version of the clear-text password.

The rand function creates s32 random bytes and stores them in a slice.

Argon2 depends on a configuration, and we will use the default set.

With the password, the salt, and the config, we can hash our clear-text password.

With this in place, we can do another test run. Open the command line and execute cargo run in the root folder of the project and send an example registration to the endpoint. Once we hit the endpoint, we check via the PSQL tool on the command line if the password was stored correctly:

```
$ curl --location --request POST 'localhost:3030/registration' \
--header 'Content-Type: application/json' \
--data-raw '{
    "email": "test@email.com",
    "password": "clearntext"
}'

$ psql rustwebdev
psql (14.2)
Type "help" for help.

rustwebdev=# select * from accounts;
      email       |
password
------------------+-----------------------------------------------------------
------------------------------------------------------------------
test@email.com |
$argon2i$v=19$m=4096,t=3,p=1$gogEn9TQPNVgSjMgDwC/JefcBmDgmyjWtuwaG1PemwA$ei
zVOyzSvnNlnvpHjmHu+d6SEQdNs3lybC4wPpYoZWo
(3 rows)

rustwebdev=#
```

9.1.5 *Handling duplicate account errors*

But what happens when we send the exact same request again? We set up our PostgreSQL accounts table in the migration file. There we specify the email field is our PRIMARY KEY. Therefore, when we try to insert the same dataset again, with the exact same email, PostgreSQL will throw an error. In our handle-files crate, we haven't treated database errors differently until now. Each error from the database will result in an HTTP code 422 to the user.

We pass up the database error from the store, through the routes back to the Warp server. If an error case exists, the Warp server will use the return_error function, which we'll implement in the handle-errors crate. In this piece of code, we go over the Error enum and check which error we are dealing with, and depending on the variant, we modify the response to the client or user.

The problem with our DatabaseQueryError so far is that we don't pass a parameter. The actual error will be logged with our Tracing library in the corresponding store function, but then we just return a generic database error with no other information.

Therefore, we have to first add a parameter to this enum variant in the handle-errors crate. Let's remember how our add_account function looks, with the error case in bold:

...

```
pub async fn add_account(self, account: Account) -> Result<bool, Error> {
    match sqlx::query("INSERT INTO accounts (email, password)
        VALUES ($1, $2)")
```

```
                        .bind(account.email)
                        .bind(account.password)
                        .execute(&self.connection)
                        .await
                {
                    Ok(_) => Ok(true),
                    Err(error) => {
                        tracing::event!(
                            tracing::Level::ERROR,
                            code = error
                                .as_database_error()
                                .unwrap()
                                .code()
                                .unwrap()
                                .parse::<i32>()
                                .unwrap(),
                            db_message = error
                                .as_database_error()
                                .unwrap()
                                .message(),
                            constraint = error
                                .as_database_error()
                                .unwrap()
                                .constraint()
                                .unwrap()
                        );
                        Err(Error::DatabaseQueryError(error))
                    }
                }
            }

        ...
```

The error we receive here is from the SQLx crate. This crate offers an `Error` enum (https://docs.rs/sqlx/latest/sqlx/enum.Error.html) that has a variant called `Database-Error` (http://mng.bz/G1Bq). Therefore, if we pass this SQLx error all the way up to our `return_error` function, we are able to check which error variant we are dealing with and then decide, based on the error code, what to do with it.

Since we are using Tracing, we can see on the command line the structure of the error we receive if a dataset with the same email already exists (highlighted in bold):

```
Finished dev [unoptimized + debuginfo] target(s) in 5.05s
Running `target/debug/practical-rust-book`
Apr 04 11:37:12.012 ERROR practical_rust_book::store: code=23505
db_message="duplicate key value violates unique constraint
\"accounts_pkey\"" constraint="accounts_pkey"
Apr 04 11:37:12.012 ERROR warp::filters::trace: unable to process request
(internal error) status=500
error=Rejection([DatabaseQueryError(Database(PgDatabaseError { severity:
Error, code: "23505", message: "duplicate key value violates unique
constraint \"accounts_pkey\"", detail: Some("Key
(email)=(testass@email.com) already exists."), hint: None, position: None,
where: None, schema: Some("public"), table: Some("accounts"), column: None,
```

```
data_type: None, constraint: Some("accounts_pkey"), file:
Some("nbtinsert.c"), line: Some(670), routine: Some("_bt_check_unique")
})), MethodNotAllowed, MethodNotAllowed, MethodNotAllowed])
```

It seems that the `duplicate key value` has a specific error code we could check against. A possible first solution is shown in the following listing.

Listing 9.13 Extending handle-errors to allow passing through `sqlx::Error`

```
...

#[derive(Debug)]
pub enum Error {
    ParseError(std::num::ParseIntError),
    MissingParameters,
    DatabaseQueryError(sqlx::Error),          ◁────  Adds a parameter to
    ReqwestAPIError(ReqwestError),                   DatabaseQueryError,
    MiddlewareReqwestAPIError(MiddlewareReqwestError),  which is the sqlx::Error
    ClientError(APILayerError),                     we want to check against
    ServerError(APILayerError)
}

...

impl std::fmt::Display for Error {
    fn fmt(&self, f: &mut std::fmt::Formatter) -> std::fmt::Result {
        match &*self {
            Error::ParseError(ref err) => {
                write!(f, "Cannot parse parameter: {}", err)
            }
            Error::MissingParameters => write!(f, "Missing parameter"),
            Error::DatabaseQueryError(_) => {
                write!(f, "Cannot update, invalid data")
            }
            Error::ReqwestAPIError(err) => {
                write!(f, "External API error: {}", err)
            }
            Error::MiddlewareReqwestAPIError(err) => {
                write!(f, "External API error: {}", err)
            }
            Error::ClientError(err) => {
                write!(f, "External Client error: {}", err)
            }
            Error::ServerError(err) => {
                write!(f, "External Server error: {}", err)
            }
        }
    }
}

...

const DUPLICATE_KEY: u32 = 23505;
```

When we try to print the error, we don't care (for now) what the actual error is.

```
#[instrument]
pub async fn return_error(r: Rejection) -> Result<impl Reply, Rejection> {
    if let Some(crate::Error::DatabaseQueryError(e)) = r.find() {
        event!(Level::ERROR, "Database query error");

        match e {
            sqlx::Error::Database(err) => {
                if err.code().unwrap().parse::<u32>().unwrap() ==
                    DUPLICATE_KEY {
                    Ok(warp::reply::with_status(
                        "Account already exsists".to_string(),
                        StatusCode::UNPROCESSABLE_ENTITY,
                    ))
                } else {
                    Ok(warp::reply::with_status(
                        "Cannot update data".to_string(),
                        StatusCode::UNPROCESSABLE_ENTITY,
                    ))
                }
            },
            _ => {
                Ok(warp::reply::with_status(
                    "Cannot update data".to_string(),
                    StatusCode::UNPROCESSABLE_ENTITY,
                ))
            }
        }
    }
...

}
```

Adds the parameter to the if clause so we can use it in the code block beneath

Matches against sqlx::Error to see if we have a database error on our hands

If it's a database error, we know we have a code field. We parse the &str to a i32 so we can compare it to the one we are looking for.

If it's the code we are looking for, we pass back a message that the account already exists.

We are not done yet. The next listing shows that we also have to pass the SQLx error up when we get one back after trying to execute the SQL in store.rs.

Listing 9.14 Passing the error up to the `Error` enum variant in store.rs

```
...
pub async fn get_questions(
    self,
    limit: Option<i32>,
    offset: i32,
) -> Result<Vec<Question>, Error> {
    ...

    {
        Ok(questions) => Ok(questions),
        Err(error) => {
            tracing::event!(tracing::Level::ERROR, "{:?}", error);
            Err(Error::DatabaseQueryError(error))
        }
    }
}
```

```
pub async fn add_question(
    self,
    new_question: NewQuestion
) -> Result<Question, Error> {
    …

            Ok(question) => Ok(question),
            Err(error) => {
                tracing::event!(tracing::Level::ERROR, "{:?}", error);
                Err(Error::DatabaseQueryError(error))
            },
        }
}

pub async fn update_question(
    self,
    question: Question,
    id: i32
) -> Result<Question, Error> {
    …

        Ok(question) => Ok(question),
        Err(error) => {
            tracing::event!(tracing::Level::ERROR, "{:?}", error);
            Err(Error::DatabaseQueryError(error))
        }
    }
}

pub async fn delete_question(self, id: i32) -> Result<bool, Error> {
    match sqlx::query("DELETE FROM questions WHERE id = $1")
        .bind(id)
        .execute(&self.connection)
        .await
    {
        Ok(_) => Ok(true),
        Err(error) => {
            tracing::event!(tracing::Level::ERROR, "{:?}", error);
            Err(Error::DatabaseQueryError(error))
        }
    }
}

pub async fn add_answer(self, answer: Answer) -> Result<bool, Error> {
    …

        Ok(_) => Ok(true),
        Err(error) => {
            tracing::event!(
                tracing::Level::ERROR,
                code = error
                    .as_database_error()
                    .unwrap()
                    .code()
                    .unwrap()
```

```
                    .parse::<i32>()
                    .unwrap(),
                db_message = error.as_database_error().unwrap().message(),
                constraint = error.as_database_error().unwrap().constraint()
                    .unwrap()
            );
            Err(Error::DatabaseQueryError(error))
        }
    }
}

pub async fn add_account(self, account: Account) -> Result<bool, Error> {
    ...
        Ok(_) => Ok(true),
        Err(error) => {
            tracing::event!(
                tracing::Level::ERROR,
                code = error
                    .as_database_error()
                    .unwrap()
                    .code()
                    .unwrap()
                    .parse::<i32>()
                    .unwrap(),
                db_message = error
                    .as_database_error()
                    .unwrap()
                    .message(),
                constraint = error
                    .as_database_error()
                    .unwrap()
                    .constraint()
                    .unwrap()
            );
            Err(Error::DatabaseQueryError(error))
        }
    }
}
```

When everything is updated, we restart the server via cargo run and try to create a new account with the same email as before:

```
$ curl --location --request POST 'localhost:3030/registration' \
    --header 'Content-Type: application/json' \
    --data-raw '{
    "email": "test@email.com",
    "password": "cleartext"
}'
Account already exsists?
```

We confirm that accounts can be created through our new API endpoint. We hash and salt the passwords, and reentering the same email won't lead to data duplication. Everything is set to go to the next step: logging new users in to our system.

9.1.6 Stateful vs. stateless authentication

Before we can write the login logic, we have to think through what a logged-in user means for us. Be aware that we're speaking in terms of the context of the book's application. And even here, you can choose different solutions for different purposes. The field of security, session handling, and authentication is vast and cannot be covered in one chapter. A great reference to consult is *API Security in Action* by Neil Madden (Manning, 2020, https://www.manning.com/books/api-security-in-action).

As we saw, the first step in the whole flow is to register a new user and save the credentials in a database. The next step is to identify an already logged-in user. This brings up the question, how can we keep a user logged in? If they want to make multiple requests, we don't always want to make them send their credentials.

One of the ways this problem is solved is through a token. A *token* can be like a key to your front door. It's a shortcut of saying, "Yes, I am the owner of this home and I prove it with the key." Our web service can therefore issue a digital key and hand it out to the user. Now with every request, the user attaches this key to the header, and we can check whether the key is valid. Figure 9.4 shows two ways of handling tokens in our application: either issuing a token and forgetting about it, or storing each issued token in a database so we can invalidate them if needed.

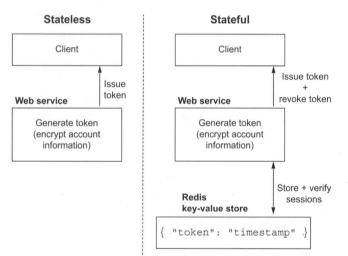

Figure 9.4   Stateless vs. stateful architecture

As with a physical key, someone can steal it, and we don't have a valid way of saying, "Wait, you are not the person I gave the key to in the first place." You can say, "I don't care; I provide a general API, and whoever has the key can make the requests." If the actual owner now wants to revoke the validity of the key (saying the key is stolen), it would be nice to have a way to invalidate the key and issue a new one.

Another solution is to hand out the key, but also store the key plus a timestamp in a database. Now every time someone tries to make a request with the authentication key attached to the header, we compare the key with the one in the database, and if it's there, we allow the request to follow through. Revoking then becomes a simple act of deleting this key from our database and therefore invalidating it.

Each scenario has tradeoffs, and in a production setting you might use a combination of these two concepts. We will have a closer look at the differences in section 9.2. For now, it is important to know that we have to hand out some form of token to the user when they log in.

In a stateless environment, there is no easy way of logging out the user. One way is to destroy the token in the frontend, so the user has to regenerate a new one with the next login. In a somewhat stateful environment where we store the tokens in a key-value store, we could simply remove the row with the token.

9.1.7 Adding the login endpoint

We continue in our authentaction.rs file and place the login function there. Listing 9.15 shows the method and the needed helper functions. We first explain the reasoning behind the implementation shown, and then cover which function we need to add to our store and the routes to make it all work together.

Listing 9.15   The login function in src/routes/authentication.rs

```
...
use crate::types::account::{Account, AccountId};          ◁── Imports the AccountID
...                                                            since we use it to create
                                                               the token

pub async fn login(
    store: Store,                                         ◁── Assumes the route handler
    login: Account                                            will get the store and login
) -> Result<impl warp::Reply, warp::Rejection> {             object passed down
    match store.get_account(login.email).await {          ◁──
        Ok(account) => match verify_password(                First checks if the user
            &account.password,                               exists in our database
            login.password.as_bytes()
        ) {                                        If the verification process is successful
            Ok(verified) => {                      (the library didn't fail), we...
                if verified {
                    Ok(warp::reply::json(&issue_token(     ◁──
                        account.id.expect("id not found"),     ...and create a
                    )))                                         token with the
                } else {                                        AccountID in it.
                    Err(warp::reject::custom(handle_errors::Error::WrongPassword))
                }
            }
            Err(e) => Err(warp::reject::custom(
                handle_errors::Error::ArgonLibraryError(e),  ◁──
            )),                                                  If the library
        },                                                       fails, we have to
        Err(e) => Err(warp::reject::custom(e)),                  send back a 500
    }                                                            to the user.
}
...
```

If it does, we verify that the password is the correct one.

...check if the password was indeed verified...

If not, we create a new error type called WrongPassword and handle this later in the handle-errors crate.

```
fn verify_password(
    hash: &str,
    password: &[u8]
) -> Result<bool, argon2::Error> {
    argon2::verify_encoded(hash, password)
}


fn issue_token(
    account_id: AccountId
) -> String {
    let state = serde_json::to_string(&account_id)
        .expect("Failed to serialize")  state");
    local_paseto(
        &state,
        None,
        "RANDOM WORDS WINTER MACINTOSH PC".as_bytes()
    ).expect("Failed to create token")
}
```

> The argon2 crate will use the salt, which is part of the hash, to verify that the hash from the database is the same as the password from the login process.

> We issue a token that takes the AccountID, stringifies it, and packs it into the paseto token.

A lot is going on in this listing. Here's the process in plain English:

- We need a login route handler to pass the email/password combination to, and to check whether a valid user is behind that combination.
- Therefore, the first step is to try to fetch the user by the given email.
- If we have the user, we need to check whether the given password matches the one from the database.
- A simple comparison is not enough since we have a hashed password in the database and a plain-text password from the user via the route handler.
- If the password matches, we create a token encapsulating the account ID, and send it back as an HTTP response.
- The account ID is helpful for us on the backend side to verify that the user is verified to access the intended resource.

The interesting bits in this listing are certainly the decisions of how to create the token and how to verify that the password is the correct one. Instead of using the widely used JWT format, we use Paseto, which generally has a stronger algorithm, and the format is more tamper proof.

We use the same crate we used to create the password hash to verify that the login password matches the one in the database. The salt is part of the password hash, and this is what the argon2 crate uses to verify the hash with the plain-text password.

What we didn't cover yet are three other parts of the codebase:

- Fetching an account from the `accounts` table
- Extending the handle-errors crate to handle the wrong password error
- Adding the login route handler to a new API path in main.rs

The get_account function is almost identical to get_questions and get_answers, except this time we just want one response and therefore add a WHERE clause to the SQL. The following listing shows the updated store.rs file.

Listing 9.16   Adding get_account to src/store.rs

```
...
    pub async fn get_account(self, email: String) -> Result<Account, Error> {
        match sqlx::query("SELECT *  from accounts where email = $1")
            .bind(email)
            .map(|row: PgRow| Account {
                id: Some(AccountId(row.get("id"))),
                email: row.get("email"),
                password: row.get("password"),
            })
            .fetch_one(&self.connection)
                .await
        {
        Ok(account) => Ok(account),
        Err(error) => {
            tracing::event!(tracing::Level::ERROR, "{:?}", error);
            Err(Error::DatabaseQueryError(error))
        }
        }
    }
}
```

We are still missing two components: adding the two new errors we implemented in the route handler and creating the route inside main.rs. The following listing shows the updated lib.rs file of the handle-errors crate.

Listing 9.17   Adding the new errors in the handle-errors crate

```
...
use tracing::{event, Level, instrument};
use argon2::Error as ArgonError;
use reqwest::Error as ReqwestError;
use reqwest_middleware::Error as MiddlewareReqwestError;


#[derive(Debug)]
pub enum Error {
    ParseError(std::num::ParseIntError),
    MissingParameters,
    WrongPassword,
    ArgonLibraryError(ArgonError),
    DatabaseQueryError(sqlx::Error),
    ReqwestAPIError(ReqwestError),
    MiddlewareReqwestAPIError(MiddlewareReqwestError),
    ClientError(APILayerError),
    ServerError(APILayerError)
}
```

...

```
impl std::fmt::Display for Error {
    fn fmt(&self, f: &mut std::fmt::Formatter) -> std::fmt::Result {
        match &*self {
            Error::ParseError(ref err) => {
                write!(f, "Cannot parse parameter: {}", err)
            }
            Error::MissingParameters => write!(f, "Missing parameter"),
            Error::WrongPassword => {
                write!(f, "Wrong password")
            }
            Error::ArgonLibraryError(_) => {
                write!(f, "Cannot verifiy password")
            }
            Error::DatabaseQueryError(_) => {
                write!(f, "Cannot update, invalid data")
            }
            Error::ReqwestAPIError(err) => {
                write!(f, "External API error: {}", err)
            }
            Error::MiddlewareReqwestAPIError(err) => {
                write!(f, "External API error: {}", err)
            }
            Error::ClientError(err) => {
                write!(f, "External Client error: {}", err)
            }
            Error::ServerError(err) => {
                write!(f, "External Server error: {}", err)
            }
        }
    }
}
```

...

```
#[instrument]
pub async fn return_error(r: Rejection) -> Result<impl Reply, Rejection> {
    ...

    } else if let Some(crate::Error::ReqwestAPIError(e)) = r.find() {
        event!(Level::ERROR, "{}", e);
        Ok(warp::reply::with_status(
            "Internal Server Error".to_string(),
            StatusCode::INTERNAL_SERVER_ERROR,
        ))
    } else if let Some(crate::Error::WrongPassword) = r.find() {
        event!(Level::ERROR, "Entered wrong password");
        Ok(warp::reply::with_status(
            "Wrong E-Mail/Password combination".to_string(),
            StatusCode::UNAUTHORIZED,
        ))
    }
    ...
}
```

The last piece is adding a new login route to our server, as shown next.

> **Listing 9.18   Adding the login route to our server in main.rs**

```
...

    let login = warp::post()
        .and(warp::path("login"))
        .and(warp::path::end())
        .and(store_filter.clone())
        .and(warp::body::json())
        .and_then(routes::authentication::login);

    let routes = get_questions
        .or(update_question)
        .or(add_question)
        .or(delete_question)
        .or(add_answer)
        .or(registration)
        .or(login)
        .with(cors)
        .with(warp::trace::request())
        .recover(return_error);

    warp::serve(routes).run(([127, 0, 0, 1], 3030)).await;

    Ok(())
}
```

Running the server with `cargo run` will compile the latest code, and we can try to log in with our email/password combination we used in the registration process:

```
$ curl --location --request POST 'localhost:3030/login' \
    --header 'Content-Type: application/json' \
    --data-raw '{
    "email": "test@email.com",
    "password": "cleartext"
  }'
"v2.local.zCW0HfFeH8ENzrX4XfSTxCzlG8z1ZudazLM6ldNeksweiwg5klJSc-
UBkuU6INGH590qlj1xaet-CI9oBAlzdQunbQvhwCk7EN0wJaW9"?
```

And it works! We can use the login path to send over our credentials, and we get a token in return. We still have to add a bit of security to our token issuance. Once the token is created, there is no way for us to invalidate this token except by changing our secret with which we create tokens. A simple first step is to add an expiry date for each token.

9.1.8   *Adding an expiry date to tokens*

Let's revisit our `issue_token` function again:

```
fn issue_token(account_id: AccountId) -> String {
    let state = serde_json::to_string(&account_id)
        .expect("Failed to serialize")  state");
```

```
    local_paseto(
        &state,
        None,
        "RANDOM WORDS WINTER MACINTOSH PC".as_bytes()
    ).expect("Failed to create token")
}
```

We use a secret to hash our tokens and send it out to the requesting client. This token is now alive forever. We must think about multiple layers of security when issuing tokens:

- How can a user invalidate the token or log out?
- For how long is a token valid?
- How does the server react to stolen tokens?
- How can we kill sessions from the server side?

A first step is to add an expiry date to our token. This should be standard practice for each public (or private) web service. We need the help of a new crate, chrono. The following listing shows the added line in the Cargo.toml file.

Listing 9.19 Adding chrono and time to our project

```
[package]
name = "practical-rust-book"
version = "0.1.0"
edition = "2021"

[dependencies]
...
rust-argon2 = "1.0"
paseto = "2.0"
chrono = "0.4.19"
```

We use this helper to create proper time formats in our codebase. We need to extend our issuance of the token method and expand it a little bit to add a timestamp, as shown here.

Listing 9.20 Adding timestamps to our tokens in src/routes/authentication.rs

```
use chrono::prelude::*;

...

fn issue_token(account_id: AccountId) -> String {
    let current_date_time = Utc::now();
    let dt = current_date_time + chrono::Duration::days(1);

    paseto::tokens::PasetoBuilder::new()
        .set_encryption_key(
            &Vec::from("RANDOM WORDS WINTER MACINTOSH PC".as_bytes()
            ))
        .set_expiration(&dt)
        .set_not_before(&Utc::now())
```

```
        .set_claim("account_id", serde_json::json!(account_id))
        .build()
        .expect("Failed to construct paseto token w/ builder!")
}
```

Instead of the local_paseto function, we use PasetoBuilder to create our token. We add account_id as a claim to the token, which can later be decrypted again. To generate the time, we need a type called DateTime. This is what the Utc::now function from the chrono crate does. We also add one day to this timestamp, since we use it as our expiration date. This added expiry gives us a bit of a piece of mind, since the worst case scenario is now that an attacker can use this token for 24 hours until it becomes useless. In section 9.2, we'll look at how to use this token in the header to verify that a request is allowed to access our routes.

9.2 Adding authorization middleware

After a successful login, we receive a token that encapsulates the account ID. With every request, we will check whether the token is set in the HTTP header, and whether it's valid. If it is, we will decrypt the token and take the account ID from it.

On the other side, to be able to check if a client is allowed to modify the underlying resource (for example, account 1 wants to modify a question), we have to check whether the question was actually created by this account. Therefore, we add a new table column to our questions and answers, which is account_id, and store with every new row the account_id. We then can check if the token from the HTTP request is allowed to modify that resource. The flow in figure 9.5 shows the added middleware.

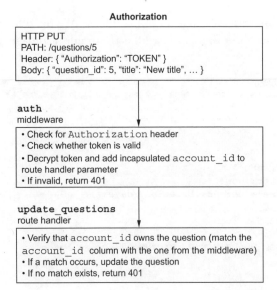

Figure 9.5   Authorization flow

Now instead of changing our migrations and dropping our complete database, we can use a new migration file for both the questions and the answers tables to add a new column.

9.2.1 Migrating the database tables

The first step is to prepare our database for the changes. We open the terminal and create two new migration files via the SQLx CLI. Make sure to execute the commands in the root folder of your project:

```
$ sqlx migrate add -r extend_questions_table;
$ sqlx migrate add -r extend_answers table;
```

These commands create four files altogether inside the migrations folder in our project. We can open each of them and add our SQL. The following listing shows the questions table migration.

> **Listing 9.21 Extending questions via migrations/**_extend_questions_table.up.rs**

```
ALTER TABLE questions
ADD COLUMN account_id serial;
```

And the following shows the reversion, dropping the column again.

> **Listing 9.22 Reverting the previous addition of the account_id column**

```
ALTER TABLE questions
DROP COLUMN account_id;
```

The code for the book shows the other two migration files to adjust the answers table (http://mng.bz/z5ea). If you start the application via cargo run, the migrations are run and add the column in the database tables of questions and answers. In the next step, we first focus on how to extract the token from an HTTP request and which part of the code we need to change so that we can verify the account ID and store it alongside our resources.

9.2.2 Creating token validation middleware

The first step in the authentication flow has to come from the client. As we see in figure 9.5, we expect a token in the HTTP Authorization header. When the request hits our web service, we can check the header, get the token out, and try to decrypt it. Since we have the private decryption key just on the server side, we can check whether the token is valid, and if it is, we can read the value from it that we put there in the first place (namely, the account ID).

We chose Warp as our web framework for this book project. And depending on your framework, this step may look slightly different. A common approach or naming convention for this type of logic is called *middleware*. Middleware is placed after the

HTTP request is accepted by a route, but just before it is passed on to the route handler. The job of middleware is to extract or add information to a request, so the route handlers can do their job.

But what exactly do we extract? In the `issue_token` function, we add `account_id` as a claim. If we inspect the token closer however, paseto is adding an expiry date and a field called `nbf`, which means "not used before this timestamp."

In a stateful environment, we would call this a *session*. Next to the account ID, we could encrypt the user role and other helpful information to decide whether the HTTP is allowed to reach certain endpoints. Therefore, in this book, we fall back to the naming convention of a session. The following listing shows the added `Session` struct we add to the account.rs file in the types folder.

Listing 9.23   **Adding a concept of a `Session` to our codebase in src/types/account.rs**

```
use serde::{Deserialize, Serialize};
use chrono::prelude::*;

#[derive(Serialize, Deserialize, Debug, Clone)]
pub struct Session {
    pub exp: DateTime<Utc>,
    pub account_id: AccountId,
    pub nbf: DateTime<Utc>,
}

#[derive(Serialize, Deserialize, Debug, Clone)]
pub struct Account {
    pub id: Option<AccountId>,
    pub email: String,
    pub password: String,
}

#[derive(Deserialize, Serialize, Debug, Clone, PartialEq, Eq, Hash)]
pub struct AccountId(pub i32);
```

Now we can concentrate on our middleware. We know we have to extract `account_id` from the `token` and store it in a new `Session`. Extracting information from an HTTP request is done through a `Filter` trait in Warp. We already created a filter for our `Store`, which we add to every route handler. This new validation middleware follows the same logic, and will add `Session` to the route handlers, or reject the request if the token is not valid. The next listing shows added functionality inside the authentication.rs file in the routes folder.

Listing 9.24   **Adding the `auth` middleware logic in src/routes/authentication.rs**

```
...

pub fn verify_token(token: String) -> Result<Session, handle_errors::Error> {
    let token = paseto::tokens::validate_local_token(
        &token,
        None,
```

```
        &"RANDOM WORDS WINTER MACINTOSH PC".as_bytes(),
        &paseto::tokens::TimeBackend::Chrono,
    )
        .map_err(|_| handle_errors::Error::CannotDecryptToken)?;

    serde_json::from_value::<Session>(token).map_err(|_| {
        handle_errors::Error::CannotDecryptToken
    })
}

...


fn issue_token(account_id: AccountId) -> String {
    let current_date_time = Utc::now();
    let dt = current_date_time + chrono::Duration::days(1);

    paseto::tokens::PasetoBuilder::new()
        .set_encryption_key(
            &Vec::from("RANDOM WORDS WINTER MACINTOSH PC".as_bytes()
        ))
        .set_expiration(&dt)
        .set_not_before(&Utc::now())
        .set_claim("account_id", serde_json::json!(account_id))
        .build()
        .expect("Failed to construct paseto token w/ builder!")
}

pub fn auth() ->
    impl Filter<Extract = (Session,), Error = warp::Rejection> + Clone {
    warp::header::<String>("Authorization").and_then(|token: String| {
        let token = match verify_token(token) {
            Ok(t) => t,
            Err(_) => return future::ready(Err(warp::reject::reject())),
        };

        future::ready(Ok(token))
    })
}
```

The auth function signature looks quite convoluted. This is the part that is Warp specific, and we have to roll with it. If we implement middleware, we have to return a type that implements the Warp Filter trait, so the framework can do further work on it (for example, passing it to the route handler afterward). Traits in Rust ensure that a type implements certain behavior so other functions can call associated functions on it. For the auth function, we return a type that implements the Filter trait (impl Filter), and this Filter trait expects the generic type Session, or an Error that implements Warp's Rejection trait. We also want to make sure we can clone the Filter that we return, so we add + Clone at the end of the signature.

NOTE This function signature looks convoluted, and it's for you to decide whether you want to just copy and paste this middleware function and adapt it for your use case, or understand at a deeper level what is going on and study it further.

The function also contains a `future::ready` call, which we have never seen before in this journey. By digging through Warp's examples (http://mng.bz/09Ox), you can find that middleware functions return an `impl Filter` signature. This lets us either extract a value and pass it on to the route handler or reject the request and skip the route handlers altogether.

A first pragmatic approach is to return a simple `Ok(token)`, which would lead to the following compiler message:

```
expected type `std::future::Ready<Result<_, Rejection>>`
   found enum `Result<Session, _>`rustcE0308
```

So we know Warp is expecting the type `std::future::Ready` back, which wraps the `Result`. The function call `future::ready` does exactly this: returns a type `Ready` with the `Result` inside it. Don't let yourself be put off by this, though. This is semantics, and once you know how to construct such a function, it becomes more of the same later when you add features.

The important pieces are that we check for the Authorization header, and if there is one, we try to decrypt it with the function `verify_token` from the paseto crate we used to encrypt the token. As you remember, we salted the password to make it unique, so how can `paseto` figure out the actual password to match it with the one given in plain text? The answer is that the salt is still part of the hash and readable; and in combination with the `&str` we used to encrypt the token, we can decrypt it. We make this filter public via the `pub` keyword, so we can use it inside our main.rs file to extend the routes with it, as shown in the following listing.

> **Listing 9.25   Adding the `auth` filter to the routes**

```
#![warn(clippy::all)]

use handle_errors::return_error;
use tracing_subscriber::fmt::format::FmtSpan;
use warp::{http::Method, Filter};

...

#[tokio::main]
async fn main() -> Result<(), sqlx::Error> {

    ...

    let get_questions = warp::get()
        .and(warp::path("questions"))
        .and(warp::path::end())
        .and(warp::query())
        .and(store_filter.clone())
        .and_then(routes::question::get_questions);
```

```
    let update_question = warp::put()
        .and(warp::path("questions"))
        .and(warp::path::param::<i32>())
        .and(warp::path::end())
        .and(routes::authentication::auth())
        .and(store_filter.clone())
        .and(warp::body::json())
        .and_then(routes::question::update_question);

    let delete_question = warp::delete()
        .and(warp::path("questions"))
        .and(warp::path::param::<i32>())
        .and(warp::path::end())
        .and(routes::authentication::auth())
        .and(store_filter.clone())
        .and_then(routes::question::delete_question);

    let add_question = warp::post()
        .and(warp::path("questions"))
        .and(warp::path::end())
        .and(routes::authentication::auth())
        .and(store_filter.clone())
        .and(warp::body::json())
        .and_then(routes::question::add_question);

    let add_answer = warp::post()
        .and(warp::path("answers"))
        .and(warp::path::end())
        .and(routes::authentication::auth())
        .and(store_filter.clone())
        .and(warp::body::form())
        .and_then(routes::answer::add_answer);

    let registration = warp::post()
        .and(warp::path("registration"))
        .and(warp::path::end())
        .and(store_filter.clone())
        .and(warp::body::json())
        .and_then(routes::authentication::register);

    let login = warp::post()
        .and(warp::path("login"))
        .and(warp::path::end())
        .and(store_filter.clone())
        .and(warp::body::json())
        .and_then(routes::authentication::login);

    ...
}
```

We verify the token just when the client is attempting to manipulate data. The get_
questions route is public, as well as login and register. Deleting, adding, or updating a question or answer requires a valid token.

Adding this filter will give us a few errors from the compiler again, because now, the routes where we added the `auth` function pass one more parameter to the route handlers (namely, the session).

9.2.3   *Extending existing routes to handle account IDs*

The first route we added the authentication filter to was `update_question`. In the route setup in main.rs, we first filter out the parameter (since we expect the path /questions/{id}) and then we added the filter. The filter, in return, extracts the Authorization header and gives us back a `Session` object. Therefore, in the function signature, we expect a `Session` parameter on the second position. The following listing shows the updated route handler.

> **Listing 9.26   Adding the `Session` parameter to the `update_question` route handler**

```
...

use crate::profanity::check_profanity;
use crate::store::Store;
use crate::types::account::Session;          ◁─────┐  Imports the Session
use crate::types::pagination::{extract_pagination, Pagination};   type from the accounts
use crate::types::question::{NewQuestion, Question};              module

...

pub async fn update_question(
    id: i32,
    session: Session,          ◁───┐  We expect the second
    store: Store,                     parameter to be the type
    question: Question,               Session, since we extract it
) -> Result<impl warp::Reply, warp::Rejection> {   via the auth middleware.
    let account_id = session.account_id;          ◁──── Gets account_id out of
    if store.is_question_owner(id, &account_id).await? {   the Session object to be
        let title = check_profanity(question.title);       able to pass a reference
        let content = check_profanity(question.content);   to later functions

        let (title, content) = tokio::join!(title, content);   ◁── A newly created
                                                                    store function
        if title.is_ok() && content.is_ok() {                       that checks if
            let question = Question {                                the question was
                id: question.id,                                     originally created
                title: title.unwrap(),                               by the same
                content: content.unwrap(),                           account
                tags: question.tags,
            };
            match store.update_question(question, id, account_id).await {   ◁──┐
                Ok(res) => Ok(warp::reply::json(&res)),
                Err(e) => Err(warp::reject::custom(e)),
            }
        } else {
            Err(warp::reject::custom(
                title.expect_err("Expected API call to have failed here"),
```

We now also pass the account_id to the store function, to fill our added account_id column in the database for each new entry.

```
            ))
        }
    } else {
        Err(warp::reject::custom(handle_errors::Error::Unauthorized))    ◀──┐
    }
}                                                                          │
}                                                                          │
```

> **If the account_id from the Session doesn't match the one from the database, we return 401 Unauthorized.**

...

The next step is to update the store functions, and in the end, add the new Unauthorized error to the handle-errors crate. We add a new function in the store to check whether the account_id matches with the one from the question we want to modify. The next listing shows the added is_question_owner function.

> **Listing 9.27   Adding an `is_question_owner` function to store.rs**

...

```
use crate::types::{
    account::{Account, AccountId},
    answer::Answer,
    question::{NewQuestion, Question, QuestionId},
};
```

...

```
    pub async fn is_question_owner(
        &self,
        question_id: i32,
        account_id: &AccountId,
    ) -> Result<bool, Error> {
        match sqlx::query(
            "SELECT * from questions where id = $1 and account_id = $2"
        )
            .bind(question_id)
            .bind(account_id.0)
            .fetch_optional(&self.connection)
            .await
        {
            Ok(question) => Ok(question.is_some()),
            Err(e) => {
                tracing::event!(tracing::Level::ERROR, "{:?}", e);
                Err(Error::DatabaseQueryError(e))
            }
        }
    }
```

Uses the SELECT query from get_questions and two WHERE clauses to it: id and account_id

fetch_optional gives us either None or one answer back.

Checks whether the result "is some," and if not, we return false

...

With each request to modify, add, or delete questions (and answers), we need to add the account_id as well. We still want to double-check if the client is allowed to modify a resource, and if we add a question or answer, we now also store the account_id. The next listing shows the new update_question function in store.rs.

Listing 9.28   Adding the `Session` parameter to `update_question` in store.rs

...

```
    pub async fn update_question(
        self,
        question: Question,
        id: i32,
        account_id: AccountId          <-
) -> Result<Question, Error> {
        println!("{}", account_id.0);
        match sqlx::query(
            "UPDATE questions SET title = $1, content = $2, tags = $3
            WHERE id = $4 AND account_id = $5     <-
            RETURNING id, title, content, tags",
        )
        .bind(question.title)
        .bind(question.content)
        .bind(question.tags)
        .bind(id)
        .bind(account_id.0)               <-
        .map(|row: PgRow| Question {
            id: QuestionId(row.get("id")),
            title: row.get("title"),
            content: row.get("content"),
            tags: row.get("tags"),
        })
        .fetch_one(&self.connection)
        .await
        {
            Ok(question) => Ok(question),
            Err(error) => {
                tracing::event!(tracing::Level::ERROR, "{:?}", error);
                Err(Error::DatabaseQueryError(error))
            }
        }
    }
```

Adds the AccountId parameter to the function that we pass down to in the route handler

Adds a WHERE clause that checks whether the question is owned by the account that wants to modify it

Binds the AccountId, which has one field that we access through the .0

...

The last step is to add an `Unauthorized` error case to the `Error` enum in the handle-errors crate. The following listing shows the addition to the code.

Listing 9.29   Adding the `Unauthorized` error case to the handle-errors crate

...

```
#[derive(Debug)]
pub enum Error {
    ParseError(std::num::ParseIntError),
    MissingParameters,
    WrongPassword,
    CannotDecryptToken,
    Unauthorized,
    ArgonLibraryError(ArgonError),
```

```
            DatabaseQueryError(sqlx::Error),
            ReqwestAPIError(ReqwestError),
            MiddlewareReqwestAPIError(MiddlewareReqwestError),
            ClientError(APILayerError),
            ServerError(APILayerError)
        }
        ...
        impl std::fmt::Display for Error {
            fn fmt(&self, f: &mut std::fmt::Formatter) -> std::fmt::Result {
                match &*self {
                    Error::ParseError(ref err) => {
                        write!(f, "Cannot parse parameter: {}", err)
                    },
                    Error::MissingParameters => write!(f, "Missing parameter"),
                    Error::WrongPassword => write!(f, "Wrong password"),
                    Error::CannotDecryptToken => write!(f, "Cannot decrypt error"),
                    Error::Unauthorized => write!(
                        f,
                        "No permission to change the underlying resource"
                    ),
                    Error::ArgonLibraryError(_) => {
                        write!(f, "Cannot verifiy password")
                    },
                    Error::DatabaseQueryError(_) => {
                        write!(f, "Cannot update, invalid data")
                    },
                    Error::ReqwestAPIError(err) => {
                        write!(f, "External API error: {}", err)
                    },
                    Error::MiddlewareReqwestAPIError(err) => {
                        write!(f, "External API error: {}", err)
                    },
                    Error::ClientError(err) => {
                        write!(f, "External Client error: {}", err)
                    },
                    Error::ServerError(err) => {
                        write!(f, "External Server error: {}", err)
                    },
                }
            }
        }


        impl Reject for Error {}
        impl Reject for APILayerError {}


        #[instrument]
        pub async fn return_error(r: Rejection) -> Result<impl Reply, Rejection> {
            ...
            } else if let Some(crate::Error::ReqwestAPIError(e)) = r.find() {
                event!(Level::ERROR, "{}", e);
                Ok(warp::reply::with_status(
                    "Internal Server Error".to_string(),
                    StatusCode::INTERNAL_SERVER_ERROR,
                ))
```

```
    } else if let Some(crate::Error::Unauthorized) = r.find() {
        event!(Level::ERROR, "Not matching account id");
        Ok(warp::reply::with_status(
            "No permission to change underlying resource".to_string(),
            StatusCode::UNAUTHORIZED,
        ))
    }
    ...
}
```

This chapter was already quite code heavy. Changing the other route handlers and store function looks very much like the changes we already made with the update question scenario. The GitHub repository for this chapter (http://mng.bz/K0nK) has all the latest changes and updates.

We can now recompile the codebase, start the application again via cargo run, and test the whole flow via either the curl commands or an app like Postman.

Creating a new question can be done via this curl:

```
$ curl --location --request POST 'localhost:3030/registration' \
    --header 'Content-Type: application/json' \
    --data-raw '{
    "email": "new@email.com",
    "password": "cleartext"
}'
```

To get a token, we have to log in first:

```
$ curl --location --request POST 'localhost:3030/login' \
    --header 'Content-Type: application/json' \
    --data-raw '{
    "email": "new@email.com",
    "password": "cleartext"
}'
"v2.local.Z9EaQ7lfPByBzKIySACj9HH8T8YLkx36aUSR2bUodwjoZzdpak6s-h8"?
```

Then we can create our very first question:

```
$ curl --location --request POST 'localhost:3030/questions' \
    --header 'Authorization:
v2.local.Z9EaQ7lfPByBzKIySACj9HH8T8YLkx36aUSR2bUodwjoZzdpak6s-h8' \
    --header 'Content-Type: application/json' \
    --data-raw '{
    "title": "How can I code better?",
    "content": "Any tips for a Junior developer?"
}'
Question added?
```

If we want to update the question, we can use this token and this curl:

```
$ curl --location --request PUT 'localhost:3030/questions/5' \
    --header 'Authorization:
```

```
v2.local.Z9EaQ7lfPByBzKIySACj9HH8T8YLkx36aUSR2bUodwjoZzdpak6s-h8' \
    --header 'Content-Type: application/json' \
    --data-raw '{
    "id": 5,
    "title": "New title",
    "content": "Any tips for a Junior developer?"
  }'
{"id":5,"title":"New title","content":" Any tips for a Junior
developer?","tags":null}?
```

And if we attempt to try this PUT call with a token from another account, we get rejected:

```
$ curl --location --request PUT 'localhost:3030/questions/5' \
    --header 'Authorization: v2.local.mrd0Bs-
5QC1BjEDXwWr1YbAY7Qf2Lj4A_Ikp3_bh3VaeFefbEbZ1TN0' \
    --header 'Content-Type: application/json' \
    --data-raw '{
    "id": 5,
    "title": "New title ",
    "content": "Any tips for a Junior developer?"
  }'
No permission to change underlying resource?
```

9.3 *What we didn't cover*

This book attempts to serve one goal: using Rust instead of your current language to get an application up and running and into production. There are so many topics and edge cases around authentication and authorization that introducing them would deviate from the goal of the book.

We didn't cover how to set up a sessions database to store tokens that you can then invalidate if a data breach occurs or the user wants to destroy them for other reasons. This falls into the software architecture category. After reading this chapter (and this book), you know how to use Rust to connect to a database, layer your code well so you can abstract over it, and use route handlers and structs to set up a workflow.

Adding a session database in this case is more of the same. Sadly, Warp doesn't have a one-size-fits-all solution here. But you could set up a Redis instance, connect to it, and with every token generation, not only send the result back to the client but also store it in a Redis key-value store.

There are more topics: resetting a user password and creating refresh tokens when the ones we handed out expire. These are topics more suited for authentication-heavy books and articles, and by the time you read this book, the best practices might have changed. Resetting a user password could be a simple process, like creating a new table for reset passwords, where you send out a link with a hash attached to the user via an email, and when the user clicks the link, open a new REST endpoint to verify that the hash exists and update the password through this workflow.

Another topic is the use of Transport Layer Security (TLS) (http://mng.bz/p6R8) for a secure connection to the client. In a larger application, this decision is best left to the infrastructure and, for example, to your NGINX instance. The ideas behind it are more security based, and it is best advised to listen to experts in each field. If this is your first foray into web development, I want to make sure you have heard of TLS and consider it before deploying your service into a production environment for everyone to access.

Summary

- Each web service has to handle authentication and authorization, whether for itself to authenticate inside a microservice architecture, or for a client/server model when offering an API of some sort.
- Make sure to hash and salt passwords before storing them in the database, and use up-to-date recommendations on which hashing algorithm to use.
- A web application offers a few endpoints that can be accessed by users who aren't authenticated.
- A registration endpoint offers a chance to send an email and password combination to the server.
- Based on the complexity of your application, you can store the email and password hash, or add user roles and other properties to an account.
- Make sure to add an ID to each entry in table so you can link resources with the respective account.
- The login endpoint is the entrance to your application. It sends back a token that is the key to authorizing future HTTP requests.
- Middleware is placed between the incoming HTTP call and the handing-off to the route handler. It checks for a valid token and extracts information out of this token.
- A token is a stateless way to do authentication. You can also choose to have a database table with all active tokens to be able to invalidate tokens in the future.
- The middleware will add a new parameter, the account ID, to the route handlers. It's their job to check whether a client is allowed to modify the underlying resource.
- You can decide if you want to establish a secure connection (TLS, for example) via your application code or in your infrastructure setup.

Deploy your application

10

After adding authentication and authorization in chapter 9, we can shift gears and leave writing business logic behind. At this stage, all code is written and done, and it is time to show the world what we built. The compiler doesn't just help us greatly in creating a solid codebase; it also shines when shipping your code to production—for example, cross-compiling the binary for various architectures or creating the smallest binary possible, so we can deploy it via Docker (or without) to different services.

Before we can do that, however, we must go through the code and look for parameters we hardcoded in our application that we have to extract and feed either from
environment variables or through CLI commands. Once we move our code from the
local machine to a third-party hosting provider, we lose control over which port we
have to listen to and how the database URL is defined. These settings are fed by the
third-party-provider (or DevOps teams) through environment variables.

Third-party providers inject IP addresses, ports, and maybe even database URLs
into our application. We have to be open to take these external requirements and use
them in our setup. Rust offers multiple ways to parse environment variables or CLI
commands, and this is exactly what we do in the first section of this chapter. Once this
is done, we have a look at how Cargo can support us in compiling a very optimized
and small binary, and even cross-compile it so you can create a binary under macOS
for a Linux machine. To finish this chapter, we will talk about Docker and how to create a more complex build process yourself.

10.1 *Setting up your application through environment variables*

Once you compile your web service into a binary, you have to be ready to hand it off to
a third party, another team, or a constantly changing environment that it's running
on. Instead of being sure about your local database port you set up on your own
machine, the server or machine it will be running on in production will have a different port assigned for the database. The same goes with logging levels and API keys,
which can change based on the current state of the application.

Therefore, your binary has to be adaptable to some degree. Outside parties
need to be able to tell your application which URL and port to use for the database, as well as the database name and the API key for the third-party service's production endpoint.

Generally, you can feed input into your application in three ways:

- Config files
- Command-line inputs when starting the application
- Dotenv (.env) files in the root folder of your application

Each of these solutions has its advantages and disadvantages. Config files are handy
because you don't have to remember all the CLI commands you need to pass and
can check how the server starts simply by looking at a JSON or TOML file. However, API keys and secrets are best not checked into the repository, which means
you always need another way of passing these to your application in production.
Figure 10.1 shows you these three options and how to access the external provided
parameters in your code.

Command-line inputs are best when you move your application through changing
environments. A different set of CLI inputs can be used in staging and production, for
example, and you don't have to maintain several config files for this. The downside of

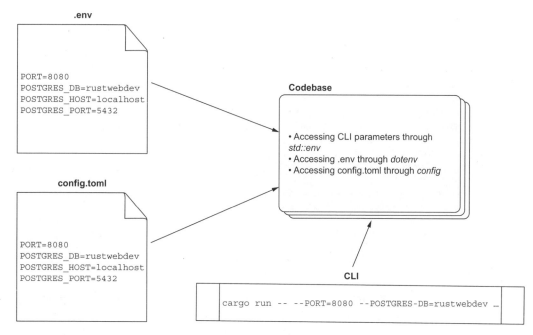

Figure 10.1 Accessing config files and parameters through crates and the standard library

this solution is that it's hard to follow what is being passed to the application simply by looking at the code.

A staple in every setup is the dotenv file. These are files with the file extension .env in the root folder of your application. Like the name suggests, these files are best kept locally and not seen by other parties. You usually store API keys and other secrets in them. The advantage is that you can deploy your application to your production machine, where another set of .env files live that supply the right secrets to your web service. The downside of this solution is that it's not easy to guess which types of commands are possible. It is therefore common practice to check in an .env file with example parameters.

10.1.1 Set up config files

Our first example implementation is handling config files. We'll use a third-party crate called config-rs, which gives us the needed tooling to parse files and read configurations. For starters, we need to add the crate to our Cargo.toml file, as shown in listing 10.1. We are coming close to finally deploying our application, so we'll do some further cleanup in the Cargo.toml file, like using 1.0.0 as the version number and changing the title of the application (highlighted in bold).

Listing 10.1 Adding config-rs to Cargo.toml

```
[package]
name = "rust-web-dev"
```

```
version = "1.0.0"
edition = "2021"

[dependencies]
warp = "0.3"
serde = { version = "1.0", features = ["derive"] }
serde_json = "1.0"
tokio = { version = "1.1.1", features = ["full"] }
handle-errors = { path = "handle-errors", version = "0.1.0" }
tracing = { version = "0.1", features = ["log"] }
tracing-subscriber = "0.2"
sqlx = { version = "0.5", features = [ "runtime-tokio-rustls", "migrate",
"postgres" ] }
reqwest = { version = "0.11", features = ["json"] }
reqwest-middleware = "0.1.1"
reqwest-retry = "0.1.1"
rand = "0.8"
rust-argon2 = "1.0"
paseto = "2.0"
config = { version = "0.13.1", features = ["toml"] }
```

We add the feature flag toml, which enables the crate to read and parse TOML files. There are also options for JSON and YAML, for example.

Next up we create a setup.toml file for storing parameters that might change along the journey of deploying and maintaining this web service. The following listing shows the new file, which we add in the root folder of the project.

Listing 10.2   Adding the setup.toml file to the root folder of the project

```
log_level = "warn"
database_host = "localhost"
database_port = 5432
database_name = "rustwebdev"
port = 8080
```

Inside the setup of the server in main.rs, we supply parameters to our Tracing library, to the setup of our database connection pools, and to the setup of the web server. All these parameters are now expressed in this file. The next step is to read these and use them inside main.rs. The following listing shows the added code, highlighted in bold.

Listing 10.3   Reading the parameters from the setup.toml file inside main.rs

```
#![warn(clippy::all)]

use config::Config;                          ◁─┐ Imports the config-rs
use handle_errors::return_error;                │ crate into our codebase
use tracing_subscriber::fmt::format::FmtSpan;
use warp::{http::Method, Filter};
use std::env;

mod profanity;
mod routes;
```

```
mod store;
mod types;


#[derive(Parser, Debug, Default, serde::Deserialize, PartialEq)]
struct Args {
    log_level: String,
    /// URL for the postgres database
    database_host: String,
    /// PORT number for the database connection
    database_port: u16,
    /// Database name
    database_name: String,
    /// Web server port
    port: u16,
}


#[tokio::main]
async fn main() -> Result<(), sqlx::Error> {
    let config = Config::builder()
        .add_source(config::File::with_name("setup"))
        .build()
        .unwrap();

    let config =  config
        .try_deserialize::<Args>()
        .unwrap();

    ...

    let log_filter = std::env::var("RUST_LOG").unwrap_or_else(|_| {
        format!(
            "handle_errors={},rust_web_dev={},warp={}",
            config.log_level, config.log_level, config.log_level
        )
    });

    let store = store::Store::new(&format!(
        "postgres://{}:{}/{}",
        config.database_host, config.database_port, config.database_name
    ))
    .await?;

    sqlx::migrate!().run(&store.clone().connection).await?;

    let store_filter = warp::any().map(move || store.clone());

    ...

    warp::serve(routes).run(([127, 0, 0, 1], config.port)).await;

    Ok(())
}
```

Creates a new type called Args, which we can use to deserialize our setup.toml file into a local variable

The config crate gives us a builder method to read our config files into the codebase.

We don't need to specify the .toml extension when parsing the file.

After reading the file, we try to map it (deserialize it) and create a new Args object.

We can now use the struct fields to supply the parameters to our function call and remove the hardcoded strings.

The same goes for the creation of the database connection pool.

Uses the config object to read the port number instead of hardcoding it

You can now try to rerun your web service via `cargo run`, and everything should work as before. The beauty of this solution is the decoupling of the parameters from the source code. A database name change, a different port number, or a different database host can now be changed without touching the code and accidently introducing bugs along the way.

You can add this TOML file to your codebase, and contributors to the repository will now know exactly what they have to set up to make the codebase run locally. They can choose to copy your parameters or use different ones for their local setup. They save a lot of time by not going through your code and trying to figure out which port to open on their database server, for example.

10.1.2 *Accept command-line inputs for your application*

You might, however, not need a complex config file for your application, or the environment you are deploying your code to is using CLI commands to supply parameters to your application. By using CLI parameters, it is also easier to quickly try different environments and configurations without always having to change and save a file.

You can either run your application via `cargo run` or do it via the built binary. Either way, programs can be run with additional parameters attached and will be provided by the operating system. Rust's standard library offers methods to read such arguments and makes them accessible in your codebase, through `std::env::args` (http://mng.bz/xMaB).

We can either use the built-in functionality or a crate that offers a bit more comfort in using command-line arguments. Depending on the complexity of your application, you can choose either. For the book, we choose `clap` (https://github.com/clap-rs/clap). Is it is well maintained and has a wide variety of possible usages.

We are using the same `Args` struct as with the example in section 10.1.1 and try to deserialize the command-line arguments into a new `Args` object. To set everything up, we add the clap crate to our Cargo.toml file. There is a special case for this version of the crate since you might run into compiler errors. A fix is shown in the following listing, where we also specify a version for the proc-macro2 crate, as it crashed our application during the creation of the codebase for this book.

> **Listing 10.4   Adding clap to our project**

```
[package]
name = "rust-web-dev"
version = "1.0.0"
edition = "2021"

[dependencies]
warp = "0.3"
serde = { version = "1.0", features = ["derive"] }
serde_json = "1.0"
tokio = { version = "1.1.1", features = ["full"] }
handle-errors = { path = "handle-errors", version = "0.1.0" }
```

```
tracing = { version = "0.1", features = ["log"] }
tracing-subscriber = "0.2"
sqlx = { version = "0.5", features = [ "runtime-tokio-rustls", "migrate",
"postgres" ] }
reqwest = { version = "0.11", features = ["json"] }
reqwest-middleware = "0.1.1"
reqwest-retry = "0.1.1"
rand = "0.8"
rust-argon2 = "1.0"
paseto = "2.0"
clap = { version = "3.1.7", features = ["derive"] }
proc-macro2 = "1.0.37"
```

Now we can try to parse arguments in our main.rs file.

Listing 10.5   Parsing command-line arguments in main.rs with clap

```
#![warn(clippy::all)]

...

use clap::Parser;

/// Q&A web service API
#[derive(Parser, Debug)]
#[clap(author, version, about, long_about = None)]
struct Args {
    /// Which errors we want to log (info, warn or error)
    #[clap(short, long, default_value = "warn")]
    log_level: String,
    /// URL for the postgres database
    #[clap(long, default_value = "localhost")]
    database_host: String,
    /// PORT number for the database connection
    #[clap(long, default_value = "5432")]
    database_port: u16,
    /// Database name
    #[clap(long, default_value = "rustwebdev")]
    database_name: String,
}

#[tokio::main]
async fn main() -> Result<(), sqlx::Error> {
    let args = Args::parse();

    let log_filter = std::env::var("RUST_LOG").unwrap_or_else(|_| {
        format!(
            "handle_errors={},rust-web-dev={},warp={}",
            args.log_level, args.log_level, args.log_level
        )
    });

    let store = store::Store::new(&format!(
        "postgres://{}:{}/{}",
```

Imports the clap parser, which lets us do the magic of parsing the CLI arguments into our Args object

Uses doc comments, with which clap will build a proper CLI interface in case the user uses the –help command

The details that will be used for the information about the CLI interface

Each field can be transformed automatically in a CLI argument with the short and long keywords, as well as set a default value in case the option is not specified when starting the application.

The parse function will read the CLI arguments and transform them into our Args object.

```
        args.database_host, args.database_port, args.database_name
    ))
    .await?

    sqlx::migrate!().run(&store.clone().connection).await?;

    …

    Ok(())
}
```

When running the application via `cargo run`, we have to add two dashes and then we are able to pass arguments:

```
$ cargo run -- --database-host localhost --log-level warn --database-name
rustwebdev --database-port 5432
```

You can also run it via the compiled binary inside the target folder:

```
$ ./target/debug/rust-web-dev --database-host localhost --log-level warn -
database-name rustwebdev --database-port 5432
```

Adding CLI parameters already gives us a lot more flexibility when operating our web service. However, we still need to cover one use case, which is reading environment variables.

10.1.3 *Read and parse environment variables into your web service*

Environment variables are different in a way, as they are set in the shell that the application is starting. We can add these environment variables via a dotenv (.env) file and use a crate that initializes this file and adds the included key-value pairs to the environment before the server starts.

If you are using third-party hosting services, these often set their specification (for example, port number and host IP) via environment variables. In your code, you have to make sure you read the right environment variables and set the IP and port of your web service accordingly.

First things first: we add a crate called dotenv to our project. This allows us to initialize .env files in our root folder and read the values in our codebase. The following listing shows the updated Cargo.toml file.

> Listing 10.6   Adding the dotenv crate to our project

```
[package]
name = "rust-web-dev"
version = "1.0.0"
edition = "2021"

[dependencies]
…
paseto = "2.0"
```

```
clap = { version = "3.1.7", features = ["derive"] }
proc-macro2 = "1.0.37"
dotenv = "0.15.0"
```

Next we add a file with the name .env in our root folder, and two key-value pairs to it. The first one is the port, since we want to see if we can accommodate a hosting provider setting. We mentioned in this chapter's introduction that these types of files are mostly used for secret keys that shouldn't be added to the repository. The next listing shows the added .env file.

Listing 10.7 The content of the .env file in the root folder of the project

```
BAD_WORDS_API_KEY=API_KEY_HIDDEN_FOR_THE_BOOK
PASETO_KEY="RANDOM WORDS WINTER MACINTOSH PC"
PORT=8080
```

Be aware to add .env to the .gitignore file in your project, so it won't get added to your branch. We can now see how parsing environment variables impacts our code. The next listing shows how we use the environment variables in our main.rs file. Since we want to make sure we added the API key for our third-party service, we want to error early and don't start the server.

Listing 10.8 Accepting environment variables inside main.rs

```
#![warn(clippy::all)]

use dotenv;                              ◁─────  Imports the
use handle_errors::return_error;                 dotenv crate
use tracing_subscriber::fmt::format::FmtSpan;
use warp::{http::Method, Filter};
use std::env;

...

/// Q&A web service API
#[derive(Parser, Debug)]
#[clap(author, version, about, long_about = None)]
struct Args {
    /// Which errors we want to log (info, warn or error)
    #[clap(short, long, default_value = "warn")]
    log_level: String,
    /// URL for the postgres database
    #[clap(long, default_value = "localhost")]
    database_host: String,
    /// PORT number for the database connection
    #[clap(long, default_value = "5432")]
    database_port: u16,
    /// Database name
    #[clap(long, default_value = "rustwebdev")]
    database_name: String,
}
```

**Initializes the .env file
via the dotenv crate**

As we see later, we
have to change our return
error to be one of our
Error enum variants from
the handle-errors crate.

```
#[tokio::main]
async fn main() -> Result<(), handle_errors::Error> {
    dotenv::dotenv().ok();

    if let Err(_) = env::var("BAD_WORDS_API_KEY") {
        panic!("BadWords API key not set");
    }

    if let Err(_) = env::var("PASETO_KEY") {
        panic!("PASETO key not set");
    }

    let port = std::env::var("PORT")
        .ok()
        .map(|val| val.parse::<u16>())
        .unwrap_or(Ok(8080))
        .map_err(|e| handle_errors::Error::ParseError(e))?;

    let args = Args::parse();

    let log_filter = std::env::var("RUST_LOG").unwrap_or_else(|_| {
        format!(
            "handle_errors={},rust-web-dev={},warp={}",
            args.log_level, args.log_level, args.log_level
        )
    });

    let store = store::Store::new(&format!(
        "postgres://{}:{}/{}",
        args.database_host, args.database_port, args.database_name
    ))
    .await
    .map_err(|e| handle_errors::Error::DatabaseQueryError(e))?;

    sqlx::migrate!()
        .run(&store.clone()
        .connection).await.map_err(|e| {
            handle_errors::Error::MigrationError(e)
        })?;

    ...

    warp::serve(routes).run(([127, 0, 0, 1], port)).await;

    Ok(())
}
```

If the API key is not
set, we won't start
the server.

**Checks for the PORT environment
variable, and if set, parses it to a
u16. If it's not set, we default
back to the 808 port or return a
custom error if the parsing fails.**

**Adds a new MigrationError
enum variant in case the
migration fails for some
reason**

**Uses the parsed
PORT environment
variable for starting
our server**

**Changes the default error, which we return from the DB pool
creation, to conform with the rest of the codebase and use our
own error defined in the Error enum in the handle-errors crate**

We also replace the hardcoded paseto encryption key with the one from the .env file,
as shown next.

```
use argon2::{self, Config};
use chrono::prelude::*;
use rand::Rng;
use std::{env, future};
use warp::{http::StatusCode, Filter};

...

pub fn verify_token(token: String) -> Result<Session, handle_errors::Error> {
    let key = env::var("PASETO_KEY").unwrap();
    let token = paseto::tokens::validate_local_token(
        &token,
        None,
        key.as_bytes(),
        &paseto::tokens::TimeBackend::Chrono,
    )
    .map_err(|_| handle_errors::Error::CannotDecryptToken)?;

    serde_json::from_value::<Session>(token).map_err(|_| {
        handle_errors::Error::CannotDecryptToken
    })
}

...

fn issue_token(account_id: AccountId) -> String {
    let key = env::var("PASETO_KEY").unwrap();

    let current_date_time = Utc::now();
    let dt = current_date_time + chrono::Duration::days(1);

    paseto::tokens::PasetoBuilder::new()
        .set_encryption_key(&Vec::from(key.as_bytes()))
        .set_expiration(&dt)
        .set_not_before(&Utc::now())
        .set_claim("account_id", serde_json::json!(account_id))
        .build()
        .expect("Failed to construct paseto token w/ builder!")
}

...
```

The missing piece is the added `Error` enum variant in the handle-errors crate. The following listing shows the added code, which we have done now multiple times in this book.

```
...

#[derive(Debug)]
pub enum Error {
```

```
        ParseError(std::num::ParseIntError),
        MissingParameters,
        WrongPassword,
        CannotDecryptToken,
        Unauthorized,
        ArgonLibraryError(ArgonError),
        DatabaseQueryError(sqlx::Error),
        MigrationError(sqlx::migrate::MigrateError),
        ReqwestAPIError(ReqwestError),
        MiddlewareReqwestAPIError(MiddlewareReqwestError),
        ClientError(APILayerError),
        ServerError(APILayerError)
    }

    ...


    impl std::fmt::Display for Error {
        fn fmt(&self, f: &mut std::fmt::Formatter) -> std::fmt::Result {
            match &*self {
                Error::ParseError(ref err) =>{
                    write!(f, "Cannot parse parameter: {}", err)
                },
                Error::MissingParameters => write!(f, "Missing parameter"),
                Error::WrongPassword => write!(f, "Wrong password"),
                Error::CannotDecryptToken => write!(f, "Cannot decrypt error"),
                Error::Unauthorized => write!(
                    f,
                    "No permission to change the underlying resource"
                ),
                Error::ArgonLibraryError(_) =>{
                    write!(f, "Cannot verifiy password")
                },
                Error::DatabaseQueryError(_) => {
                    write!(f, "Cannot update, invalid data")
                },
                Error::MigrationError(_) => write!(f, "Cannot migrate data"),
                Error::ReqwestAPIError(err) => {
                    write!(f, "External API error: {}", err)
                },
                Error::MiddlewareReqwestAPIError(err) => {
                    write!(f, "External API error: {}", err)
                },
                Error::ClientError(err) => {
                    write!(f, "External Client error: {}", err)
                },
                Error::ServerError(err) => {
                    write!(f, "External Server error: {}", err)
                },
            }
        }
    }

    ...


    }
```

We also added the `BAD_WORDS_API_KEY` to the .env file, but just check if the key-value pair exists. Let's read the value where we need it, inside the profanity.rs file. The following listing shows how we use it in our external API call.

> **Listing 10.11 Using the API key from the .env file in the `check_profanity` function**

```
use std::env;

...

#[instrument]
pub async fn check_profanity(
    content: String
) -> Result<String, handle_errors::Error> {
    // We are already checking if the ENV VARIABLE is set inside main.rs,
    // so safe to unwrap here
    let api_key = env::var("BAD_WORDS_API_KEY").unwrap();

    let retry_policy =
        ExponentialBackoff::builder().build_with_max_retries(3);
    let client = ClientBuilder::new(reqwest::Client::new())
        .with(RetryTransientMiddleware::new_with_policy(retry_policy))
        .build();

    let res = client.post("https://api.apilayer.com
            /bad_words?censor_character={censor_character}"
        )
        .header("apikey", api_key)
        .body(content)
        .send()
        .await
        .map_err(handle_errors::Error::MiddlewareReqwestAPIError)?;

    ...
}
```

You can now play around with different environment variables and see how the endpoint and your code behaves. You will recognize that if you add the `BAD_WORDS_API_KEY` key in the .env file but no value, the code will not fail. You also need to check that the variable to which you assigned the value is not empty. The reading of environment variables concludes the first section of this chapter. No matter in which environment your application is going to be used, you can feed it variables from files, command-line arguments, or other environments and can therefore react dynamically to different environments and requirements.

These are really the last code adjustments we need to make before we can leave our codebase alone and focus on the building and deploying part. We will now have a look at how Cargo can help us prepare our codebase for various environments.

10.2   *Compiling your web service for different environments*

Rust's package manager, Cargo, packs a lot of features. In this section, we'll look at how it can help target and optimize your build binary. It has two main profiles: `dev` and `release`. When you run `cargo build`, Cargo uses the `dev` profile by default, and if you want to build your application for a release, you can add the `--release` flag. Figure 10.2 highlights the differences.

We'll also look at how to cross-compile your binary. Whenever you run `cargo build`, it uses the libraries from the underlying operating system to build the binary. Whenever you execute the binary, it depends on this exact operating system to be able to perform the task. But what if you compile your application on macOS and want to run it on a Linux server?

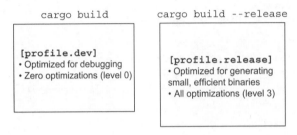

Figure 10.2   **Cargo uses the `dev` profile by default, and will optimize the binary if the `--release` flag is attached.**

In larger companies, a build pipeline is triggered remotely to compile your application on the target machine, so this won't be an issue. But it is important to know that if you develop locally and ship the code "by hand" or have other use cases where the machine the application is built on doesn't have the same configuration as the one it is running on in production, cross-compilation comes to the rescue.

10.2.1   *Development vs. release flag when building your binary*

We saw that the `dev` flag is used by default with `cargo build`. This command will simply use a default profile with the name `dev` (http://mng.bz/WMY0). The settings can be changed inside your Cargo.toml file, but the default parameters are shown here:

```
[profile.dev]
opt-level = 0
debug = true
split-debuginfo = '...'  # Platform-specific.
debug-assertions = true
overflow-checks = true
lto = false
panic = 'unwind'
incremental = true
codegen-units = 256
rpath = false
```

The first setting, `opt-level` (http://mng.bz/82BP), is important. With the value set to 0, the compiler doesn't apply any optimization when compiling your code. This results in faster compile times but also larger binaries.

It is not always straightforward, but generally 3 stands for all optimizations and should result in the fastest produced binary, while 1 and 2 offer "basic optimization" and "some optimization."

The `release` profile (http://mng.bz/E0AJ) looks as follows:

```
[profile.release]
opt-level = 3
debug = false
split-debuginfo = '...'  # Platform-specific.
debug-assertions = false
overflow-checks = false
lto = false
panic = 'unwind'
incremental = false
codegen-units = 16
rpath = false
```

The Cargo documentation has a great up-to-date explanation of the settings (http://mng.bz/N5QD). It is good to know that you can add a [profile.dev] or [profile .release] section to your Cargo.toml file and add individual settings via the key-value pair.

Since the optimization depends largely on your environment and codebase, you can either take the default settings or play around with values to see if you gain a smaller binary size or a more performant one.

The general advice is to use the `--release` flag when you compile your codebase before you ship it to a production environment. The binary size will be smaller, and your code should run more efficiently with that profile.

10.2.2 Cross-compile your binary for different environments

The binary size is not the only consideration when compiling Rust code. During compilation, the compiler uses operating system libraries to build the binary. Each build is dependent on the underlying API calls to the operating system it is running on. If you are on macOS, the binary you are producing will also run on macOS. If you try to copy the code over to a Linux machine and run it, it will fail.

Rust supports the compilation for various environments, called *targets* (http://mng .bz/DDBE). You can get a list of available targets via the command `rustup target list`:

```
$ rustup target list
aarch64-apple-darwin (installed)
aarch64-apple-ios
aarch64-apple-ios-sim
aarch64-fuchsia
aarch64-linux-android
...
```

A full list can be found via the Platform Support section of the Rustc documentation website (http://mng.bz/lR8y). You have to first add an additional target to your toolchain via Rustup before you can build your codebase for this specific environment. So, if you are on a macOS M1 machine and want to build a binary for an Intel Mac, you have to add the target first and then specify it at the build step:

```
$ rustup target install x86_64-apple-darwin
$ cargo build --release --target x86_64-apple-darwin
```

Another common use case is to create cross-compiled binaries. The terms used in this scenario are *dynamically linked* vs. *statically linked* binaries. When building a dynamically linked binary, the created executable will not pack every library it needs into itself but remembers the address spaces to call to when needing to make a system call to the operating system. The differences are shown in figure 10.3.

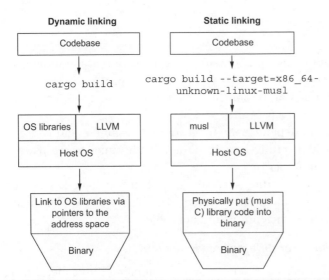

Figure 10.3   Dynamically vs. statically linking in binaries

This makes the binary smaller, but also means it relies on the exact operating system it is built on. If you use a statically linked process, the libraries will be put into the binary, so you don't have to rely on the operating system to provide the exact code and don't have to rely on the memory address of your current host machine.

Rust offers a target for a cross-compiled Linux binary called x86_64-unknown-linux-musl. You can add this to your Rustup toolchain and build it:

```
$ rustup target install x86_64-unknown-linux-musl
$ cargo build --release --target=x86_64-unknown-linux-musl
```

The musl project (www.musl-libc.org/intro.html) provides an implementation of the standard C library optimized for static linking. Build systems can use musl to make system calls to the operating systems, and musl translates the calls to the operating system it is currently running on.

This also means that your current operating system must have this library installed, so the Rust compiler can integrate it into your binary. The installation process depends on which operating system you are running on, and this book can't offer musl installation instructions that remain up-to-date. If you run into problems, keep in mind that if you want to create a statically linked binary, you need musl installed on your machine, and sometimes tell your operating system explicitly (sometimes through environment variables in your shell) which environment you are targeting.

10.3 *Using build.rs in your build process*

Now that you know about targeting different environments in your build process, and using the optimization flag `--release` when compiling your Rust codebase into a binary, we have one more ace up our sleeves before we can get this produced binary onto different servers.

Sometimes a simple `cargo build --release` is not enough. Suppose you want to provide a build ID to your environment variable that can be provided to your codebase, or you want to compile other, non-Rust code that your Rust code depends on. Putting this release-dependent code directly into your codebase feels wrong, since it has nothing to do with the business logic of your application. You could write a bash script, but then you lose the type-safety aspect of Rust along the way.

The team behind Cargo has you covered. If you create a file with the name build.rs, Cargo will run the code in this file before it compiles your application code. Since it's a Rust file, we get all the benefits of the compiler making sure everything works in the correct and intended way, and we profit from the Rust standard library as well.

One important aspect of using build.rs is the setting of environment variables for your CI/CD pipeline. You can use the `cargo:rustc-env=VAR=VALUE` (http://mng.bz/BZBJ) command to set an environment variable from within the build script (like the hash of the current Git HEAD or commit). An example of this usage is in a crate called substrate, which uses build.rs to generate a unique build version (http://mng.bz/de8Q). We use this code as an example in our codebase. The following listing shows the added build.rs in our repository.

> **Listing 10.12 Adding a build.rs file in the root folder of our codebase**

```
use platforms::*;
use std::{borrow::Cow, process::Command};

/// Generate the `cargo:` key output
pub fn generate_cargo_keys() {
    let output = Command::new("git")
            .args(&["rev-parse", "--short", "HEAD"])
            .output();
```

```rust
        let commit = match output {
            Ok(o) if o.status.success() => {
                let sha = String::from_utf8_lossy(&o.stdout).trim().to_owned();
                Cow::from(sha)
            }
            Ok(o) => {
                println!(
                    "cargo:warning=Git command failed with status: {}",
                    o.status
                );
                Cow::from("unknown")
            },
            Err(err) => {
                println!(
                    "cargo:warning=Failed to execute git command: {}",
                    Err
                );
                Cow::from("unknown")
            },
        };

        println!(
            "cargo:rustc-env=RUST_WEB_DEV_VERSION={}",
            get_version(&commit)
        );
}


fn get_platform() -> String {
    let env_dash = if TARGET_ENV.is_some() { "-" } else { "" };

    format!(
        "{}-{}{}{}",
        TARGET_ARCH.as_str(),
        TARGET_OS.as_str(),
        env_dash,
        TARGET_ENV.map(|x| x.as_str()).unwrap_or(""),
    )
}


fn get_version(impl_commit: &str) -> String {
    let commit_dash = if impl_commit.is_empty() { "" } else { "-" };

    format!(
        "{}{}{}-{}",
        std::env::var("CARGO_PKG_VERSION").unwrap_or_default(),
        commit_dash,
        impl_commit,
        get_platform(),
    )
}


fn main() {
 generate_cargo_keys();
}
```

This is an extended way of generating a unique ID, which includes the commit hash and information from the operating system it is running on. The line

```
println!("cargo:rustc-env=RUST_WEB_DEV_VERSION={}", get_version(&commit))
```

adds the outcome of the functions to an environment variable called RUST_WEB_DEV_VERSION, which in turn is set by the command cargo:rustc-env. To be able to read the information from the targeting system, we need a crate called platforms. Now, just adding it into Cargo.toml won't work. We have to add a new section in the Cargo file so the build.rs file can access it. This section is [build-dependencies], shown in the following listing.

> **Listing 10.13 Adding the platforms as a build dependency**

```
[package]
name = "rust-web-dev"
version = "1.0.0"
edition = "2021"

[dependencies]
...


[build-dependencies]
platforms = "2.0.0"
```

With this environment variable set, we try to access it in our codebase. We want to use the Tracing library to produce a log every time the application is started, which displays this exact version number. Each time we find a bug or anything, we can combine it with the exact hash of the commit, so we always know where the problem happened. The next listing shows the added line inside main.rs.

> **Listing 10.14 Adding tracing info with our application version**

```
...

#[tokio::main]
async fn main() -> Result<(), handle_errors::Error> {
    ...

    tracing::info!("Q&A service build ID {}", env!("RUST_WEB_DEV_VERSION"));

    warp::serve(routes).run(([127, 0, 0, 1], port)).await;

    Ok(())
}
```

We use the env! macro that comes with the standard library to access the environment variable. This is also stated in the Cargo documentation (http://mng.bz/rnvX).

When you rerun the application with `cargo run`, you would expect to see the version number on your terminal. But there is none. Why? As you may remember, we set the log level variable to `warn`. We can now see the power of using CLI parameters that we implemented in section 10.1 to allow changing variables dynamically without touching the code again.

We can use this command to lower the log level and then see the expected output:

```
$ cargo run -- --log-level info
   Compiling rust-web-dev v1.0.0
     (/Users/gruberbastian/CodingIsFun/RWD/code/ch_10)
    Finished dev [unoptimized + debuginfo] target(s) in 3.29s
     Running `target/debug/rust-web-dev --database-host localhost -
-log-level info --database-name rustwebdev --database-port 5432`
Apr 19 12:49:37.745  INFO rust_web_dev: Q&A service build ID 1.0.0-c15dd9e-
    aarch64-macos
Apr 19 12:49:37.746  INFO Server::run{addr=127.0.0.1:8080}: warp::server:
    listening on http://127.0.0.1:8080
```

The text in bold highlights the changes. We pass the log level to the application, which produces two logs. The first is our unique ID for this exact build we are running, and the second one is a Warp built-in log.

10.4 *Creating the right Docker image for your web service*

The preceding section unlocked a new superpower to our deployment flow. What these last two sections cover are also Rust-specific ways of getting your code out there. When it comes to deployment, we can't cover every possible solution. Plenty of books cover this. What we can cover, however, is preparing your code as best as you can so its deployment, maintenance, and monitoring is as flawless as possible.

One way Rust code has to be packaged in is a Docker container. We won't go into the details of how Docker works (a great resource for that is *Docker in Action* by Jeff Nickoloff and Stephen Kuenzli [Manning, 2019, www.manning.com/books/docker-in-action-second-edition]). But we will look through the creation of a Docker file and the effects it has on your code. Since we also have a database, we have to think about how to bootstrap PostgreSQL next to our codebase Docker container to have a quickly bootstrapped development environment. Figure 10.4 shows the whole process of preparing and deploying a Docker container.

The Docker container is not used just for the local development environment but also in your deployment pipeline. The official Docker website has a great introduction to Docker if you are not familiar with the concept: https://docs.docker.com/get-started/. It also includes the basic Docker setup for your operating system so you can follow along with the code examples.

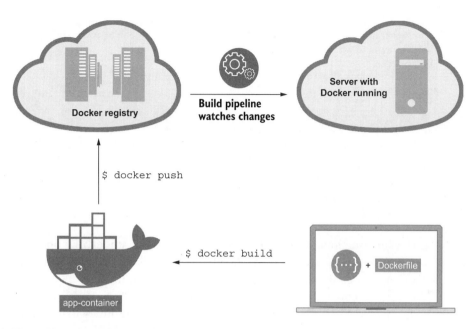

Figure 10.4   A possible workflow for a Docker deployment

10.4.1 Create a statically linked Docker image

We'll take the cross-compilation approach from section 10.2 and prepare our container to be run on various machines. Listing 10.15 shows the Docker file we are going to use, which we put in the root folder of the project. As of this writing, all the code presented is developed on a macOS operating system based on an M1 chip, which is ARM based.

> **Listing 10.15   The Dockerfile we use inside our root folder**

```
FROM rust:latest AS builder

RUN rustup target add x86_64-unknown-linux-musl
RUN apt -y update
RUN apt install -y musl-tools musl-dev
RUN apt-get install -y build-essential
RUN apt install -y gcc-x86-64-linux-gnu

WORKDIR /app

COPY ./ .

// For a musl build on M1 Macs, these ENV variables have to be set
ENV RUSTFLAGS='-C linker=x86_64-linux-gnu-gcc'
ENV CC='gcc'
ENV CC_x86_64_unknown_linux_musl=x86_64-linux-gnu-gcc
ENV CC_x86_64-unknown-linux-musl=x86_64-linux-gnu-gcc
```

```
RUN cargo build --target x86_64-unknown-linux-musl --release

// We create the final Docker image "from scratch"
FROM scratch

WORKDIR /app

// We copy our binary and the .env file over to
// the final image to keep it small
COPY --from=builder /app/target/x86_64-unknown-linux-musl/release/rust-web-
dev ./
COPY --from=builder /app/.env ./

// Executing the binary
CMD ["/app/rust-web-dev"]
```

Each Docker container is based on an *image,* which is the underlying operating system or composition of tooling you might need for this particular use case. Rust has an official Docker image that you can use to run your application.

We want to cover a special case of creating a statically linked Docker container. This gives us the chance to create a smaller, self-contained binary that we can put on a very bare-bones Docker image.

Therefore, we add the musl target to Rustup and install the libraries needed to statically link the created binary. We create a working directory and copy all current files into it, before we set the needed environment variables for the musl library. The last two steps are running the build command via Cargo, which targets our cross-compilation musl target with the release profile, and the command that executes the binary. A simple version targeting the current machine is shown in the following listing.

Listing 10.16 The simplest Dockerfile possible for our use case

```
FROM rust:latest

COPY ./ ./

RUN cargo build --release

CMD ["./target/release/rust-web-dev"]
```

10.4.2 *Set up a local Docker environment with docker-compose*

We have one caveat, though: we need a PostgreSQL instance running that we can connect to for our database tables. We can either try to connect to our local PostgreSQL server through the Docker container, or use a tool called Docker Compose, which can create a network of Docker containers and connect them with one another. This tool is great when it comes to replicating a more complex environment locally you can test against. We need to create a file called docker-compose.yml in our root directory.

Listing 10.17   Creating docker-compose.yml to replicate our database and web server

```
version: "3.7"
services:
  database:
    image: postgres
    restart: always
    env_file:
      - .env
    ports:
      - "5432:5432"
    volumes:
      - data:/var/lib/postgresql/data
  server:
    build:
      context: .
      dockerfile: Dockerfile
    env_file: .env
    depends_on:
      - database
    networks:
      - default
    ports:
    - "8080:8080"
volumes:
  data:
```

After creating this file, you can open your terminal, navigate to your code directory, and execute docker-compose up. This will create the PostgreSQL image first, and then create our web service image, based on the Dockerfile we created earlier. However, you will see that some things are not right:

```
ch_10-server-1    | Error: DatabaseQueryError(Io(Os { code: 99, kind:
AddrNotAvailable, message: "Address not available" }))
```

Because we operate in a different environment now, we have to consider several issues:

- The PostgreSQL server inside the Docker container requires a username and password.
- In our web service, we still try to connect to the PostgreSQL server running on localhost, instead of the one we just started via docker-compose.
- Since the PostgreSQL server requires a username/password combination, we also have to supply this to the connection URL in our codebase.
- We start the web server behind the IP address 127.0.0.1. However, operating from within a container, we need access from the outside, so we have to change the address to 0.0.0.0, which means "all IP4 addresses on the local machine."

The following listing shows the changes to be made to main.rs to accommodate the Docker container setup.

...

```rust
/// Q&A web service API
#[derive(Parser, Debug)]
#[clap(author, version, about, long_about = None)]
struct Args {
    /// Which errors we want to log (info, warn or error)
    #[clap(short, long, default_value = "warn")]
    log_level: String,
    /// Which PORT the server is listening to
    #[clap(short, long, default_value = "8080")]
    port: u16,
    /// Database user
    #[clap(long, default_value = "user")]
    db_user: String,
    /// URL for the postgres database
    #[clap(long, default_value = "localhost")]
    db_host: String,
    /// PORT number for the database connection
    #[clap(long, default_value = "5432")]
    db_port: u16,
    /// Database name
    #[clap(long, default_value = "rustwebdev")]
    db_name: String,
}

#[tokio::main]
async fn main() -> Result<(), handle_errors::Error> {
    ...

    let db_user = env::var("POSTGRES_USER")
        .unwrap_or(args.db_user.to_owned());
    let db_password = env::var("POSTGRES_PASSWORD").unwrap();
    let db_host = env::var("POSTGRES_HOST")
        .unwrap_or(args.db_host.to_owned());
    let db_port = env::var("POSTGRES_PORT")
        .unwrap_or(args.db_port.to_string());
    let db_name = env::var("POSTGRES_DB")
        .unwrap_or(args.db_name.to_owned());

    let log_filter = std::env::var("RUST_LOG").unwrap_or_else(|_| {
        format!(
            "handle_errors={},rust_web_dev={},warp={}",
            args.log_level, args.log_level, args.log_level
        )
    });

    let store = store::Store::new(&format!(
        "postgres://{}:{}@{}:{}/{}",
        db_user, db_password, db_host, db_port, db_name
    ))
    .await
    .map_err(|e| handle_errors::Error::DatabaseQueryError(e))?;
```

```
...

    warp::serve(routes).run(([0, 0, 0, 0], port)).await;

    Ok(())
}
```

We add the option to read every environment variable via the .env file, or if it's not set, via CLI parameters (made available through our `Args` struct). If they are not set by the .env file nor by the CLI, we use the default parameter from `Args`. The next listing shows the updated .env file.

Listing 10.19   Adding variables to the .env file for the database access

```
BAD_WORDS_API_KEY=API_KEY_FROM_APILAYER
PASETO_KEY="RANDOM WORDS WINTER MACINTOSH PC"
PORT=8080
POSTGRES_USER=user
POSTGRES_PASSWORD=password
POSTGRES_DB=rustwebdev
POSTGRES_HOST=localhost
POSTGRES_PORT=5432
```

We could also add a default value for the PostgreSQL password, but we keep the strict requirement of not putting credentials directly in the codebase. You can use the build command from Docker Compose to rebuild the changed containers:

```
$ docker-compose build
$ docker-compose up
```

Keep in mind that we changed our server port to `8080`. After Docker Compose is done building and getting the new containers up and running, we can check via the following curl command if everything still works as expected:

```
$ curl --location --request GET 'localhost:8080/questions'
[]
```

We run on a complete new and empty database, so all users and questions have to be created again. With the code changes in place, we have the flexibility to supply our application with variables from either the environment or the command line. If we forget both, we use the default parameter set in the codebase (except the two secret keys we just have in the .env file).

10.4.3   Extract the configuration of the web server into a new module

Now the setting and getting of the environment seems a bit convoluted and is making our main.rs file even longer and somewhat more difficult to read. We can extract the setting of these configuration parameters into a new module called config. The following listing shows the new module, which is located just inside the src folder.

Listing 10.20   The new config module in src/config.rs

```
use std::env;
use clap::Parser;
use dotenv;

/// Q&A web service API
#[derive(Parser, Debug)]
#[clap(author, version, about, long_about = None)]
pub struct Config {
    /// Which errors we want to log (info, warn or error)
    #[clap(short, long, default_value = "warn")]
    pub log_level: String,
    /// Which PORT the server is listening to
    #[clap(short, long, default_value = "8080")]
    pub port: u16,
    /// Database user
    #[clap(long, default_value = "user")]
    pub db_user: String,
    /// Database user
    #[clap(long)]
    pub db_password: String,
    /// URL for the postgres database
    #[clap(long, default_value = "localhost")]
    pub db_host: String,
    /// PORT number for the database connection
    #[clap(long, default_value = "5432")]
    pub db_port: u16,
    /// Database name
    #[clap(long, default_value = "rustwebdev")]
    pub db_name: String,
}

impl Config {
    pub fn new() -> Result<Config, handle_errors::Error> {
        dotenv::dotenv().ok();
        let config = Config::parse();

        if let Err(_) = env::var("BAD_WORDS_API_KEY") {
            panic!("BadWords API key not set");
        }

        if let Err(_) = env::var("PASETO_KEY") {
            panic!("PASETO_KEY not set");
        }

        let port = std::env::var("PORT")
            .ok()
            .map(|val| val.parse::<u16>())
            .unwrap_or(Ok(config.port))
            .map_err(|e| handle_errors::Error::ParseError(e))?;

        let db_user = env::var("POSTGRES_USER")
            .unwrap_or(config.db_user.to_owned());
```

```
        let db_password = env::var("POSTGRES_PASSWORD").unwrap();
        let db_host = env::var("POSTGRES_HOST")
            .unwrap_or(config.db_host.to_owned());
        let db_port = env::var("POSTGRES_PORT")
            .unwrap_or(config.db_port.to_string());
        let db_name = env::var("POSTGRES_DB")
            .unwrap_or(config.db_name.to_owned());

        Ok(Config {
            log_level: config.log_level,
            port,
            db_user,
            db_password,
            db_host,
            db_port: db_port.parse::<u16>().map_err(|e| {
                handle_errors::Error::ParseError(e)
            })?,
            db_name,
        })
    }
}
```

With that in place, we can shorten our main.rs file and have just one line for generating a new config.

Listing 10.21   The updated main.rs file with the initialization of the config variable

```
#![warn(clippy::all)]

use handle_errors::return_error;

use tracing_subscriber::fmt::format::FmtSpan;
use warp::{http::Method, Filter};

mod routes;
mod types;
mod config;
mod profanity;
mod store;

#[tokio::main]
async fn main() -> Result<(), handle_errors::Error> {
    let config = config::Config::new().expect("Config can't be set");

    let log_filter = format!(
        "handle_errors={},rust_web_dev={},warp={}",
        config.log_level, config.log_level, config.log_level
    );

    let store = store::Store::new(&format!(
        "postgres://{}:{}@{}:{}/{}",
        config.db_user,
        config.db_password,
        config.db_host,
```

```
        config.db_port,
        config.db_name
))
.await
.map_err(|e| handle_errors::Error::DatabaseQueryError(e))?;

...

warp::serve(routes).run(([0, 0, 0, 0], config.port)).await;

Ok(())
}
```

What we have to think about, though, is what happens when we start the server without Docker. We now require a database user and password for the database. Depending on your setup, you should have a username and a database with the same name as the username created for you by the installation script you used to install PostgreSQL on your machine.

You can try this by logging into PSQL with your username:

```
$ sudo -u <USERNAME> psql
```

If this doesn't work, you can use the following command to create a database for you:

```
$ createdb
```

Now you can log in, create a new user with a password, and add this information to your .env file in your code folder:

```
$ sudo -u <USERNAME> psql
<USERNAME>=# create user username with encrypted password 'password';
CREATE ROLE
<USERNAME>=# grant all privileges on database rustwebdev to username;
GRANT
<USERNAME>=#
```

These commands are enough to create a new PostgreSQL user with the given password and grant them access to our database called `rustwebdev`. On the command line, we are not allowed to call a user `user`, because it is a reserved keyword for PostgreSQL. Therefore, we also adjust the .env file.

Listing 10.22   Adjusting the database username in .env

```
...
PORT=8080
POSTGRES_USER=username
POSTGRES_PASSWORD=password
POSTGRES_DB=rustwebdev
POSTGRES_HOST=localhost
POSTGRES_PORT=5432
```

With this in place, we can start our web server both inside Docker and without Docker through the CLI:

```
$ cargo run -- --db-host localhost --log-level info --db-name rustwebdev -
db-port 5432 --db-password password
    Finished dev [unoptimized + debuginfo] target(s) in 0.13s
     Running `target/debug/rust-web-dev --db-host localhost --log-level
info -db-name rustwebdev -db-port 5432 -db-password password`
Apr 20 13:33:35.664  INFO rust_web_dev: Q&A service build ID 1.0.0-c15dd9e-
aarch64-macos
Apr 20 13:33:35.665  INFO Server::run{addr=0.0.0.0:8080}: warp::server:
listening on http://0.0.0.0:8080
```

We have now created a very dynamic codebase, which we can feed variables into based on the environment we are operating in. Our API keys and hashing secret are removed from the codebase and stored privately in an .env file, which is not getting checked into the repository (through an added entry in the .gitignore file). The added config module lets us quickly get an overview of the possible adjustments we can make through parameters in our codebase. All of our code is now able to be deployed, inspected, and maintained, which lets us tackle the last chapter of the book, focused on testing.

Summary

- When it comes to deployments, nearly endless possibilities exist to package and deliver your code.
- To prepare for different scenarios, we can open up our codebase to dynamic changes via environment variables or CLI parameters.
- We can remove hardcoded strings in our code and read values from config files, .env files, or CLI parameters.
- The server's IP address and port, the database URL, and API keys are good candidates for replacing hardcoded strings with outside variables.
- Once we can dynamically change key parameters in our codebase, we determine which options to use to compile the binary.
- The package manager Cargo offers various profiles, depending on the goal.
- A common way of building a Rust binary for production is to add a `--release` flag to the `cargo build` command, which triggers a more optimized build profile.
- We also have the option of targeting different platforms.
- The Rustup tool supports various targets, which we can add via `rustup target add`.
- We then can use `cargo build --release --target NAME_OF_TARGET` to build for a different operating system than the one we are currently operating on.
- With the help of a library called musl, we can package the needed system libraries in our binary and generate a statically linked and therefore portable binary.
- A common way of releasing code is through deploying Docker containers.

- We can use a multistage Docker container to create smaller images.
- If we operate in a more complex setup, Docker Compose helps us generate a network of running Docker containers that are networked together.
- The added config module gives us the chance to remove the reading and parsing of environment variables and config files from the main.rs file and lets us tinker with the logic without interfering with the rest of the code.

Testing your
Rust application

This chapter covers

- Assessing the testing needs for our web service
- Using Rust's built-in testing capabilities to create unit tests
- Setting up a conditional testing environment
- Creating a mock server that we can remotely shut down
- Using Warp's built-in testing framework to test our filters
- Writing integration tests against our running web service

This topic of this last chapter of the book is, for some developers, the most important aspect of writing applications: testing. You can practice test-driven development, where you write tests first. You can choose to write tests directly after having implemented the business logic, or can wait until a large part of the application logic is written before testing it. No one-size-fits-all process exists, and your choice depends on the size of the application and the circumstances you are writing it in.

The same goes for the types of tests you are writing and whether you want to cover 100% of your codebase. The most important point is that you have tests, and that they cover the most critical workflow of your application. Another aspect you should have in mind is to thoroughly test the most complex code. If you change a piece of code you barely understand or that has many side effects throughout your application, that's the area where you want to have many tests, to ideally cover all possible outcomes.

The Rust compiler is great in making sure you have exhaustive match patterns, return the right type, and take care of results that could have errors popping up. What it can't test, though, is business logic, and whether out of the hundred possible errors, we return the right one for the right use case. Especially in web applications, it is important to ensure that the user gets the right response or gets a response at all.

The engineering world has a variety of testing strategies, which also swap over to the software engineering side. The two most common used strategies are unit testing and integration testing. *Unit testing* refers to a piece of code (a function, for example), that has a set of defined inputs and a possible list of outputs. You use this type of testing when the function in question has no side effects. An example is our extract_pagination function, which has the following signature:

```
pub fn extract_pagination(
    params: HashMap<String, String>
) -> Result<Pagination, Error>
```

We pass a hash map into the function and expect either a Pagination type back or an Error. Inside the function body, there are no calls to other functions, and we don't manipulate any type of state. We can imagine having a set of input parameters the user can pass, and we want to test whether we cover all of these inputs with a valid response.

The next type of testing is *integration testing*. This is used when we want to make sure that an incoming HTTP request is being processed in the right way, with all the database changes made along the way, and that we get the expected HTTP response back. One example is the login endpoint. Figure 11.1 highlights the different scopes of unit and integration testing.

We can test the login flow via unit tests, to check whether the filters are working as expected, whether we run a database query with the email and password combination from the request, and whether we return, based on the parameters, the right response. Or we can simply bootstrap the server, have a test function make a login request, and expect an HTTP response with certain parameters. In this case, we don't care about the details of the implementation and treat our code more like a black box.

When it comes to testing, Rust offers a few tools to make our life easier. The package manager Cargo has a test command, and there is a test attribute (#[test]) you

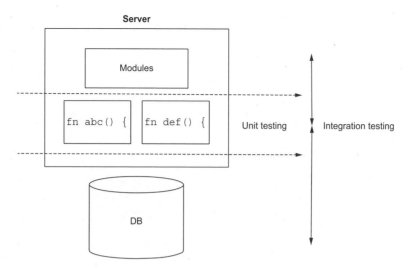

Figure 11.1 Unit testing focuses on isolated functions, whereas integration testing focuses on the interaction between modules and functions.

can put on top of a function, so the compiler knows not to add this piece of code to the binary. In addition, Rust offers a few `assert` macros (`assert_eq!`, for example), which check whether the right and left sides of the arguments are equal.

Everything else is basically standard Rust code. A few extra crates can help you do more advanced mocking of functionality. Here's some advice before we start, however: see how far you can get with the Rust standard library before adding more crates to your codebase.

11.1 Unit testing our business logic

We start our testing journey with encapsulated, self-contained tests. We want to make sure the business logic works as expected. You will see that with each test case, we will run into new challenges. Nothing is "just write a few more lines of code and you are done." We deal with external API calls, environment variables, and library-specific implementations like the Warp filters.

Following along, you will learn a great deal about writing mocking servers, dealing with tests running in parallel, and running asynchronous functions inside a test module, which Rust doesn't support.

11.1.1 Testing the pagination logic and dealing with custom errors

We'll start small so you can become familiar with the ideology behind testing in Rust. We'll pick isolated functions that have no side effects for our first unit tests. A perfect candidate, as mentioned in the chapter intro, is the `extract_pagination` function.

Listing 11.1 The `extract_pagination` function inside src/types/pagination.rs

...

```
pub fn extract_pagination(
    params: HashMap<String, String>
) -> Result<Pagination, Error> {
    // Could be improved in the future
    if params.contains_key("limit") && params.contains_key("offset") {
        return Ok(Pagination {
            // Takes the "limit" parameter in the query
            // and tries to convert it to a number
            limit: Some(
                params
                    .get("limit")
                    .unwrap()
                    .parse()
                    .map_err(Error::ParseError)?,
            ),
            // Takes the "offset" parameter in the query
            // and tries to convert it to a number
            offset: params
                .get("offset")
                .unwrap()
                .parse()
                .map_err(Error::ParseError)?,
        });
    }

    Err(Error::MissingParameters)
}
```

The function takes `HashMap<String, String>` as input and returns `Result<Pagination, Error>`. Rust makes sure that we can't pass a `HashMap` object with `i64`, for example, and that we return the proper `Result`. We have a few possible scenarios:

- Everything works as expected: The hash map has two strings that we can parse as numbers and return a `Pagination` object.
- The hash map doesn't have a `limit` or `offset` key, and we return a `MissingParameters` error.
- The hash map has both a `limit` and an `offset` key, but either one of the values cannot be parsed as a number and we return a `ParseError` error.

It is common practice in Rust to have the tests in the same file as the actual code—at least in the case of unit tests. The following listing shows the first test setup with the "everything as expected" case.

Listing 11.2 Creating the test module inside the pagination.rs file

...

```
#[cfg(test)]
```

⊲ Uses the test attribute to signal the compiler that this is test code that doesn't need to be included into the binary

Creates a new module, which you
can give any name you want

Since we opened a new module, we have
to import the functions and types from
the pagination.rs file via use super.

```
mod pagination_tests {
    use super::{HashMap, extract_pagination, Pagination, Error};

    #[test]
    fn valid_pagination() {
        let mut params = HashMap::new();
        params.insert(String::from("limit"), String::from("1"));
        params.insert(String::from("offset"), String::from("1"));
        let pagination_result = extract_pagination(params);
        let expected = Pagination {
            limit: Some(1),
            offset: 1
        };
        assert_eq!(pagination_result.unwrap(), expected);
    }
}
```

The test macro annotates functions
that should be run when we use
cargo test on the command line.

Creates
normal Rust
functions that
should have
expressive
names

Creates a variable that represents
the state of our Result after we
call extract_pagination

Compares our expected Result
with the one from the function
call via the assert_eq macro

The whole codebase looks like usual Rust code. You can even find the `assert_eq!` macro in a codebase where the developer wants to make sure a certain state is expected and panics if not. You can see the test module as another part of the codebase that uses functions and logic you have written previously, sort of as a library or web service user. Since it's normal Rust code with no third-party libraries, it is easier to read and understand.

We covered our best-case scenario where all the parameters were set right, and the function returns a `Pagination` object. Let's now add the error cases, where either of the parameters is missing or wrong. The following listing shows the test for the missing offset parameter.

Listing 11.3 Adding the error test cases for a missing offset parameter

We are expecting an error since we are just adding the limit
key/value to the HashMap, and our extract_pagination
function fails. We transform this error into a string,
so we can compare it to the expected error case.

```
#[test]
fn missing_offset_parameter() {
    let mut params = HashMap::new();
    params.insert(String::from("limit"), String::from("1"));

    let pagination_result = format!(
        "{}",
        extract_pagination(params).unwrap_err()
    );
    let expected = format!("{}", Error::MissingParameters);

    assert_eq!(pagination_result, expected);
}
```

Uses the impl Display
trait implementation
to transform the
MissingParameters error
into a string so we can
compare it later

Passes both strings to the
assert_eq! macro, and if both
match, the test was a success

Even this small test case offers a variety of ways to implement the logic. We create a hash map and insert a key-value pair with a limit and a number. We create an error case in which we won't insert the offset key-value pair and therefore make the function fail. The question now is how do we want to compare errors?

Our errors originate from the handle-errors crate, and we need to implement another trait if we want to compare the enum variants—namely, PartialEq (http:// mng.bz/p6X8). We could use the derive macro to implement the trait for us, but we also use errors from external libraries like SQLx, for which the trait can't be automatically implemented. The following code snippet shows the added trait to the derive macro:

```
...

#[derive(Debug, PartialEq)]
pub enum Error {
    ParseError(std::num::ParseIntError),
    MissingParameters,
    WrongPassword,
    CannotDecryptToken,
    Unauthorized,
    ArgonLibraryError(ArgonError),
    DatabaseQueryError(sqlx::Error),
    MigrationError(sqlx::migrate::MigrateError),
    ReqwestAPIError(ReqwestError),
    MiddlewareReqwestAPIError(MiddlewareReqwestError),
    ClientError(APILayerError),
    ServerError(APILayerError)
}
...
```

This results in an error. One of the errors points to the sqlx::Error type, for which we can't implement the PartialEq trait automatically:

```
binary operation `==` cannot be applied to type `sqlx::Error`rustcE0369
lib.rs(13, 17): Error originated from macro call here
```

We have, however, implemented the Display trait by hand for all our variants:

```
...

impl std::fmt::Display for Error {
    fn fmt(&self, f: &mut std::fmt::Formatter) -> std::fmt::Result {
        match &*self {
            Error::ParseError(ref err) => {
                write!(f, "Cannot parse parameter: {}", err)
            },
            Error::MissingParameters => write!(f, "Missing parameter"),
            Error::WrongPassword => write!(f, "Wrong password"),
            Error::CannotDecryptToken => write!(f, "Cannot decrypt error"),
```

```
        Error::Unauthorized => write!(
            f,
            "No permission to change the underlying resource"
        ),
        Error::ArgonLibraryError(_) => {
            write!(f, "Cannot verifiy password")
        },
        Error::DatabaseQueryError(_) => {
            write!(f, "Cannot update, invalid data")
        },
        Error::MigrationError(_) => write!(f, "Cannot migrate data"),
        Error::ReqwestAPIError(err) => {
            write!(f, "External API error: {}", err)
        },
        Error::MiddlewareReqwestAPIError(err) => {
            write!(f, "External API error: {}", err)
        },
        Error::ClientError(err) => {
            write!(f, "External Client error: {}", err)
        },
        Error::ServerError(err) => {
            write!(f, "External Server error: {}", err)
        },
    }
  }
}

...
```

We therefore can use the `String` version of the error via the `format!` macro:

```
...
let pagination_result = format!("{}", extract_pagination(params).unwrap_err());
let expected = format!("{}", Error::MissingParameters);
assert_eq!(pagination_result, expected);
...
```

The strings implemented the `PartialEq` trait (http://mng.bz/O6WR), and therefore can be used in the `assert_eq!` macro. The standard library also has the `kind` function implemented onto its errors: http://mng.bz/YKvB. You can access the kind of error and then compare them with each other. The rest of the test cases for the pagination function can be found in the book's repository: http://mng.bz/G1Dv.

11.1.2 *Testing the Config module with environment variables*

In the previous section, we learned how to handle custom errors and compare them. This section offers another interesting tidbit about testing in Rust: by default, all tests are run in parallel. This is great for performance and speed, but can introduce side effects that you have to be aware of. One of these side effects, as you will soon see while testing the Config module, is that setting and removing environment variables in one test function has an impact on other tests. If we look at the implementation of the Config struct in the following listing, we see that we fail early if either the paseto key or the API key is not set.

Listing 11.4   The first few lines of the impl config in src/config.rs

```
...

impl Config {
    pub fn new() -> Result<Config, handle_errors::Error> {
        dotenv::dotenv().ok();
        let config = Config::parse();

        if let Err(_) = env::var("BAD_WORDS_API_KEY") {
            panic!("BadWords API key not set");
        }

        if let Err(_) = env::var("PASETO_KEY") {
            panic!("PASETO_KEY not set");
        }

    ...
```

We have to consider this when testing the associated new function. We somehow have to figure out when the environment variables are set, and how to set or unset them in our test module. The first line of the function calls the dotenv crate, which brings the environment variables from the .env file in the environment, where we can pick them up via the env::var call.

Every time we call the new function, we also set all the environment variables. There is no real reason for this since we can do this in our main function when starting the server. Leaving out the first line also makes this function side-effect free. We therefore remove the first line in our codebase:

```
...

impl Config {
    pub fn new() -> Result<Config, handle_errors::Error> {
        dotenv::dotenv().ok();
        let config = Config::parse();

        if let Err(_) = env::var("BAD_WORDS_API_KEY") {
            panic!("BadWords API key not set");
        }

        if let Err(_) = env::var("PASETO_KEY") {
            panic!("PASETO_KEY not set");
        }

    ...
```

We add it instead to our `main` function inside main.rs:

```
...

#[tokio::main]
async fn main() -> Result<(), handle_errors::Error> {
    dotenv::dotenv().ok();

    let config = config::Config::new().expect("Config can't be set");

    let log_filter = format!(
...
```

With this out of the way, we can focus on writing our first tests. The following listing shows the added test module at the end of the config.rs file.

Listing 11.5   Adding a test module to src/config.rs

```
...


#[cfg(test)]
mod config_tests {
    use super::*;

    #[test]
    fn unset_api_key() {
        let result = std::panic::catch_unwind(|| Config::new());
        assert!(result.is_err());
    }
}
```

We import all the module's functions and structs via `super::*`, and write our first test, which captures the case of the API key not being set through the environment variable. We removed the `dotenv::dotenv.ok` call earlier, so by calling `Config::new`, no variable from the .env should be brought into the scope.

We also add a new trick to our toolbox, which is the `catch_unwind` call from the standard library. This neat function lets us capture panics in the code without bringing down the program. It also encapsulates why the panic happened in the first place. For our use case, however, it's important that we catch the error, and with a simple `assert!(result.is_err())`, we check that the creation of a new `Config` object errored.

Running `cargo test` on the command line gives us a green light, and all tests pass. Now we can go on to the use case when we set the environment variable and want a valid `Config` object back. The following listing shows the added test.

Listing 11.6   Adding a positive test to the config module

```
...
#[cfg(test)]
mod config_tests {
    use super::*;
```

```
fn set_env() {
    env::set_var("BAD_WORDS_API_KEY", "yes");
    env::set_var("PASETO_KEY", "yes");
    env::set_var("POSTGRES_USER", "user");
    env::set_var("POSTGRES_PASSWORD", "pass");
    env::set_var("POSTGRES_HOST", "localhost");
    env::set_var("POSTGRES_PORT", "5432");
    env::set_var("POSTGRES_DB", "rustwebdev");
}

#[test]
fn unset_api_key() {
    let result = std::panic::catch_unwind(|| Config::new());
    assert!(result.is_err());
}

#[test]
fn set_api_key() {
    set_env();

    let expected = Config {
        log_level: "warn".to_string(),
        port: 8080,
        db_user: "user".to_string(),
        db_password: "pass".to_string(),
        db_host: "localhost".to_string(),
        db_port: 5432,
        db_name: "rustwebdev".to_string(),
    };

    let config = Config::new().unwrap();

    assert_eq!(config, expected);
}
}
```

Here, we create a new helper function within the test module, which sets all environment variables manually. We call this function and try to create a new config object afterward. We then check whether the created config is equal to the one we created manually. Running cargo test shows some weird behavior:

```
$ cargo test
…

test config::config_tests::set_api_key ... ok
test config::config_tests::unset_api_key ... FAILED
```

The set_api_key test, which we just added, is green, but now the previous test, unset_api_key, fails. We already mentioned that Rust tests are running in parallel; we start the config test module and execute both functions at the same time. The set_api_key test will set all the environment variables, but we expected in our other test that those are not set, and therefore the Config::new function call should panic.

So what does a solution look like? We need to make sure to run the failing test first and then set the environment variables afterward.

One solution could be not to run the tests in parallel. The official Rust book teaches us (http://mng.bz/z5zB) that we can run the tests consecutively:

```
$ cargo test -- --test-threads=1
```

However, all tests would stop running in parallel, and this is not what we want. Another solution is not to create two separate functions, but one, and pack both test cases in the same. The next listing shows our solution.

Listing 11.7   Combining the two config tests so the environment variables don't interfere

```
...
    #[test]
    fn unset_and_set_api_key() {
        // ENV VARIABLES ARE NOT SET
        let result = std::panic::catch_unwind(|| Config::new());
        assert!(result.is_err());

        // NOW WE SET THEM
        set_env();

        let expected = Config {
            log_level: "warn".to_string(),
            port: 8080,
            db_user: "user".to_string(),
            db_password: "pass".to_string(),
            db_host: "localhost".to_string(),
            db_port: 5432,
            db_name: "rustwebdev".to_string(),
        };

        let config = Config::new().unwrap();

        assert_eq!(config, expected);
    }
}
```

Rerunning the tests makes them green again, and the code all works. We can choose to unset all the environment variables again via `env::remove_var("")`.

11.1.3   Testing the profanity module with a newly created mock server

The first round of tests was a great warm-up. We will enter a new level of complexity when dealing with the profanity module. As you may remember, we use the `check_profanity` function to send our question (or answer) title and content to a third-party API to check for profane words (which sends us back a censored version of the content).

We want to test the behavior of this function. Although not much business logic is happening, we handle multiple error and success cases, and we want to return the right responses. The challenge here is the HTTP call to the third-party API, which we somehow have to deal with.

There are basically two (main) concepts when dealing with such a case:

- We could replace the Reqwest library with our own dummy logic.
- We can change the API URL, and instead of the real URL, target a mock server running on localhost with predefined responses.

Generally, it is good advice not to replace too much code, since you want to test the real source code. We choose to write our own mock server that we can run and tear down again after the test. We can preset some JSON responses for our tests so we can check different errors and responses. Figure 11.2 shows two different mocking strategies you can use.

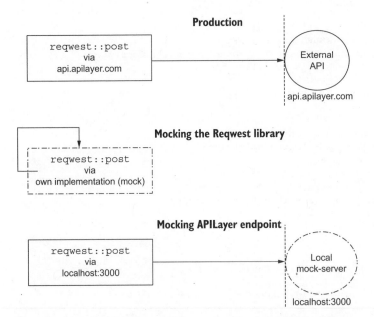

Figure 11.2   In these mocking strategies, we can call the library itself or the endpoint.

Here we are. We thought we were done with writing a huge amount of new code and could focus on a little test code here and there. But creating this mock server will leave you with a great tool in your toolchain, which you can use in your own projects in the future.

We start by creating a new Rust project *within our root folder* (the same as we did with the handle-errors crate):

```
$ cargo new --lib mock-server
```

We created a new library, which we can add to our Cargo.toml file.

Listing 11.8   Adding the new mock-server to our Cargo.toml file

```
[package]
name = "rust-web-dev"
version = "1.0.0"
edition = "2021"

[dependencies]
handle-errors = { path = "handle-errors", version = "0.1.0" }
mock-server = { path = "mock-server", version = " 0.1.0" }
warp = "0.3"
...
```

Now we have to think about what a mock server should look like. What are its features? We want to do the following:

- Start it on command on a specific port and address
- Have the same route as our third-party server, so we can just switch the URL from api.apylayer.com to localhost when testing
- Accept the same parameters as the real API
- Introduce the possibility of responding with different error and OK cases
- Shut down the server again from within our tests after we are done testing

It seems like we are building almost a normal web server again, with the added simplicity of predefined answers and the possibility to shut it down when we are done testing. It is exactly this "remotely shutting down a server" that is the interesting part about this solution; the rest of the mock server is more of the same as what we are already doing throughout the book.

Listing 11.9 shows the updated lib.rs file in our mock-server crate. The code in bold demonstrates the functionality we use to remotely send a message to the server for it to shut down.

Listing 11.9   Using a oneshot channel to signal to the server it can shut down now

```
use serde_json::json;
use std::net::SocketAddr;
use tokio::sync::{oneshot, oneshot::Sender};
use warp::{http, Filter, Reply};
use bytes::Bytes;
use std::collections::HashMap;

#[derive(Clone, Debug)]
pub struct MockServer {
    socket: SocketAddr,
}

pub struct OneshotHandler {
    pub sender: Sender<i32>,
}
```

```
impl MockServer {
    pub fn new(bind_addr: SocketAddr) -> MockServer {
        MockServer {
            socket: bind_addr,
        }
    }

    async fn check_profanity(
        _: (),
        content: Bytes,
    ) -> Result<impl warp::Reply, warp::Rejection> {
        let content = String::from_utf8(content.to_vec())
            .expect("Invalid UTF-8");
        if content.contains("shitty") {
            Ok(warp::reply::with_status(
                warp::reply::json(&json!({
                    "bad_words_list": [
                        {
                            "deviations": 0,
                            "end": 16,
                            "info": 2,
                            "original": "shitty",
                            "replacedLen": 6,
                            "start": 10,
                            "word": "shitty"
                        }
                    ],
                    "bad_words_total": 1,
                    "censored_content": "this is a ****** sentence",
                    "content": "this is a shitty sentence"
                })),
                http::StatusCode::OK))
        } else {
            Ok(warp::reply::with_status(
                warp::reply::json(&json!({
                    "bad_words_list": [],
                    "bad_words_total": 0,
                    "censored_content": "",
                    "content": "this is a sentence"
                })),
                http::StatusCode::OK,
            ))
        }
    }

    fn build_routes(&self) -> impl Filter<Extract = impl Reply> + Clone {
        warp::post()
            .and(warp::path("bad_words"))
            .and(warp::query())
            .map(|_: HashMap<String, String>| ())
            .and(warp::path::end())
            .and(warp::body::bytes())
            .and_then(Self::check_profanity)
    }
```

```
    pub fn oneshot(&self) -> OneshotHandler {
        let (tx, rx) = oneshot::channel::<i32>();
        let routes = Self::build_routes(&self);

        let (_, server) = warp::serve(routes)
            .bind_with_graceful_shutdown(self.socket, async {
                rx.await.ok();
            });

        tokio::task::spawn(server);

        OneshotHandler {
            sender: tx,
        }
    }
}
```

As you can see, the build_routes functionality and the check_profanity route handler look exactly like what we already did multiple times in this book. We just built another web server with the tools we know, and instead of having a database and more sophisticated middleware, we simply want to return mock data to provide sufficient test cases for the integration test to cover all possible lines of code.

The highlighted code in bold is the interesting bit. We start inspecting the endpoint we opened up, and then talk about the functionality we added to be able to remotely shut down the server. The API layer has the following endpoint: /bad_words?censor_character={{censor_character}}. When starting the server, we just want to replace the host from api.apilayer.com to localhost, and therefore we have to mimic the endpoint word for word. The query parameters are hardcoded and can't be changed. We therefore expect a query parameter, but do nothing with it (therefore, the .map(|_: HashMap<String, String>…).

The API we are using expects the body not in JSON format but raw. That's the reason we expect the body in our Warp server as bytes. We use a third-party crate, called bytes, which we add to the Cargo.toml file of the mock server (listing 11.10). Inside the route handler, we use this line to transform the bytes into a string:

```
let content = String::from_utf8(content.to_vec()).expect("Invalid UTF-8");
```

Listing 11.10 The Cargo.toml of our mock-server project

```
[package]
name = "mock-server"
version = "0.1.0"
edition = "2021"

[dependencies]
tokio = { version = "1.1.1", features = ["full"] }
warp = "0.3"
serde_json = "1.0"
bytes = "1.1.0"
```

With the endpoint and route handler in place, we can focus on the other new piece of code you learned, which provides the ability to gracefully shut down a server. Warp gives us the ability to start a server with the added function `bind_with_graceful_shutdown`, which takes a socket address and a signal that has to be a future. Whenever this signal is received, the server will start to shut down. Figure 11.3 illustrates the concept of sending a signal through an open channel.

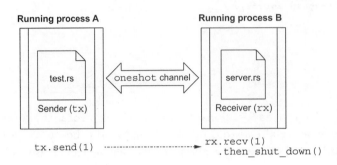

Figure 11.3 A `oneshot` channel to send exactly one message can be used to trigger a shutdown from the receiver side of the message.

Now this signal could be the Ctrl-C command on the command line (depending on the operating system). If we hit this, Warp will make sure to tear everything down in a proper way, and maybe empty some address spaces, instead of performing a forceful shutdown. Since we are "far away" from the command line, however (we want to start and stop the server from within a different project, remotely, within our tests), we need a signal that we can send to the running server.

This is where channels come into play. *Channels* can be created between two instances, and then the two parties can communicate through them. The Tokio website has a great overview and tutorial about channels (https://tokio.rs/tokio/tutorial/channels). In this case, we use a `oneshot` channel, which is meant to send one single value between the sender and the receiver. Other channels are meant to be kept up, maybe even indefinitely.

Therefore, this line creates the channel and gives us a `tx` (for sender) and an `rx` (receiver) object back:

```
let (tx, rx) = oneshot::channel::<i32>();
```

We `await` the signal on `rx` in the `bind_with_graceful_shutdown` function and create a `OneshotHandler` object with the created sender (`tx`). When we create a new `MockServer` later, through `MockServer::new`, we get a new object back, on which we can call the function `oneshot`. This will start the server, and give a sender back, which we can use to send a simple message (`i32`), and once this message is sent, the server will start shutting down. Let's see it in action, as we add the tests for the profanity module.

...

```
#[instrument]
pub async fn check_profanity(content: String)
    -> Result<String, handle_errors::Error> {
    // We are already checking if the ENV VARIABLE is set inside main.rs,
    // so safe to unwrap here
    let api_key = env::var("BAD_WORDS_API_KEY")
        .expect("BAD WORDS API KEY NOT SET");
    let api_layer_url = env::var("API_LAYER_URL")
        .expect("APILAYER URL NOT SET");

    let retry_policy = ExponentialBackoff::builder()
        .build_with_max_retries(3);
    let client = ClientBuilder::new(reqwest::Client::new())
        // Trace HTTP requests. See the tracing crate to make use of
        // these traces.Retry failed requests.
        .with(RetryTransientMiddleware::new_with_policy(retry_policy))
        .build();

    let res = client
        .post(format!(
            "{}/bad_words?censor_character=*",
            api_layer_url
        ))
        .header("apikey", api_key)
```

...

```
#[cfg(test)]
mod profanity_tests {
    use super::{check_profanity, env};

    use mock_server::{MockServer, OneshotHandler};

    #[tokio::test]
    async fn run() {
        let handler = run_mock();
        censor_profane_words().await;
        no_profane_words().await;
        let _ = handler.sender.send(1);
    }

    fn run_mock() -> OneshotHandler {
        env::set_var("API_LAYER_URL", "http://127.0.0.1:3030");
        env::set_var("BAD_WORDS_API_KEY", "YES");

        let socket = "127.0.0.1:3030"
            .to_string()
            .parse()
            .expect("Not a valid address");
        let mock = MockServer::new(socket);
```

```
        mock.oneshot()
    }

    async fn censor_profane_words() {
        let content = "This is a shitty sentence".to_string();
        let censored_content = check_profanity(content).await;
        assert_eq!(censored_content.unwrap(), "this is a ****** sentence");

    }

    async fn no_profane_words() {
        let content = "this is a sentence".to_string();
        let censored_content = check_profanity(content).await;
        assert_eq!(censored_content.unwrap(), "");
    }
}
```

We have one run function, which is the only one triggered by `cargo test`. In it, we start the mock server (and receive the `oneshot` handler with the sender back). We run two tests, calling our real implementation of the `check_profanity` function, and after the two functions run, we send an arbitrary integer over the `oneshot` channel to signal the mock server to shut down.

The `run_mock` function has another important piece of code, though. We have to be able to change the URL that the `check_profanity` function is calling. We can replace the host from api.apilayer.com on the fly through an environment variable. We have to add this environment variable to our .env file.

Listing 11.12   Adding the API layer URL in the .env file

```
BAD_WORDS_API_KEY=API_KEY
PASETO_KEY="RANDOM WORDS WINTER MACINTOSH PC"
API_LAYER_URL="https://api.apilayer.com"
PORT=8080
POSTGRES_USER=username
POSTGRES_PASSWORD=password
POSTGRES_DB=rustwebdev
POSTGRES_HOST=localhost
POSTGRES_PORT=5432
```

With the added test for the profanity module, we can run `cargo test` again to see all our tests in action:

```
$ cargo test
    Finished test [unoptimized + debuginfo] target(s) in 0.08s
     Running unittests (target/debug/deps/rust_web_dev-125890e6530d6a57)

running 7 tests
test types::pagination::pagination_tests::valid_pagination ... ok
test types::pagination::pagination_tests::missing_offset_paramater ... ok
test types::pagination::pagination_tests::wrong_limit_type ... ok
test types::pagination::pagination_tests::missing_limit_paramater ... ok
test types::pagination::pagination_tests::wrong_offset_type ... ok
```

```
test config::config_tests::unset_and_set_api_key ... ok
test profanity::profanity_tests::run ... ok

test result: ok. 7 passed; 0 failed; 0 ignored; 0 measured; 0 filtered out;
finished in 0.00s
```

The three modules we just finished testing cover a variety of techniques you will use again and again in your future Rust codebases. You might decide not to unit-test smaller modules like config, but for the purposes of the book, this gave us a chance to look at the parallelism of Rust testing, and how to handle environment variables.

The pagination module gave us a chance to see how not so straightforward it is to compare errors, and the last one, profanity, had the largest impact, since we created a mock server from scratch. But it's one you can take with you everywhere you go. With these tests in place, we can focus on the next step of our testing journey: the Warp filters.

11.2 Testing our Warp filters

Before we pass on incoming HTTP requests to our route handlers, we go through the authentication filter to make sure an Authorization header exists, and it has a valid token inside. Testing this piece of code is crucial for the security of our application. Now it would be great to test this piece of code without having to start the server and run requests through it.

We have two ways of testing this:

- Testing the authentication function separately
- Using the integrated warp::test module to test the endpoints without starting the server

We will go for the second method, since we can go through the various endpoints and make sure they will include the auth middleware and can see how the test module in Warp behaves. The code in question is the following part of the authentication.rs file, where the code in bold is the actual filter function we use in our routes:

```
...

pub fn verify_token(token: String) -> Result<Session, handle_errors::Error> {
    let key = env::var("PASETO_KEY").unwrap();
    let token = paseto::tokens::validate_local_token(
        &token,
        None,
        key.as_bytes(),
        &paseto::tokens::TimeBackend::Chrono,
    )
    .map_err(|_| handle_errors::Error::CannotDecryptToken)?;

    serde_json::from_value::<Session>(token).map_err(|_| {
        handle_errors::Error::CannotDecryptToken
    })
}
```

```
fn issue_token(account_id: AccountId) -> String {
    let key = env::var("PASETO_KEY").unwrap();

    let current_date_time = Utc::now();
    let dt = current_date_time + chrono::Duration::days(1);

    paseto::tokens::PasetoBuilder::new()
        .set_encryption_key(&Vec::from(key.as_bytes()))
        .set_expiration(&dt)
        .set_not_before(&Utc::now())
        .set_claim("account_id", serde_json::json!(account_id))
        .build()
        .expect("Failed to construct paseto token w/ builder!")
}

pub fn auth()
    -> impl Filter<Extract = (Session,), Error = warp::Rejection> + Clone {
    warp::header::<String>("Authorization").and_then(|token: String| {
        let token = match verify_token(token) {
            Ok(t) => t,
            Err(_) => return future::ready(Err(warp::reject::custom(
                handle_errors::Error::Unauthorized
            ))),
        };

        future::ready(Ok(token))
    })
}
```

Instead of spinning up a test server to run requests against, we can use the mentioned warp::test module, build a request, set the Authorization header, and see if the auth filter behaves as we expect. The following listing shows our first test for the auth filter.

Listing 11.13   Testing the `auth` filter in src/routes/authentication.rs

```
...                              Imports the needed structs
                                 and functions from the
#[cfg(test)]                     authentication module         We have to set the
mod authentication_tests {                                     PASETO_KEY env variable;
    use super::{auth, env, issue_token, AccountId};  ◁─────    otherwise, the issue_token
                                                               function, which auth calls in
    #[tokio::test]                                             the background, would fail.
    async fn post_questions_auth() {
        env::set_var("PASETO_KEY", "RANDOM WORDS WINTER MACINTOSH PC");  ◁───
        let token = issue_token(AccountId(3));  ◁───
                                                     Issues a new token that we
        let filter = auth();                         can pass to your test request
                                                     in the Authorization header
        let res = warp::test::request()
            .header("Authorization", token)          Calls create-a-test request with a
            .filter(&filter);           ◁───         header and passes it to the filter,
                                                     which is our auth function
```

```
        assert_eq!(res.await.unwrap().account_id, AccountId(3));      ◁──────────┐
    }
}
```
**Awaits the response and gets a session back,
where we compare the account_id from the
session with the one we issued the token with**

As we explored with the previous tests, you always find some tidbits you didn't know before. In this case, if you implement this test and run it, you will see that every now and then, the test fails:

```
$ cargo test
    Finished test [unoptimized + debuginfo] target(s) in 0.07s
     Running unittests (target/debug/deps/rust_web_dev-125890e6530d6a57)

running 8 tests
test types::pagination::pagination_tests::missing_offset_paramater ... ok
test types::pagination::pagination_tests::wrong_limit_type ... ok
test types::pagination::pagination_tests::wrong_offset_type ... ok
test types::pagination::pagination_tests::missing_limit_paramater ... ok
test types::pagination::pagination_tests::valid_pagination ... ok
test config::config_tests::unset_and_set_api_key ... ok
test routes::authentication::authentication_tests::post_questions_auth ...
FAILED
test profanity::profanity_tests::run ... ok

failures:

---- routes::authentication::authentication_tests::post_questions_auth
stdout ----
thread 'routes::authentication::authentication_tests::post_questions_auth'
panicked at 'called `Result::unwrap()` on an `Err` value:
Rejection(Unauthorized)', src/routes/authentication.rs:113:30


failures:
    routes::authentication::authentication_tests::post_questions_auth

test result: FAILED. 7 passed; 1 failed; 0 ignored; 0 measured; 0 filtered
out; finished in 0.00s
```

This test also proves how testing can uncover new insights in your codebase. For tests that fail every so often, we can have two assumptions:

- Another test, run at the same time, has some side effects on our auth test.
- The timing of the token issuance has something to do with the failing test.

As it turns out, both assumptions are right. We have to single out which tests might interfere, and the only ones where we set and delete environment variables are the config tests. We could comment them out first and see if this has an impact on our tests. If we do so, and rerun the tests, we get the feeling that it's getting better. The tests pass more often, but still, not all the time.

Let's inspect how the token is issued (we highlight the pieces of code that have a timestamp associated with them):

```
fn issue_token(account_id: AccountId) -> String {
    let key = env::var("PASETO_KEY").unwrap();

    let current_date_time = Utc::now();
    let dt = current_date_time + chrono::Duration::days(1);

    paseto::tokens::PasetoBuilder::new()
        .set_encryption_key(&Vec::from(key.as_bytes()))
        .set_expiration(&dt)
        .set_not_before(&current_date_time)
        .set_claim("account_id", serde_json::json!(account_id))
        .build()
        .expect("Failed to construct paseto token w/ builder!")
}
```

We can identify that when we issue the token, we set a set_not_before field. The timestamp of the not_before field is Utc::now. So can it be that we try to use the token before the Utc::now timestamp? We can try to delete the set_not_before setting on the token and see if it has an impact. As it turns out, our auth test is now failing all the time. We inspect further and realize that when we verify the token, we try to deserialize it via Serde into a new Session object. To finalize our change, we change the Session struct and remove the nbf field:

```
#[derive(Serialize, Deserialize, Debug, Clone, PartialEq)]
pub struct Session {
    pub exp: DateTime<Utc>,
    pub account_id: AccountId,
    pub nbf: DateTime<Utc>,
}
```

With the config tests still commented out, and the removal of the nbf field on the token and session, we rerun the tests:

```
$ cargo test
    Finished test [unoptimized + debuginfo] target(s) in 0.07s
     Running unittests (target/debug/deps/rust_web_dev-125890e6530d6a57)

running 7 tests
test types::pagination::pagination_tests::missing_limit_paramater ... ok
test types::pagination::pagination_tests::valid_pagination ... ok
test types::pagination::pagination_tests::missing_offset_paramater ... ok
test types::pagination::pagination_tests::wrong_offset_type ... ok
test types::pagination::pagination_tests::wrong_limit_type ... ok
test routes::authentication::authentication_tests::post_questions_auth ... ok
test profanity::profanity_tests::run ... ok

test result: ok. 7 passed; 0 failed; 0 ignored; 0 measured; 0 filtered out;
finished in 0.00s
```

It's green all the way through, on every run. Uncommenting the config tests results again in failing tests every now and then. Inspecting the tests further, we can see that we set the `PASETO_KEY` environment variable to `YES`. Before we go on and try to isolate the tests better, we change the example value to the proper key, and rerun the tests again:

```
...
#[cfg(test)]
mod config_tests {
    use super::*;

    fn set_env() {
        env::set_var("BAD_WORDS_API_KEY", "yes");
        env::set_var("PASETO_KEY", "yes");
        env::set_var("PASETO_KEY", "RANDOM WORDS WINTER MACINTOSH PC");
...
```

We hit all green again, on every test run:

```
$ cargo test
    Finished test [unoptimized + debuginfo] target(s) in 0.07s
      Running unittests (target/debug/deps/rust_web_dev-125890e6530d6a57)

running 8 tests
test types::pagination::pagination_tests::missing_offset_paramater ... ok
test types::pagination::pagination_tests::wrong_offset_type ... ok
test types::pagination::pagination_tests::wrong_limit_type ... ok
test types::pagination::pagination_tests::valid_pagination ... ok
test routes::authentication::authentication_tests::post_questions_auth ... ok
test config::config_tests::unset_and_set_api_key ... ok
test types::pagination::pagination_tests::missing_limit_paramater ... ok
test profanity::profanity_tests::run ... ok

test result: ok. 8 passed; 0 failed; 0 ignored; 0 measured; 0 filtered out;
finished in 0.00s
```

This was a lot of changing and figuring out for a simple filter test. But in the end, we got to know our code better, changed the actual codebase, and feel more confident in the inner workings of our application. We're ready to go on to the last section of our testing journey, this chapter, and the whole book: integration testing.

11.3   Creating an integration testing setup

When we talk about *integration testing* in this book, we mean launching the web service on localhost or inside a Docker environment, having a local database setup, and mocking our external API endpoints. We want to make sure each module is cooperating as it should, and the whole registration, login, and creating-a-question workflow is working as expected. The modules and processes included in an integration testing setup are shown in figure 11.4.

There is a distinction between integration testing and end-to-end testing. For this book integration testing is the connection between the modules in our application. For example: can I send an HTTP POST request to create a new question in our web

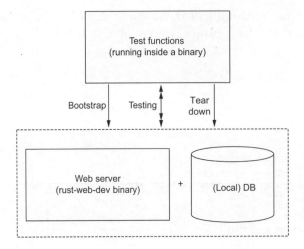

Figure 11.4   Setting up the server and database before the integration test and tearing it down again

service and get the appropriate response? This can also mean mocking the external API calls to third parties.

This step also depends highly on your development environment. You have options:

- Setting up a bash script that bootstraps a Docker environment and tears it down at the end
- Setting up the Docker environment through your codebase and tearing it down there as well
- Using a local setup without Docker and having the tests run inside your current codebase
- Creating a subfolder or new Cargo project to put your integration tests there and run them against your local setup

We choose the last option (creating subfolders for our integration tests), as shown in figure 11.5.

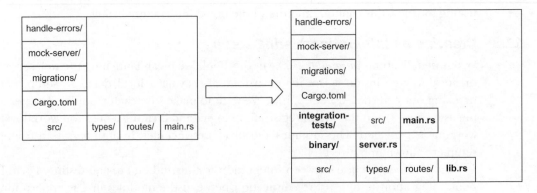

Figure 11.5   Restructuring our codebase to offer a library and a binary at the same time

This book focuses on the Rust part of the problem. Each topic (building an API, adding authentication, setting up a testing environment) has a variety of outside factors and best practices, which are sometimes changing quite fast. Therefore, we choose to stay with our local environment and explore what one solution to an integration testing setup will look like.

We are attempting to do the following:

- Create a new Cargo project called integration-tests within the root folder of our project
- Create a lib.rs file out of our main.rs file and create a binary folder with the rest of the main.rs file
- Add a `oneshot` function to our newly created lib.rs file so we can bootstrap a server and shut it down on the fly
- Set up a local database and drop it after each integration test from within the Rust codebase
- Write test functions in the form of normal Rust functions and send HTTP requests against our running web server

Figure 11.6 shows splitting up the main.rs file and what the new server.rs and lib.rs files will include.

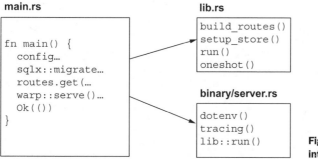

Figure 11.6   Splitting main.rs into server.rs and lib.rs

This big restructure of our codebase (splitting main.rs into lib.rs) will teach you a lot about how to further parameterize the setup of our server. Much of the code splitting we will do in the next few pages will actually be the first thing you will attempt to do when starting a project from scratch.

11.3.1 Splitting up the codebase into a lib.rs and a binary

We want to create both a library and a binary out of our codebase. This will allow us to use public functions and structs from outside this codebase (and in our new integration-test project), and still be able to execute `cargo run` to start the server, and use `cargo build` to create the binary version of the codebase. The first step is renaming the main.rs to lib.rs, and in a second step, creating functions to create the store and the routes, and run the server. The following listing has all the details.

Listing 11.14 Renaming main.rs to lib.rs and grouping functionality

```rust
#![warn(clippy::all)]

…

async fn build_routes(store: store::Store)
    -> impl Filter<Extract = impl Reply> + Clone {
    let store_filter = warp::any().map(move || store.clone());

    let cors = warp::cors()
        .allow_any_origin()
        .allow_header("content-type")
        .allow_methods(&[Method::PUT, Method::DELETE]);

    let get_questions = warp::get()
        .and(warp::path("questions"))
        .and(warp::path::end())
        .and(warp::query())
        .and(store_filter.clone())
        .and_then(routes::question::get_questions);


        …

    get_questions
        .or(update_question)
        .or(add_question)
        .or(delete_question)
        .or(add_answer)
        .or(registration)
        .or(login)
        .with(cors)
        .with(warp::trace::request())
        .recover(handle_errors::return_error)
}

pub async fn setup_store(
    config:
    &config::Config
) -> Result<store::Store, handle_errors::Error> {
    let store = store::Store::new(&format!(
        "postgres://{}:{}@{}:{}/{}",
        config.db_user,
        config.db_password,
        config.db_host,
        config.db_port,
        config.db_name
    ))
    .await
    .map_err(handle_errors::Error::DatabaseQueryError)?;
```

```
sqlx::migrate!()
    .run(&store.clone().connection)
    .await
    .map_err(handle_errors::Error::MigrationError)?;

let log_filter = format!(
    "handle_errors={},rust_web_dev={},warp={}",
    config.log_level, config.log_level, config.log_level
);

tracing_subscriber::fmt()
    // Use the filter we built above to determine which traces to record.
    .with_env_filter(log_filter)
    // Record an event when each span closes.
    // This can be used to time our
    // routes' durations!
    .with_span_events(FmtSpan::CLOSE)
    .init();

Ok(store)
}

pub async fn run(config: config::Config, store: store::Store) {
    let routes = build_routes(store).await;
    warp::serve(routes).run(([0, 0, 0, 0], config.port)).await;
}
```

We now create a folder called bin in our src folder and add a file called server.rs. This will be the place which `cargo run` will execute and build from in the future. The following listing shows the new file.

Listing 11.15   The new server.rs file inside the new src/bin folder

```
use rust_web_dev::{config, run, setup_store};

#[tokio::main]
async fn main() -> Result<(), handle_errors::Error> {
    dotenv::dotenv().ok();

    let config = config::Config::new().expect("Config can't be set");
    let store = setup_store(&config).await?;

    tracing::info!("Q&A service build ID {}", env!("RUST_WEB_DEV_VERSION"));

    run(config, store).await;

    Ok(())
}
```

We will initialize our .env files via dotenv::dotenv().ok, create a config, which we pass to the setup_store function inside lib.rs, and call the run function with both the store and the config object that will internally build the routes and start the server.

The first line of the file tells you that we now access the library called rust_web_dev (our project name) and import public functions from there.

The renaming has other consequences as well. If we want to import modules from inside the library, we have to use the `crate` keyword now. The next listing shows the updated authentication.rs file as an example.

Listing 11.16 **Importing library code via the `crate` keyword in authentication.rs**

```
use argon2::{self, Config};
use chrono::prelude::*;
use rand::Rng;
use std::{env, future};
use warp::Filter;

use crate::store::Store;
use crate::types::account::{Account, AccountId, Session};

pub async fn register(
    store: Store,
    account: Account
) -> Result<impl warp::Reply, warp::Rejection> {
    let hashed_password = hash_password(account.password.as_bytes());

...
```

We have to do the same inside three more files (updated code can be found at https://github.com/Rust-Web-Development/code/tree/main/ch_11):

- routes/answer.rs
- routes/question.rs
- store.rs

Running the code via `cargo run` should work now as before. This change creates the foundation for our new integration-test crate inside the project, where we can now better control the server. The next section will add the missing pieces.

11.3.2 *Creating the integration-test crate and the oneshot server implementation*

To run integration tests, we need to be able to start and stop our web server on command. We will use the trick we learned from our mock server and create a oneshot channel between the integration test and the web server. We already created a lib.rs file, where we now are able to add functionality and further customize our server on demand. The following listing shows the addition of the oneshot functionality.

Listing 11.17 **Adding a `oneshot` channel to our server inside src/lib.rs**

```
#![warn(clippy::all)]

use handle_errors;
```

```
use tokio::sync::{oneshot, oneshot::Sender};
use tracing_subscriber::fmt::format::FmtSpan;
use warp::{http::Method, Filter, Reply};

...

pub struct OneshotHandler {
    pub sender: Sender<i32>,
}

...

pub async fn run(config: config::Config, store: store::Store) {
    let routes = build_routes(store).await;
    warp::serve(routes).run(([0, 0, 0, 0], config.port)).await;
}

pub async fn oneshot(store: store::Store) -> OneshotHandler {
    let routes = build_routes(store).await;
    let (tx, rx) = oneshot::channel::<i32>();

    let socket: std::net::SocketAddr = "127.0.0.1:3030"
        .to_string()
        .parse()
        .expect("Not a valid address");

    let (_, server) = warp::serve(routes).bind_with_graceful_shut-
      down(socket, async {
        rx.await.ok();
    });

    tokio::task::spawn(server);

    OneshotHandler { sender: tx }
}
```

There is nothing really new here that we didn't already see in our mock-server implementation. We build the routes, create the channel, and return a `OneshotHandler`
that holds the sender object, which we will use to send an integer over to the server via
the channel when we want to shut it down.

Now is the time to create our new integration-tests crate inside the root folder of
the project:

```
$ cargo new integration-tests
```

We will need to add a few dependencies to our Cargo.toml file (listing 11.18). It's
important to note that we also add our rust-web-dev library (our project) to the
dependency list. We need to access the `oneshot` function, for example, as well as the
config module to create our server.

Listing 11.18   The Cargo.toml file for the integration-tests crate

```
[package]
name = "integration-tests"
version = "0.1.0"
edition = "2021"

[dependencies]
rust-web-dev = { path = "../",  version = "1.0.0" }
dotenv = "0.15.0"
tokio = { version = "1.1.1", features = ["full"] }
reqwest = { version = "0.11", features = ["json"] }
serde = { version = "1.0", features = ["derive"] }
serde_json = "1.0"
```

The next listing shows the first version of main.rs, which gives us a first look at what we want to achieve when setting up our server.

Listing 11.19   A first attempt at bootstrapping the server from within integration-tests

```
use rust_web_dev::{config, handle_errors, oneshot, setup_store};

#[tokio::main]
async fn main() -> Result<(), handle_errors::Error> {
    dotenv::dotenv().ok();
    let config = config::Config::new().expect("Config can't be set");

    let store = setup_store(&config).await?;

    let handler = oneshot(store).await;

    // register_user();
    // login_user();
    // post_question();

    let _ = handler.sender.send(1);

    Ok(())
}
```

We import the needed functions and modules from our project, where the compiler throws the first error. The config module as well as the handle_errors module are not public, and limited to the library so far. We change that by adding a pub keyword in front of them inside the lib.rs file:

```
#![warn(clippy::all)]

pub use handle_errors;

use tokio::sync::{oneshot, oneshot::Sender};
use tracing_subscriber::fmt::format::FmtSpan;
use warp::{http::Method, Filter, Reply};
```

```
pub mod config;
mod profanity;
mod routes;
```

...

We will also need to copy over the .env file from the project folder into the integra-tion-tests crate, since this is where the dotenv helper library will look for the file when it is invoked:

```
$ cd BOOK_PROJECT
$ cp .env integration-tests/
```

We are now ready to write our first integration test.

11.3.3 Adding the registration test

We need to start our web service and send an HTTP request to it with an email/pass-word combination. The following listing shows the implementation details.

Listing 11.20   Adding the registration HTTP call in integration-tests/main.rs

```
use rust_web_dev::{config, handle_errors, oneshot, setup_store};
use serde::{Deserialize, Serialize};
use serde_json::Value;

#[derive(Serialize, Deserialize, Debug, Clone)]
struct User {
    email: String,
    password: String,
}

#[tokio::main]
async fn main() -> Result<(), handle_errors::Error> {
    dotenv::dotenv().ok();
    let config = config::Config::new().expect("Config can't be set");

    let store = setup_store(&config).await?;

    let handler = oneshot(store).await;

    let u = User {
        email: "test@email.com".to_string(),
        password: "password".to_string(),
    };

    register_new_user(&u).await?;

    let _ = handler.sender.send(1);

    Ok(())
}
```

```
async fn register_new_user(user: &User) {
    let client = reqwest::Client::new();
    let res = client
        .post("http://localhost:3030/registration")
        .json(&user)
        .send()
        .await
        .unwrap()
        .json::<Value>()
        .await
        .unwrap

    assert_eq!(res, "Account added".to_string());
}
```

This test seems trivial. We start our web server via the `oneshot` function, create a dummy user, and create a function called `register_new_user`, where we send out an HTTP request via Reqwest. If you look carefully, this function differs from the one we usually write:

- There is no return type (`Result` of some form).
- We don't do any error handling but unwrap the `Result` directly.
- We end the function with an `assert_eq!` macro.

Why would we do that? Well, for one, we don't care about any error handling or further processing the results. We want to check whether we can create an account, and if we can, the integration test was successful. If not, we fail and want to say, "Something is wrong!"

And if we think one step further: what does it mean to fail? We have to clearly stop the mock server, and we have to stop the other test functions from running. We need a way of gracefully shutting down both the mock server and our own application. We will see shortly how we can achieve this.

But let's handle two other, more obvious problems first. We can run the tests via navigating into the integration-tests folder, and execute `cargo run` on the command line.

We will run into two problems:

- We are getting a database error, telling us the user already exists.
- The response from the HTTP request can't be parsed since it's not valid JSON.

Let's tackle the second problem first. We check inside src/routes/authentication.rs to see what we return, and find that we return a string instead of a valid JSON:

```
pub async fn register(
    store: Store,
    account: Account
) -> Result<impl warp::Reply, warp::Rejection> {
    ...

    match store.add_account(account).await {
        Ok(_) =>
```

```
            Ok(warp::reply::with_status("Account added", StatusCode::OK)),
        Err(e) => Err(warp::reject::custom(e)),
    }
}
```

We are changing this line to `warp::reply::json()` like that:

```
pub async fn register(
    store: Store,
    account: Account
) -> Result<impl warp::Reply, warp::Rejection> {
    ...

    match store.add_account(account).await {
        Ok(_) => Ok(warp::reply::json(&"Account added".to_string())),
        Err(e) => Err(warp::reject::custom(e)),
    }
}
```

This solves our parsing of the response as a JSON value. The first error we got, that the account already exists, might be a local problem to each of you. We are currently reusing the database we used for the whole book, and you might have chosen the same email before. However, that's not a satisfying situation. We need to do the following:

- Create a new test database that we use only for our integration tests.
- Connect to this test database every time we run the tests.
- Clean up the database after each integration test run.

First, we change our .env file inside the integration-tests crate and connect to a database called `test` instead:

```
...
PORT=8080
POSTGRES_USER=username
POSTGRES_PASSWORD=password
POSTGRES_DB=test
POSTGRES_HOST=localhost
POSTGRES_PORT=5432
```

Now we have to find a way of creating and deleting the database for each run. We could create it manually via the command line and then use an SQL statement inside the code to delete all the data after each test. For simplicity's sake and to learn something new, we will try to execute a CLI command from within the code via the Rust standard library. The following listing shows how.

Listing 11.21 Dropping and creating the `test` database for each test run

```
use std::process::Command;        ◁─┐  The standard library offers the
use std::io::{self, Write};          │  Command module, which we can use
                                     │  to translate CLI commands into code.
```

```
use rust_web_dev::{config, handle_errors, oneshot, setup_store};
use serde::{Deserialize, Serialize};
use serde_json::Value;

#[derive(Serialize, Deserialize, Debug, Clone)]
struct User {
    email: String,
    password: String,
}

#[tokio::main]
async fn main() -> Result<(), handle_errors::Error> {
    dotenv::dotenv().ok();
    let config = config::Config::new().expect("Config can't be set");

    let s = Command::new("sqlx")
        .arg("database")
        .arg("drop")
        .arg("--database-url")
        .arg(format!("postgres://{}:{}/{}",
            config.db_host, config.db_port, config.db_name
        ))
        .arg("-y")
        .output()
        .expect("sqlx command failed to start");

    io::stdout().write_all(&s.stderr).unwrap();

    let s = Command::new("sqlx")
        .arg("database")
        .arg("create")
        .arg("--database-url")
        .arg(format!("postgres://{}:{}/{}",
            config.db_host, config.db_port, config.db_name
        ))
        .output()
        .expect("sqlx command failed to start");

    io::stdout().write_all(&s.stderr).unwrap();

    ...
}
...
```

Specifies arguments that we pass to the sqlx command

Creates a new command, which is our SQLx CLI tool we call to drop and create a database

Adds a -y parameter, which automatically answers the CLI question if we are sure to drop a database, with yes

The output function will create the final command, which we can use to execute later.

Uses the stdout function to write our command to the command line and execute it

We translate the following two CLI commands to the Command builder structure from the Rust standard library:

```
sqlx database drop --database-url postgres://localhost:5432/test -y
sqlx database create --database-url postgres://localhost:5432/test
```

And then we execute via the `write_all` command, where we can also specify that we want to print out errors if they happen via the `stderr` field:

```
io::stdout().write_all(&s.stderr).unwrap();
```

After this is done, we can try again to run the binary via `cargo run` and send out the HTTP request to register a new user. If you see no output at all, the tests worked, and we registered a new user and added it to the database.

11.3.4 Unwinding in case of an error

We could create a new account, and the call was successful. But we also have to plan for the case that a test fails. Since we write plain Rust and just call our application integration-tests, we don't get any support from Rust test helper logic to bootstrap and wind down the application in a proper way in case of an error. We have to handle this ourselves. The next listing shows the resulting code, which we will explain right after.

Listing 11.22 Unwinding a possible failing integration test

```
use std::process::Command;
use std::io::{self, Write};

use futures_util::future::FutureExt;          Needs the help of the futures_util
                                              crate for the catch_unwind function
                                              to use on our async test functions
...

#[tokio::main]                                                      Uses the
async fn main() -> Result<(), handle_errors::Error> {      AssertUnwindSafe
    ...                                                      wrapper from the
                                                          Rust standard library
    print!("Running register_new_user...");                 to wrap our function
                                                                  and variables
    let result = std::panic::AssertUnwindSafe(register_new_user(&u))
        .catch_unwind().await;

    match result {                            Matches the result of our
        Ok(_) => println!("√"),               register_new_user function
        Err(_) => {
            let _ = handler.sender.send(1);   In case it was successful, we
            std::process::exit(1);            print a checkmark symbol
        }                                     on the command line.
    }

    let _ = handler.sender.send(1);           If the function panics, we catch
                                              it via catch_unwind earlier,
    Ok(())                                    and stop the process here.
}

...
```

In programming, *unwinding* means to remove the functions and variables from the stack in reverse order, to leave a clean slate in case of an exception. If we expect a panic from a function call, we can use the `catch_unwind` call from the Rust standard library (http://mng.bz/K0dj). In our case, we use the wrapper `AssertUnwindSafe` (http://mng.bz/9VJ7), which signals that the variables we use are safe to unwind. We wrap our function call with it, and call `catch_unwind` (http://mng.bz/jA9r) from the futures_util crate, which "catches unwinding panics while polling the future."

If the `register_new_user` function panics (since we don't handle errors and unwrap them), and if something else goes wrong during our testing, we unwind the stack, stop the mock server, and end the process.

11.3.5 *Testing the login and posting questions*

We can now add the login test and the first question. The following listing shows the missing pieces.

Listing 11.23 Adding the login and `add_question` tests

```
...

#[derive(Serialize, Deserialize, Debug, Clone)]
struct User {
    email: String,
    password: String,
}

#[derive(Serialize, Deserialize, Debug, Clone)]
struct Question {
    title: String,
    content: String,
}

#[derive(Serialize, Deserialize, Debug, Clone)]
struct QuestionAnswer {
    id: i32,
    title: String,
    content: String,
    tags: Option<Vec<String>>,
}

#[derive(Serialize, Deserialize, Debug, Clone)]
struct Token(String);

#[tokio::main]
async fn main() -> Result<(), handle_errors::Error> {
    ...

    print!("Running login...");
    match std::panic::AssertUnwindSafe(login(u)).catch_unwind().await {
        Ok(t) => {
            token = t;
            println!("✓");
        },
        Err(_) => {
            let _ = handler.sender.send(1);
            std::process::exit(1);
        }
    }
```

```
        print!("Running post_question...");
        match std::panic::AssertUnwindSafe(post_question(token))
            .catch_unwind().await {
            Ok(_) => println!("√"),
            Err(_) => {
                let _ = handler.sender.send(1);
                std::process::exit(1);
            }
        }

        let _ = handler.sender.send(1);

        Ok(())
}

...

async fn login(user: User) -> Token {
    let client = reqwest::Client::new();
    let res = client
        .post("http://localhost:3030/login")
        .json(&user)
        .send()
        .await
        .unwrap();

    assert_eq!(res.status(), 200);

    res
        .json::<Token>()
        .await
        .unwrap()
}

async fn post_question(token: Token) {
    let q = Question {
        title: "First Question".to_string(),
        content: "How can I test?".to_string(),
    };

    let client = reqwest::Client::new();
    let res = client
        .post("http://localhost:3030/questions")
        .header("Authorization", token.0)
        .json(&q)
        .send()
        .await
        .unwrap()
        .json::<QuestionAnswer>()
        .await
        .unwrap();

    assert_eq!(res.id, 1);
    assert_eq!(res.title, q.title);
}
```

And this is it: we verified the registration and login routes, and can create new questions. With the knowledge learned over the course of the book, it should not be hard to create failing tests (a missing token, for example, when creating questions) and use the `assert` macro to check for the right error code.

Improvements could still be made, and this is left as an exercise for you:

- Print out the name of each test (function) when it is run and put a checkmark or x when it's successful or fails.
- Drop the database after each run instead of before.
- Add more failing tests to the test suite.

The changes made throughout this chapter not only verified a working web service, but also changed quite a lot of our codebase to accommodate the testing environment. We spotted a few problems (for example, we didn't return JSON for each HTTP response we sent out) and moved the creation of the store and the routes into their own functions. The resulting code is cleaner and more adaptable to future changes.

Summary

- Self-contained functions are well suited for unit tests, where we can feed the functions with different parameters and can always rely on side-effect free responses.
- When trying to compare results, we need to implement the `PartialEq` trait on our structs.
- Comparing errors is not always trivial, and the easiest solution is to compare the `String` the error produces (via the `Display` trait and the `.to_string` function).
- Rust runs tests in parallel, which has side effects when testing different environment variables. This will impact all tests that rely on these environment variables and therefore need to be as self-contained as possible.
- We don't have to mock external API calls; we can change the URL they are calling to localhost and run a mock server on our own, where we control the response.
- A mock server can be shut down via opening a channel between the test function and the server, where we can send over a signal that triggers a graceful shutdown of the server.
- A oneshot channel is a great tool for communicating with a different part of the system (like a mock server) and triggering functions (like a shutdown) through messages.
- Testing middleware is partly dependent on the web framework you are using. It is ideal if it allows testing routes without starting the server, like the `warp::test` module does.
- Integration tests are large-scale tests that test functionality (partly) end to end in a local environment.

- You can use your own folder or crate, or put them with the rest of your codebase.
- You need to be able to start and stop the server and clean the database before and after each integration test run. This can be achieved through a bash file that starts a Docker environment, or through your own codebase via a oneshot channel and the Command module in the standard library.

appendix
Thinking about security

When developing an API or other web services, you have to think about how to secure your endpoints, validate the data that comes in, and understand how an attacker might abuse your application. These topics span multiple books and can't be covered here. However, what we can do in the scope of this book is introduce tools you can use to inspect and verify your Rust code, so at least this aspect of the security audit can be done.

A.1 *Verify your dependencies for security issues*

Building a Rust codebase involves pulling in sometimes hundreds of dependencies. Verifying them all by hand is tedious and, dare I say it, impossible. A CLI tool called Cargo-crev can help you with that task. This code review system enables users to review third-party dependencies and publish their findings.

The latest setup steps can be found in the project's GitHub repository: https://github.com/crev-dev/cargo-crev. You can install and set up Cargo-crev via these steps:

```
$ cargo install cargo-crev
$ cargo crev trust --level high https://github.com/dpc/crev-proofs
$ cargo crev repo fetch all
```

The next step is to run the tool in your Rust project folder:

```
$ cargo crev verify --show-all
```

This will generate a table with all your crates, the versions, and any issues other reviewers found. For example, a crate we pull in called traitobject has an open issue:

```
status reviews issues owner       downloads     loc lpidx geiger flgs crate
none      0   4   0   0  0  1 16318K  72935K     577  140      0  ____
version_check                    0.9.4                        ↓0.9.3
```

```
none      0   0   0    0   0   2   6698K   42472K      529   119      112 CB__
futures-task                         0.3.21
none      1   1   0    1   0   1   6374K    7712K       96    70       88 ____
traitobject                          0.1.0
```

We can use this information to go into the details of the issue via this command:

```
$ cargo crev repo query issue traitobject 0.1.0
```

This generates the following output:

```
---
kind: package review
version: -1
date: "2020-02-10T17:11:03.187657396+01:00"
from:
  id-type: crev
  id: tjxgceP0Tp8LrAEV_onFfMwoEKFqSMWWfN-1f-HnzIw
  url: "https://github.com/Nemo157/crev-proofs"
package:
  source: "https://crates.io"
  name: traitobject
  version: 0.1.0
  digest: mrCxpjxVETR7m06rtGmx71d6R5kQ_dlH25_WncE0UOk
review:
  thoroughness: none
  understanding: none
  rating: negative
issues:
- id: "https://github.com/reem/rust-traitobject/issues/5"
  severity: medium
  comment: ""
flags:
  unmaintained: true
comment: |-
  Has future compat warnings over a year old,
      and given that it is unmaintained
  there is very little possibility that these will be fixed.

  ```
  warning: conflicting implementations of trait `Trait` for type
    `(dyn std::marker::Send + std::marker::Sync + 'static)`: (E0119)
    |
  71 | unsafe impl Trait for ::std::marker::Send + Sync { }
    | --
      first implementation here
  72 | unsafe impl Trait for ::std::marker::Send + Send + Sync { }
    | ^^
      conflicting implementation for
      `(dyn std::marker::Send + std::marker::Sync + 'static)`
    |
    = note: `#[warn(order_dependent_trait_objects)]` on by default
    = warning: this was previously accepted by the compiler
      but is being phased out; it will become a hard error
```
```

```
           in a future release!
     = note: for more information,
         see issue #56484 <https://github.com/rust-lang/rust/issues/56484>
     ```
```

Based on the information we get, we can decide (or try) not to use this crate or try to go to the repository and push a change. Currently, the feature set is limited. We can't, for example, easily see which dependency in our Cargo.toml file is pulling in this one.

Another crate that you can use is called Cargo Audit (http://mng.bz/VyO5). This tool will check dependencies against the RustSec Advisory Database (https://github .com/RustSec/advisory-db/) and report any found vulnerability. You can install it via cargo install:

```
$ cargo install cargo-audit
```

After that, run it:

```
$ cargo audit
```

This tool will show you the dependency tree and offer a solution:

```
$ argo audit
    Fetching advisory database from
        `https://github.com/RustSec/advisory-db.git`
      Loaded 417 security advisories
        (from /Users/gruberbastian/.cargo/advisory-db)
    Updating crates.io index
    Scanning Cargo.lock for vulnerabilities (214 crate dependencies)
Crate:     hyper
Version:   0.14.7
Title:     Integer overflow in `hyper`'s parsing
    of the `Transfer-Encoding` header leads to data loss
Date:      2021-07-07
ID:        RUSTSEC-2021-0079
URL:       https://rustsec.org/advisories/RUSTSEC-2021-0079
Solution:  Upgrade to >=0.14.10
Dependency tree:
hyper 0.14.7
??? warp 0.3.1
    ??? practical-rust-book 0.1.0
    ??? handle-errors 0.1.0
        ??? practical-rust-book 0.1.0

Crate:     hyper
Version:   0.14.7
Title:     Lenient `hyper` header parsing of `Content-Length`
             could allow request smuggling
Date:      2021-07-07
ID:        RUSTSEC-2021-0078
URL:       https://rustsec.org/advisories/RUSTSEC-2021-0078
Solution:  Upgrade to >=0.14.10
```

In this case, upgrading Hyper to version 0.14.10 would fix our problem.
```

A.2 Verify your own code

When it comes to developing a Rust application, make sure to follow guidelines. The online "Secure Rust Guidelines" guide (http://mng.bz/xMYB) helps with best practices and recommendations.

Always develop on the latest, updated Rust stable branch, and switch to nightly if you really have to. You can verify this by running the `toolchain list` command via Rustup:

```
$ rustup toolchain list
stable-aarch64-apple-darwin (default)
beta-aarch64-apple-darwin
nightly-aarch64-apple-darwin
```

The version you are using is set by default. Make sure to regularly check for updates to the stable version of Rust:

```
$ rustup update
```

You can do a lot by using Clippy to lint, and the Rust formatter Rustfmt to format your code (as explained in chapter 5). A clean and easy-to-read codebase helps find bugs faster. One step further, and you can verify your actual code.

A crate called semval lets you "validate complex data structures at runtime" (https://github.com/slowtec/semval). You can implement validation checks indicating what it means for your application to have a valid phone number or email address, for example. Other crates let you help check inputs to your functions and cover edge cases: http://mng.bz/AVRW.

A.3 Closing words

When it comes to security, this book can cover the basic setup and offer further resources. But the whole topic is worth way more than one book, and my advice is to consult a security expert on issues you are not comfortable tackling yourself.

The Rust Secure Code Working Group has a list of crates and projects you can use: https://github.com/rust-secure-code/projects. As a rule of thumb, checking against vulnerabilities in your dependencies is a first, very important step. The next step is linting and formatting your code, so you can easily reason about it and can be sure you cover the basics.

The next step after that is validating your function inputs. And if you have an API endpoint, check what unexpected parameters and JSON can do to your application. Inputting sanitizing libraries can help with that as well. For a full-rounded check read the literature and consult an expert to teach you or do the work for you.

index